Vigilante Islamists

Vigilante Islamists

Religious Parties and Anti-State Violence in Pakistan

Joshua T. White

OXFORD
UNIVERSITY PRESS

Oxford University Press is a department of the University of Oxford.
It furthers the University's objective of excellence in research, scholarship,
and education by publishing worldwide. Oxford is a registered trade mark of
Oxford University Press in the UK and in certain other countries.

Published in the United States of America by Oxford University Press
198 Madison Avenue, New York, NY 10016, United States of America.

CIP data is on file at the Library of Congress

ISBN 9780197814147

ISBN 9780197814130 (hbk.)

DOI: 10.1093/9780197814178.001.0001

Paperback Printed by Integrated Books International, United States of America

Hardback Printed by Bridgeport National Bindery, Inc., United States of America

The manufacturer's authorised representative in the EU for product safety is
Oxford University Press España S.A., Parque Empresarial San Fernando de Henares,
Avenida de Castilla, 2 – 28830 Madrid (www.oup.es/en).

Contents

Acknowledgments

This book would not have been possible without the support of a great many people. I am indebted to an extraordinary group of advisors and mentors at the Johns Hopkins School of Advanced International Studies, most notably Walter Andersen, Jonah Blank, Eliot Cohen, Karl Jackson, and Sunil Khilnani. My interest in South Asia would never have amounted to anything were it not for Robert, Margaret Ann, and Chris Seiple. I also owe a debt of gratitude to Anita Weiss, Nadeem Akbar, and the entire staff of the American Institute of Pakistan Studies, which provided me a generous grant for fieldwork in Pakistan; Nadia Schadlow and Allan Song at the Smith Richardson Foundation, who twice funded my research into Pakistani Islamism; Andrew Wilder at the U.S. Institute of Peace, who graciously hosted me during my Jennings Randolph Peace Scholar fellowship; Rasul Bakhsh Rais and Mohammad Waseem, who invited me to the Lahore University of Management Sciences; the late Mumtaz Ahmad at the International Islamic University Islamabad, who provided me encouragement and a spectacular guesthouse in the shadow of the Faisal Mosque; the Mustard Seed Foundation; and many unnamed politicians, bureaucrats, military officers, and experts who facilitated my research on the ground.

Special thanks to Shuja Ali Malik, a superb research assistant and friend; M. Asif Gul, who provided excellent research support in Peshawar as well as Pashto translations; and Raja Qaisar, who ably assisted with document collection and Urdu translation. I was also fortunate to have been given the opportunity to conduct some interviews alongside Mariam Mufti and Niloufer Siddiqui, two exceptional scholars of Pakistani politics.

I owe a great debt to my long-suffering wife Jennifer, who put up with my frequent travels, and kept my focus on what mattered; to my parents Tom and Terri, who faithfully taught me both religion and diplomacy; to David McBride and the superb editorial team at Oxford University Press; and to my mentors and colleagues Qibla Ayaz, C. Christine Fair, Peter Lavoy, Daniel Markey, Hasan-Askari Rizvi, Ashley Tellis, Marvin Weinbaum, and the late Stephen Cohen and Michael Krepon.

I dedicate this book to my late grandparents, Selman and Esther Tempchin, who gave me a love of world politics and the tenacity to pursue it.

A Note on Transliteration

All Urdu transliterations have been made in accordance with the schema employed by the *Ferozsons Urdu-English Dictionary*.[1] This schema is identical to the latest Library of Congress (LOC) romanization table,[2] with the following substitutions that are in wide use:

For ث, s̤ in place of s;
for ض, ẓ in place of z̤;
for ظ, z̤ in place of ẓ;
for ں, ṅ in place of n; and
for the *iẓāfat*, -e in place of -i.

The transposition of transliterated letters for ض and ظ is in conformity with most Urdu-specific transliteration tables, and likely is "reversed" in the LOC tables to maintain backward compatibility with the Arabic LOC schema. The *Ferozsons* renderings of ں and the *iẓāfat* are also closer to renderings used by Urdu-specific publications, such as the *Annual of Urdu Studies*.[3]

Foreign terms will generally be transliterated and italicized on first use, and printed in roman script with simplified spelling thereafter. For example, *jihād* will be rendered jihad, and *'ulamā'* as ulama. As a general rule, author and organization names may be transliterated fully in the footnotes, but simplified in the body text. For example, "Maulānā Faẓl ur-Raḥmān" in a footnote citation may be rendered in the body text simply as "Fazl ur-Rahman" or "Rahman." Similarly, "taḥrīk" (movement) may rendered simply as "tahrik," even if other transliterations such as "tehreek" are in common use. Note that the definite article will typically be transliterated as *al-*, *as-*, *at-*, and so forth, but will be rendered *ur-* or *ul-* in proper names when it is customary to do so.

[1] *Ferozsons Urdu-English Dictionary: A Comprehensive Dictionary of Current Vocabulary*, rev. ed. (Lahore: Ferozsons, 1988).

[2] "ALA-LC Urdu Romanization Table" (Library of Congress and the American Library Association, 2012), http://www.loc.gov/catdir/cpso/romanization/urdu.pdf.

[3] "A Note on Transliteration," *Annual of Urdu Studies* (2007), http://www.urdustudies.com/pdf/22/01TitleTranslit.pdf.

PART 1

1
"Democratic Islamists" and the Anti-State Turn

1.1 Introduction

One of the most striking developments of the last four decades in Pakistan has been the rise of violent anti-state religious movements that have justified their actions on the basis of Islamic law. Anti-state violence is not a new phenomenon in Pakistan. In the pre-independence period, British officials faced dozens of tribal "jihadi" uprisings that challenged colonial rule in starkly Islamic terms.[1] And following the partition of British India in 1947, the Pakistani state encountered many forms of violent resistance, including ethno-nationalist agitations, separatist insurgencies, and vigilante activities by religious and political movements. Some of these were severe: The Bengali nationalist movement of 1971 rent the state in two. Many were precipitated or given succor by the martial state's own heavy-handed mismanagement of domestic affairs, or its clumsy attempts to instrumentalize fringe movements against the country's political elite.

Beginning in the 1990s, however, Pakistan began to face newly potent forms of anti-state violence from religious movements which, in various ways and to varying degrees, challenged the state's legitimacy and justified vigilantism and more severe violence against the government on the basis of Islamic legal discourse. The rise of the Tahrik-e-Nifaz-e-Shariat-e-Muhammadi (TNSM) movement in the early 1990s in the northern Pakistani tribal agency of Swat was, in retrospect, a bellwether of these new movements. But it was not until the extraordinary spasm of internal violence that unfolded across Pakistan between 2004 and 2018—a period which saw, among other things, the rebirth of the TNSM, the rise of the violent Tahrik-e-Taliban Pakistan, a movement of vigilante violence in the heart of the capital, Islamabad, and the assassination

[1] Abdul Rauf, "The British Empire and the Mujāhidīn Movement in the N.W.F.P. of India, 1914–1934," *Islamic Studies* 44, no. 3 (2005): 409–439; Dietrich Reetz, *Islam in the Public Sphere: Religious Groups in India, 1900–1947* (New Delhi: Oxford University Press, 2006), 251ff; Sana Haroon, *Frontier of Faith: Islam in the Indo-Afghan Borderland* (New York: Columbia University Press, 2007); Ayesha Jalal, *Partisans of Allah: Jihad in South Asia* (Cambridge: Harvard University Press, 2008).

Vigilante Islamists. Joshua T. White, Oxford University Press. © Oxford University Press (2025).
DOI: 10.1093/9780197814178.003.0001

of the governor of Punjab province by a radical Sunni Barelvi activist—that the public began to pay close attention to this new class of violent actors who, in whole or in part, targeted the state and its symbols on ostensibly religious grounds.

Although there is a vast literature on the evolution of Pakistan's Islamic political identity and on the instrumental uses of Islam by both state and non-state actors for political ends, scholars are still beginning to grapple with this more recent period of extraordinary violence in Pakistan. To the extent that they have done so, it has largely been to begin to chronicle the emergence of these groups and explore their ideological and organizational antecedents.[2]

This book takes a complementary approach to the study of this anti-state violence. Rather than examining the groups that have come to inhabit the radical fringe, it studies some of their most important enablers, interlocutors, and competitors: Pakistan's Islamic political parties. The central question of the book is how and why these parties enable religiously justified anti-state violence—how they deal with anti-state organizations on the radical fringe, and with vigilante impulses within their own party structures; how they navigate their dual and often conflicting interests in democratic participation and state Islamization; and what their decisions might mean for the trajectory of anti-state discourse and violence in Pakistan.

It is not at first obvious that Pakistan's Islamic political parties—or "Islamist parties," as they will be described and defined in Chapter 2—are particularly consequential to addressing the larger question of anti-state violence. This study examines the most prominent of these parties: the Jamaat-e-Islami (JI), Jamiat Ulama-e-Islam (Fazl ur-Rahman faction) (JUI-F), Jamiat Ulama-e-Islam (Sami ul-Haq faction) (JUI-S), the Tahrik-e-Labbaik Pakistan (TLP), and, when relevant, several minor parties. Taken together, they constitute a relatively small subset of the country's political class. Why should one care about parties that have never garnered more than 12 percent of the national vote, have only thrice formed governments at the provincial level, quarrel among themselves almost constantly, and have virtually no chance of decisively capturing state power?[3] Indeed, why care about small parties at all, when politics in Pakistan is conducted in the shadow of the state's

[2] See, for example, Mona Kanwal Sheikh, *Guardians of God: Inside the Religious Mind of the Pakistani Taliban* (New Delhi: Oxford University Press, 2016); C. Christine Fair, *Mapping Pakistan's Internal Dynamics: Implications for State Stability and Regional Security* (Seattle: National Bureau of Asian Research, 2016); Farhat Haq, *Sharia and the State in Pakistan: Blasphemy Politics* (Milton: Taylor & Francis Group, 2019).

[3] Islamist parties together garnered 12 percent of National Assembly seats in the 2002 general election. They have thrice formed provincial governments: the first was in 1972, when the JUI governed the erstwhile North-West Frontier Province (NWFP) for nine months; the second was in 2002, when a coalition of Islamist parties governed NWFP and joined a coalition government Balochistan, ruling until 2007; the third began in 2013, when the JI joined the Pakistan Tahrik-e-Insaf (PTI) as a coalition partner in Khyber Pakhtunkhwa, an arrangement that continued until 2018.

powerful army that both suppresses and sponsors militancy, oversees one of the world's fastest-growing nuclear arsenals, and for decades has promoted Islamic ideology in the service of its obsession with India?[4]

Further, even if one accepts the value of studying the Islamist parties, why focus specifically on anti-state violence to the exclusion of, for example, instrumental political violence? Why limit the study to religiously justified violence, to the exclusion of cases in which Islamist parties might enable violence by other organizations which make ethnic, linguistic, or nationalist claims against the state? These are all worthwhile questions and areas of research. There are, however, three important reasons why it is worth understanding the drivers and limitations of Islamist parties' embrace of anti-state violence in the name of Islam.

First, while Islamist parties have since Pakistan's earliest days acted as opposition gadflies to civilian and military governments alike, their support to violent anti-state movements could presage *organic* threats to the state—not to its territorial control directly, but to its ability to justify its institutions and actions as legitimately Islamic in the face of violent opposition groups that claim the mantle of religion. Government elites, and the army in particular, have long put forward Islam as the state's unifying ideology and fountainhead of political legitimacy. Islamist parties may never be influential enough to act as decisive arbiters of state legitimacy, but they do wield influence that far outstrips their collective size. Were they to begin more decisively rejecting the political order, the government would face an even higher bar to justifying police and military action against militant groups.

Second, as organizations that often bridge the worlds of respectable democratic politics and vigilante activism, the Islamist parties are in a position to wield influence over important non-state actors to either stoke or rein in anti-state violence. (Or, if they prefer, to remain passive.) Most directly, they can do so through their affiliated social and educational institutions. The JUI parties have deep links with influential madrassah networks representing the Deobandi Sunni school of thought across Pakistan. The Jamaat-e-Islami has its own network of affiliated schools, but also reaches deep into universities through its affiliate, the Islami Jamiat Talaba (IJT), which at times has been Pakistan's most effective (or at least feared) student organization. The TLP serves as a public face for an array of radical Barelvi groups. These parties do not always exert directive control over their affiliates; like any political

[4] The role of the Pakistani state in instrumentalizing militancy and religious radicalism has been widely documented. For a historically and theoretically grounded summary, see Husain Haqqani, *Pakistan: Between Mosque and Military* (Washington: Carnegie Endowment for International Peace, 2005); S. Paul Kapur and Sumit Ganguly, "The Jihad Paradox: Pakistan and Islamist Militancy in South Asia," *International Security* 37, no. 1 (Summer 2012): 111–141; C. Christine Fair, *Fighting to the End: The Pakistan Army's Way of War* (New York: Oxford University Press, 2014).

organization, they are to some extent captive to their own constituencies. Nonetheless, they wield substantial influence in shaping the religious narratives, political activism, and violent activities of these important movements.

Somewhat further afield, Pakistan's Islamic parties exert influence over—and are themselves shaped by—their longstanding interactions with militants. As described throughout this book, these parties have since the early days of the state cultivated symbiotic relationships with militant organizations: The parties provide mobilization support and political cover for the militants, and the militants provide credibility and deniable violence for the parties. As with their educational affiliates, the parties are to some extent captive to the interests of their militant collaborators, but also have a role in shaping their actions in the public domain.

The third and final reason for investigating the relationships between religious parties and fringe anti-state movements in Pakistan is that they have wider implications for Islamic democracy in diverse parts of the world. From Turkey to Egypt to Malaysia, self-identified Islamist parties have staked their reputations on accepting the constitutional and pluralistic "rules of the road" governing democratic participation. They regularly disavow subversive and antinomian agendas, and they steer clear of overt links with Islamic organizations employing violence against the state. Like many of their counterparts around the world, Islamic political parties in Pakistan operate under constraints imposed by a strong central government, function primarily as opposition actors, and face political and legal risks in supporting fringe movements that perpetrate anti-state violence or vigilantism. Indeed, one of the insights that emerges from the political science literature on "anti-system" parties is that even anti-establishment political organizations such as Islamist parties typically operate under significant constraints, are pressured to "walk on the minefields between normal and anti-democratic opposition," and have the difficult task of criticizing the political order without rendering quixotic their own attempts to enter it.[5] Lessons from these parties' dalliances with anti-state extremists in Pakistan can serve to highlight both the influence and vulnerabilities of Islamist parties similarly positioned in the Muslim-majority world.

Within its immediate neighborhood, the Islamic political shifts in Pakistan discussed in this book could interact in important ways with Islamic politics in neighboring Afghanistan. The JUI parties share with the Afghan Taliban religious, historical, ethnic, educational, and political links. Indeed, the leadership of the JUI-F and JUI-S repeatedly suggested to this author that they had long encouraged the Taliban to pursue a JUI-style party in Afghanistan.

[5] Andreas Schedler, "Anti-Political-Establishment Parties," *Party Politics* 2, no. 3 (July 1996): 303.

Not surprisingly, the JUI parties celebrated the Afghan Taliban's victory in 2021. Although the domestic contexts in Afghanistan and Pakistan are quite different, both the Afghan Taliban leadership and the leadership of Pakistan's Islamist parties face similar challenges from the radical fringe—particularly from groups such as the Islamic State—that will likely shape their policy ambitions, rhetoric, and relationships with other Islamist organizations.

Some have dismissed the small Islamic political parties as inconsequential players in Pakistan's democratic process, or as mere proxies for—depending on the arc of one's conspiratorial worldview—the army or various groups that identify as "Taliban." This book, by contrast, will argue that these parties' relationships with violent anti-state Islamic movements do indeed matter. These relationships affect the legitimacy of military and state institutions; influence the policy positions of other parties; delimit the political space available to civilian and military leaders to act against extremism; regulate political access and protections afforded to affiliated militant organizations; and condition public discourse on issues as diverse as suicide bombing, religious education, fiscal policy, and U.S.–Pakistan relations. In short, they have avenues of influence that neither scholars nor policymakers can afford to ignore.

1.2 The Arguments

At the heart of this book is a question: *Why, and under what conditions, do Pakistan's Islamist parties enable religiously justified anti-state violence?* The book seeks to answer this question through an exploration of the most prominent Islamist parties. It explores why and how these parties enable violence through various kinds of support—sometimes with rhetoric, and sometimes with material assistance—and through various means of support—sometimes directly facilitating actors within their own party structures, and sometimes indirectly facilitating third parties. Even as the book discusses the relationship of these parties more broadly to the use of violence, it focuses on the ways in which they enable violence that is directed against state institutions, and that is publicly justified with reference to advancing some conception of *shari'ah* (Islamic law).

From this overarching question flow two major lines of inquiry that will be taken up in the chapters that follow. The first is *why* Pakistan's Islamist parties, each of which has a history of participating in electoral politics, would risk enabling anti-state violence by publicly endorsing or materially supporting a violent anti-state movement, or by allowing their own party members or affiliates to engage in violent anti-state vigilantism. At first blush, it would seem that challenging state institutions, including the country's powerful army and security services, would preclude these parties from securing gains that flow from political participation, including patronage and legitimacy.

The existing literature provides a framework for categorizing these behaviors. An "anti-system" or "semi-loyal" party is one "whose supporters or members engage in unconventional, illegal or violent behavior," or one that is willing "to encourage, tolerate, cover up, treat leniently, excuse, or justify the actions of other participants that go beyond the limits of peaceful, legitimate patterns of politics in a democracy."[6] In the South Asian context, Philip Oldenburg has argued that Islamist parties are among those actors in Pakistan who have at times behaved "semi-loyally."[7] In his study of the geography of conflict in India, Adnan Naseemullah has helpfully distinguished between sovereignty-neutral and sovereignty-challenging types of violence, a difference that turns on whether the violence is intended to fundamentally challenge the structures of state power.[8] Beyond South Asia, there is a robust literature on the role of anti-system or semi-loyal parties and their respective relationships with the state, in countries as varied as Indonesia and Lebanon.[9] And there is a growing body of work on vigilantism and its relationship to democratic politics.[10]

As valuable as this literature is, much of it is effectively descriptive in nature. It does not directly address the *benefits* that Islamist parties might seek to secure by operating on the margin between responsible democratic participation, and support for violence and extra-legal activities. There is a sophisticated body of work on electoral violence, and the ways in which parties instrumentalize violence to polarize communities for electoral gain, or to intimidate or coerce them into certain voting behaviors.[11] But in Pakistan, Islamist parties have not been particularly successful at the ballot box, and on

[6] Giovanni Capoccia, "Anti-System Parties: A Conceptual Reassessment," *Journal of Theoretical Politics* 14, no. 1 (2002): 12; Juan Linz, *The Breakdown of Democratic Regimes: Crises, Breakdown and Reequilibrium* (Baltimore, MD: Johns Hopkins University Press, 1978), 32–33. See also Robert R. Barr, "Populists, Outsiders and Anti-Establishment Politics," *Party Politics* 15, no. 1 (January 2009): 29–48; Mattia Zulianello, "Anti-System Parties Revisited: Concept Formation and Guidelines for Empirical Research," *Government and Opposition* 53, no. 4 (October 2018): 653–681.

[7] Philip Oldenburg, "Loyalty, Disloyalty, and Semi-Loyalty in Pakistan's Hybrid Regime," *Commonwealth & Comparative Politics* 55, no. 1 (2017): 86.

[8] Adnan Naseemullah, "Riots and Rebellion: State, Society and the Geography of Conflict in India," *Political Geography* 63 (2018): 104–115.

[9] See Zachary Abuza, *Political Islam and Violence in Indonesia* (London: Routledge, 2007), 66; Rosita Di Peri, "Islamist Actors from an Anti-System Perspective: The Case of Hizbullah," *Politics, Religion & Ideology* 15, no. 4 (October 2, 2014): 491–2.

[10] See most notably Regina Bateson, "The Politics of Vigilantism," *Comparative Political Studies* 54, no. 6 (2021): 923–55; Dara Kay Cohen, Danielle F. Jung, and Michael Weintraub, "Introduction: Collective Vigilantism in Global Comparative Perspective," *Comparative Politics* 55, no. 2 (January 1, 2023): 239–61.

[11] For two superb introductions to this literature, see Paul Staniland, "Violence and Democracy," *Comparative Politics* 47, no. 1 (2014): 99–118; Sarah Birch, Ursula Daxecker, and Kristine Höglund, "Electoral Violence: An Introduction," *Journal of Peace Research* 57, no. 1 (2020): 3–14. See also Paul R. Brass, *The Production of Hindu-Muslim Violence in Contemporary India* (Seattle: University of Washington, 2003); Steven Wilkinson, *Votes and Violence: Electoral Competition and Ethnic Riots in India* (Cambridge: Cambridge University Press, 2004); Pippa Norris, *Why Elections Fail* (Cambridge: Cambridge University Press, 2014).

prominent occasions when they have, it has been because the military and security services—rather than the parties themselves—coerced or threatened politicians and bureaucrats.[12] As Niloufer Siddiqui rightly notes, "much of the [Islamist] parties' violent activity seems, at least at first glance, unrelated to electoral activity."[13] She goes on to posit that, in addition to supporting the parties' electoral ambitions, their violence can also be in service of advancing their policy objectives and their ideological aims.

I will argue in the course of this book that the Islamist parties, as semi-loyal participants in the democratic process, enable anti-state violence for the same set of reasons that often compel so-called mainstream parties to do so, although for Islamist parties the pressures are frequently more acute:

- Ideological Sympathy. Political parties may choose to enable anti-state violence out of sympathy for the stated objective of furthering the Islamic character of the Pakistani state, even if they do not condone the means by which that "Islamization" takes place.
- Opposition Targeting. Political parties may choose to enable anti-state violence because they derive advantages from establishing symbiotic (and occasionally deniable) relationships with anti-state militants, on whom they might rely to carry out politically advantageous acts of violence against shared opponents, and to whom they might provide in exchange some measure of political protection.
- Competition Management. Political parties may choose to enable anti-state violence because, fearing defection of their own party cadres to more radical anti-state organizations, they decide to publicly support those organizations rather than risk challenging them.

The second and more significant line of inquiry is *under what conditions and in what ways* Islamist parties enable religiously justified anti-state violence. That is, how can we explain the observed variation in Islamist party behavior toward this kind of violence. In the chapters that follow I will examine puzzling cases of within-party variation, in which a single Islamist party adopts notably divergent postures toward different anti-state movements. For example, why was it that the Jamaat-e-Islami was initially critical of the disruptive vigilante activities of the leaders of the Red Mosque in Islamabad in 2007, but came out in support of the vigilante killing of Punjab governor Salman Taseer in 2011? We will also observe numerous cases of between-party variation, in which different Islamist parties adopt divergent postures toward the same anti-state movement. For example, Chapter 9

[12] These cases, notably from the late 1990s and early 2000s, are described in greater detail in Chapter 2.
[13] Niloufer Siddiqui, "Strategic Violence Among Religious Parties in Pakistan," *Oxford Research Encyclopedia of Politics* (London and New York: Oxford University Press, March 2019).

narrates an episode in which the JI and JUI-F adopted strikingly divergent public postures toward the anti-state TTP following a drone strike that killed the movement's leader, Hakimullah Mehsud, in 2013.

Broadly speaking, there are two compelling approaches to explaining these kinds of party behaviors. One approach emphasizes the role of ideational and ideological factors in party decision-making. An expansive literature explores the ideological and theological genealogies of South Asia's various Islamic traditions. I examine this literature in depth in Chapter 3, with particular reference to those ideological principles and positions that might help to explain Islamist parties' postures toward anti-state violence.

An alternative approach privileges the role of structural and material factors in explaining party behavior. This approach draws on a somewhat different literature, which emphasizes the instrumental utility of political violence, the role of party organization in shaping leaders' behaviors, the importance of patron-client relations, the path-dependent effects of linkage patterns that a party forms with its constituents, and the opportunity structures available to parties to advance their agendas. I explore this literature in Chapters 4 and 5, focusing on the structural roots of Islamist party behavior. In particular, I develop a structural framework for evaluating a party's vulnerabilities to two of its key interlocutors: state institutions and anti-state movements.

Ultimately, in order to make sense of the patterns of Islamist party behavior toward anti-state violence, I propose two main hypotheses. **Hypothesis 1** is that an Islamist party's willingness to enable anti-state violence in the name of advancing Islamic law is principally a function of its structural vulnerabilities to the state and to anti-state movements, rather than a function of its ideological commitments. This is not to say that ideology is inconsequential, but rather that much of Islamist parties' behavior toward anti-state violence and anti-state movements, much of the time, can be explained through material factors. I then describe two ways in which I believe that structural vulnerabilities shape these parties' behaviors:

- **Corollary 1a**: When Islamist parties feel that they are vulnerable to the state, from which they might fear financial or legal retaliation, they will be cautious about *publicly endorsing* anti-state violence by party members, affiliates, and outside movements.
- **Corollary 1b**: When Islamist parties feel that they are vulnerable to violent anti-state movements, from whom they might fear defection of their own party cadres or physical violence, they will seek to undermine those movements even if their public rhetoric remains positive.

Taken together, these two corollaries suggest a generalized pattern of Islamist party behavior, illustrated here in Figure 1.1, which I will test in the case

Vulnerability to the state ↓ / Vulnerability to the anti-state movement →	Low	High
Low	Strategy: **Praise and support** (*Most supportive rhetoric and action toward anti-state movement*)	Strategy: **Praise and undermine** (*Least supportive action toward anti-state movement*)
High	Strategy: **Criticize** (*Least supportive rhetoric toward anti-state movement*)	Strategy: **Prevaricate and undermine**

Figure 1.1 Islamist Party Strategies Toward Anti-State Movements Engaged in Religiously Justified Violence.

chapters that follow. When an Islamist party's vulnerabilities to both the state and to an anti-state movement engaged in religiously justified violence are relatively low, it has incentives to praise and support the movement. In doing so it can bolster its standing with its own cadres as being serious about Islamization, while incurring only modest risk of reprisals from the state. When, however, the party has high vulnerabilities to the state, its incentives shift; regardless of whether it provides material support to the anti-state movement, it has ample reason to criticize it so as to forestall pressure from the state.

In the third case, in which a party has low vulnerability to the state but high vulnerability to an anti-state movement, its incentives become particularly complex; it is likely to engage in what I call "praise for protection" behavior, in which its adulatory public rhetoric is designed to mitigate the risk of defection by its own cadres or of direct attacks from anti-state elements. Effectively, the party is seeking to avoid being ideologically outflanked or out-recruited by a more strident movement that can claim a mantle of greater purity. In such cases, the Islamist party may praise the anti-state movement while quietly and actively working to undermine it. (This naturally has limits; if an anti-state movement begins to openly condemn party leaders and subject them to violence, the party may begin to question its "praise for protection" strategy. The JUI-F arguably reached this inflection point with the TTP, as described in Chapter 9.) In the fourth case, when a party faces significant vulnerabilities to both the state and an anti-state movement, it predictably prevaricates in public, while doing what it can to limit any direct risks to its own party organization.

Lastly, given that my core argument pertains to the importance of the structural vulnerabilities of Islamist parties, I put forward a second group of hypotheses that propose ways of thinking about the underlying roots of these vulnerabilities. These hypotheses draw heavily on the literatures relating to party linkages and organizational coherence and are explored in greater depth in Chapter 4. **Hypothesis 2a** is that Islamist parties that rely on clientelist party linkages are more vulnerable to the state than those that rely on programmatic party linkages. That is to say, parties that are obliged to provide financial patronage to their members, or other clientelist benefits such as protection, are naturally more susceptible to compellence by state institutions than are those parties whose linkages with their members are anchored in matters of policy or ideology.

Hypothesis 2b is that Islamist parties that are weakly institutionalized are more vulnerable both to the state and to violent anti-state movements than those that are strongly institutionalized. As described in Chapters 4 and 5, parties that lack organizational coherence, strong centralization, or independent sources of financing are susceptible to manipulation by the government. Moreover, parties without systems of internal control and accountability may feel particularly vulnerable to being out-recruited by more dynamic and aggressive movements, and they will take steps to neutralize new political challengers—publicly or privately. This risk of cadre defection may be especially acute if the challenger is active in a region in which the party is electorally competitive.

1.3 Methodology

In order to test these hypotheses, I drew on a range of sources that illuminated the political, organizational, and ideological drivers of Islamist party behavior in Pakistan. I relied first on a number of qualitative sources, the first of which was newspaper and magazine archives, primarily but not exclusively in English, which provided a rich contemporaneous reading of political events for the five case studies that are described here. Although official censorship and self-censorship by journalistic organizations have waxed and waned since the 1990s, Pakistan has had a relatively vibrant press that has reported on political and religious matters. Second, I examined a number of Urdu publications produced by the parties themselves, with emphasis on the JI and JUI-F. The richest vein of material was in the form of weekly and monthly magazines published by the parties, most notably the JI's monthly *Tarjumān al-Qur'ān* (Interpretation of the Quran) and *Haft Rozah Aishyā* (Weekly Asia); the JUI-S's monthly *al-Ḥaq* (The Truth); and the JUI-F's flagship monthly *al-Jam'iyat* and its monthly student publication, *'Azm-e-Nau* (New Resolve). These latter two publications in particular have received extremely limited attention from among the scholarly community. In addition, I examined an array of other party publications in English and Urdu including various constitutions, pamphlets, and manifestos.

Third, I reviewed parliamentary debates related to the first three case studies described here. These included National Assembly and Senate debates, transcribed in a mix of English and Urdu and accessed at the National Assembly Library in Islamabad; and the Khyber Pakhtunkhwa Provincial Assembly debates, transcribed in a mix of English and Pashto and accessed at the Provincial Assembly Library in Peshawar. Fourth, I took advantage of a limited set of legal records in English and Urdu pertaining to the *sharī'ah* (Islamic law) cases in question, including draft legislation and court rulings. Fifth, I drew on a small set of U.S. State Department cables reporting on the 1994 events in Malakand. These communications were declassified by the Department on request under the Freedom of Information Act (FOIA).

Finally, this research drew on a set of several dozen semistructured interviews with scholars, journalists, party members, elected officials, and government functionaries. These interviews were conducted largely in Lahore, Islamabad, and Washington. I also drew on a set of related interviews conducted for prior research on Islamic politics in Pakistan between 2005 and 2009, many of which took place in Khyber Pakhtunkhwa province.[14] These interviews were conducted in English, Urdu, or often a mixture of both languages, and often on a not-for-attribution basis. While the interviews were a particularly valuable source of information on party structure and operations, they were also subject to the widest number of potential limitations, largely in the form of response biases. Islamist party figures had significant incentives to downplay their party's relationships to anti-state violence and anti-state movements, particularly in the course of their interactions with an American interlocutor. These interviews thus had utility in corroborating certain kinds of information, but I treated them with significant skepticism on sensitive matters relating to parties' relationships with anti-state violence.

Keeping in mind Kay Lawson's admonition that those who collect quantitative data on party organization often find that their "results are likely to be more quantifiable than credible," there were several discrete types of quantitative data that proved useful in addressing the key questions posed by this study.[15] The most notable of these related to party membership. Political

[14] The North-West Frontier Province (NWFP) was renamed Khyber Pakhtunkhwa (KP) province in 2010.

[15] Kay Lawson, "Political Parties: Inside and Out," *Comparative Politics* 23, no. 1 (October 1990): 107.

parties in Pakistan typically do not release their membership information, possibly for reasons related to political competition. I was, however, able to obtain for the JI 2009–10 top-line membership data from the party secretariat in Mansurah, Punjab.[16] These figures, analyzed in Chapter 4, provide a breakdown of membership on the basis of the party's various membership categories, from the lowest to the highest: members, workers, rukn (full member) candidates, and rukn. By comparing this membership data to the contemporaneous electoral rolls, I was able to calculate the party's membership density by province.

Gathering membership data from Pakistan's other major Islamist party, the JUI-F, proved to be considerably more difficult. The party does not publish any broad-based membership information, and it lacks a well-organized central secretariat to tabulate detailed party data. I was, nonetheless, able to calculate relatively comprehensive party membership figures indirectly by examining a copy of the party's 2011 leadership directory, a 270-page tome produced for party leaders.[17] It provides names, addresses, and titles for every party leadership body across the country, down to the district level. The JUI-F electoral structure is such that the party elects a national general council (markazī majlis-e-'umumī) on a strict proportional basis. For every 3,000 members in a district, the party will send one representative to the national general council.[18]

Having tabulated the national general council members by district, I was thus able to calculate the JUI-F's minimum district party membership for every district in the country. These figures were also standardized, this time against the district-level contemporaneous electoral rolls, to produce a measure of JUI-F party density by district. These data—both the absolute membership, and the membership density—were mapped using GIS software onto the extant (2011-delimited) district and provincial boundaries.[19] I used these data to identify key districts in which the party had large numbers of members, or high levels of membership density. Although the JI's overall membership figures are widely known, these analyses provide the most detailed picture ever of the JUI-F's constituencies and geographic distribution.

[16] Jamā'at-e Islāmī Pākistān, "afrādī quvat jamā'at-e islāmī pākistān [Personnel Strength of Jamaat-e Islami Pakistan]" (Jamā'at-e Islāmī Pākistān, October 2009).

[17] Maulānā Maḥbūb ur-Raḥmān Qureshī, ed., *ḍā'irekṭrī jami'yat 'ulamā'-e islām pākistān 2011 tā 2013* (Rawalpindi: Ṣadā'e Qur'ān Publīkeshanz, 2011).

[18] Muḥammad Akrām al-Qādrī, "ruknsāzī ke b'ad ab hamāre karne ke kām! ek jā'izah [After Recruitment, The Things for Us to Do! An Analysis]," *al-Jam'iyat* 11, no. 11 (August 2010): 10–12.

[19] The directory, based on the party's 2011 elections, took into account the government's district delimitation revisions that had taken place in recent years in Sindh and Balochistan. The data extrapolated from the directory were compared against the 2011 Draft Electoral Rolls, Election Commission of Pakistan, "List of District Wise Verified/Unverified/Augmented Voters," 2012, https://archive.org/details/voter-stats-ecp-2012.

Information derived from the JUI-F directory also formed the basis for other analyses. It allowed, first, a comparison of which provinces were over- and under-represented in the national leadership council (markazī majlis-e-shūrá), which is not chosen on a proportional basis. Second, I conducted a detailed count of the names and personal titles of members of the national leadership council, to assess the percentage of party leaders, by province, who held earned religious titles (e.g., maulana), as opposed to honorary religious titles or titles indicating a professional background (e.g., doctor).

Finally, I compiled a database of Provincial Assembly and National Assembly electoral returns for the 2002, 2008, 2013, and 2018 elections. These data provide a useful picture of the Islamist parties' relative electoral strengths and the geographic distribution of their influence. The data also helpfully disaggregate the returns related to candidates who ran under electoral alliances (such as the MMA in 2002), by re-coding a candidate based on his or her original party affiliation (e.g., JI, JUI-F, or JUI-S). Some of these qualitative and quantitative data sources are used to answer general questions about party structure and behaviors. Others were specifically collected to support the five case studies, detailed later in Chapters 6 through 10.

These cases were selected by first identifying the universe of cases, from the advent of the new era of electoral politics in 1988 following the death of General Zia ul-Haq until 2023, in which a movement or political party engaged in religiously justified anti-state violence that was sustained and organizationally condoned. I selected this time period because, while the chapter that follows chronicles the activities of a number of anti-state movements from the pre-Partition era through Pakistan's first few decades, it was not until the late 1980s that this form of religiously justified violence against the Pakistani state emerged prominently.

Reviewing the period 1998 through 2023, I identified a total of five significant cases that met the above criteria.[20] A number of potential cases were considered and rejected for not meeting one or both elements: Some cases, including many involving sectarian violence, included religious justifications but were directed toward individuals or groups rather than state entities. Other cases, including some that centered on ethnic or tribal separatist violence, were directed toward state entities but were justified principally on nonreligious grounds. It is worth noting that four of the five identified cases occurred after the watershed events of September 11, 2001. Given this book's efforts to trace and interpret the rise of anti-state violence over the past several decades, the preponderance of cases after 2001 does not diminish their

[20] The second case only partially meets these criteria, because the anti-state violence was not as obviously sustained or organizationally condoned but was included for reasons described later in this chapter.

Table 1.1 Case Studies

Case	Violence Enabled	Location	National Regime
(1) TNSM (from 1994)	By an outside movement	Khyber Pakhtunkhwa	Elected
(2) MMA (from 2005)	By/within an Islamist party	Khyber Pakhtunkhwa	Martial
(3) Red Mosque (from 2007)	By an outside movement	Islamabad	Martial
(4) TTP (from 2005)	By an outside movement	Nationwide	Elected
(5) TLP (from 2011)	By/within an Islamist party	Select cities	Elected

applicability or relevance, but it does require that these cases in question be properly situated, as I have sought to do in the case study chapters that follow, in the context of Pakistan's post-9/11 geopolitical circumstances—often simultaneously as a partner and antagonist of the United States.

The five resulting cases, presented here in Table 1.1 and summarized in the section that follows, helpfully provide some analytic diversity with respect to the types of cases (direct versus indirect means of enabling anti-state violence), the locations involved, and the types of national government regime against which the anti-state violence was directed.

In the chapters that follow, I will for each of these cases explore whether there is evidence that Islamist parties publicly endorsed or materially supported religiously justified anti-state violence or allowed their own party members or affiliates to engage in such violence.

1.4 Structure of the Book

Chapter 2 surveys Pakistan's Islamic political landscape. It begins by providing a working definition of "Islamist parties," and introduces the universe of parties that will be addressed in this book. It then provides a succinct history of the role that these Islamist parties have played in Pakistani politics, from the pre-Partition era until 2023.

Chapter 3 focuses on the parties' respective ideological moorings. It begins with an overview of the various theological interpretive traditions from which the Islamist parties emerged and describes how these traditions have shaped the parties' views of ritual practice and certain aspects of Islamic law. The second part of the chapter explores in depth a set of theological and ideological debates related to interpretation and enforcement of shariah that might have more direct bearing on the parties' decisions to endorse anti-state violence and various forms of vigilantism. Even though this book argues that ideological differences among the parties have limited power to explain their divergent behaviors, this chapter helps to describe the patterns of ideological affinities and affiliations that figure prominently in the parties' relationships with militant groups and with the state.

The fourth and fifth chapters present a detailed look at the structural drivers of Islamist party behavior. I begin by examining the organizational coherence and institutionalization of the Islamist parties. The second section explores their relationships with their constituents, and with affiliate groups including student wings and madrassah organizations. The third, beginning in Chapter 5, maps the parties' relationships with militant organizations. The final section evaluates the parties' respective relationships with the state, and their vulnerabilities to state influence and institutions. These chapters in particular try to illuminate the ways in which Islamist parties differ—in structure, relationships, and vulnerabilities—from so-called mainstream parties.

Part II of the book contains five chapters that present concise case studies in roughly chronological order, each of which explore the conditions under which Pakistan's Islamist parties choose to enable religiously justified anti-state violence. Each chapter is similarly structured, with an introduction, a background to the case, a section describing the roles and behaviors of the Islamist parties, and a conclusion that explores the "logics of anti-state violence" as practiced by the parties and the implications of the case for the wider research project.

The first case, in Chapter 6, presents a study of the Tahrik-e-Nifaz-e-Shariat-e-Muhammadi (TNSM), an Islamic movement that emerged in 1989 in northwest Pakistan, led by Maulana Sufi Muhammad. Based in the northern Malakand Division of Pakistan's Khyber Pakhtunknwa province (the erstwhile North-West Frontier Province), the TNSM called for implementation of a vague "shariah" agenda. Its movement gained momentum in 1994, and when the government refused to meet its demands, the TNSM took to the streets in violent protest, clashing with police and precipitating a military operation against the group. Eventually, the government proffered a package of shariah measures, which was tentatively approved but quickly bogged down in the court system. The TNSM had, and continued to have for the subsequent two decades, complex relationships with local Islamist parties, as well as a contentious relationship with the central government. This chapter traces the first TNSM uprising, from late 1993 through early 1995, an episode which—despite being one of the earliest and most foundational cases of anti-state Islamic mobilization in Pakistan—has received rather limited attention in the academic literature.

The second case, in Chapter 7, explores a period in which a coalition of Islamist parties governing in the erstwhile NWFP episodically supported vigilantism that challenged the authority of the state. This case is somewhat different from the other four, in that the anti-state violence was not as obviously sustained or organizationally condoned. The case specifically examines a period in which the Muttahida Majlis-e-Amal (MMA) Islamic alliance, following its unprecedented victory in the provincial elections in 2002 and continuing through the end of its elected tenure in 2008, wrestled with decisions about whether to pursue its agenda through vigilante violence or legal means. Although this episode does not fully conform to the case criteria, it is a valuable addition because it provides insight into the organizational incentive structures of the various Islamist parties, and how those structures are influenced by the parties' positions in elected office.

Chapter 8 tells the story of the 2007 Lal Masjid crisis through the lens of Islamist party decision-making. The Lal Masjid, or Red Mosque, sits in the heart of Islamabad, and has long been patronized by government officials. In 2007, a dispute broke out when the leaders of the mosque—who had increasingly been challenging the government and the military—mobilized their students to begin enforcing their conception of Islamic law through vigilante means throughout the capital. Eventually, the army stormed the mosque in an ill-fated operation, resulting in a militant backlash across the country. This case study traces the Red Mosque crisis, particularly from mid-2006 through late 2007. Islamist parties became deeply involved in the crisis—as advocates for the Red Mosque leadership, as intermediaries, and as street protestors. Moreover, some of them faced internal dissension about how they should handle the crisis, and whether they should support the call for shariah. In some respects a microcosm of how Islamist parties can be caught between the government and anti-state vigilantes, this crisis illuminated the risks that religious parties face in inserting themselves between state and non-state actors.

The fourth case study, in Chapter 9, examines Islamist party responses to the rise of new movements that identified themselves as "Taliban" in northwest Pakistan beginning around 2005. These new movements received intermittent support from Pakistan's religious parties but were also viewed with skepticism for their anti-democratic ideology and their spectacular attacks on the Pakistani state. This chapter traces in particular the Islamist parties' responses and attempts at mediation during the complex negotiations between the Tahrik-e-Taliban Pakistan (TTP) and the Pakistani government that unfolded—ultimately unsuccessfully—in 2013 and 2014. The narrative examines debates within the religious parties about how to deal with the rise of anti-state Taliban organizations and highlights the sometimes counterintuitive "praise for protection" strategies that the parties employed to navigate the increasingly dangerous political landscape.

The final case study, in Chapter 10, explores the rise of Barelvi activism and vigilantism. The Barelvis are a Sunni sect with a large following in Pakistan, though historically Barelvism and its associated Sufi practices have found political representation in so-called mainstream parties rather than Islamist parties, which have been dominated by the Deobandi sect. The 2011 assassination of Punjab Governor Salman Taseer by his Barelvi bodyguard, who was upset by the governor's support for a Christian woman accused of blasphemy, sparked a revival of Barelvi activism and forced the established Deobandi Islamist parties to take a position on vigilantism being carried out by their ideological rivals. Following the execution of Taseer's assassin in 2016, Barelvi leader Allama Khadim Hussain Rizvi registered the Tahrik-e-Labbaik Pakistan (TLP) as a political party and in 2017 organized protests that paralyzed the capital for weeks. The party won only a couple of provincial seats in the 2018 election but garnered more than two million votes overall. When the Christian woman, Asia Bibi, was acquitted later that year, the TLP again launched protests, this time openly challenging military and judicial organs as well. Rizvi and many senior party members were subsequently arrested and charged by the anti-terrorism court. This case study focuses on two key episodes in this story: the Islamist parties' responses to the 2011 assassination, and the TLP's own decision-making regarding its protests, vigilantism, and challenges to state authority during the 2017–2018 period.

The concluding chapter brings together the analytical material in Chapters 2 through 5 with the case study evidence from Chapters 6 through 10 to evaluate the hypotheses outlined in this opening chapter. The conclusion considers the wider implications of this research for the study of Pakistani politics and, more broadly, the incentive structures that shape Islamist organizations' relationships with religiously justified political violence.

2
The Islamist Party Landscape

2.1 Pakistan's Islamist Parties

This chapter begins by defining "Islamism" and "Islamist" parties, and based on those definitions introduces the universe of parties that will be discussed in this book. The section that follows sets these parties in their historical context, tracing their emergence in Pakistan and their political trajectories.

Throughout this book I will use the term "Islamism" to describe an ideological expression of Islamic thought or practice that privileges politics, and "Islamist" to describe those individuals or organizations that advance or practice Islamism.[1] Scholars have proposed a host of definitions of Islamism, including those that emphasize Islam's role as a "guide in political action";[2] as a form of political theory and practice that seeks a state "whose governmental principles, institutions, and legal system derive directly from the *shari'ah*";[3] or as "a form of instrumentalization of Islam."[4] Each of these has flaws. The first is too generic and does little to separate Islamism from the more common phenomenon of Muslim participation in politics writ large. The second is too broad, given that desire for an Islamic political order of some kind is now almost so accepted as to be beyond contest in much of the Muslim-majority world.[5] And the third is too cynical, leaving the reader the impossible task of discerning the underlying motives of actors who have both political and religious ambitions.

[1] For a multifaceted typology of Islamists in Pakistan and their relation to democratic politics, see Haroon K. Ullah, *Vying for Allah's Vote: Understanding Islamic Parties, Political Violence, and Extremism in Pakistan* (Washington: Georgetown University Press, 2013).

[2] Ann-Kristin Jonasson, *At the Command of God? On the Political Linkage of Islamist Parties* (Göteborg: Göteborg Studies in Politics, 2004), 3.

[3] Peter Mandaville, *Global Political Islam* (London: Routledge, 2007), 57.

[4] Guilain Denoeux, "The Forgotten Swamp: Navigating Political Islam," *Middle East Policy* 9, no. 2 (June 2002): 61.

[5] Olivier Roy's definition of Islamism as "the brand of modern political Islamic fundamentalism that claims to re-create a true Islamic society, not simply by imposing sharia, but by establishing first an Islamic state through political action" also suffers from being overly broad. Olivier Roy, *Globalized Islam: The Search for a New Ummah* (New York: Columbia University Press, 2006), 58. See also Olivier Roy, *The Failure of Political Islam*, trans. Carol Volk (Cambridge, MA: Harvard University Press, 1994).

Vigilante Islamists. Joshua T. White, Oxford University Press. © Oxford University Press (2025).
DOI: 10.1093/9780197814178.003.0002

I will adopt instead a more bounded definition put forward by Frédéric Volpi, who modified a popular definition by Graham Fuller to highlight the fact that Islamism is best defined by the *emphasis* it places on political dynamics: "an Islamist is one who believes that Islam as a body of faith has something *crucial* to say about how politics and society should be ordered in the contemporary *ummah* and who seeks to implement this idea in some fashion *as a matter of priority*."[6] This line of logic helpfully distinguishes between those Muslims who generically support public Islamization measures, and those for whom the advancement of such measures is both a matter of compulsion and, to use Muhammad Qasim Zaman's phrase, a "single-minded concern."[7] Unlike some scholars, I do not limit the label Islamist to technocratic or anticlerical parties and movements; the working definition above is capacious enough to include so-called modernist Islamist parties such as the Jamaat-e-Islami, as well as clerical parties such as the Jamiat Ulama-e-Islam, who also place a notable emphasis on politics and the state.

Although debates about politics have long occupied Islamic scholars, Islamism and its emphasis on state centricity borrows heavily from twentieth-century ideologies—including, in some cases, Marxist-Leninist theories of political organization—and came of age in the 1970s as an expression of Islam that combined both traditional and modern aspects.[8] As I note below, in the Pakistani context, a variety of organizations and political parties representing various interpretive schools and traditions have adopted the basic tenets of Islamism, all in their own ways prioritizing political change as a crucial task of the Muslim community.

Just as Islamism is not synonymous with traditionalism or modernism, neither is it synonymous with extremism or an embrace of instrumental violence. Islamism as an idea does not necessarily presume, and neither does it necessarily prescribe, that the transformation of the state requires violence. Some Islamist groups, including some of the parties studied in this book, do legitimize or enable violence for political ends. But an embrace of those tactics is not what makes them Islamist.

In the Pakistani context, there are a number of formally registered political parties for whom Islamic political change is central to their mission and

[6] Frédéric Volpi, *Political Islam Observed* (New York: Columbia University Press, 2010), xi.

[7] Muhammad Qasim Zaman, "Pakistan: Shari'a and the State," in *Shari'a Politics*, ed. Robert W. Hefner (Bloomington: Indiana University Press, 2011), 236.

[8] Barry M. Rubin, "An Introduction to Assessing Contemporary Islamism," in *Guide to Islamist Movements*, ed. Barry M. Rubin, vol. 1 (Armonk, NY: M.E. Sharpe, 2010), xvii; Irfan Ahmad, "Genealogy of the Islamic State: Reflections on Maududi's Political Thought and Islamism," *Journal of the Royal Anthropological Institute* 15, no. s1 (2009): S147. Some also see the emergence of Islamism as a product of the nineteenth-century "subjugation" of Muslims in the Indian subcontinent and further afield. See Mohammed Ayoob, *The Many Faces of Political Islam: Religion and Politics in the Muslim World* (Ann Arbor: University of Michigan Press, 2008), 9.

identity. These are referred to in this book as Islamist parties, and those with national profile are described below. The "Islamist party" shorthand is useful, but confounded somewhat by the fact that other, so-called mainstream political parties in Pakistan have come to adopt to varying degrees the rhetoric of Islamism. This is due in part to the influence that the Islamist parties have exerted, with support from the military establishment, since the early days of the Pakistani state, and these relationships will be explored in greater detail later in this chapter.

Broadly speaking, Pakistan's Islamist parties can be divided into five main categories, based loosely on sectarian identity.

The first is the **Jamaat-e-Islami (JI).** The JI was founded by Sunni cleric Maulana Abul Ala Maududi in 1941. Opposed to the Muslim League, the JI was Maududi's attempt to institutionalize a movement of Islamic renewal among Muslims in India. Maududi's ideology emphasized the importance of reforming and indeed capturing the state and its legal apparatus, and his focus on political transformation and, to quote Oliver Roy, "providing an alternative viable model to the different ideologies promoted by the West," influenced the writings of Arab Islamist intellectuals including Hassan al-Banna and Sayyid Qutb.[9] The JI has come to see itself as nonsectarian or suprasectarian, rising above the divisions that have characterized the factionalized Sunni landscape.[10]

Unlike the clerical political parties in the pre-Partition era, the JI sought from the beginning to recruit technocrats and activists, and drew its support predominantly from the "devout middle classes" of Pakistan's urban centers.[11] The party has remained largely urban, highly centralized, and focused on the legal Islamization of the state. It has also retained links with a wider family of Jamaat-e-Islami parties in the subcontinent, the United Kingdom, and further afield, and with likeminded modernist Islamist parties such as the Muslim Brotherhood.

The second category comprises the Deobandi Sunni parties, principally, the various clerical **Jamiat Ulama-e-Islam (JUI)** parties. As described in Chapter 3, Deobandism is a Sunni *maslak* (interpretive school; literally "path" or "way") that has its roots in late nineteenth-century India. The Jamiat Ulama-e-Islam (Assembly of Clerics of Islam; JUI) parties are the successors

[9] Olivier Roy, "The Failure of Political Islam Revisited," in *Pathways to Contemporary Islam*, ed. Mohamed Nawab Mohamed Osman (Amsterdam: Amsterdam University Press, 2020), 169. It was through Sayyid Qutb that many of Maududi's ideas eventually made their way to the Arab world.

[10] Other Sunni groups do not always agree with this characterization, and see the JI as theologically ungrounded and insufficiently deferential to the classical interpretive traditions.

[11] This phrase is borrowed from Gilles Kepel, *Jihad: The Trail of Political Islam*, trans. Anthony F. Roberts (Cambridge, MA: Belknap Press of Harvard University Press, 2002), 103.

to the Jamiat Ulama-e-Hind (Assembly of Clerics of India; JUH), which was established in 1919. As the dominant political branch of the Deobandi school of thought, the JUI parties have drawn from a largely rural and clerical support base, and their interests have been deeply intertwined with their vast *madrassah* (religious school; plural *madāris*) networks.

The JUI parties experienced a major factional split in the early 1980s; the dominant faction led by Maulana Fazl ur-Rahman became the JUI-F, and the considerably smaller faction led by Maulana Sami ul-Haq became the JUI-S.[12] There have been other short-lived splinter groups, including the JUI-Nazryati (ideological) faction based in Balochistan province, which broke away from the JUI-F in 2007 and largely merged back into the party in 2016.[13]

Although it is not principally organized to contest elections, the virulently anti-Shia Deobandi militant group **Ahl-e-Sunnat Wal Jamaat (ASWJ)** has a history of episodically participating in politics. Its antecedent, the militant organization Sipah-e-Sahabah Pakistan (SSP), contested seats in Punjab in the 1990s, and one of its leaders even secured an appointment as a provincial minister.[14] Although notionally banned by the Pakistani government, the ASWJ sought to contest in the 2018 general election; the government lifted restrictions on the organization's leader, Maulana Ahmed Ludhianvi, who subsequently ran for a National Assembly seat as an independent and placed second.[15] The ASWJ was ultimately not registered by the Election Commission of Pakistan in the 2018 cycle, but the organization nonetheless fielded candidates, some as independents, and some under an agreement to use the extant registration of the Pakistan Rah-e-Haq Party (PRHP), which had been founded by an SSP member in 2012.[16]

The third category of Islamist parties is those associated with the Barelvi Sunni school of interpretation. Barelvism is a school of Sunni Islamic thought and practice that nominally traces its roots to the writings of the

[12] Sohail Mahmood, *Islamic Fundamentalism in Pakistan, Egypt and Iran* (Lahore: Vanguard, 1995), 373ff. Note that the JUI-F officially registered its name as the Jamiat Ulama-e-Islam (JUI) with the Election Commission of Pakistan in March 2020, but is still commonly referred to as the JUI-F, and will be referred to as such in this volume.

[13] "Two JUI Factions Merge After Patch-Up," *Dawn*, February 26, 2016.

[14] Mariam Abou Zahab, "The Regional Dimension of Sectarian Conflicts in Pakistan," in *Pakistan: Nationalism Without a Nation?*, ed. Christophe Jaffrelot (New York: Zed Books, 2002), 119; Arif Rafiq, "Sunni Deobandi-Shi'i Sectarian Violence in Pakistan: Explaining the Resurgence Since 2007" (Washington: Middle East Institute, December 2014), 24ff.

[15] Sohail Chaudhry, "Govt Lifts Ban on AWJ, Unfreezes Assets of Its Chief Ahmed Ludhianvi," *Express Tribune*, June 27, 2018; Asad Hashim, "Quetta Hazaras Despair as Religious Supremacists Contest Election," *Al Jazeera*, July 15, 2018, https://web.archive.org/web/20240528140419/https://www.aljazeera.com/features/2018/7/15/quetta-hazaras-despair-as-religious-supremacists-contest-election.

[16] Qadeer Tanoli, "'Rent-a-Party' Phenomenon Emerges on Political Landscape," *Express Tribune*, July 11, 2018; Munir Ahmed, "A Look at the Main Candidates in Pakistan National Elections," *Associated Press*, July 24, 2018.

nineteenth-century cleric Ahmed Raza Khan Barelvi. Barelvis, who typically prefer the generic Sunni label *Ahl-e-Sunnat Wal Jamaat* (not to be confused with the above-mentioned Deobandi militant organization) are associated with shrine-based forms of popular devotion and have links to various Sufi brotherhoods in the subcontinent.[17] This school of interpretation is particularly prominent in Punjab and Sindh provinces.

Barelvi political parties have never been particularly strong in Pakistan, though Barelvi interests have arguably been well represented by other parties such as the Pakistan Peoples Party (PPP) and the Karachi-based Muttahida Qaumi Movement (MQM). This book will examine two main clusters of Barelvi Islamist parties. The first is a group of small parties led by clerics who use the **Jamiat Ulama-e-Pakistan (JUP)** name. The JUP was founded in 1948 as a collective of Barelvi clerics who sought to advance the interests of their sect and their madrassah network.[18] The party had some modest electoral successes in the 1970s, but even that influence has waned over time; it suffered a major factional split in 1990, and again in 2003 following the death of its longtime leader Maulana Shah Ahmad Noorani.[19] The JUP parties further fragmented, and occasionally recombined, settling into two major factions: JUP-Imam Noorani (JUP-IN), the dominant faction, which has sustained closer relationships with the JUI-F; and the JUP-Noorani (JUP-N), which is more closely aligned with the JI.[20] (There is also a separate Barelvi umbrella organization, the Sunni Ittihad Council, that was formed in 2009 and registered with the Election Commission of Pakistan as a political party, but it has never garnered significant votes.)

The second important Barelvi Islamist party has more recent origins. The **Tahrik-e-Labbaik Pakistan (TLP)** was founded in 2015 by the cleric Allama Khadim Hussain Rizvi, and it rose to prominence by organizing protests against the execution of Mumtaz Qadri, who assassinated Punjab Governor Salman Taseer in 2011.[21] Less institutionally tied to the Barelvi shrine and madrassah networks than the JUP, the TLP seized as its raison d'être

[17] See Joshua T. White, "Beyond Moderation: Dynamics of Political Islam in Pakistan," *Contemporary South Asia* 20, no. 2 (June 2012): 179–94.

[18] Mujeeb Ahmad, *Jam'iyyat 'Ulama-i-Pakistan, 1948–1979* (Islamabad, Pakistan: National Institute of Historical and Cultural Research, 1993), 3ff.

[19] Abdul Basit, "Barelvi Political Activism and Religious Mobilization in Pakistan: The Case of Tehreek-e-Labaik Pakistan (TLP)," *Politics, Religion & Ideology* 21, no. 3 (2020): 376. For a deeper history of the institutional development of the JUP, see Alix Philippon, *Soufisme et Politique au Pakistan: Le Mouvement Barelwi à L'heure de "La Guerre Contre Le Terrorisme"* (Paris: Éditions Karthala and Sciences Po Aix, 2011), chaps. 2–3.

[20] International Crisis Group, "Islamic Parties in Pakistan," Asia Report 216 (Islamabad: International Crisis Group, December 12, 2011), 15ff; Ali Arqam, "Divine Intervention," *Newsline*, July 2018; Election Commission of Pakistan, "List of Enlisted Political Parties" (Government of Pakistan, May 19, 2020).

[21] K. K. Shahid, "Rise of the TLP," *Newsline*, October 2018.

its resistance to blasphemy and its public advocacy for the protection of the honor of the prophet Muhammad. The party, which was first registered just a year prior to the 2018 general election, received the fifth-highest number of votes, and won two Provincial Assembly seats in Sindh, but it gained a national profile on account of its protests and its complex relationship to the military as described in detail in Chapter 10.

Finally, it is worth noting that **Sunni Tahrik**, a Barelvi militant organization, has at times been registered as a political party, but is not principally organized to contest elections, and has never won a parliamentary seat. It is discussed later in this chapter and in Chapter 10.

The fourth group of Islamist parties is those associated with the Shia branch of Islam. Shia parties have historically not been politically influential in Pakistan. Some evidence suggests that Shiite voters have typically patronized the left-of-center PPP.[22] In response to General Zia ul-Haq's Islamization measures, some leaders in the Shia community founded the Tahrik-e-Nifaz-e-Fiqh-e-Jafariah (Movement for the Implementation of Jafariah Law; TNFJ) in 1979, and launched major protests in 1980 challenging the government's imposition of automatic *zakāt* (obligatory almsgiving) deductions.[23] The TNFJ underwent various splits, and in 1993, it was renamed the Tahrik-e-Jafariah Pakistan (TJP).[24]

Worried about the rise of anti-Shia militancy of Sunni organizations such as SSP and Lashkar-e-Jhangvi (LeJ), a group of TJP activists broke away from the party in the early 1990s to form the Shia militant organization Sipah-e-Muhammad Pakistan (SMP).[25] TJP, along with SSP, were banned by General Pervez Musharraf as terrorist organizations in 2002, though TJP continued operating as a political party under the new name **Islami Tahrik Pakistan (ITP)**.[26] The ITP, led by Sajid Naqvi, was a mainstay member of the Muttahida Majlis-e-Amal (MMA) electoral alliance, and won several seats in the

[22] Frédéric Grare, "The Evolution of Sectarian Conflicts in Pakistan and the Ever-Changing Face of Islamic Violence," *South Asia: Journal of South Asian Studies* 30, no. 1 (April 2007): 128–30; Hassan Abbas, "Shiism and Sectarian Conflict in Pakistan: Identity Politics, Iranian Influence, and Tit-for-Tat Violence," Occasional Paper Series (West Point, NY: Combatting Terrorism Center at West Point, September 22, 2010), 23ff.

[23] See Muhammad Qasim Zaman, "Sectarianism in Pakistan: The Radicalization of Shi'i and Sunni Identities," *Modern Asian Studies* 32, no. 3 (July 1998): 689–716; Andreas Rieck, *The Shias of Pakistan: An Assertive and Beleaguered Minority* (Oxford: Oxford University Press, 2015), 207–20; Simon Wolfgang Fuchs, *In a Pure Muslim Land: Shi'ism between Pakistan and the Middle East* (Chapel Hill: University of North Carolina Press, 2019), 137ff.

[24] Muhammad Qasim Zaman, *The Ulama in Contemporary Islam: Custodians of Change*, Princeton Studies in Muslim Politics (Princeton: Princeton University Press, 2002), 115ff; Mariam Abou Zahab, *A Kaleidoscope of Islam* (New York: Oxford University Press, 2020), 50.

[25] "Sipah-e-Mohammed Pakistan, Terrorist Group of Pakistan," South Asia Terrorism Portal, 2014, https://www.satp.org/satporgtp/countries/pakistan/terroristoutfits/SMP.htm.

[26] International Crisis Group, "Islamic Parties in Pakistan," 19.

Gilgit-Baltistan assembly elections in 2015. Naqvi, however, has been the only member of the party with a sustained national profile. The ITP lacks a strong organizational base, and one close observer noted that it functions more like an advocacy group than a party, and sometimes informally encourages its followers to vote for the PPP.[27]

Other small Shia parties vie for influence in provincial elections and at the local level. The **Majlis Wahadat-e-Muslimin Pakistan** (Council of Unity of Muslims; MWMP)[28] was founded in 2008 with the backing of the Imamia Students Organization, which exercises significant clout in Shia politics.[29] In 2013 the party won a single Provincial Assembly seat in Balochistan, in a district that had a significant proportion of Hazara Shiite voters.[30] The party received only about 20,000 National Assembly votes in 2018, and won no National or Provincial Assembly seats.[31]

The fifth group of Islamist parties are those associated with the Ahl-e-Hadith (People of the Tradition) sect. Unlike the Deobandis and Barelvis, who follow the Hanafi school of *fiqh* (jurisprudence), the Wahhabi-influenced Ahl-e-Hadith reject the jurisprudential schools and instead privilege the *ḥadīth* (prophetic traditions).[32] For years the only meaningful Ahl-e-Hadith political party in Pakistan was the **Markazi Jamiat Ahl-e-Hadith** (Central Assembly of Ahl-e-Hadith; MJAH). The party has deep roots in pre-Partition India, tracing its history to the 1906 All India Ahl-e-Hadith Conference, but it became involved in politics only in the 1970s.[33] The MJAH has had a very small electoral footprint; it joined the MMA coalition in 2002, but has had few prominent political figures.[34] Tellingly, Sajid Mir, who became the party's president in 1992, served multiple terms in Pakistan's Senate with a ticket from the mainstream PML-N rather than his own party.[35]

[27] Talib Rizvi, interview by Joshua White, Shuja Malik, and Niloufer Siddiqui, English, March 6, 2011.

[28] International Crisis Group, "Islamic Parties in Pakistan," 29ff; Rieck, *The Shias of Pakistan*, 311.

[29] Abbas, "Shiism and Sectarian Conflict in Pakistan: Identity Politics, Iranian Influence, and Tit-for-Tat Violence," 24ff; Zia Ur Rehman, "Political Parties in Talks to Woo Shia Voters," *The News*, July 7, 2018.

[30] Arqam, "Divine Intervention."

[31] Election Commission of Pakistan, "Party Wise Vote Bank—National Assembly," 2018, https://web.archive.org/web/20201205085504/https://www.ecp.gov.pk/frmVotebank.aspx.

[32] Dietrich Reetz, "Migrants, Mujahedin, Madrassa Students: The Diversity of Transnational Islam in Pakistan," *South Asia Chronicle* 1 (2011): 175; C. Christine Fair, Rebecca Littman, and Elizabeth R. Nugent, "Conceptions of Shari'a and Support for Militancy and Democratic Values: Evidence from Pakistan," *Political Science Research and Methods* 6, no. 3 (July 2018): 4.

[33] International Crisis Group, "Islamic Parties in Pakistan," 14.

[34] For more on the MJAH, see Mariam Abou Zahab, "Salafism in Pakistan: The Ahl-e Hadith Movement," in *Global Salafism: Islam's New Religious Movement*, ed. Roel Meijer (New York: Oxford University Press, 2014), 130–33; Samina Yasmeen, *Jihad and Dawah: Evolving Narratives of Lashkar-e-Taiba and Jamat Ud Dawah* (London: Hurst & Company, 2017), 41.

[35] Sajid Mir, "Nomination Form-I, Sajid Mir" (Election Commission of Pakistan, October 2, 2015).

A more recent entrant to the Ahl-e-Hadith political scene has been the **Milli Muslim League** (National Muslim League; MML). The MML was created in 2017 by Hafiz Saeed, the leader of Lashkar-e-Taiba (LeT), as a bespoke public-facing entity designed to appear distinct from the militant group.[36] LeT and its other front organizations such as Jamaat ud-Dawa (JuD) operate with the support of, and in the service of, the Pakistani military. Although Saeed and other functionaries claimed that MML was an independent party, it plainly operated as part of the extended LeT/JuD family of organizations, and was led at its founding by Saifullah Khalid, a close associate of Saeed's.[37] The creation of MML was unexpected, not least because Saeed had a long record of publishing elaborate theological arguments rejecting democratic politics and criticizing the JI and other Islamist parties.[38] His about-face suggests that the MML was birthed for the purpose of serving state interests rather than for advancing any independent ideological or political agenda.

With the LeT and JuD designated as terrorist organizations by the international community, and listed on various (functionally ineffectual) watchlists by the Pakistani state, the MML's electoral registration was challenged in Pakistani courts. After the Election Commission of Pakistan rejected the MML's registration, the party effectively contested the 2018 general election under the Allah-o-Akbar Tahrik (God is Great Movement; AAT) party name, winning no seats.[39] The emergence of the MML was a notable development in Pakistan's Islamist party landscape, particularly given the party's clear links to internationally designated terrorist organizations and its close ties with the state. The very nature of these ties, however, and the LeT/JuD's history of abjuring violence against the Pakistani state, make the MML somewhat peripheral to the central research questions of this book, which focus on the ways in which Islamist parties justify anti-state violence.

Not all of the Islamist parties listed in this five-fold typology hold equal influence—electorally or otherwise. In terms of size and system influence, the JI and JUI-F have historically been the most consequential, and thus receive

[36] U.S. Department of the Treasury, "Treasury Targets Terrorist Group Lashkar-e Tayyiba's Political Party," April 2, 2018, https://web.archive.org/web/20240918185542/https://home.treasury.gov/news/press-releases/sm0335.

[37] C. Christine Fair, "The Milli Muslim League: The Domestic Politics of Pakistan's Lashkar-e-Taiba," *Current Trends in Islamist Ideology*, June 3, 2018.

[38] See Joshua T. White, "A Cooperative Jihad? The Religious Logic of Hafiz Muhammad Saeed and the Limits of Pan-Sunni Cooperation in Pakistan," in *Pakistan's Enduring Challenges*, ed. C. Christine Fair and Sarah J. Watson (Philadelphia: University of Pennsylvania Press, 2015), 55–71; Fair, "The Milli Muslim League."

[39] Tanoli, "'Rent-a-Party' Phenomenon Emerges on Political Landscape"; Frud Bezhan and Daud Khattak, "'Terrorist' Turned Candidate: Pakistani Extremists Contest National Elections," *RadioFreeEurope/RadioLiberty*, July 24, 2018, https://web.archive.org/web/20240918190002/https://www.rferl.org/a/from-terrorist-to-candidate-pakistani-extremists-contest-elections/29388270.html.

significant attention in this book. The more recent entrants, notably the TLP and the MML, with their evident links to vigilante and militant organizations, and complex links to the military and state institutions, could grow in importance and will be discussed in this book in the context of their relationships to religiously justified anti-state violence.

2.2 Islamist Parties in Historical Context

2.2.1 Pre-1947: The Emergence of Islamist Parties

All of Pakistan's Islamist parties have antecedents in pre-1947 India. The major clerical parties that operate today—the JUI, JUP, and MJAH—emerged from clerical associations founded in the early part of the twentieth century.

Of these, the Deobandis were on balance the most politically active. Deobandism traces its roots to modern-day Uttar Pradesh, where a group of clerics founded the Dar ul-Ulum Deoband in 1866. Established in the wake of the failed uprising against the British in 1857, this madrassah became the focal point of a wider religious revivalist movement that sought to reconsolidate and refocus the religious and cultural life of the Muslim community on the subcontinent. Far from being political, the early Deobandis were mostly, in the words of Barbara Metcalf, "inward-looking and primarily concerned with the Islamic quality of individual lives."[40] Deobandism emphasized a rigorous devotional ethic and an austere interpretation of religious practice. Although many of the early Deobandis belonged to Sufi orders, over time the movement developed a suspicion of mystical practice and became both critical of, and competitive with, Barelvi Sunnis who oriented their devotional practices around the Sufi shrine culture.

Through the First World War, most Deobandi clerics remained apolitical. Some, however, came to believe that the revivalist message that began at Deoband had to be broadened beyond its pietistic vision to include a political restoration of the Muslim community. Several of the clerics sought a military response to the dual problems of British rule and Muslim disenfranchisement, most notably through their participation in the so-called Silk Letter Conspiracy that attempted to raise an Islamic army of Pashtun tribesmen against the British. Others—perhaps the majority of the politically minded Deobandis—entered the political realm by means of the failed

[40] Barbara D. Metcalf, *Islamic Revival in British India: Deoband, 1860–1900* (Princeton: Princeton University Press, 1982), 86.

Khilafat movement, begun in 1919, which agitated against the proposed abolition of the Ottoman caliphate.[41] Of these clerics, a great number eventually formalized their political participation by joining the Jamiat Ulama-e-Hind (Assembly of Indian Clerics; JUH), a party established in 1919.

Throughout the 1920s, the JUH clerics struggled to define their political agenda and their role in the anti-British agitation. The party's activist energy, however, could not be sustained after the failure of the Khilafat movement. From the late 1920s until the mid-1940s, the JUH again turned inward, focused (as in the early days of the Dar ul-Ulum) on cultural renewal and improving the conditions of the Muslim minority in India.

By the mid-1940s, however, the majority of the Deobandi ulama were no longer debating whether they ought to engage in politics; the question before them was, "Politics toward what end?" Despite their common opposition to British rule, the ulama were divided on the "two-nation theory" proposed by Muhammad Ali Jinnah and the Muslim League and their call for Pakistan as a homeland for Muslims of the Indian subcontinent.[42] In 1945, the JUH split over this issue: the pro-Muslim League faction became the Jamiat Ulama-e-Islam (JUI), and the JUH maintained its affiliation with the Indian National Congress party, arguing that the creation of Pakistan would divide and dangerously weaken the Muslims of India.[43]

Despite support from the British, who sought to blunt the influence of pro-Congress politics in the largely Pashtun North-West Frontier Province (NWFP), the JUI performed poorly in the 1946 elections. The results, in any case, were short-lived. The competition between the JUH and JUI continued right up until the partition of 1947, and neither party was able to gain the overwhelming support of Muslims living in the areas that would become the new state of Pakistan. The Deobandi ulama were divided as to whether the establishment of Pakistan was truly in their interest, and whether its creation reflected legitimate Islamic principles.[44] The JUI began in the new state with limited influence, but would in time emerge as one of Pakistan's leading Islamist parties.

[41] The Muslims sought to persuade Britain to protect the defeated Ottoman Empire, and thus the sultan who also held the title of caliph. In an extraordinary show of solidarity, Mahatma Gandhi also advocated on behalf of the Khilafat movement.

[42] See Barbara D. Metcalf, "Maulana Husain Ahmad Madani and the Jami'at 'Ulama-i-Hind: Against Pakistan, Against the Muslim League," in *Muslims Against the Muslim League: Critiques of the Idea of Pakistan*, ed. Ali Usman Qasmi and Megan Eaton Robb (Cambridge, UK: Cambridge University Press, 2017), 35–64, https://doi.org/10.1017/9781316711224.002.

[43] See, for example, Zia ul-Hasan Faruqi, *The Deoband School and the Demand for Pakistan* (London: Asia Publishing House, 1963), 110–11.

[44] See Ayesha Jalal, *Self and Sovereignty: Individual and Community in South Asian Islam Since 1850* (London: Routledge, 2000), 458ff.

The JUP similarly emerged out of a pre-Partition clerical association, but the Barelvi clerical elite from which it formed were more skeptical of efforts at political mobilization and disinclined to challenge British rule. Ahmad Raza Khan Barelvi, the central figure around whom the Barelvi movement coalesced in the late nineteenth century, was deeply critical of Deobandi and Ahl-e-Hadith clerics on theological grounds, but also rejected much of the Deobandis' political activism.[45] Even as anti-British sentiment gained momentum in the first two decades of the twentieth century, Ahmad Raza held to his view that because British India permitted Muslims to live in accordance with Muslim law, it was within the *dār ul-Islām* (abode of Islam) and not the *dār ul-ḥarb* (abode of war), and thus did not need to be challenged directly.[46]

Ahmad Raza and other leading Barelvi clerics declined to join the JUH or support the Deobandi-led activism on the Khilafat issue, which they considered both inappropriate and ineffectual. Deeply suspicious of what they saw as a growing Hindu assertiveness, they also opposed the way in which many of the Deobandi elite welcomed the cooperation of Hindus.[47] Following Ahmad Raza's death in 1921, leadership of the Barelvi movement diffused among Ahmad Raza's sons and other clerics, most notably Naeem ud-Din Muradabadi. In 1925, Muradabadi founded the All-India Sunni Conference (AISC), a Barelvi association designed to contest the influence of the JUH.[48] Over the two decades that followed, the AISC articulated not only its opposition to Deobandi fiqh, but to Muslim–Hindu cooperation against the British. By the 1940s, the AISC had declared its support for the "two nation theory" and a Muslim state independent of both British and Hindu domination, thereby joining with the Muslim League in a demand for Pakistan.[49]

The MJAH is the only Ahl-e-Hadith Islamist party that can directly trace its roots to pre-Partition India. It has its origins in the All India Ahl-e-Hadith Conference of 1906 in modern-day Bihar.[50] Ahl-e-Hadith clerics generally supported the Muslim League's call for an independent Muslim state, and

[45] These maslak identities were, in the late nineteenth century, still nascent.

[46] Usha Sanyal, *Devotional Islam and Politics in British India: Ahmad Riza Khan Barelwi and His Movement, 1870–1920*, New Perspectives on Indian Pasts (New Delhi: Yoda Press, 2010), 273ff.

[47] Sanyal, *Devotional Islam and Politics in British India*, 290–91.

[48] William Kesler Jackson, "A Subcontinent's Sunni Schism: The Deobandi–Barelvi Rivalry and the Creation of Modern South Asia" (PhD, Syracuse, NY, Syracuse University, 2013), 193.

[49] Mohamed Nawab bin Mohamed Osman, "The Ulama in Pakistani Politics," *South Asia: Journal of South Asian Studies* 32, no. 2 (August 2009): 234; Jackson, "A Subcontinent's Sunni Schism," 197ff. Note that there were a minority of prominent Barelvi clerics, including Ahmad Raza's son Mustafa Raza, who voiced skepticism about Partition, concerned that it would lead to the abandonment of shrines and mosques. Usha Sanyal, "Generational Changes in the Leadership of the Ahl-E Sunnat Movement in North India During the Twentieth Century," *Modern Asian Studies* 32, no. 3 (July 1998): 648n37.

[50] Zahab, "Salafism in Pakistan," 130–31.

after Partition they hewed close to the Pakistan Muslim League, though the MJAH did not emerge as an active political party until the 1980s.[51]

The fourth major Islamist party that traces its roots to the pre-Partition era is the Jamaat-e-Islami, founded by Maulana Maududi in 1941. As described later in this chapter, Maududi championed a robustly political vision for the global Islamic community. He opposed British rule in India, but also rejected the political visions of both the Indian National Congress and the Pakistan Muslim League. Maududi notably reversed his opposition to the new state of Pakistan, however, once it had become a reality.[52]

2.2.2 1947–1969: State Formation and Islamic Identity

The first two decades of Pakistan's history were a formative period for the country's two largest Islamist parties, the JUI and the JI, as each sought to shape the future of the world's first modern Islamic state. Key leaders in both parties had chosen to support the "wrong" side in the years leading up to 1947: Members of the pro-Congress JUH who ended up in Pakistan after Partition pivoted to join the JUI, which adopted a more state-centric view of Islamization; while Maulana Maududi, who had outright opposed not only the creation of Pakistan (believing that "he should be the one to found and lead the Muslim state of Pakistan if there had to be one")[53] but also the Kashmiri jihad in 1948, chose to compensate for those decisions by recasting himself as the leading advocate for an Islamist Pakistan.

Once these two parties came to terms, politically speaking, with the creation of the state of Pakistan, they set out to influence its early development. One of the first major opportunities to do so came in the framing and debates over the Objectives Resolution, a statement of principles that was eventually adopted as an annex to Pakistan's first constitution in 1956.[54] The resolution was first put before the constituent assembly in March 1949, and it contained several clauses anchoring the new state's relationship with Islam, most notably: "Whereas sovereignty over the entire universe belongs to God Almighty alone and the authority which He has delegated to the State of

[51] Zahab, *A Kaleidoscope of Islam*, 105.

[52] Ali Usman Qasmi, "Differentiating Between Pakistan and Napak-istan: Maulana Abul Ala Maududi's Critique of the Muslim League and Muhammad Ali Jinnah," in *Muslims Against the Muslim League: Critiques of the Idea of Pakistan*, ed. Ali Usman Qasmi and Megan Eaton Robb (Cambridge, UK: Cambridge University Press, 2017), 124ff, https://doi.org/10.1017/9781316711224.005.

[53] Seyyed Vali Reza Nasr, *The Vanguard of the Islamic Revolution: The Jama'at-i Islami of Pakistan* (Berkeley: University of California Press, 1994), 6.

[54] For more on these debates see Leonard Binder, *Religion and Politics in Pakistan* (Berkeley: University of California Press, 1961), 116ff.

Pakistan through its people for being exercised within the limit prescribed by Him is a sacred trust"; "Wherein the principles of democracy, freedom, equality, tolerance and social justice, as enunciated by Islam, shall be fully observed"; and "Wherein the Muslims shall be enabled to order their lives in the individual and collective spheres in accord with the teachings and requirements of Islam as set out in the Holy Quran and the Sunna."[55]

Maulana Shabbir Ahmed Usmani, a leading Deobandi cleric and JUI's first president, was influential in shaping the text of the Objectives Resolution and championing its approval by the constituent assembly.[56] The JI was also eager to have a hand in crafting a foundational constitutional document, but its ambitions were complicated by its contentious relationship with the Liaqat Ali Khan government. In the summer of 1948 Maududi had run afoul both of leading Muslim League figures and the army by his unwillingness to swear allegiance to the state. Viewed as subversive, he was jailed, party offices were shuttered, and the government undertook efforts to purge JI members from the civil service.[57] Notwithstanding these disadvantages, Maududi quietly reached out to the Deobandi ulama, including Shabbir Usmani, and was able to indirectly influence the crafting of the Objectives Resolution.

The Islamists had won an important victory, but the debate over the new state's relationship with Islam continued to play out as Pakistan struggled in the years that followed to craft a constitution. The dividing lines were ideological—"two rival discourses of Islam"—but also organizational: Relatively secular bureaucratic elites saw Pakistan as above all a refuge for Muslims in the subcontinent, whereas a coalition of Islamists, led by the JI and JUI, believed that Pakistan could be and ought to be the modern world's leading exemplar of an Islamic state.[58]

Although the JI had supported the Objectives Resolution, Maududi was dissatisfied that the resolution failed to mention shariah explicitly. He had long argued that individual and social reformation were not possible in the absence of an Islamic state structure.[59] His blueprint for an Islamic state, as articulated in 1948 just following the creation of Pakistan, insisted that

[55] "The Constituent Assembly of Pakistan Debates: Official Report, Volume V" (Karachi: Constituent Assembly of Pakistan, March 1949).

[56] Muhammad Qasim Zaman, *Islam in Pakistan: A History* (Princeton: Princeton University Press, 2018), 95ff.

[57] Nasr, *Vanguard*, 122–23.

[58] See Farzana Shaikh, *Making Sense of Pakistan* (New York: Columbia University Press, 2009), 11.

[59] For a comparison of the Jamaat-e-Islami and the Tablighi Jamaat, see Mumtaz Ahmad, "Islamic Fundamentalism in South Asia: The Jamaat-i-Islami and the Tablighi Jamaat of South Asia," in *Fundamentalisms Observed*, ed. Martin E. Marty and R. Scott Appleby (Chicago: University of Chicago Press, 1991). See also Joshua T. White and Niloufer Siddiqui, "Syed Abul A'ala Maududi," in *The Oxford Handbook of Islam and Politics*, ed. John L. Esposito and Emad El-Din Shahin (Oxford: Oxford University Press, 2012), 144–156.

shariah be "the basic law of the land."[60] Convinced that Islamic rule under the days of the early caliphates had been nothing short of glorious, he "wanted to have Islam, as he understood it, tried again; he was sure it would work," and that for it to work, it must be declared the sole basis of law.[61]

Both the JI and the JUI were further disappointed by Pakistan's first constitution, ratified in 1956. The constitution included a so-called repugnancy clause, stipulating that no law could contravene the Quran or Sunna; it incorporated the Objectives Resolution, adding a reference to Muhammad Ali Jinnah's assertion that Pakistan would be "a democratic State based on Islamic principles of social justice"; and declared the state an Islamic Republic. Nonetheless, the JI, in line with its statist and technocratic approach, was unhappy about the tractability of the new constitutional language. Far from being established as the sole basis of law, shariah was not even explicitly mentioned, and the repugnancy clause was to be adjudicated not by the Supreme Court but the National Assembly. Maududi eventually accepted the constitution, but not without reservations.[62] The JUI was displeased for somewhat different reasons, concerned that the Pakistani legal system, which incorporated large portions of British colonial codes, did not delineate a prominent role for *clerics* to shape the interpretation of law, or to adjudicate what was properly Islamic. The ulama viewed this as their prerogative, and their vision of the Islamic state naturally included a significant role for the clerical class.[63]

The contestation over Pakistan's religious identity during this period did not play out solely in the legal domain. In 1953, Maududi and the JI were instrumental in stirring up deadly riots against the minority Ahmadi sect, a movement which considered itself Muslim but which, on account of its claims that the nineteenth-century cleric Ghulam Mirza had received divine revelation, many Sunni apologists deemed heterodox.[64] Although Maududi had in the early 1950s worried that, as a tactical matter, the rising anti-Ahmadi agitation that was being driven by the populist Majlis-e-Ahrar-e-Islam might serve

[60] Quoted in Marc Gaborieau, "Religion in the Pakistani Polity," in *Pakistan: The Contours of State and Society*, ed. Soofia Mumtaz, Jean-Luc Racine, and Imran Anwar Ali (Karachi: Oxford University Press, 2002), 48.

[61] Freeland Abbott, *Islam and Pakistan* (Ithaca, NY: Cornell University Press, 1968), 180.

[62] Sayyid Abul A'la Maududi, *Islamic Law and Constitution*, trans. Khurshid Ahmad, 2nd ed. (Lahore: Islamic Publications, 1960), 383ff; Matthew J. Nelson, "Islamic Law in an Islamic Republic," in *Constitution Writing, Religion and Democracy*, ed. Asli U. Bali and Hannah Lerner (Cambridge, UK: Cambridge University Press, 2017), 235–63.

[63] See, for example, Ali Usman Qasmi, "God's Kingdom on Earth? Politics of Islam in Pakistan, 1947–1969," *Modern Asian Studies* 44, no. 6 (2010): 1218, https://doi.org/10.1017/S0026749X09000134.

[64] See Binder, *Religion and Politics in Pakistan*, 259ff; Abbott, *Islam and Pakistan*, 147ff. For an Ahmadi view of the events, see Hazrat Mirza Tahir Ahmad, *Murder in the Name of Allah*, trans. Syed Barakat Ahmad (Cambridge, UK: Lutterworth Press, 1989).

as a distraction from the JI's ambition to shape the formation of an Islamic constitution, his party by 1953 decided to champion a public and virulent anti-Ahmadi agenda. The party played a key role in the riots that followed, and which led to a brief imposition of martial law in Punjab.[65]

The government's investigation into the rioting, known as the Munir Report, was critical of the role of the JI and other political and religious groups in stirring up violence. It also made a broader argument that likely contributed the muted Islamic language in the 1956 constitution; namely, that one cannot reasonably organize an Islamic state based on a narrow sectarian definition of Muslim identity.[66] The report noted that some Sunni clerics had deemed Shias as *kāfir* (apostate), and some Shia clerics considered Sunnis as kafir; it continued:

> The net result of all this is that neither Shias nor Sunnis nor Deobandis nor Ahl-i-Hadith nor Barelvis are Muslims and any change from one view to the other must be accompanied in an Islamic State with the penalty of death if the Government of the State is in the hands of the party which considers the other party to be *kafirs.* And it does not require much imagination to judge of the consequences of this doctrine when it is remembered that no two *ulama* have agreed before us as to the definition of a Muslim.[67]

Although the JI portrayed itself as suprasectarian, its embrace of the politics of apostícization laid bare the more fundamental interests that would characterize its behavior in the decades that followed: sustaining its public relevance in the face of competition, and pressuring the state to articulate ever-narrower definitions of Islamic law.

In Pakistan's first two decades, the Jamaat-e-Islami clashed frequently with state elites. The JI's early experiences of confrontation with the martial state anticipated its future interactions with the military and bureaucratic elite. When Governor-General Iskander Mirza declared martial law in October 1958 and appointed General Ayub Khan as Chief Martial Law Administrator, he did so in part to thwart the designs of the JI and its growing involvement in the political process.[68] And when Ayub Khan took control from Mirza later that month, inaugurating his own martial law government, the result was the banning of political parties. Although Maududi chose to follow a pragmatic

[65] Nasr, *Vanguard*, 136–37.

[66] Nelson, "Islamic Law in an Islamic Republic," 244.

[67] M. Munir and M. R. Kayani, "Report of the Court of Inquiry Constituted Under Punjab Act II of 1954 to Enquire Into the Punjab Disturbances of 1953" (Lahore: Superintendent, Government Printing, Punjab, 1954), 219.

[68] Nasr, *Vanguard*, 148.

path that avoided direct confrontation with the military regime—perhaps because he was aware of the fate of the Muslim Brotherhood in Egypt—the JI remained a strident opponent of Ayub's martial rule.

To most appearances, Ayub Khan was uniformly hostile both to the Islamist vision of the JI and the JUI's interests in expanding clerical influence in the political and legal domains.[69] He initially sought to roll back even the modestly symbolic Islamism of the 1956 constitution, removing the word "Islamic" from the official name of the state. (He was forced under pressure to capitulate and roll back the change with a constitutional amendment.) He appointed modernist Islamic scholar Fazlur Rahman to the Central Institute of Islamic Research and clearly preferred modernists like Rahman to both the clerical elite and the Jamaat-e-Islami.[70] He also angered many clerics with the West Pakistan Waqf Properties Ordinance in 1959, granting the government the power to nationalize mosques, shrines, and other religious institutions.[71]

Although he was a modernist and in some respects a liberal who aligned Pakistan with the West, Ayub was not strictly a secularist. He was inclined, as Husain Haqqani has written, "to do what he perceived was good for the state and declare it as Islamic."[72] Drawing heavily on the Islamic political philosopher Muhammad Iqbal, he articulated in religious language the need for a distinctly Pakistani national ideology.[73] Even as he sought to reduce the influence of most religious elites—in particular, and explicitly, the ulama—he took steps to institutionalize a form of state Islamism that validated this ideology.[74] As Stephen Cohen noted, "If there was a role for Islam" in Ayub's ideology, "it was to assist in the mobilization of the state apparatus, particularly the armed forces" in its competition with India.[75] To that end, he created a centralized bureaucracy to promote the ideology of Pakistan and laid the groundwork for a national education system with standardized textbooks in which "Hindu-Muslim relations were painted as intrinsically hostile."[76]

[69] Qasmi, "God's Kingdom on Earth?," 1227–28.

[70] For more on Fazlur Rahman and the debate between his modernist approach and that of the ulama, see Zaman, *Islam in Pakistan*, chap. 2.

[71] Jamal S. Malik, "Waqf in Pakistan: Change in Traditional Institutions," *Die Welt Des Islams* (1990), 64.

[72] Husain Haqqani, *Pakistan: Between Mosque and Military* (Washington: Carnegie Endowment for International Peace, 2005), 41.

[73] See, for example, Mohammed Ayub Khan, "Pakistan Perspective," *Foreign Affairs* 38, no. 4 (July 1960): 547–56.

[74] Mohammad Ayub Khan, *Friends Not Masters: A Political Autobiography* (New York: Oxford University Press, 1967), chap. 11.

[75] Stephen Cohen, *The Idea of Pakistan* (Washington: Brookings Institution, 2004), 61.

[76] Haqqani, *Pakistan: Between Mosque and Military*, 40.

Ayub's relationship with Barelvi religious figures was complex. His Waqf ordinance of 1959, superseded by an ordinance in 1961 that further extended the authorities of the Auqaf Department, gave the state wide latitude to take control of religious institutions including Sufi shrines. Ayub's objectives were simultaneous to weaken the hold of hereditary *pīrs* (saints) on the politics of rural West Pakistan, and to elevate and co-opt Sufism in service to Pakistan's national ideology. Even where the Ayub government chose to nationalize shrines, it was often less successful in diluting the religious influence of the pirs and the families who served as caretakers to those shrines. Some Barelvi clerics benefited from the government's new efforts to directly patronize shrines and shrine-affiliated social welfare facilities, but others were effectively disenfranchised. The government's attempts to leverage Sufism—for example, by promoting the *'urs* celebrations as "national rather than regional affairs," and sanitizing the traditional hagiographies of Sufi saints by downplaying their mystical powers—may not have done much to shift public perceptions of religious practice, but reflect early efforts by the state to co-opt religious institutions and leaders to defend an ideology that buttressed the legitimacy of the state.[77]

Although Ayub's policies propagated a loosely Islamic state ideology, the Jamaat-e-Islami was displeased by his perceived secularism. The basic political orientation of the party during the Ayub era was pro-democracy, anti-militarist, and above all, "anti-secularist." Its popular slogan in the 1960s, "*Tajaddud Band Karo!*" (Stop the innovations!), expressed the spirit of its protest and its fear of a polity modeled increasingly along Western lines.[78] Cooperating with the JUI, the JI took to the streets to protest the Muslim Family Laws Ordinance of 1961, which put limits on polygyny and declared illegal the "much abused practice of divorce by repudiation."[79] The party's antipathy toward a perceived secularism in the Ayub era was part and parcel of its antipathy toward the West. Maududi saw the secularizing trends in the Arab and Persian world, and feared that, with America's help, the Ayub regime was charting a similar course. In language that very much foreshadowed the party's rhetoric four decades later, he claimed in 1960 that America "[does] not want Muslim nations to remain Muslim"; that the Americans "most unscrupulously . . . support dictatorships against democracy"; and that their policies are "possessed by the devil called Jewry." In spite

[77] Katherine Ewing, "The Politics of Sufism: Redefining the Saints of Pakistan," *Journal of Asian Studies* 42, no. 2 (February 1983): 258ff.

[78] Ahmad, "Islamic Fundamentalism," 474.

[79] Mumtaz Ahmad, "The Muslim Family Laws Ordinance of Pakistan," *International Journal on World Peace* 10, no. 3 (1993): 41.

of his strident opposition to the atheism of the communist bloc, he concluded that the Western countries "loom upon Islam as a greater menace than communism."[80]

The ideological differences between the JI and Ayub Khan did not entirely preclude them from cooperating where and when they found a convergence of interests relating to Pakistan's neighbors. The 1965 war with India brought the JI and Ayub onto the same page for a short while, with Maududi deciding that "it was now the religious duty of the Muslims to wage a holy war or jihad against the enemy," adding that "I can think of no other way of forcing India to withdraw from Kashmir."[81]

2.2.3 1970–1977: Zulfikar Ali Bhutto and Islamization

Two trends arose in the 1970s that would shape the role of Islamist parties in Pakistani politics. The first was the increasingly instrumental use of Islam by military and elected elites. Yahya Khan, who succeeded Ayub as the third president of Pakistan, ruled during a short but tumultuous period from early 1969 through late 1971, when he stepped down in the wake of the East Pakistan catastrophe. Building on Ayub's efforts to leverage Islamic language in support of the military, Yahya's advisor General Sher Ali employed a conscious strategy of emphasizing the "glory of Islam" to bolster the army's standing.[82] In the run-up to the elections of 1970, Yahya allegedly used the intelligence agencies to persuade Islamic scholars to declare socialism and secularism to be *kufr* (disbelief) as a means to discredit the Pakistan Peoples Party (PPP) and Awami League, respectively.[83]

In the lead-up to the 1971 war, the military also forged an alliance with the Jamaat-e-Islami and its youth wing, both of which were active in East Pakistan. As Vali Nasr noted, "Both sides saw gains to be made from their alliance. The army would receive religious sanction for its increasingly brutal campaign, and the Jama'at would gain prominence."[84] It did indeed gain prominence, and the war helped temper the embarrassment associated with the party's opposition to the first Kashmir war. But the JI's involvement was

[80] Sayyid Abul A'la Maududi, "Interview with Chiragh-e Rah, Karachi, December 1960," in *Selected Speeches & Writings of Maulana Maududi*, trans. S. Zakir Aijaz, vol. 2 (Karachi: International Islamic Publishers, 1982), 62–64.

[81] Sayyid Abul A'la Maududi, "Interview with The Asia, Lahore, September 6, 1966," in *Selected Speeches & Writings of Maulana Maududi*, trans. S. Zakir Aijaz, vol. 2 (Karachi: International Islamic Publishers, 1982), 144–45.

[82] Haqqani, *Pakistan: Between Mosque and Military*, 55.

[83] Haqqani, *Pakistan: Between Mosque and Military*, 58.

[84] Nasr, *Vanguard*, 169.

also costly; thousands of party workers and affiliates were held as prisoners of war, and the party leadership in East Pakistan faced—and was dogged for decades in Bangladesh by—credible accusations of war crimes.

Zulfikar Ali Bhutto was, at least initially, somewhat less reliant upon Islamic rhetoric than his predecessor. The "Islamic socialism" of the PPP had a strong populist appeal, and Bhutto took power at a time when the military was at the low ebb of its reputation. Within a few years, however, Bhutto would also come to appreciate the instrumental value of divisive religious issues. In 1974, clashes between Sunni and Ahmadi students in Punjab precipitated anti-Ahmadi demonstrations that were larger in scale than those in 1953.[85] These demonstrations were organized and promoted by a diverse coalition of Islamic activists from across the ideological spectrum, and included Deobandi, Barelvi, and Jamaat-e-Islami leaders, among others.[86] Bhutto originally opposed the demands for a debate on the Ahmadi issue in parliament. But, responding to this pressure campaign, he soon relented and agreed to an amendment to the constitution that effectively declared Ahmadis to be non-Muslims.[87]

Sadia Saeed observes in her incisive study of this episode that "[in] agreeing to place the demand before the National Assembly, Bhutto did not simply accede to a religious demand. He endorsed a political *claim* about the boundaries of the political community."[88] This proved to be a major capitulation to activists, and one that emboldened Islamist parties to further constrict the political space available to religious minorities.

Shortly thereafter, Bhutto established the Ministry of Religious Affairs, which became a bastion of Islamist influence within successive governments.[89] Three years later, when after the rigged elections of 1977 Bhutto faced growing pressure from political opponents on the right, he again capitulated to demands from the Islamist parties, proffering a new shariah measure and bans on alcohol and gambling. The moves did not placate his opposition, and Bhutto was overthrown by Zia ul-Haq in a coup in July 1977.

Though it was not apparent at the time, Bhutto's tenure also marked the beginning of a new phase of leveraging Islamists to advance Pakistani objectives in Afghanistan. Bhutto stood up a secret Afghan Cell in 1973 and

[85] Saadia Sumbal, *Islam and Religious Change in Pakistan: Sufis and Ulema in 20th Century South Asia* (London and New York: Taylor & Francis Group, 2021), 115ff.

[86] See Ali Usman Qasmi, *The Ahmadis and the Politics of Religious Exclusion in Pakistan* (London: Anthem Press, 2014), chap. 6.

[87] Sadia Saeed, *Politics of Desecularization: Law and the Minority Question in Pakistan*, Cambridge Studies in Social Theory, Religion and Politics (Cambridge, UK: Cambridge University Press, 2017), chap. 3, https://doi.org/10.1017/9781316492420.

[88] Saeed, *Politics of Desecularization*, 124.

[89] Haqqani, *Pakistan: Between Mosque and Military*, 107.

directed the intelligence services to undertake covert actions in Afghanistan. Some Afghan Islamist leaders, fleeing Daoud's rule, were invited to Pakistani training camps in the tribal areas—an effort that prefigured, and laid the groundwork for, the much broader mobilization of Islamist groups during the jihad of the 1980s. During the mid-to-late 1970s, these Afghan Islamist figures forged ties with Pakistani Islamist parties, in particular the JI and JUI.[90] These ties would grow throughout the subsequent two decades.

The second trend during this period required the Islamist parties to grapple internally with the rising popularity of leftist ideologies. Forced to confront the emergence of a new mass politics, the Islamists split on the issue of socialism: the more politically minded Madani faction of the Deobandis insisted that socialist thought was consistent with the populism and anti-imperialism of the pre-Partition Jamiat Ulama movements, while the less politically active Thanwi faction of the Deobandis joined with the Jamaat-e-Islami in arguing that socialism amounted to kufr.[91] The JI waged a vigorous antisocialist campaign against Bhutto, and mobilized its youth and university affiliate organizations to put pressure on Bhutto's political strongholds in Sindh and Punjab. The party was, however, unable to translate this grassroots activism into political power. The Madani Deobandis, by contrast, were adept at adapting their politics to the leftism of the time, and did so in a way that solidified their faction's leading role in Deobandi politics and provided them with a brief opportunity to exercise power.

Few expected that it would be Mufti Mahmud who would take up the mantle of leftist Deobandi politics in Pakistan. Born in the southern NWFP district of Dera Ismail Khan in 1919, he studied at a Deobandi seminary in Muradabad in the United Provinces, where he became involved in the JUH before returning north to teach at a madrassah in Mianwali, a Pashtun-dominated district adjacent to Dera Ismail Khan. During the 1940s, Mahmud formed close ties with the pro-Congress Maulana Husain Ahmad Madani

[90] See Rizwan Hussain, *Pakistan and the Emergence of Islamic Militancy in Afghanistan* (Hampshire, England: Ashgate, 2005), 101; C. Christine Fair, *Fighting to the End: The Pakistan Army's Way of War* (New York: Oxford University Press, 2014), 121–22.

[91] Vali R. Nasr, "The Rise of Sunni Militancy in Pakistan: The Changing Role of Islamism and the Ulama in Society and Politics," *Modern Asian Studies* 34, no. 1 (February 2000): 173. For the history of this split, see Sayyid A. S. Pirzada, *The Politics of the Jamiat-i-Ulema-i-Islam Pakistan 1971–1977* (Karachi: Oxford University Press, 2000), 52ff; Metcalf, "Maulana Husain Ahmad Madani and the Jami'at 'Ulama-i-Hind," 48. This conflict between the viewpoints of the clerical and the non-clerical Islamists became unusually bitter: Mufti Mahmud claimed that the real threat to Pakistan was "Maududiyyat" (a reference to Maulana Maududi) which was "worse than socialism," and insisted—in a claim that today seems rather bizarre—that JI was secretly working for the Americans. The amount of propaganda put out by JUI to reinforce this notion, according to one hyperbolic observer at the time, "is so huge that if put together, even without a commentary, it could make a book running into thousands of pages." Pirzada, *The Politics of the Jamiat-i-Ulema-i-Islam*, 222.

(traveling with him in NWFP in 1943) and began building a political base in his home district. By the late 1960s, Mahmud had inherited the socialist-leaning Madani wing of the JUI and had developed an active Pashtun constituency in southern NWFP and the tribal agencies.[92]

When it came time for the 1970 elections, Mufti Mahmud's JUI captured six National Assembly seats in the NWFP, with Mahmud himself scoring an upset victory over Zulfikar Ali Bhutto, chairman of the PPP, in the hotly contested constituency from Dera Ismail Khan.[93] The Mufti's political stature and influence among the JUI ulama, particularly in the Pashtun-dominated NWFP, paid off when Bhutto came to power in late 1971, following the war that saw the creation of Bangladesh. Seeking to form a government, Bhutto signed a tripartite agreement in 1972 that established a joint government in NWFP with Mufti Mahmud and Abdul Wali Khan's National Awami Party (NAP). On May 1, 1972, Mufti Mahmud was sworn in as chief minister.

The JUI-NAP government lasted only ten months.[94] It was, however, the first instance of an Islamist party forming a government in a province, and it represented a high water mark for Deobandi influence in the political arena. Mufti Mahmud's agenda as chief minister would set the tone for the next four decades of JUI politics. He began a vigorous Islamization program; banned alcohol; introduced an Islamic reform of the inheritance law; and mandated the observance of Ramadan. He further (though unsuccessfully) set out to grant interest-free loans; establish an ulama advisory board; make reading of the Quran and study of Arabic compulsory for university admission; require women to be veiled in public; insist that the *shalwar kamiz* tunic be mandatory for government servants; ban the dowry; and prohibit gambling.[95]

Mahmud's tenure was brief and largely unsuccessful, but once his government fell he continued to champion divisive Islamic measures. His politics in

[92] For a history of Deobandism in the NWFP, and the role of Mufti Mahmud, see Sana Haroon, "The Rise of Deobandi Islam in the North-West Frontier Province and Its Implications in Colonial India and Pakistan 1914–1996," *Journal of the Royal Asiatic Society* 18, no. 1 (2008): 47–70. For a discussion of the JUI's engagement with leftist politics, see Sayyid A. S. Pirzada, "Islam and Socialism in the 1970 General Elections: A Case Study of the Jam'iat Ulama-i-Islam Pakistan," *Journal of the Pakistan Historical Society* 41, no. 4 (October 1, 1993): 397–404.

[93] Craig Baxter, "Pakistan Votes—1970," *Asian Survey* 11, no. 3 (March 1971): 197–218; Javed Kamran Bashir, *N.W.F.P. Elections of 1970: An Analysis* (Lahore: Progressive Publishers, 1973).

[94] The NWFP coalition government resigned in protest over Z. A. Bhutto's dismissal of the JUI-NAP government in Balochistan following accusations over its involvement in the "London Plan" to break up Pakistan. Pirzada, *The Politics of the Jamiat-i-Ulema-i-Islam*, 73; Shuja Nawaz, *Crossed Swords: Pakistan, Its Army, and the Wars Within* (Karachi: Oxford University Press, 2008), 331ff; Syed Mujawar Hussain Shah, *Religion and Politics in Pakistan (1972–88)* (Islamabad: National Institute of Pakistan Studies, Quaid-i-Azam University, 1996), 142–45.

[95] This is a partial list. See Pirzada, *The Politics of the Jamiat-i-Ulema-i-Islam*, 67.

the final years of Bhutto's government involved the proposal of increasingly sweeping and stringent Islamic-oriented legislation. In 1974, he took the lead with Maulana Yusuf Binori of the famous Madani-influenced Binori madrassah in Karachi to once again raise—this time successfully—legislation that would declare Ahmadis as non-Muslims.[96]

By the time Zia ul-Haq took power in 1977, the JUI of Mufti Mahmud had grown into a serious and strident political voice in Pakistan. Its association with the leftist PPP and its promotion of an Islamist legal agenda led many to dismiss it as hypocritical, and cynically pragmatic—a movement that "was only committed to keeping itself alive, and not an ideological organization fighting for a given cause."[97] The early reticence by Madani Deobandis to create an Islamic society "from above" had been washed away by the opportunities that Partition presented them to redefine their politics and make themselves newly relevant.

2.2.4 1977–1988: Zia ul-Haq and Islamization

General Zia ul-Haq seized power in a coup d'état in July 1977, and quickly declared martial law. His tenure marked a period of tremendous expansion of Islamist influence in Pakistani politics, the contours of which are now well known. Zia ul-Haq undertook efforts to further Islamize Pakistan's institutions, from the army to the courts to the bureaucracy. He propagated the Hudood Ordinance, which made it even more difficult for a woman to prove an allegation of rape; revised the penal code to make blasphemy a capital crime; and promulgated a number of Islamic "reforms" that reinforced the ideological character of the state.[98] It was a program that he would continue for eleven years, until his death in 1988.[99]

[96] See "Mufti Mehmood," Khyber.org, accessed April 29, 2011, https://web.archive.org/web/20110429032908/http://www.khyber.org:80/people/ulema/MuftiMehmood.shtml.

[97] Pirzada, *The Politics of the Jamiat-i-Ulema-i-Islam*, 232.

[98] The Hudood ordinance made it difficult for a woman to prove an allegation of rape, requiring four adult male witnesses. If the woman cannot prove rape, she is open to the charge of adultery, which carries a lower standard of evidence. See especially Anita M. Weiss, *Islamic Reassertion in Pakistan: The Application of Islamic Laws in a Modern State*, Contemporary Issues in the Middle East (Syracuse, NY: Syracuse University Press, 1986), 97–113; Asma Jahangir and Hina Jilani, *The Hudood Ordinances: A Divine Sanction?* (Lahore: Sang-e-Meel Publications, 2003); Rahat Imran, "Legal Injustices: The Zina Hudood Ordinance of Pakistan and Its Implications for Women," *Journal of International Women's Studies* 7, no. 2 (November 2005): 78–100; Martin Lau, "Twenty-Five Years of Hudood Ordinances—A Review," *Washington and Lee Law Review* 64, no. 4 (September 2007): 1291–314.

[99] For an examination of Zia's Islamization, see Seyyed Vali Reza Nasr, *Islamic Leviathan: Islam and the Making of State Power* (Oxford: Oxford University Press, 2001), 130–57; Haqqani, *Pakistan: Between Mosque and Military*, 139ff.

The Jamaat-e-Islami's domestic policy during this era was consumed with the question of whether to give precedence to Zia ul-Haq's program of Islamization, or to hold to the party's democratic principles and insist on civilian governance. After much internal disagreement, Maududi's successor Mian Tufail decided that the opportunity to do away with Bhutto and institutionalize the legal Islamization program of the JI was too appealing to pass up: the party became a partner with Zia ul-Haq and contributed several cabinet members to his government.[100]

The JI's influence during the early years of Zia ul-Haq's regime was, on the whole, modest. Aside from Khurshid Ahmad—who promoted new policies for *zakat* and banking—the ministers were unable to stir the federal bureaucracy into implementing their shariah agenda.[101] Their influence was more pronounced, however, in the Council of Islamic Ideology, where the party's nominees helped to formulate a new package of Islamic penal reforms; and, most of all, in the military, where they were given unprecedented access to the senior officer ranks. This became most evident during the Afghan jihad. The jihad, as noted above, predated Zia ul-Haq's regime; it was Bhutto who began the work of consolidating the various pro-Pakistan militias that could fight in Afghanistan.[102] Under ul-Haq, however, the JI was mobilized to take on a significant role.[103]

Even though the early years of the Afghan jihad represented the apex of the JI's influence in official circles, some elements within the party continued to worry that the opportunities that came from partnership with Zia ul-Haq were a distraction from the real political vision of the movement. Indeed, the JI leadership soon became disillusioned with its stepchild role in the military government and in the jihad operations.[104] By 1982, the relationship had begun to sour. General ul-Haq was feeling more confident in his support from the United States and from the ulama, and at the same time more concerned about the potential for the JI to mobilize its well-organized student base against him.[105] After the 1985 non-party elections, in which JI-affiliated candidates performed poorly, the rupture was complete. The results demonstrated to Zia ul-Haq that the party had lost its influence, and he turned to other parties for popular support.[106]

[100] Ahmad, "Islamic Fundamentalism," 480.
[101] Ahmad, "Islamic Fundamentalism," 480.
[102] See Khalid Mahmud Arif, *Working With Zia: Pakistan's Power Politics* (Oxford: Oxford University Press, 1995), 306.
[103] Nasr, *Vanguard*, 195.
[104] Nasr, *Vanguard*, 194.
[105] Ahmad, "Islamic Fundamentalism," 483.
[106] Nasr, *Vanguard*, 199–200.

JUI had more limited engagement with Zia ul-Haq's government. Most of the party leadership quickly grew disillusioned with the general's reforms, and began agitating for a return to civilian rule. A small minority faction, led by Maulana Sami ul-Haq, chancellor of the Dar-ul Uloom Haqqaniya seminary in NWFP, sought to maintain closer ties to the Zia regime and split away in the mid-1980s to form the JUI-S.[107] (The majority faction, led by Maulana Fazl ur-Rahman, was rechristened the JUI-F.) As Mashal Saif has noted, although the Deobandi ulama may not have been insiders in Zia ul-Haq's regime, they were often successful in pressuring his government to enact the above-mentioned Islamization measures and revisions to the Pakistani penal code.[108]

Outside of formal political channels, the two JUI parties—both of whose core constituencies were composed of Deobandi clerics—were themselves shaped in profound ways during the Zia ul-Haq era by clerical participation in the Afghan jihad, and by the patronage Deobandi seminaries received from the state. The jihadi campaign against Soviet forces in Afghanistan, funded by the Americans and Saudis, managed by the Pakistani intelligence services, and carried out by a confederation of Afghan parties and militant factions, spurred the establishment of hundreds of madaris throughout Pakistan's north-west frontier and Balochistan.

The Afghan jihad altered the face of Deobandism, particularly in the Pashtun-majority areas of NWFP and Balochistan. In many madaris, the careful and comprehensive curriculum designed by the founders at Dar ul-Ulum Deoband decisively gave way to mass education that was more ideological in character, prioritizing assertive jihad as a central pillar of the faith.[109] Many of the *mujāhidīn* were trained in NWFP, either by or with Deobandi compatriots. Leading Deobandi ulama including Mufti Mahmud in Dera Ismail Khan and Maulana Yusuf Binori in Karachi issued *fatāwa* (legal rulings) encouraging jihad against the Soviet infidels. These legitimating ideologies were not entirely novel—Pashtun Deobandi clerics in the 1920s and 1930s had issued calls for jihad against the British—but, backed by state funding and support, they took on a primacy during the 1980s.

The expansion of madaris during the 1980s also laid the groundwork for a more entrepreneurial and competitive clerical culture in the decade

[107] International Crisis Group, "Islamic Parties in Pakistan," 11.

[108] Mashal Saif, *The 'Ulama in Contemporary Pakistan: Contesting and Cultivating an Islamic Republic* (Cambridge, UK: Cambridge University Press, 2020), 52–54.

[109] See, for example, Yahia Baiza, *Education in Afghanistan: Developments, Influences and Legacies Since 1901* (Oxford: Taylor & Francis Group, 2013), chap. 6; Hassan Abbas, *The Taliban Revival: Violence and Extremism on the Pakistan-Afghanistan Frontier* (New Haven: Yale University Press, 2014), chap. 3; Nafay Choudhury, "The Localised Madrasas of Afghanistan: Their Political and Governance Entanglements," *Religion, State and Society* 45, no. 2 (April 3, 2017): 120–40, https://doi.org/10.1080/09637494.2017.1311512.

that followed.[110] Lower-level ulama had benefited only indirectly from state patronage during Zia ul-Haq's jihad. Following the end of the war and the withdrawal of foreign involvement, these clerics—many poorly trained—found themselves unemployable, or at least discouraged by the bleak prospects available outside of the jihadi line of work.[111] These ulama, Vali Nasr has argued, "began to stake out their own claim to power and wealth—satiating appetites for power, status and wealth that Islamization had whetted but left unsatiated."[112]

In this sense the Afghan jihad opened the door to new forms of Islamist mobilization. It brought to the forefront a new clerical class, largely Deobandi in orientation, which was both more diffuse and more ideologically entrepreneurial than its predecessors. It was these "petty ulama"—many of whom had only loose connections to the scholarly Deobandi establishment—who in part carried on the most destructive aspects of the jihad into the post-Zia ul-Haq era, including the entrenchment of sectarian movements and their ideologies-of-difference;[113] and, perhaps most dangerously, the creation of a vast cadre of both ideological and opportunistic veteran jihadis beholden only tenuously to the Pakistani state. In the short term, these developments seemed to redound to the benefit of the JUI parties, which were able to serve as the political face of a newly energized and increasingly Pashtun-dominated network of Deobandi madaris. As described later in this chapter, the JUI parties were able to cultivate productive ties with the array of new Kashmir-oriented Deobandi jihadi groups that were, following the Afghan jihad, enjoying robust patronage from the state. But these advantages came with risks that would become clear only in the decades that followed, when some of the party's loose affiliates in the militant community began questioning the legitimacy of the JUI parties and their sympathetic orientation toward the state.

2.2.5 1988–1999: Fragmented Politics

The first two civilian governments that came to power in Islamabad after more than a decade of martial rule faced a host of problems in asserting their independence over an entrenched military-bureaucratic complex. This was

[110] Haqqani, *Pakistan: Between Mosque and Military*, 190ff.
[111] See, for example, Abdul Salam Zaeef, *My Life with the Taliban* (New York: Oxford University Press, 2011), 103.
[112] Nasr, "The Rise of Sunni Militancy in Pakistan," 150.
[113] See, for example, Nasr, "The Rise of Sunni Militancy in Pakistan," 144ff.

a period of relatively minimal political involvement for the Deobandi clerics, and one of indecision for the Jamaat-e-Islami, which was torn between its anti-martial idealism and the pressures of political expediency.

Benazir Bhutto's PPP garnered a plurality of votes in the elections held after Zia ul-Haq's death in 1988, and managed to form a government in the face of a rival electoral alliance orchestrated by the Inter-Services Intelligence directorate—the Islami Jamhuri Ittihad (Islamic Democratic Alliance; IJI)—which included the JI and pro-military mainstream parties.[114] The IJI employed Islamist rhetoric, played on fears of a female prime minister, and argued for the necessity of continuing the jihad in Afghanistan. Even in defeat, the IJI parties continued to be a thorn in Bhutto's side: her government, which lasted less than two years, was hobbled by an awkward power-sharing arrangement with President Ghulam Ishaq Khan and Chief of Army Staff Aslam Beg, as well as local competition from Punjab Chief Minister Nawaz Sharif.

Although the JI had played a major role in the IJI's election campaign, it was never entirely comfortable with its place in the pro-military alliance. In 1987 Qazi Hussain Ahmad had taken over leadership of the party from Maududi's successor, Mian Tufail. As an ethnic Pashtun, Qazi Hussain was the first non-Muhajir to lead the party since its inception in 1941, and was more sympathetic than his predecessors to populist political mobilization.[115] Under his leadership the JI retained its ideological focus on Islamization of the state, but broadened its political agenda to include populist agitation and more rhetoric on socioeconomic issues. This orientation did not always fit comfortably with the IJI's political approach.

The JI's ambivalent relationship with the pro-military block in the post-Zia ul Haq era was also accelerated by domestic political realignments that were threatening its hold on a traditional base of support among the Muhajir community. The rise of the Muhajir Qaumi Movement (MQM) in Karachi in the late 1980s—a rise engineered in part by Zia ul-Haq and the army to weaken the JI—left the party casting about for new constituencies. Qazi Hussain's ethnic background and Islamic populism allowed the JI to broaden its base of support among the non-Muhajir middle classes in Punjab and, perhaps most importantly, into the Pashtun frontier areas of what was then the North-West Frontier Province.

[114] Vali Nasr, "Military Rule, Islamism and Democracy in Pakistan," *Middle East Journal* 58, no. 2 (Spring 2004): 198ff; "ISI Collected Rs140m, Gave 70m to IJI, Says Asad Durrani," *Nation*, November 10, 2012; Iftikhar Muhammad Chaudhry, Jawwad S. Khawaja, and Khilji Arif Hussain, Human Rights Case No. 19 of 1996 (Supreme Court of Pakistan October 19, 2012).

[115] The term Muhajirs refers to Urdu-speaking refugees from India who settled in Pakistan after 1947.

As a result of these shifts, the JI played a vocal but relatively insignificant role in the five years following the return to democratic rule. Its politics were consistently contrarian. During the 1988 campaign, it reluctantly joined the pro-military IJI. In March 1990, upset at the IJI's pressure on the army to overthrow the PPP government, the party looked for an excuse to back away from the alliance. It found it, as it so often did, by pivoting around a foreign policy issue and announcing its "principled" intention to stand with Benazir Bhutto in her support of the Kashmiri independence movement.[116] When it became clear several months later that the IJI was on track to win the upcoming elections, the JI again took advantage of an international issue to pivot domestically away from the ruling party—in this case, by highlighting the U.S. decertification of Pakistan under the Pressler Amendment.

The Jamaat-e-Islami again quickly became disillusioned. Dissatisfied with the IJI's failure to carry out Islamic reforms, the party once again turned to foreign policy in order to provide a convenient cover for its pivot with respect to domestic politics. When the IJI government decided to accept a settlement to the conflict in Afghanistan, the JI crowed that it was selling out the mujahidin and betraying the path of jihad. It quit the IJI in May 1992 and began agitation against the Nawaz Sharif government that lasted until its fall in April 1993.

The final six years of democratic governance in the late 1990s saw second terms for Benazir Bhutto (1993–1996) and Nawaz Sharif (1996–1999). This was a period full of significant developments, including a financial crisis; Pakistan's first nuclear test; the rise of the Taliban in Afghanistan; an attempt by Nawaz Sharif to bolster his political standing with a robust shariah amendment to the constitution, and a limited war in the Kargil sector of Kashmir.[117] From the perspective of religious politics, both the Deobandis and the JI played important roles during this era in facilitating the emergence of new Islamist movements.

The most visible of these new movements was the Taliban, led by Mullah Muhammad Omar. The Taliban emerged from the extensive network of Deobandi madaris that had sprung up in the Pakistani frontier areas after the Afghan jihad. A number of the prominent students who eventually joined the Taliban had studied at Sami ul-Haq's Dar ul-Ulum Haqqania madrassah at

[116] Nasr, *Vanguard*, 212. The JI had extensive involvement with the Kashmir insurgency during this period, and the struggle in Kashmir became one of the most effective means for rallying the party's Muhajir and Punjabi constituencies.

[117] The proposed fifteenth amendment to the constitution would have enshrined shariah as the law of the land, granted the prime minister extraordinary powers to interpret and act upon Quranic injunctions, and lowered the effective bar for substantive shariah measures from the level required for constitutional amendments (two-thirds of each house of parliament) to that of ordinary bills (a majority of each house). "Constitution (Fifteenth Amendment) Bill, 1998," *Dawn*, August 29, 1998; Owen Bennett Jones, *Pakistan: Eye of the Storm*, 3rd ed. (New Haven: Yale University Press, 2009), 18.

Akora Khattak outside of Peshawar, and many others at Madani Deobandi madaris in Karachi.[118] At the time, senior JUI leaders went out of their way to highlight their connections with, and influence over, the burgeoning Taliban movement.[119]

In reality, their influence on the new movement was often overstated. The clerical establishment in Pakistan, recognizing the increasingly entrepreneurial and decentralized character of Deobandi politics, gravitated toward the role of broker, trading on access, influence, and rhetoric to mediate between institutions (governments, madaris, political parties) and new movements such as the Taliban. Perhaps no political figure was so adept at this as Maulana Fazl ur-Rahman, son of Mufti Mahmud, who threw his support behind Benazir Bhutto during her second term, but was also, like nearly every element of the Pakistani military–political establishment—including Bhutto herself—providing rhetorical and logistical support to the Taliban.[120]

As described in greater detail later, the Deobandi establishment was, throughout the 1990s, also active in supporting jihadi groups operating outside of Afghanistan. These included Kashmir-oriented groups such as Harkat ul-Mujahidin, and sectarian groups such as Jaish-e-Muhammad, Lashkar-e-Jhangvi, Sipah-e-Sahabah, and their many successor factions.[121] Many such groups also benefited from the patronage of the Pakistani state, resulting in multiple spheres of policy convergence between the JUI parties and the Pakistani security establishment. Indeed, the vast majority of the jihadi groups that flourished in Kashmir in the 1990s were Deobandi in orientation, and they relied on Deobandi madaris for recruitment and on the JUI parties for political support.

Although the JI was not at the forefront of the Taliban's advance into Afghanistan, it did play a role in the emergence of two important Islamist movements during this period. The first was the Kashmiri militant group Hizb ul-Mujahidin, which the party supported under the aegis of its affiliate

[118] Mahmood, *Islamic Fundamentalism in Pakistan, Egypt and Iran*, 373–75.

[119] The JUI and, more broadly, the Deobandi ulama, maintained close ties to the Taliban, but nonetheless "were never unanimously euphoric" about the movement's successes in Afghanistan. Zaman, *The Ulama in Contemporary Islam*, 136–43.

[120] Fazl ur-Rahman was given the Chairmanship of the Standing Committee on Foreign Affairs in the National Assembly, from which he was able to promote the Taliban and build contacts in the Gulf. For background on the Taliban's connection with the Deobandis and in particular the JUI-S, see Ahmed Rashid, *Taliban: Militant Islam, Oil, and Fundamentalism in Central Asia* (New Haven: Yale University Press, 2000), 88–94. For Bhutto's role in supporting the Taliban, see Steve Coll, *Ghost Wars: The Secret History of the CIA, Afghanistan, and Bin Laden, from the Soviet Invasion to September 10, 2001* (New York: Penguin Press, 2004), 298ff.

[121] Zahab, "The Regional Dimension of Sectarian Conflicts in Pakistan."

the Jamaat-e-Islami Jammu and Kashmir.[122] Although the party has in recent years distanced itself from the Hizb ul-Mujahidin specifically, and Kashmiri militancy more generally, many party members continue to express sympathy for the group, and there is evidence that the JI's ties with Kashmiri organizations have not been completely severed.[123]

The second movement with which the JI played a significant albeit indirect role was the Tahrik-e-Nifaz-e-Shariat-e-Muhammadi (TNSM), or Movement for the System of the Shariah of Muhammad. The TNSM was established in 1989 in district Dir, part of the Malakand administrative division in the northern mountainous region of what is now Khyber Pakhtunkhwa province. This movement, which we will examine in considerable detail in Chapter 6, clashed with government authorities throughout the mid-1990s over the implementation of shariah, and re-emerged after 2001 and the U.S. military actions in Afghanistan. Although the JI did not formally support the TNSM, and in fact was threatened by its emergence, it interacted extensively with the group during and after its rise to prominence.

2.2.6 1999–2007: Musharraf, the MMA, and New Anti-State Challengers

Pervez Musharraf's coup in October 1999 brought a return of direct military rule, which lasted until Musharraf's resignation under pressure from the Lawyer's Movement in 2008. This nine-year period saw three significant developments for the Islamist parties.

The first was Musharraf's selective policy of "enlightened moderation," in which he publicly positioned himself as a champion of a more liberal society while at the same time continuing vigorous state support for Kashmiri militant groups and the Afghan Taliban.[124] (Kashmiri groups were also active in Afghanistan at that time, with Pakistani support. The 1998 U.S. cruise missile

[122] Yoginder Sikand, "The Emergence and Development of the Jama'at-i-Islami of Jammu and Kashmir (1940s–1990)," *Modern Asian Studies* 36, no. 3 (2002): 705–51. For an astute exploration of the ideological and political foundations of the early 1990s jihad in Kashmir, see Ashutosh Varshney, "India, Pakistan, and Kashmir: Antinomies of Nationalism," *Asian Survey* 31, no. 11 (1991): 997–1019, https://doi.org/10.2307/2645304.

[123] Interviews by the author with numerous JI party workers, 2006–2011.

[124] In May 2000, Musharraf publicly attested to his support for the Taliban: "I just want to say that there is a difference of understanding on who is a terrorist. The perceptions are different in the United States and in Pakistan, in the West and what we understand is terrorism . . . .Afghanistan's majority ethnic Pashtuns have to be on our side. This is our national interest. . . . The Taliban cannot be alienated by Pakistan. We have a national security interest there." Ahmed Rashid, *Descent Into Chaos: The United States and the Failure of Nation Building in Pakistan, Afghanistan, and Central Asia* (New York: Viking, 2008), 50–51.

strike on Khost did not kill al-Qaeda operatives as intended, but reportedly did kill many Deobandi Pakistani militants associated with Harakat ul-Jihad-e-Islami.[125]) The Deobandi political establishment, well-connected to the Pakistani intelligence services and heavily invested in the Taliban, had by and large only a muted response to Musharraf's coup.[126] They rejected his "enlightened moderation" discourse but recognized that the army coup was at least in part an attempt by the military to forestall a change by then-Prime Minister Nawaz Sharif to Pakistan's policy toward the Taliban.[127]

The Jamaat-e-Islami, by contrast, had considerably less political investment in the Taliban movement and realized that, for all of the state's support for Taliban and Kashmiri Islamist proxies, Musharraf would be unlikely to make even half-hearted attempts at expanding the reach of Islamist legal or political influence. The party thus organized to conduct protests following the coup; its amir, Qazi Hussain Ahmad, was temporarily banned from the NWFP, and party activities were closely monitored by the government to prevent domestic unrest.[128]

The attacks of September 11, 2001, prompted both the JUI-F and the JI to recalibrate their politics. In the wake of Musharraf's about-face and decision to join the Global War on Terror coalition, the Islamist parties worked opportunistically to exploit public sympathies for al-Qaeda and against the United States, but took care to distance themselves from any direct ties to terrorist organizations, lest they incur legal jeopardy. The JI, as described later in this volume, appeared to have informal links with al-Qaeda; and the JUI parties had significant and often overt ties with Jaish-e-Muhammad, which Musharraf banned in 2002 following the militant group's attack on the Indian parliament in late 2001.[129]

The second significant development for Islamist parties during this period was their ability to take advantage of the post-9/11 environment to come together under a common electoral banner to contest the 2002 general elections. The Muttahida Majlis-e-Amal (MMA) alliance, comprising six Islamist parties, was unexpectedly successful, winning forty-five National Assembly seats, capturing a majority of the NWFP Provincial Assembly, and serving

[125] Zahab, "The Regional Dimension of Sectarian Conflicts in Pakistan."

[126] Human Rights Watch, "Afghanistan: Crisis of Impunity: The Role of Pakistan, Russia, and Iran in Fueling the Civil War" (Human Rights Watch, July 2001).

[127] Douglas Frantz, "Supplying the Taliban: Pakistan Ended Aid to Taliban Only Hesitantly," *New York Times*, December 8, 2001.

[128] "Qazi's Entry in NWFP Banned," *Dawn*, October 24, 1999.

[129] Thomas Houlahan, "Commentary: Musharraf's Anti-Terror Moves," *UPI*, January 30, 2002, http://www.upi.com/Top_News/2002/01/30/Commentary-Musharrafs-Anti-Terror-Moves/UPI-51891012407971/.

as a coalition partner in the Balochistan provincial government.[130] Although the MMA failed to implement many of the promises on which it campaigned, it did advance a populist agenda that fused Islamic political reforms with a pro-poor discourse.

The MMA, whose rise and tenure is explored in detail in Chapter 7, represented the high-water mark for Islamist influence in Pakistan's electoral process, and produced the first example of an Islamist party or alliance forming a provincial government that served out the balance of its five-year term. The MMA's remarkable rise was due to a confluence of factors. The American invasion of Afghanistan in late 2001 immediately became the *cause célèbre* of the Islamist parties, and gave them an electoral issue with strong regional, ethnic, and religious appeal. Not surprisingly, it was Pashtun Islamist politicians such as Maulana Fazl ur-Rahman of the JUI-F, Maulana Sami ul-Haq of the JUI-S, and Qazi Hussain Ahmad of the JI who were best positioned to make instrumental use of "Islamic rage" in the wake of American operations against the Pashtun Taliban in Afghanistan.[131] As described later in this book, the military and intelligence services also played important roles, both in promoting the MMA and sidelining its potential rivals.

The third major development for the Islamist parties during this period was the rise of new competitors in the form of militant movements that challenged the authority of the Pakistani state. One such movement, explored in greater detail in Chapter 8, centered around Islamabad's Red Mosque. Another, broader and more potent, began circa 2005 as a spillover of militancy from the troubled Waziristan tribal agencies into the southern settled districts of then-NWFP—precipitated in part by the failed peace deals between the government and self-described Taliban groups operating in the tribal areas—but became within about a year's time a more coherent movement that threatened the political stability of northwest Pakistan.[132] This new militant movement, which became known as the Pakistani Taliban and which eventually coalesced in late 2007 as the Tahrik-e-Taliban Pakistan (TTP), was distinct from both the Afghan Taliban and from mainstream Pakistani Islamists such as the JUI parties and the Jamaat-e-Islami, though it had linkages with both. As detailed in Chapter 9, the Islamist parties found themselves directly threatened, and occasionally attacked, by the TTP, who considered them too closely aligned with the government.

[130] Mohammad Waseem, *Democratization in Pakistan: A Study of the 2002 Elections* (Oxford: Oxford University Press, 2006), 164.

[131] Khaled Ahmed, "Three Angry Pushtuns," *Friday Times*, August 16, 2002.

[132] See, for example, Behroz Khan, "Settled NWFP Areas Also Under Threat of Talibanisation," *The News*, September 30, 2006; Nicholas Schmidle, "Next-Gen Taliban," *New York Times Magazine*, January 6, 2008.

2.2.7 2008–2023: The Return of Hybrid Rule

Two-time prime minister Benazir Bhutto was widely expected to return to the premiership in the 2008 general election by way of a power-sharing deal with President Musharraf. Her assassination in December 2007 by the TTP upended that plan, but her party nonetheless won the election and formed a government under Yousuf Raza Gilani in February. Under pressure from the Lawyer's Movement, President Musharraf announced his resignation in the summer of 2008, paving the way for Bhutto's widower Asif Ali Zardari to be elected president. Musharraf's resignation marked the beginning of a new era of hybrid rule, in which elected civilian governments combined the public appearance of autonomy with a de facto deference to the military establishment.[133]

Under this hybrid rule, the Islamist parties were unable to replicate their electoral successes from the Musharraf era. But even as their electoral standing receded, they sustained some influence. The JUI-F continued to leverage its position as a swing bloc in parliamentary coalition politics, and all of the major Islamist parties mobilized their voters to pressure the government on issues related to their Islamization agenda. They also faced new competition from both anti-state Deobandi elements in the form of the TTP (discussed in Chapter 9), and anti-state Barelvi elements in the form of the TLP (discussed in Chapter 10).

The Islamist parties performed poorly in the 2008 elections. The MMA technically contested in the elections, but due to a boycott by the JI, only the JUI-F meaningfully participated. At the national level, the parties won only six National Assembly seats, compared with forty-five in 2002. At the provincial level, the governing MMA alliance was resoundingly defeated in NWFP, winning only ten seats, compared with forty-eight in the prior election. It also lost its leading role in the Balochistan coalition government, securing only seven seats.[134]

Seeking to remain relevant in spite of its diminished status the JUI-F, breaking with the JI and its other MMA partners, decided to join the PPP-led coalition at the center in exchange for three federal ministerial appointments. Its participation in the coalition was, however, short-lived. It joined

[133] For a review of the debate about Pakistan's hybrid regime, see Katharine Adeney, "How to Understand Pakistan's Hybrid Regime: The Importance of a Multidimensional Continuum," *Democratization* 24, no. 1 (2017): 119–37, https://doi.org/10.1080/13510347.2015.1110574.

[134] Waseem Ahmad Shah, "MMA Tally in NWFP PA Rises to 68: Names for Reserved Seats Notified," *Dawn*, November 3, 2002; Election Commission of Pakistan, "General Election 2008: Party Position Including Reserved Seats: Provincial Assemblies" (Islamabad, March 18, 2008), https://web.archive.org/web/20080409121415/http://www.ecp.gov.pk/PAPosition.pdf.

the opposition in 2010, but retained its party's chairmanships of the Council of Islamic Ideology and the National Assembly's special committee on Kashmir, chaired by JUI-F leader Maulana Fazl ur-Rahman.

The PPP-led government's tenure was tumultuous, and marked by increasingly high levels of terrorist violence against civilians by TTP and other anti-state groups.[135] The Islamist parties took particular advantage of events in 2011—the fatal shooting of two Pakistanis by U.S. security contractor Raymond Davis, the Bin Laden raid in Abbottabad, and U.S.-led NATO forces' inadvertent attack on a Pakistani border checkpost at Salala—to criticize the government's cooperation with the United States. The Jamaat-e-Islami and JUI-S joined the Jamaat ud-Dawa (the political arm of the banned Lashkar-e-Taiba militant group), the Ahl-e-Sunnat Wal Jamaat (the banned militant anti-Shia organization Sipah-e-Sahabah, operating under a new name), the Pakistan Tahrik-e-Insaf (PTI), and several dozen smaller organizations in late 2011 to form the Difa-e-Pakistan Council (DPC).[136] Widely suspected of being a front for Pakistani intelligence agencies, the DPC agitated for the continued closure of U.S. supply lines to Afghanistan, and against efforts by the PPP government to advance trade liberalization with India.[137]

The PPP's tenure was also marked by a rise in Barelvi political mobilization, spurred by the assassination of Punjab governor Salman Taseer by his bodyguard in January 2011, and the return to Pakistan from Canada of Barelvi cleric Muhammad Tahir-ul-Qadri in 2012, who agitated against the PPP government.

The PML-N won the May 2013 general elections comfortably, bolstered by an overwhelming victory in Punjab province.[138] The Islamist parties performed better than in the previous general election, but far from their high-water mark in 2002. The parties could not agree on terms for joining forces

[135] Terrorism-related civilian casualties exceeded 1,000 annually for the first time in 2007, and did not decrease below that threshold until 2015. See data from 2000 to the present at South Asia Terrorism Portal, "Terrorism in Pakistan—Yearly Fatalities," May 8, 2021, https://web.archive.org/web/20240805035456/https://satp.org/datasheet-terrorist-attack/fatalities/pakistan.

[136] The JUI-F was notable for its absence; its leader Maulana Fazl ur-Rahman had been particularly critical of the military establishment throughout the preceding year. See Arif Rafiq, "The Emergence of the Difa-e-Pakistan Islamist Coalition," *CTC Sentinel* 5, no. 3 (2012): 20–22; White, "A Cooperative Jihad?"

[137] Difa-e-Pakistan Council, "About Us," April 15, 2012, https://web.archive.org/web/20120415170455/http://www.difaepakistan.com/about-us.html; Difa-e-Pakistan Council, "Govt Warned Against Restoring NATO Supplies," January 9, 2012, https://web.archive.org/web/20120113023337/http://difaepakistan.com/news/18-govt-warned-against-restoring-nato-supplies.html.

[138] See Election Commission of Pakistan, "General Elections 2013 Report: Volume II" (Islamabad, 2016), 5–6, https://web.archive.org/web/20210427013008/https://www.ecp.gov.pk/Documents/General%20Elections%202013%20report/Election%20Report%202013%20Volume-II.pdf. The PML-N secured a plurality in the National Assembly and was able to form a government after independent candidates caucused with the party.

under an MMA-like alliance, and thus each party contested individually. The JUI-F won eight National Assembly seats—all in KP, the Federally Administered Tribal Areas (FATA), and Balochistan—and the JI won three seats from KP. The parties' showings in the provincial assemblies were similarly mediocre: the JUI-F and JI together won twenty seats in the KP assembly, six in Balochistan and, apart from a single JI seat in Bahawalpur, were shut out of Sindh and Punjab.

Once again, as it had during the PPP government, the JUI-F sought to negotiate a place for itself in the PML-N governing coalition. This time, the JUI-F was given two ministerial positions, and Fazl ur-Rahman was granted the status of a federal minister for his chairmanship of the Kashmir committee.[139] The JI, with only three seats at the national level, and an atrophying electoral apparatus, had less to offer the PML-N coalition and preferred a place in the opposition where it could be vocally critical of the ruling party. It did decide to join the Pakistan Tahrik-e-Insaf coalition provincial government in Khyber Pakhtunkhwa.

Anti-state violence, much of it targeting civilians, peaked around 2013, and began to decline following aggressive military operations.[140] The attack on the Army Public School in Peshawar, which killed over 130 schoolchildren, catalyzed political support for army action against the TTP. As discussed in Chapter 9, the Islamist parties generally supported the military's campaign against the TTP, but they were concerned that the proposed text of the twenty-first amendment of the constitution, designed to enable the use of military courts for terrorist offenses, might be used to target members of registered Islamist parties.

The populist PTI, led by former cricket star Imran Khan, won the 2018 general elections. Khan attracted broad-based support as a reformist candidate, but his path to victory was smoothed by the military's continued interference in domestic politics.[141] Nawaz Sharif resigned in July 2017 after the Supreme Court disqualified him in a corruption case, and he and his daughter were later arrested on corruption charges. The military was widely accused of promulgating these charges and intimidating political elites in order to clear the way for Imran Khan's victory.[142]

[139] "JUI-F Represented: Three New Ministers Take Oath," *Express Tribune*, January 16, 2014.

[140] See, for example, South Asia Terrorism Portal, "Number of Terrorism Related Incidents Year Wise: Pakistan," accessed May 28, 2021, https://web.archive.org/web/20240228101009/https://satp.org/datasheet-terrorist-attack/incidents-data/pakistan.

[141] See Gilani Research Foundation, "Pakistan's 11th General Election 2018: Who Voted for Whom and Why" (Islamabad: Gallup Pakistan, March 2019); Aqil Shah, "Pakistan: Voting Under Military Tutelage," *Journal of Democracy* 30, no. 1 (2019): 128–42, https://doi.org/10.1353/jod.2019.0010.

[142] Mohammad Taqi, "Pakistan: An Election Heist and Beyond," *The Wire*, July 29, 2018, https://web.archive.org/web/20240918190438/https://thewire.in/politics/pakistan-elections-imran-khan.

The Islamist parties that constituted the MMA chose to revive their once-potent alliance in the lead-up to the 2018 general elections, but still managed to win only twelve National Assembly seats, similar to their showing five years prior. Looking beyond the top-line figure, however, the election results revealed that there were significant changes taking place in the Islamic political landscape.

First, the JI, which had been in electoral decline since 2002, nearly collapsed as an electoral force in 2018, winning a single National Assembly seat and two Provincial Assembly seats. The party's leader, Siraj ul-Haq, lost his own seat from Lower Dir. The JI's abysmal performance raised questions about the future utility of an alliance in which only one party, the JUI-F, consistently won more than a handful of seats. The MMA's weakness in the KP Provincial Assembly elections, and its poor showing in the more densely concentrated areas of the Peshawar valley, suggested that the JUI-F's strength was also waning, though MMA candidates (largely from the JUI-F) remained modestly competitive, recording second-place showings in about two dozen National Assembly seats across the country. Both major parties in the MMA likely suffered from PTI's success in co-opting their longstanding policy discourse on Islamization, sympathy for the Afghan Taliban, and criticism of the West.

Second, the TLP emerged with a surprisingly large share of votes, more than 4 percent nationally, which placed it fifth among parties overall. Combining the TLP's vote share with that of the MMA, the overall share for Islamist parties reached about 9 percent, not far from the high-water mark of 11.4 percent in 2002. Strikingly, however, the TLP's vote bank was sufficiently diffuse that it was not able to translate those votes into seats.[143] It was shut out of the National Assembly and managed to win only two Provincial Assembly elections in Karachi districts.[144] Exit polling suggests that the TLP's strength in Punjab may have benefited PTI candidates by drawing away significant support from the PML-N, which explains why the TLP was seen by some observers as a tool by which the military eased the PTI into power in a key province.[145]

The third notable development was the JUI-F's decision not to join the PTI's coalition government at the national or provincial levels. The JUI-F had participated in some form in every government since 2002, but it chose in this case to launch early protests against the new government. Maulana Fazl ur-Rahman, who had on numerous occasions over the previous two decades

[143] Zahid Hussain, "The Politics of Religion," *Dawn*, August 8, 2018.

[144] Iftikhar A. Khan, "PTI Secures Lead of Four Million Votes Over PML-N," *Dawn*, July 29, 2018; Erum Haider, "The Barelvi Vote," *Dawn*, August 15, 2018.

[145] Sib Kaifee, "Rapid Rise of Far-Right TLP Poses Dilemma for Pakistan," *Arab News*, August 2, 2018, https://web.archive.org/web/20181211165716/http://www.arabnews.com/node/1350111/world.

benefited from the quiet support of the military establishment, framed his agitation as a protest against not only the PTI but also the Army's interference on its behalf.[146] Rahman led a high-profile but ultimately ineffectual march in Islamabad in October 2019, and he played a prominent role leading the fractious Pakistan Democratic Movement opposition alliance.

[146] Javed Hussain, "Multi-Party Conference Rejects Results of July 25 Polls 'with Consensus', Demands Re-Election," *Dawn*, July 27, 2018; Mohammad Taqi, "Who Is Fazl-Ur-Rehman, and Can He Topple Pakistan's Hybrid Regime?," November 3, 2019, https://web.archive.org/web/20240918190712/https://thewire.in/south-asia/who-is-fazl-ur-rehman-and-can-he-topple-pakistans-hybrid-regime.

3
Ideology and Islamist Party Behavior

3.1 Introduction

Pakistan's Islamist parties emerged from several distinct ideological and theological traditions, and they hold divergent views on a range of issues. This chapter will explore some of those differences, with an eye toward discerning whether there are compelling ideational drivers for the parties' decisions to enable religiously justified anti-state violence. This analysis will focus on delineating the parties' understandings of Islamic law, as well as the key areas of differentiation and dispute.

The first section explores the parties' ideological and theological moorings, with particular reference to their interpretive traditions and some of the foundational theological differences by which they are defined and can be categorized. It then briefly provides examples of topics in which these differences are apparent—matters related to ritual practice, views of the prophet Muhammad, and the application of family law.

The second section focuses on theological and ideological debates that might have more direct bearing on the parties' endorsement of anti-state violence. It explores two such interrelated debates, organized around simple framing questions: (1) Who should interpret shariah? (2) Who can enforce shariah? And can one rebel against the state if it does not do so? Pakistan's Islamist parties have often provided inconclusive or fragmentary answers to these questions, but the ways in which they—and leading figures within their traditions—have grappled with them in theological discourse provides insights into the salience of ideational factors in shaping their behaviors in the public domain.

One of the overarching arguments of this book is that there are indeed meaningful ideological differences among Pakistan's Islamist parties, but that their ideological and theological disputes do not explain in systematic and satisfying ways their postures toward anti-state movements and anti-state violence. Why then devote a chapter to the role of ideology in Islamist party behavior? There are several compelling reasons.

Vigilante Islamists. Joshua T. White, Oxford University Press. © Oxford University Press (2025).
DOI: 10.1093/9780197814178.003.0003

In the first place, this analysis can help us understand the limits of the explanatory power of ideological differences. In the chapters that follow, I will argue that structural factors, such as the parties' perceived vulnerabilities to anti-state groups and the state itself, are more persuasive than ideological ones in explaining the parties' often-ambivalent behavior toward violent movements. At the same time, ideological positions can influence a party's perceived vulnerabilities. A party, for example, that has demonstrated a willingness to publicly justify vigilantism on theological grounds could find itself at decreased risk of being targeted by violent anti-state groups, and at greater risk of being subject to legal or financial retaliation by government institutions.

Second, this chapter's exploration of ideology helps to explain how, where, and why Islamist parties may develop sympathies with violent groups that reject democratic politics, or even attack the parties themselves. Political parties of all stripes, as I argued in the previous chapter, sometimes choose to enable anti-state violence out of sympathy for the stated objective of furthering the Islamic character of the Pakistani state, even if they do not condone the means by which that "Islamization" takes place. These incentives apply to mainstream parties in Pakistan, but even more so to parties that place Islamization at the center of their political discourse. Moreover, it is clear that parties' rhetorical repertoires—the ways in which they describe their Islamization agendas, their relationships to the state, and their critiques of their political adversaries—are drawn in large part from their ideological and theological traditions.

Third and finally, mapping the Islamist ideological landscape in Pakistan helps us make sense of the affinities and affiliations that Islamist parties choose to cultivate. The next two chapters explore in depth the parties' relationships with one another, with mainstream parties, and with various classes of armed affiliates and militant groups. These relationships are deeply conditioned by the parties' respective ideological and theological traditions, as well as the epistemic communities that they inhabit.

3.2 Ideological Differentiation

3.2.1 The Interpretive Traditions

There are five principal Islamic interpretive traditions in Pakistan. Four are Sunni: Barelvi, Deobandi, Ahl-e-Hadith, and Jamaat-e-Islami. The fifth is Shia. Each maslak emerged out of a particular historical context, and reflects a distinctive though not unitary set of "shared sensibilities" regarding Islamic authority, interpretation, jurisprudence, and normative practices.[1] There are no reliable data on the prevalence of these *masālik* (pl. of maslak) among the Pakistani population, and information on sectarian identity is not collected as part of the national census. Most popular sources assert, without much evidence, that the Barelvi maslak is dominant, and indeed Barelvi shrines are widespread throughout the country. If, however, one measures by the number of madaris, the Deobandi maslak appears dominant.[2] As a matter of self-identification, survey research suggests that the largest group of Pakistanis identify generically as Sunni Muslim (*Ahl-e-Sunnat*) rather than with any particular maslak.[3]

The masalik should not be confused with the various jurisprudential schools, or *madhhab*s, which took shape in the ninth and tenth centuries.[4] The Deobandi and Barelvi traditions both follow Hanafi fiqh, which is dominant throughout much of South and Central Asia, while the Ahl-e-Hadith reject the established schools of fiqh and emphasize interpreting afresh from the prophetic traditions. The Jamaat-e-Islami postures itself as suprasectarian, but draws generously from the Hanafi tradition. And most of Pakistan's Shia community subscribes to the Ja'fari fiqh.[5]

3.2.2 The Barelvis

Barelvism is a school of Sunni thought and practice that traces its roots to Ahmed Raza Khan Barelvi (b. 1856), a prominent scholar and cleric who founded the movement in present-day Uttar Pradesh. Broadly speaking, Barelvis embrace popular devotional practices, and while they are by no means the sole inheritors of the Sufi tradition in the subcontinent, they are closely associated with adherence to Sufi brotherhoods and ritual

[1] Brannon D. Ingram, *Revival from Below: The Deoband Movement and Global Islam* (Berkeley: University of California Press, 2018), 22.

[2] See Qazi Faez Isa, "Quetta Inquiry Commission Report" (Islamabad: Supreme Court of Pakistan, 2016), 50, https://web.archive.org/web/20240716131117/https://www.supremecourt.gov.pk/downloads_judgements/press_release/QuettaInquiryCommissionReport.pdf.

[3] C. Christine Fair, Neil Malhotra, and Jacob N. Shapiro, "Islam, Militancy, and Politics in Pakistan: Insights From a National Sample," *Terrorism and Political Violence* 22, no. 4 (2010): 504–6.

[4] For a history of their emergence, see Wael B. Hallaq, *The Origins and Evolution of Islamic Law*, Themes in Islamic Law 1 (Cambridge, UK: Cambridge University Press, 2005), 150ff; Devin J. Stewart, "Shari'a," in *Islamic Political Thought: An Introduction*, ed. Gerhard Bowering (Princeton, NJ: Princeton University Press, 2015).

[5] Simon Wolfgang Fuchs, "Third Wave Shi'ism: Sayyid 'Arif Husain al-Husaini and the Islamic Revolution in Pakistan," *Journal of the Royal Asiatic Society* 24, no. 3 (2014): 493–510.

participation at Sufi shrines. As noted in the previous chapter, the Barelvi ulama and charismatic figures never successfully mobilized as a political party (the JUP and its factions remain bit players in Pakistani politics), but Barelvi religious figures have held prominent roles, including high elected office, as part of mainstream parties, particularly the PPP.

The Barelvi interpretative tradition is grounded in Hanafi fiqh, but often gives special emphasis to the role of miracles and wonders in the prophetic literature and to devotional practices honoring the life of Muhammad.[6] Although popular discourse about Barelvis sometimes associates them pejoratively with "folk Islam" and suggests that they are relatively unconcerned about shariah, that view is belied by a long tradition of rigorous Barelvi legal pronouncements and polemics, dating to the writings of Ahmed Raza Khan himself.[7] More recently, as discussed in Chapter 10 of this book, Barelvi elites have complicated longstanding assumptions about the benign nature of the movement's orthopraxis by leading often violent agitation against individuals whom they deem to have dishonored the prophet Muhammad.

3.2.3 The Deobandis

The Deobandi school of Sunni interpretation also has its roots in north India and emerged in the latter half of the nineteenth century. This was a period in which the minority Muslim community was, following the formal abolition of the Mughal empire by the British, facing newfound insecurities. Centered around a madrassah in Deoband, in present-day Uttar Pradesh, Deobandism spread as a revivalist movement organized around what became a vast network of madaris committed to a pedagogy centered on the hadith literature and on Hanafi fiqh.[8] From the beginning, the Deobandis were characterized by more austere norms of religious practice than their Barelvi counterparts and criticized some of the popular piety associated with Barelvi shrine culture.

Deobandism has had a complex relationship with Sufism. Although many of the founders of the Dar ul-Ulum Deoband were prominent Sufis, the Deobandi movement at large has, since the late nineteenth century, evolved

[6] Dietrich Reetz, *Islam in the Public Sphere: Religious Groups in India, 1900–1947* (New Delhi: Oxford University Press, 2006), 303.

[7] Ingram, *Revival from Below*, 8.

[8] Barbara D. Metcalf, *Islamic Revival in British India: Deoband, 1860–1900* (Princeton, NJ: Princeton University Press, 1982); Muhammad Qasim Zaman, *The Ulama in Contemporary Islam: Custodians of Change*, Princeton Studies in Muslim Politics (Princeton, NJ: Princeton University Press, 2002), 68.

to become more critical of Sufi practice.[9] This is particularly true in Pakistan's Khyber Pakhtunkhwa and Balochistan provinces, where Deobandi clerics are frequently heard criticizing Sufi-inspired devotional practices such as celebration of the prophet Muhammad's birthday; the seeking out of mystical healers; the use of amulets; and the ecstatic repetition of the names of God, or *zikr*.[10]

It is not widely appreciated that many Deobandi clerics in Punjab and Sindh—including leaders of the Deobandi JUI-F—continue to belong to Sufi orders, and engage in limited Sufi devotional practices. At Jamia Ashrafiya, perhaps Lahore's most famous Deobandi madrassah, virtually all of the faculty are affiliated with at least one Sufi order. Most of these belong to the Chishti brotherhood, and visit shrines regularly, but will not participate in many shrine festivals; they claim, moreover, to recite only those zikr that are from the Quran, and to listen only to music that draws its lyrics directly from the Quran.[11] These practices, while consistent with historic Deobandism, are nonetheless somewhat out of step, both culturally and theologically, with the ethnically Pashtun Deobandis who dominate the JUI parties. (As a result, Deobandi ulama and political figures have tended to downplay their adherence to Sufi practices and affiliation with Sufi brotherhoods.)

This gradual "Pashtunization" of the Deobandi movement—that is, both the dramatic expansion of Deobandi madaris in the ethnic Pashtun areas in northwest Pakistan and Afghanistan, and the rising prominence of Pashtun ulama in Deobandi politics—probably traces to the 1970s, but accelerated during the Afghan jihad in the 1980s when Deobandi militant groups were heavily supported by the Pakistani state and its foreign backers.[12] The militarization of the madaris during this period further weakened the movement's traditional pedagogies. (As explored in the next chapter, the majority of militant groups operating in, or from, Pakistan remain Deobandi.) Although Deobandism remains a relatively diverse tradition, it has become intertwined in the public imagination with austere and conservative Pashtun tribal norms,

[9] See Sana Haroon, "The Rise of Deobandi Islam in the North-West Frontier Province and Its Implications in Colonial India and Pakistan 1914–1996," *Journal of the Royal Asiatic Society*, 3, 18, no. 1 (2008): 47–70.

[10] See, for example, Thomas K. Gugler, "Islamization and Barelvis in Pakistan," in *Faith-Based Violence and Deobandi Militancy in Pakistan*, ed. Jawad Syed et al. (London: Palgrave Macmillan UK, 2016), 375–78.

[11] Muhammad Abu Bakar, interview by Joshua White, Urdu, trans. Shuja Malik, May 19, 2011; Muhammad Akram Kashmiri, interview by Joshua White, Urdu, trans. Shuja Malik, May 22, 2011.

[12] Ahmed Rashid, *Taliban: Militant Islam, Oil, and Fundamentalism in Central Asia* (New Haven, CT: Yale University Press, 2000); Haroon, "The Rise of Deobandi Islam," 66–69; Tariq Rahman, "Denizens of Alien Worlds: A Survey of Students and Teachers at Pakistan's Urdu and English Language-Medium Schools, and Madrassas," *Contemporary South Asia* 13, no. 3 (2010): 311, https://doi.org/10.1080/0958493042000272212.

especially those relating to gender, and with the draconian interpretations of shariah imposed by the Afghan Taliban who emerged from Pakistan's Deobandi madaris. Deobandi ulama, reflecting this conservative bent, have been on the forefront of public criticism of music, television, women's public participation in sports, and even the playing of chess.[13]

3.2.4 The Ahl-e-Hadith

The Ahl-e-Hadith (lit. people of the hadith) emerged as a distinctive maslak in South Asia in the late nineteenth century reflecting the Salafi interpretive tradition.[14] Salafism, which calls its adherents to pursue the ways of the pious ancestors (*al-salaf al-ṣāliḥ*) of the first three generations of Muslims, is a relatively small movement in Pakistan. Ahl-e-Hadith political parties, such as the MJAH and MML described in the previous chapter, have been almost inconsequential electorally, but the movement has become influential in other ways. The Ahl-e-Hadith militant organization Lashkar-e-Taiba, and its allegedly "charitable" affiliates, have long received state support for their targeted violence against India and operate openly within Pakistan. Groups with even more extreme Salafi ideologies, such as al-Qaeda, have operated in Pakistan, influencing the evolution of sectarian Deobandi organizations and anti-state movements such as the Pakistani Taliban.[15]

The Ahl-e-Hadith seek to purify Muslim society by returning to the ways of the early generations of the faithful.[16] Unlike the Deobandis and the Barelvis, they reject the established schools of fiqh, and assert that interpretation of Islamic law be derived afresh from only the Quran and the canonical Sunni hadith collections.[17] Further, they combine this hypertextualism and rejection of interpretative traditions with an intense criticism of *bid'ah* (innovations),

[13] Muhammad Moj, *The Deoband Madrassah Movement: Countercultural Trends and Tendencies* (London: Anthem Press, 2015), 160ff; Mufti Muhammad Taqi Usmani, "Sports and Entertainment in Islam," *Deoband.Org* (blog), June 17, 2010, https://web.archive.org/web/20240301211057/https://www.deoband.org/2010/06/theology-rulings/sports-and-entertainment-in-islam/. For a deeper historical perspective of the debates within Deobandism regarding technology and piety, see Naveeda Khan, "The Acoustics of Muslim Striving: Loudspeaker Use in Ritual Practice in Pakistan," *Comparative Studies in Society and History* 53, no. 3 (July 2011): 571–94, https://doi.org/10.1017/S0010417511000259; Ali Altaf Mian, "Troubling Technology: The Deobandī Debate on the Loudspeaker and Ritual Prayer," *Islamic Law and Society* 24, no. 4 (October 3, 2017): 355–83, https://doi.org/10.1163/15685195-00244P03.

[14] Yoginder Sikand, "Stoking the Flames: Intra-Muslim Rivalries in India and the Saudi Connection," *Comparative Studies of South Asia, Africa and the Middle East* 27, no. 1 (2007): 96ff.

[15] C. Christine Fair, *In Their Own Words: Understanding Lashkar-e-Tayyaba* (London: Hurst & Co., 2018), 67.

[16] Bernard Haykel, "On the Nature of Salafi Thought and Action," in *Global Salafism: Islam's New Religious Movement*, ed. Roel Meijer (New York: Oxford University Press, 2014), 33–34.

[17] Haykel, "On the Nature of Salafi Thought and Action," 38–39.

much of which is directed toward Sufi devotional practices and the Shia community at large.[18] Although the label Ahl-e-Hadith gained wide currency in British India by the mid-nineteenth century, the movements' critics in the subcontinent have long called them "Wahhabis" in an effort to discredit their ideas.[19] (The Wahhabis of Arabia share some commonalities with the Ahl-e-Hadith, and are generally considered part of the Salafi movement, but adhere to the Hanbali fiqh.[20])

Internal disputes have left the Ahl-e-Hadith highly fragmented, with over a dozen organizations operating in Pakistan alone.[21] Some of these disputes center on contention for leadership; some are the product of minor theological differences, compounded by the Salafis' decentralized view of interpretive authority; and some, described later in this chapter, concern more fundamental disagreements. The spectrum of views among South Asian Salafis on matters of politics and violence is particularly expansive, from quietists who reject political engagement, to parties like the MJAH that are involved in electoral politics, to so-called Salafi-Jihadis who espouse violence for the purpose of overthrowing existing Islamic states, including Pakistan.[22]

3.2.5 The Jamaat-e-Islami

The Jamaat-e-Islami, as a political party and reform movement, does not consider itself to be a maslak, and its leaders describe it as a suprasectarian organization that is broadly in the Sunni tradition. It leaders also tend to downplay the ideological differences among the Islamist parties; one of them argued to me, unconvincingly, that "there is no objective basis for ideological difference" between the parties.[23] This gloss notwithstanding, the Jamaat-e-Islami has a distinctive ideology and interpretive tradition, developed out of the capacious writings of its founder Maulana Abul Ala Maududi.[24] One of

[18] Mariam Abou Zahab, "Salafism In Pakistan: The Ahl-e Hadith Movement," in *Global Salafism: Islam's New Religious Movement*, ed. Roel Meijer (New York: Oxford University Press, 2014), 126–42. The Deobandi ulama also critique bid'ah, though often in a more qualified manner than the Ahl-e-Hadith. See Moj, *The Deoband Madrassah Movement*, 120–23.

[19] Usha Sanyal, "Al-Huda's Intellectual Foundations," in *Scholars of Faith*, by Usha Sanyal (Oxford University Press, 2020), 282, https://doi.org/10.1093/oso/9780190120801.003.0008.

[20] For a history of the term Ahl-e-Hadith in the subcontinent, see Bashir Ahmad Khan, "From 'Wahabi' to 'Ahl-i-Hadith': A Historical Analysis," *Proceedings of the Indian History Congress* 61 (2001): 747–60.

[21] Zahab, "Salafism In Pakistan," 130.

[22] See Haykel, "On the Nature of Salafi Thought and Action," 48ff.

[23] Asif Luqman Qazi, interview by Joshua White, English, May 25, 2011.

[24] Maududi followed Hanafi fiqh but was dismissive of the view that the ulama had the exclusive right to interpret shariah. Anis Ahmad, "Mawdudi's Concept of Shari'ah," *The Muslim World* 93, no. 3–4 (July 2003): 533–45, https://doi.org/10.1111/1478-1913.00036.

the leading "modernist" Islamic theorists, Maududi championed an expansive vision for the Islamic state, and one in which the ulama would necessarily play a secondary role to a new vanguard of ideologues and technocrats.[25]

One Maududi's most important contributions to public discourse was his view—what Andrew March has called a "high utopian Islamism"—that Islam constitutes a complete system of life, a totalizing ideology that ought to encompass not only ritual practice, but the spheres of economics, politics, and law.[26] For Maududi, and for the Jamaat-e-Islami, the traditional Islamic jurisprudence of the Deobandi and Barelvi ulama was too narrowly focused on personal and family matters, and gave insufficient attention to questions of state and public life.[27] To that end the party and its associated research centers and affiliates have generated a vast corpus of literature on subjects such as Islamic economics and foreign policy.

3.2.6 The Shia

The Shia are a minority in Pakistan. No reliable data exist on the size of the community, but it is thought to be less than 20 percent of the overall population. Most Pakistani Shias follow the Twelver school of thought, though there are small populations of other sects such as the Ismaili. Unlike the interpretive schools described above, the Shia did not emerge out of a colonial or postcolonial milieu, but from a much older dispute over leadership of the Muslim community that dates to the years following the prophet Muhammad's death in 632.[28]

The community of Shias in Pakistan operate under a separate system of personal law, with distinct ritual practices and a more hierarchical structure of interpretive authority than is found among the Sunni ulama. As a minority, the Shia have guarded their legal prerogatives, and challenged the view that there should be a unitary—namely, Hanafi—jurisprudence guiding the

[25] This generated tension between the nascent Jamaat-e-Islami and the ulama. See Seyyed Vali Reza Nasr, *Mawdudi and the Making of Islamic Revivalism* (Oxford: Oxford University Press, 1996), 115–22. For more on the modern Islamist posture toward the ulama see Wael B. Hallaq, *Shari'a: Theory, Practice, Transformations* (Cambridge, UK: Cambridge University Press, 2009), 475–76.

[26] Andrew F. March, *The Caliphate of Man: Popular Sovereignty in Modern Islamic Thought* (Cambridge, MA: Harvard University Press, 2019), 75; see also Joshua T. White and Niloufer Siddiqui, "Syed Abul A'ala Maududi," in *The Oxford Handbook of Islam and Politics*, ed. John L. Esposito and Emad El-Din Shahin (Oxford: Oxford University Press, 2012).

[27] For a more detailed review of Maududi's ideology, see Nasr, *Mawdudi and the Making of Islamic Revivalism*; Sayyid Abul A'la Maududi, *Islamic Law and Constitution*, trans. Khurshid Ahmad, 2nd ed. (Lahore: Islamic Publications, 1960); Charles J. Adams, "Mawdudi and the Islamic State," in *Voices of Resurgent Islam*, ed. John L. Esposito (New York: Oxford University Press, 1983), 113ff.

[28] Francis Robinson, "Varieties of South Asian Islam" (Coventry: Centre for Research in Ethnic Relations, University of Warwick, September 1988).

state's decisions on matters of personal law, and civil and criminal conduct. The TNFJ's manifesto, issued in 1987, reflects these concerns, advocating that each "recognized" school of thought or sect be governed by its own interpretation of the Quran and Sunnah; and that the Shia be permitted their own ritual practices (especially the observance of Muharram).[29]

3.2.7 Views of the Prophet and Certain Ritual Practices

Some of the most prominent areas of disagreement among the Sunni interpretive traditions pertain, in the words of scholar SherAli Tareen, to their "competing views of the Prophet's charisma and the limits of his normative model" and the implications of those views for certain ritual practices related to his veneration.[30] One foundational debate between Barelvis and Deobandis has been over the question of the prophet's basic nature. Barelvis assert that Muhammad is *nūr* (light), whereas most Deobandis believe that the prophet was merely *bashar* (human), and that Quranic verses that refer to light, to the extent that they might refer to Muhammad, are to be interpreted metaphorically.[31] There is a related debate as to whether the prophet remains alive in his grave, or is dead. The Ahl-e-Hadith generally believe the latter, but the Deobandi ulama have long been split on this question, between the majority *Ḥayātī* (lit. alive) and the minority *Mamātī* (lit. dead) schools of interpretation.[32] Deobandi and Barelvi polemics have also fiercely debated whether the prophet has *'ilm-e-ghaib* (knowledge of the unknown), or whether that knowledge is exclusive to Allah alone; and whether Muhammad is *ḥāẓir-o-nāẓir* (present and watching), that is, able to be present at the same time at multiple locations.[33]

These debates may be esoteric, but they have formed the basis of the ulamas' legal injunctions about contentious ritual practices and have helped to define the boundaries of legitimate practice within and between the masalik. For

[29] Zaman, *The Ulama in Contemporary Islam*, 116.

[30] SherAli Tareen, *Defending Muḥammad in Modernity* (Notre Dame, IN: University of Notre Dame Press, 2020), 172.

[31] See Gugler, "Islamization and Barelvis in Pakistan," 375–78; Moj, *The Deoband Madrassah Movement*, 131–33.

[32] See Charles M. Ramsey, "Anti-Saint or Anti-Shrine? Tracing Deoband's Disdain for the Sufi in Pakistan," in *Sufism, Pluralism and Democracy*, ed. Clinton Bennett and Sarwar Alam (Sheffield, MA: Equinox Publishing, 2017), 108–12.

[33] Some early Deobandi ulama were somewhat accepting of the view that Muhammad was *hāzir-o-nāzir*, but Deobandi views later hardened against it. See Moj, *The Deoband Madrassah Movement*, 133–36; Mohammad Waqas Sajjad, "For the Love of the Prophet: Deobandi-Barelvi Polemics and the Ulama in Pakistan" (Dissertation, Berkeley, September 2018), 397–98. See also Tareen, *Defending Muḥammad in Modernity*, 301ff.

example, Ahl-e-Hadith or Deobandi clerics who hold the mamati position are likely to be particularly suspicious of the practice of invoking the prophet's presence with "Yā Muhammad!" or "Yā Rasūl Allāh." And those who reject the concept of Muhammad as hazir-o-nazir will naturally question whether he can, limited to one location in space, intercede for all those who call upon him.

Barelvi devotional practice places a particular emphasis on rituals that venerate the prophet Muhammad and honor Sufi saints. Critics of the Barelvis, including many Deobandis and virtually all Ahl-e-Hadith, reject many such practices, arguing that they represent unacceptable bid'ah and are—or can lead to—*shirk* (polytheism).[34] These disputes have centered on a number of ritual practices that are widespread in South Asia, such as celebration of the birthday of the prophet; visiting, circumambulating, or kissing shrines; and participating in *'urs* festivals marking the death anniversary of a Sufi saint.[35]

Unlike the Ahl-e-Hadith scholars, whose views on these devotional practices are often unsparing and unequivocal, there has traditionally been among the Deobandi ulama a wider range of views and responses. On one end of the spectrum, Deobandi militant organizations across Pakistan and Afghanistan have attacked Sufi shrines and destroyed other Barelvi holy sites. But Deobandi scholarship, reflecting its early Sufi roots, is often more equivocal. Brannon Ingram cites a collection of *fatāwa* (legal rulings; pl. of fatwa) from Dar-ul Uloom Haqqaniya in northwest Pakistan—a madrassa where many of the Afghan Taliban leaders studied, and which prides itself on its connections to militant Deobandi organizations. The fatawa, perhaps surprisingly, "[regard] Sufism as an essential part of Muslim piety" and rule that "un-Islamic" practices at a shrine do not justify killing the shrine's custodian.[36] This can hardly be read as an endorsement of Barelvi shrine practices, but it points to some of the tensions within Deobandi communities between the ulama's promulgated doctrine and the activities of Deobandi militant organizations. (The Jamaat-e-Islami, while also critical of what it views as the excesses of Barelvi devotional practice, has largely considered Sufism to be legitimate.[37])

[34] Muhammad Qasim Zaman, "Tradition and Authority in Deobandi Madrasas of South Asia," in *Schooling Islam: The Culture and Politics of Modern Muslim Education*, ed. Robert W. Hefner and Muhammad Qasim Zaman (Princeton, NJ: Princeton University Press, 2007), 62.

[35] Ingram, *Revival from Below*, 65; Moj, *The Deoband Madrassah Movement*, 144ff.

[36] Brannon D. Ingram, "Is the Taliban Anti-Sufi? Deobandi Discourses on Sufism in Contemporary Pakistan," in *Modern Sufis and the State: The Politics of Islam in South Asia and Beyond*, ed. Katherine Pratt Ewing and Rosemary R. Corbett (New York: Columbia University Press, 2020), 86.

[37] See Muhammad Qasim Zaman, *Islam in Pakistan: A History* (Princeton, NJ: Princeton University Press, 2018), 214–15.

3.2.8 The Application of Islamic Law in Pakistan

The meaning of "shariah" has, of course, varied widely across time, location, and community. Traditionally, however, much of the accepted body of law that has become known as "shariah" has been rather limited in scope, applied in the main to private community affairs and devotional questions, and focused heavily on issues such as inheritance and matters that are now considered in many countries to be under the aegis of "personal law."[38] Throughout the classical period it frequently existed alongside a welter of other regulations, laws, and edicts issued by the ruling caliphs and their designees.[39] An examination of a classical fiqh text will demonstrate this in abundance: Most of the subjects pertain to what would now be considered private law rather than matters of broad public concern or statecraft.[40]

In most locales in which traditional Islamic legal systems came into conflict with Western legal norms (beginning, by many accounts, with the Ottoman and Mughal empires in the mid-nineteenth century), shariah underwent a process of *étatization*, in which the state changed, codified, and displaced Islamic law.[41] This process was accelerated under British rule in India through the formation of so-called Anglo-Muhammadan law that, in the words of Scott Alan Kugle, "regulate[d] and justifie[d] the raw exercise of power" by the British to advance their political ends.[42] As the British progressively codified, systematized, and Anglicized this body of law, they simultaneously circumscribed the power of the ulama. When Pakistan became a state in 1947, it inherited this legal template for shariah. The Pakistani legal system, derived from Anglo-Muhammadan law, largely relegated shariah to the margins (though it adopted certain elements that would become prominent and contentious, such as statutes on blasphemy). The shariah that *was*

[38] See, for example, Robert W. Hefner, "Introduction: Shari'a Politics—Law and Society in the Modern Muslim World," in *Shari'a Politics*, ed. Robert W. Hefner (Bloomington: Indiana University Press, 2011); Matthew J. Nelson, *In the Shadow of Shari'ah: Islam, Islamic Law, and Democracy in Pakistan* (New York: Columbia University Press, 2011), 264ff.

[39] For discussion of this legal pluralism, see Hefner, "Introduction: Shari'a Politics," 17–18.

[40] See Bernard G. Weiss, *The Spirit of Islamic Law*, pbk. ed. (Athens: University of Georgia Press, 2006), 172. As Wael Hallaq notes, there is indeed a branch of Islamic law that deals with "offenses against life, body, morality, public conduct and property," but it is imprecise and anachronistic to call it "criminal" or "penal" law. Hallaq, *Shari'a*, 308.

[41] See Wael B. Hallaq, *An Introduction to Islamic Law* (Cambridge, UK: Cambridge University Press, 2009), 167ff; Hallaq, *Shari'a*, 361ff; Frank Griffel, "Introduction," in *Shari'a: Islamic Law in the Contemporary Context*, ed. Abbas Amanat and Frank Griffel (Stanford, CA: Stanford University Press, 2007). And for a somewhat contrasting view of the relationship between Islamic law and "state" law in the Ottoman period, see Samy A. Ayoub, *Law, Empire, and the Sultan: Ottoman Imperial Authority and Late Ḥanafī Jurisprudence*, Oxford Islamic Legal Studies (New York: Oxford University Press, 2020), chap. 2.

[42] Scott Alan Kugle, "Framed, Blamed and Renamed: The Recasting of Islamic Jurisprudence in Colonial South Asia," *Modern Asian Studies* 35, no. 2 (April 2001): 257, https://doi.org/10.1017/S0026749X01002013.

incorporated was of a form that would be unrecognizable to Indian Muslim scholars of the nineteenth century. Under British rule of the subcontinent, shariah was codified so as to make it conform in structure to the norms of British law. Islamic criminal law was almost fully displaced by British codes; the principle of stare decisis was introduced; the decisions of centuries of Islamic jurists were codified arbitrarily; and the scope of shariah's jurisdiction was severely circumscribed.[43]

The place of shariah in Pakistan's legal system began to evolve with the 1956 Constitution, which incorporated the Objectives Resolution's general commitment to bringing about an Islamic society, as well as a set of Directive Principles of State Policy, "to enable the Muslims of Pakistan individually and collectively to order their lives in accordance with the Holy Quran and Sunnah."[44] The constitution itself, however, declared the Directive Principles to be nonjusticiable, and thus there was no legal mechanism to Islamicize the laws. During Ayub Khan's tenure, a constitutional amendment established an Advisory Council of Islamic Ideology, but as its name suggests, it had no power to enforce its recommendations.[45] The 1973 Constitution redesignated the body as the Council of Islamic Ideology (CII), but it retained its purely advisory function.[46] More significant than the new constitution was the passage in 1974 of the Second Amendment, which declared Ahmadis as non-Muslims. As noted above, this constitutional change followed months of riots and attacks on Ahmadi holy sites and was driven by Islamist parties and their youth wings in coalition with some mainstream parties.[47] Although it directly affected only a small number of Pakistanis, it was a watershed in that it defined legal boundaries for determining who was a Muslim, and who therefore could interpret Islamic law.[48]

The first systematic attempt at the Islamicization of the legal system was undertaken by Zia ul-Haq following his coup d'état in 1977. He promulgated the so-called Hudood ordinances, under which certain categories of offenses—most notably sexual offenses, theft, and the consumption of

[43] For superb accounts of this transformation, see Rudolph Peters, *Crime and Punishment in Islamic Law: Theory and Practice from the Sixteenth to the Twenty-First Century*, Themes in Islamic Law 2 (Cambridge, UK: Cambridge University Press, 2005), 109ff; Hallaq, *Shari'a*, 378ff.

[44] Constitution of the Islamic Republic of Pakistan, 1956, Art. 25(1).

[45] Martin Lau, "Islam and Constitutional Development In Pakistan," *Yearbook of Islamic and Middle Eastern Law* 6 (2000, 1999): 47.

[46] See Sarah Holz, *Governance of Islam in Pakistan: An Institutional Study of the Council of Islamic Ideology* (Brighton, UK: Sussex Academic Press, 2023), chap. 3.

[47] Seyyed Vali Reza Nasr, *The Vanguard of the Islamic Revolution: The Jama'at-i Islami of Pakistan* (Berkeley: University of California Press, 1994), 181–82.

[48] See Ali Usman Qasmi, *The Ahmadis and the Politics of Religious Exclusion in Pakistan* (London: Anthem Press, 2014); Farahnaz Ispahani, *Purifying the Land of the Pure: Pakistan's Religious Minorities* (Noida: HarperCollins Publishers India, 2015), chap. 4.

alcohol—were dealt with under Islamic criminal law in parallel shariah courts whose jurisdiction was limited to those offenses.[49] The Federal Shariat Court (FSC), established by presidential order in 1980, holds appellate jurisdiction over Hudood cases, as well as original jurisdiction to "examine and decide the question whether or not any law or provision of law is repugnant to the injunctions of Islam, as laid down in the Holy Quran and Sunnah of the Holy Prophet."[50] Its influence is nonetheless limited, as its jurisdiction was circumscribed to exclude the constitution, the Muslim Personal Law, and other matters; and its decisions are subject to review by the Shariat Appellate Bench of the Supreme Court, which is made up of three members of the Court and up to two clerics from the FSC or independently appointed.[51] These limitations notwithstanding, Zia ul-Haq's Islamization of the legal system had wide-ranging effects, from the draconian Hudood punishments that further disadvantaged women, to the notorious Ordinance XX in 1984 that revised the Pakistan Penal Code to criminalize Ahmadi religious practices.

In the years following Zia ul-Haq's rule, there were three other important milestones in the legal debates over Islamization: the 1990 Qisas and Diyat Ordinance, the 1991 Shariah Act, and the 2006 Women's Protection Bill. The 1990 ordinance, promulgated under an interim government, applied the principles of *qiṣāṣ* (retaliation in kind) and *diyat* (blood money) to murder and certain other offenses in the Pakistani Penal Code, allowing those convicted to pursue private settlements with the victims or their families and avoid imprisonment.[52]

Throughout Zia ul-Haq's tenure, the JUI and the JI had proposed bills and constitutional amendments that would have expanded the reach of the shariah courts to include jurisdiction over Muslim Personal Law. These efforts were largely opposed by the PML and PPP and were ultimately unsuccessful.[53] Zia himself promulgated an "Enforcement of Shariah" Ordinance in 1988, but it was not passed by the legislature and thus lapsed. Several years later, the right-of-center IJI alliance, which was led by Nawaz Sharif and included the Jamaat-e-Islami, revived the substance of Zia ul-Haq's ordinance, and eventually passed it on partisan lines as

[49] Martin Lau, *The Role of Islam in the Legal System of Pakistan* (Leiden: Martinus Nijhoff, 2006), 9.

[50] Constitution of the Islamic Republic of Pakistan, 1973, as amended, Art. 203D(1). The Protection of Woman Act 2006, described below, curtailed the FSC's jurisdiction.

[51] Hallaq, *Shari'a*, 484.

[52] See Tahir Wasti, *The Application of Islamic Criminal Law in Pakistan: Sharia in Practice* (Leiden: Brill, 2009); Hassan Javid, "Reforming the Qisas and Diyat Laws," *The Nation*, February 4, 2018.

[53] Matthew J. Nelson, "Islamic Law in an Islamic Republic," in *Constitution Writing, Religion and Democracy*, ed. Asli U. Bali and Hannah Lerner (Cambridge, UK: Cambridge University Press, 2017), 257–58.

the 1991 Shariah Act.[54] The Act was a political success for the IJI, but it did nothing to change the FSC's jurisdiction and had a negligible legal impact. It did, notably, mandate that "the recognized principles of interpretation and explanation" of the Quran and Sunnah be followed, "and the expositions and opinions of recognized jurists of Islam belonging to prevalent Islamic schools of jurisprudence may be taken into consideration."[55] This language did not provide proactive guidance as to how Pakistani jurists should navigate the differences among various schools of fiqh, but it did suggest that judges had the freedom to engage in *ijtihād* (interpretation) and not limit themselves to the dominant school of interpretation.[56]

The last, and most recent, major legal skirmish over the role of shariah in the Pakistani legal system came in response to the introduction of the Women's Protection Bill in 2004. Some Islamic scholars and activists had long argued that the Zia ul-Haq-era Hudood ordinances were flawed in that they misinterpreted Islamic principles and allowed rape victims to be charged with adultery or fornication. The Council of Islamic Ideology took up the issue in 2002, and issued a critical report in 2006, deeming the ordinances to be repugnant to the teachings of the Quran and Sunnah and in need of revision.[57] The Islamist parties, and many ulama, were firmly opposed to changing the ordinances. The Muttahida Majlis-e-Amal (MMA) alliance of Islamist parties refused to participate in the parliamentary committee reviewing the Women's Protection Bill and argued that it was un-Islamic.[58] The Musharraf government recruited leading Deobandi ulama, including Muhammad Taqi Usmani, to negotiate with the MMA on the issue, but even these clerics held reservations about the text of the bill on both Islamic and procedural grounds, and they continued to criticize it after it became law as the The Protection of Women Act of 2006.[59]

Although the major Islamist parties were generally aligned in their ideological and jurisprudential critiques of the bill, and used the issue to bolster their public standing and to put pressure on the Musharraf government, there were

[54] Charles H. Kennedy, "Repugnancy to Islam: Who Decides? Islam and Legal Reform in Pakistan," *The International and Comparative Law Quarterly* 41, no. 4 (October 1992): 799.

[55] See Enforcement of Shari'ah Act, 1991, section 2.

[56] Muhammad Munir, "Precedent in Islamic Law with Special Reference to the Federal Shariat Court and the Legal System in Pakistan," *Islamic Studies* 47, no. 4 (2008): 458.

[57] Martin Lau, "Twenty-Five Years of Hudood Ordinances—A Review," *Washington and Lee Law Review* 64, no. 4 (September 2007): 1298ff; Muhammad Khalid Masud, "Modernizing Islamic Law in Pakistan: Reform or Reconstruction?," *Journal of South Asian and Middle Eastern Studies* 42, no. 2 (2019): 79–80, https://doi.org/10.1353/jsa.2019.0006.

[58] Lau, "Twenty-Five Years of Hudood Ordinances—A Review," 1306.

[59] Muhammad Qasim Zaman, "Pakistan: Shari'a and the State," in *Shari'a Politics*, ed. Robert W. Hefner (Bloomington: Indiana University Press, 2011), 224–25.

limits to their political convergence. The MMA parties had repeatedly threatened to resign from the parliament if the Women's Protection Bill passed; once it did, however, the rift between the two leading parties continued to grow, with the JI in favor of resigning and the JUI-F opposed. (The JI boycotted the 2008 general elections that followed, and the MMA disbanded shortly thereafter.)

In summary, it is clear that while the Pakistani legal system is still largely Anglo-Muhammadan in character, with Islamic provisions limited in scope and the jurisdiction of shariah courts circumscribed, the Islamist parties have played a vocal role in advocating for legal Islamization and have led efforts to oppose revisions to some of the most controversial elements of Zia-ul Haq's legal legacy. The Deobandi and Barelvi parties, which follow Hanafi fiqh, have generally shared similar views about their desired legal reforms. Although they have not articulated proposals for a dramatic expansion of shariah across the scope of state "public" functions, they have routinely sought to privilege the role of ulama in adjudicating Islamic principles in the legal system. The Jamaat-e-Islami, since the founding of Pakistan, has been heavily focused on legal Islamization, but as a nonclerical party does not see the ulama as the proper locus of interpretive authority. The Shia and Ahl-e-Hadith parties have, as minorities, feared that the Islamization of the legal system would privilege Hanafi fiqh at their expense, and they have pressed to preserve the legal prerogatives of their respective communities while bandwagoning where possible with the major Islamist parties in coalition.[60]

When there have been debates among the major Islamist parties about state Islamization, it has often been over politics rather than legal substance. In the mid-1980s, during the Zia ul-Haq regime, the Islamist parties were divided over the shariah bills pending in the National Assembly, with the JI and one JUI faction supporting it, and a Barelvi party and another JUI faction opposing it. Far from being theological in nature, the dispute was related to political posturing over the legitimacy of the referendum.[61] And as noted earlier, the JUI-F and JI held similar views of the Women's Protection Bill but had differences about how best to politically instrumentalize their opposition to it.

[60] The Ahl-e-Hadith, for example, hold legal doctrines on marriage and divorce that are somewhat different from those in the Hanafi fiqh (and in some cases strengthen the position of women). See Martin Riexinger, "How Favourable Is Puritan Islam to Modernity? A Study of the Ahl-i Hadīs in Late Nineteenth/Early Twentieth Century South Asia," in *Colonialism, Modernity, and Religious Identities*, ed. Gwilym Beckerlegge (New York: Oxford University Press, 2008), 149.

[61] See Syed Mujawar Hussain Shah, *Religion and Politics in Pakistan (1972–88)* (Islamabad: National Institute of Pakistan Studies, Quaid-i-Azam University, 1996), 289.

3.3 Who Should Interpret Shariah?

Among Pakistan's Islamist parties there are two principal disagreements regarding the question of who should interpret shariah. The first concerns the proper locus of authority in interpreting Islamic law. The Deobandi clerics, and by extension the JUI parties, believe that interpretive authority lies principally with the ulama. The ulama are, to use a definition proposed by Muhammad Qasim Zaman, "those educated in institutions of traditional Islamic learning and basing their claims to religious authority on a sustained engagement with the historically articulated Islamic scholarly tradition."[62] As a community characterized chiefly by its engagement with classical jurisprudence, they are generally cautious about interpretive innovations. The ulama traditionally hold that only clerics who have completed the standard course of instruction at a madrassah, such as the eight-year *shahādat al-ʿālamiyah*, are qualified to comment on shariah, and that their commentary must be based upon one of the classic schools of fiqh.[63] Many ulama further hold that in order to move beyond commentary and issue fatwas, one must have obtained an even more advanced degree in Islamic jurisprudence, commonly known as the *qāẓī* course.

The Barelvi, too, generally privilege the place of the ulama in matters of interpretation, and rely on their own madrassah networks to produce clerics. Within Sufi devotional culture there are, however, other notable and sometimes competing sources of authority. These include Sufi saints or pirs affiliated with one of the orders active in Pakistan; and caretakers of shrines, which are positions that are often hereditary in nature. Moreover, some prominent Barelvi figures who have written and spoken on Islamic legal interpretation, such as Tahir ul-Qadri profiled in Chapter 10, were educated largely outside of the traditional seminaries; they and their followers would not necessarily defer to the traditional Barelvi ulama on matters of interpretation.

The Jamaat-e-Islami has taken a strikingly different view of the locus of authority in interpreting shariah. Although he was addressed as "maulana" as a title of respect, Maududi's education was eclectic and not grounded in traditional madrassah studies. In his writings he was particularly disparaging of the ulama and their traditions, and found their fiqh to be insufficiently

[62] Zaman, "Pakistan: Shariʿa and the State," 236.

[63] See C. Christine Fair, "The Madrassah Challenge: Militancy and Religious Education in Pakistan" (Washington, DC: U.S. Institute of Peace, March 2008).

attentive to matters of the state.[64] More overtly, he took the ulama to task for "still living in the eighteenth century," complaining that they "still breathe, live and think in that old world, and talk in terms that could have meaning and relevance only in that world."[65] Like other Islamic modernists Maududi tended to see shariah as, to borrow Olivier Roy's phrase, "more a project than a corpus," and to express skepticism at the apparent interpretive complacency of the clerical class.[66] In keeping with their more egalitarian view of interpretation, Jamaat-e-Islami leaders have vigorously defended the right of those educated in modern subjects to comment critically on the Quran and matters of Islamic law.

In one respect, this difference of views between the ulama and the JI is a dispute over the proper role of ijtihad, in which the JI is considerably less cautious.[67] It can also be seen, however, as part of a wider competition—which includes sectarian or other radical organizations—"to gain ascendancy as the arbiters of Islamic practice."[68] In this competition, the ulama have certain natural advantages, not least of which is their historically recognized ability to speak authoritatively on matters of Islam.[69] The ulama-based Islamist parties, notably the JUI-F, JUI-S, and JUP, may have their own political objectives, but have incentives to guard the prerogatives of the ulama.

The second principal disagreement about who should interpret shariah concerns the centrality of the state as an arbiter of Islamic practice. Put simply, the Jamaat-e-Islami places the state—shaping it, and capturing it—at the center of its religio-political ideology. As Vali Nasr has argued in his authoritative treatment of Maududi's life and ideology:

> In traditional Islam there had been a balance between religion as individual piety and religion as social order. It was the piety of men that created and sustained a religious order. In Mawdudi's formula, although individual piety featured prominently, in the final analysis, it was the society and the political order that guaranteed the

[64] Mohammed Ayoob, *The Many Faces of Political Islam: Religion and Politics in the Muslim World* (Ann Arbor: University of Michigan Press, 2008), 72.

[65] Syed Abul A'la Maududi Maududi, *West Versus Islam*, trans. S. Waqar Ahmad Gardezi and Abdul Waheed Khan, 2nd ed. (Lahore: Islamic Publications, 1992), 42–43.

[66] Olivier Roy, *The Failure of Political Islam*, trans. Carol Volk (Cambridge, MA: Harvard University Press, 1994), 38.

[67] Mumtaz Ahmad, "Islamic Fundamentalism in South Asia: The Jamaat-i-Islami and the Tablighi Jamaat of South Asia," in *Fundamentalisms Observed*, ed. Martin E. Marty and R. Scott Appleby (Chicago: University of Chicago Press, 1991), 463.

[68] Dale F. Eickelman and James P. Piscatori, *Muslim Politics*, 2nd pbk. ed, Princeton Studies in Muslim Politics (Princeton, NJ: Princeton University Press, 2004), 44.

[69] Shahram Akbarzadeh and Abdullah Saeed, eds., "Islam and Politics," in *Islam and Political Legitimacy* (London: RoutledgeCurzon, 2003), 9ff.

piety of the individual: "a very large part of the Islamic system of law, however, needs for its enforcement in all its details the coercive power and authority of the state."[70]

In the early years after Partition, the party put forward a vision of the ideal state as an Islamic institution, with the shariah as the substantive basis of its legal code. Maududi went so far as to argue quite improbably that the injunctions of shariah are "so comprehensive that we can frame detailed laws for every emergency and every fresh problem."[71] The party's ideology was, and remains, a synthesis of revivalist Islam—with an emphasis on preserving the Muslim community in the face of colonial and neocolonial pressures—and a modern, institutionalist, quasi-technocratic Islamic vision not unlike that of Egypt's Muslim Brotherhood.

Maududi's emphasis on capturing state power did not emerge fully formed when the party was founded in the early 1940s. But after the establishment of Pakistan, Maududi became convinced that the state was the proper and indeed indispensable vehicle for Islamic revival.[72] His view of the inseparable relation of Islam and the state has since the 1940s been dismissed by critics as highly ahistorical.[73] And his view of divinely delegated sovereignty, *ḥākimiyyah*—the Quranic basis for much of his political vision—has been harshly criticized by scholars for its anachronistic and misleading rendering of key Quranic texts.[74] With a state-centric view of Islamization, the Jamaat-e-Islami has preferred to support clerics who press the government for legal changes rather than those who are content with discharging narrowly construed educational and interpretive obligations on behalf of the state.[75]

The Deobandi ulama in Pakistan, by contrast, have traditionally focused as a matter of priority on reforming the individual and society, and have been more consistently pragmatic and reluctant to challenge political authority.[76] In their view, the role of the state is to empower the clerical class to

[70] Nasr, *Mawdudi and the Making of Islamic Revivalism*, 57. The quotation is from a work by Mawdudi in 1955.

[71] Maududi, *Islamic Law and Constitution*, 58.

[72] For a more detailed review of Maududi's ideology, see Nasr, *Mawdudi and the Making of Islamic Revivalism*; Maududi, *Islamic Law and Constitution*; Adams, "Mawdudi and the Islamic State," 113ff.

[73] See Irfan Ahmad, "Genealogy of the Islamic State: Reflections on Maududi's Political Thought and Islamism," *Journal of the Royal Anthropological Institute* 15, no. s1 (2009): S145–62.

[74] See, for example, Bernard Lewis, *The Political Language of Islam* (Chicago: University of Chicago Press, 1988), 36; Griffel, "Introduction," 15; Adams, "Mawdudi and the Islamic State," 118ff.

[75] Abdullah Saeed, "The Official Ulema and Religious Legitimacy of the Modern Nation State," in *Islam and Political Legitimacy* (London: RoutledgeCurzon, 2003), 26.

[76] On the ulama's collective posture toward political authority, see Zaman, "Pakistan: Shari'a and the State," 217.

adjudicate disputes regarding Islamic law. As Zaman notes wryly, for the ulama "an Islamic state without a central role for those drawn from within their own ranks would be inconceivable."[77] For this reason, the ulama were often unenthusiastic about the Zia ul-Haq's Islamic legal reforms, which limited the jurisdiction of the shariah courts and deferred to nonclerical jurists on the Supreme Court to make appellate decisions on shariah cases.[78]

Although the Jamaat-e-Islami has been disappointed by the pace of legal Islamization in Pakistan and has forged for itself only a minor role in electoral politics, it has played an outsized role in shaping the ways in which Pakistani religious figures and political parties discuss their aspirations for Islamic law. As Khalid Masud, former chairman of the CII and critic of much of the Jamaat-e-Islami's agenda, observed, the ulama in Pakistan has had to "rely on JI to express itself in modern terms," and the same holds for the ulama parties, and even anti-state militant groups demanding the enforcement of shariah. In modern Pakistan, Masud went on to argue, "You cannot logically frame your ideas [about shariah] without the help of the JI."[79] These disparate groups have all drawn from Maududi's lexicon about the need for a comprehensive "Islamic state"; about "Islam as a complete way of life"; about shariah as a panacea for a corrupt and Westernizing society; and about the imperative for devout political leadership.[80]

The influence of Maududi's discourse has been so profound that most political elites—even relatively liberal politicians—commonly argue that Pakistan is and ought to be an Islamic state, that shariah (however they define it) is and ought to be the guiding instrument of law, and that state institutions have a necessary role in interpreting Islamic law. The substance of what shariah demands is, of course, often both ill-defined and contested. Most polling in Pakistan has reported high levels of public support for shariah, but has not interrogated respondents' views about what shariah actually means. Survey research conducted by Fair, Littman, and Nugent suggests Pakistani views of shariah are multidimensional: "One conceptualization [of an Islamic government guided by shariah] supposes a government that is transparent, fair, and provides services. The other articulates a government that imposes *hudud* punishments and restricts participation of women in civic life."[81] These views

[77] Zaman, *The Ulama in Contemporary Islam*, 104.
[78] Zaman, *The Ulama in Contemporary Islam*, 89.
[79] Khalid Masud, interview by Joshua White, English, February 22, 2011.
[80] For more on the widespread use of Maududi's conceptual template for modern Islamism, see White and Siddiqui, "Syed Abul A'ala Maududi."
[81] C. Christine Fair, Rebecca Littman, and Elizabeth R. Nugent, "Conceptions of Shari'a and Support for Militancy and Democratic Values: Evidence From Pakistan," *Political Science Research and Methods* 6, no. 3 (July 2018): 443.

are not mutually exclusive, but they suggest a wide range of public opinions about shariah, most of which probably assume a substantial role for the state in interpreting Islamic law.

3.4 Who Can Enforce Shariah? And Can One Rebel Against the State if It Does Not Do So?

3.4.1 Reckoning with the Interpretive Traditions

The question of who is qualified to enforce shariah, and under what conditions, is for the purposes of this study the most complex and important matter of ideological contention among Islamist parties, as well as between those parties and violent anti-state groups. These questions are rarely framed around *whether* shariah should be implemented, but almost always around *how* to implement it.[82] The theological touchstone of the debate centers on a concept that appears throughout the Quran and the secondary literature: commanding the right and forbidding the wrong. Most scholars, both classical and modern, agree that this obligation is incumbent upon the state or legitimate political authority. Some commentators place the responsibility upon the ruler himself, but more commonly it is seen as an authority delegated to a *muḥtasib* (ombudsman) who "forbids the wrong" on behalf of the political ruler.[83]

To what extent, however, does the Muslim community itself have the authority or the obligation to command the good and forbid the wrong within Muslim society, particularly if the state is deemed to have failed in its obligation to do so? Most references to this concept in the Quran seem to refer to the community or to individuals as the primary actors, not the political leader as such. For example, one commonly cited verse commands, "Let there arise out of you a band of people inviting to all that is good, enjoining what is right, and forbidding what is wrong: They are the ones to attain felicity."[84] For a theological matter that has taken on great importance within the Sunni community, there is a notable dearth of historical commentary on the subject. Hanafi jurists virtually ignore the topic in their fiqh and, given the concept's

[82] Muhammad Qasim Zaman, "Pluralism, Democracy, and the 'Ulama," in *Remaking Muslim Politics: Pluralism, Contestation, Democratization*, ed. Robert W. Hefner, Princeton Studies in Muslim Politics (Princeton, NJ: Princeton University Press, 2005), 67.
[83] Michael Cook, *Commanding Right and Forbidding Wrong in Islamic Thought* (Cambridge, UK: Cambridge University Press, 2000), 471.
[84] *Qur'ān*, 3:104.

vague character in the Quran, those who adopt an expansive interpretation have few sources to which they can turn.[85]

Most Muslim scholars have been cautious about extending the prerogative of "forbidding the wrong" to individuals or to the community as a whole. Even the Egyptian ideologue Sayyid Qutb, whose writings inspired radical groups such as al-Qaeda, cautioned that only the state could carry out this obligation.[86] Mainstream Sunni clerics have occasionally framed this question as whether or not an individual can right wrongs "with the hand" (i.e., his own hand) apart from the authority of the state. In doing so, they typically also urge caution: The influential Egyptian Sheikh Tantawi worried that allowing such action could easily lead to anarchy.[87] (This precise concern, we will see in Chapter 7, was echoed by the Supreme Court and the Council of Islamic Ideology with respect to the Hisbah Bill proposed by Islamist parties in northwest Pakistan.)

One permutation of this question that has taken on new relevance is whether, and under what conditions, Muslims can act to enforce shariah against those who are *kāfir*, or unbelievers. This term was originally reserved for non-Muslims, but its usage has expanded, and it is now used by some commentators to include Muslims who hold allegedly heterodox beliefs, or who fail to implement shariah as they ought.[88] Debate over this *takfīrī* ideology—that is, an ideology characterized by the willingness to declare other Muslims as unbelievers—is at the center of disputes between so-called moderates and radicals throughout the Islamic world. It remains a fault-line between the Muslim Brotherhood in Egypt and groups such as al-Qaeda and ISIS. In Pakistan, as described later, the logic of takfirism has been used by Sunni militant groups to justify targeting of Shia communities, and by Barelvi militants to justify violence against those they assert have engaged in blasphemy against Muhammad.

The second major contested dynamic behind "commanding the right and forbidding the wrong" is the question of whether Muslims can rebel against a state that rejects Islam or fails to implement shariah in a manner that they consider suitable. The traditional orientation of Sunni clerics toward political authority has been deferential. Citing Quran 4:59, which admonishes "Obey Allah, and obey the Messenger, and those charged with authority among you,"

[85] Cook, *Commanding Right*, 309–310.
[86] Cook, *Commanding Right*, 528.
[87] Cook, *Commanding Right*, 524.
[88] Katherine P. Ewing, "Ambiguity and Sharī'at: A Perspective on the Problem of Moral Principles in Tension," in *Sharī'at and Ambiguity in South Asian Islam*, ed. Katherine P. Ewing (Berkeley: University of California Press, 1988), 2.

clerics have historically counseled loyalty to the imam or caliph, except in cases in which he explicitly ordered them to reject Islam.[89]

Medieval scholars from the various schools of fiqh dilated at length on the differences between banditry and rebellion (agreeing that banditry was typically more condemnable) but generally avoided enumerating the conditions under which rebellion was justified.[90] Compared to the Shafis and the Hanbalis, Hanafi scholars were somewhat less tolerant of rebels, but even most of them held that those who rebelled for a plausible reason "should not be held liable for property or life destroyed during the course of their rebellion."[91]

Among Islamic interpreters, there has been a minority tradition of validating the person "for whom forbidding wrong entail[s] rebellion" against the state.[92] In the modern period, this view was taken up most visibly by Ayatollah Ruhollah Khomeini in his revolution overthrowing the Shah of Iran in 1979. Other modern ideologues who have made a case for rebellion often draw on the works of the fourteenth-century Hanbali scholar Ibn Taymiyyah, whose writings came into fashion again in the 1920s and 1930s among Egyptian Islamists. Ibn Taymiyyah was a fierce critic of the Mongols, who, though Muslim, were threatening Egypt and Syria in the late thirteenth century. His position on the legitimacy of rebellion was nuanced and generally deferential to authority, but he is read by some modern interpreters to have argued that a Muslim ruler must keep the shariah in order to be truly Muslim.[93]

Several decades later, in the 1950s, Muslim Brotherhood ideologue Sayyid Qutb seized upon this intimation of a test for Muslim rulers and, through an act of "creative interpretation," developed from it an ideology that legitimated confrontation against an ostensibly Islamic political authority.[94] In order to

[89] Saeed, "The Official Ulema," 18–20; Sadia Tabassum, "Discourse on the Legality of Rebellion in the Manuals of Creed with Focus on the Hanafi and Shafi'i Jurists," *Islamic Studies* 59, no. 4 (2020): 437.

[90] Khaled Abou El Fadl, *Rebellion and Violence in Islamic Law* (Cambridge, UK: Cambridge University Press, 2001), 189ff.

[91] Abou El Fadl, *Rebellion and Violence in Islamic Law*, 272. For more on Hanafi views of rebellion, see Tabassum, "Discourse on the Legality of Rebellion in the Manuals of Creed with Focus on the Hanafi and Shafi'i Jurists."

[92] Cook, *Commanding Right*, 51–52.

[93] Emmanuel Sivan, *Radical Islam: Medieval Theology and Modern Politics*, Enlarged (New Haven, CT: Yale University Press, 1990), 96ff; Abou El Fadl, *Rebellion and Violence in Islamic Law*, 274–78; Griffel, "Introduction," 10. Some scholars of Ibn Taymiyyah have argued that he has been wildly misread on this point, and that his critique of the Mongol converts was only incidentally about their misapplication of shariah, and more substantially about their gross heterodoxy. For a scholarly examination of this debate, see Mona Hassan, "Modern Interpretations and Misinterpretations of a Medieval Scholar: Apprehending the Political Thought of Ibn Taymiyya," in *Ibn Taymiyya and His Times* (Oxford: Oxford University Press, 2010), 338–66.

[94] Sivan, *Radical Islam*, 94.

obviate the charge that his actions would be fomenting *fitnah* (division), he crafted an ideology that cleverly skirted the matter:

> The task Sayyid Qutb set for himself was to legitimize revolt in terms of mainstream Sunni thought. He had, in a word, to ban the specter of fitna . . . . [Thus, when interrogated by the Egyptian authorities he claimed,] "If I do my religious duty and a fitna ensues, the burden of responsibility is to be borne by he who had driven me underground and not by myself."[95]

This argument, in one derivative form or another, has become the signature justification of anti-state violence among modern Islamists. It has enabled Islamists to challenge the Egyptian state or the Pakistani state on the grounds that its rulers are kafir.[96]

Less commonly, militant groups targeting Islamic states have justified their rebellion using the doctrine of *jihād*. In early juristic works, jihad referred to "military campaigns by the Abode of Islam against the Abode of War, this latter defined as territory inhabited and ruled by non-Muslims" and was undertaken for the primary purpose of converting unbelievers.[97] These early works have limited applicability to contemporary cases in which Islamic groups are challenging an Islamic state.

In the modern period, however, debates over the conditions and requirements for undertaking jihad have become more contentious among Islamic scholars, and the term itself has become more fungible. Most prominent Pakistani clerics and Islamist party leaders would agree that defensive jihad is an obligation of all believers, but might disagree as to whether that obligation includes defense of Muslim coreligionists abroad.[98] There is also disagreement as to whether offensive jihad is obligatory, whether it applies to some or all Muslims, and who the legitimate targets ought to be. The respected Deobandi cleric Taqi Usmani, for example, has argued that offensive jihad is justified by the power differential between the West and the Muslim states, but does not endorse jihad against Muslim rulers.[99] Militant groups such as ISIS go much further, arguing that offensive jihad is mandatory for all believers against states like Pakistan that they deem to be led by unbelievers.

[95] Sivan, *Radical Islam*, 92–93.

[96] Even within the Brotherhood there are debates regarding the conditions under which individuals or parties can legitimately challenge the state. Sami Zemni and Koenraad Bogaert, "Egyptian Muslim Brotherhood and Competitive Politics," in *Interpreting Islamic Political Parties*, ed. M. A. Mohamed Salih (New York: Palgrave Macmillan, 2009), 161.

[97] Hallaq, *Shari'a*, 325, 333.

[98] See Muhammad Mushtaq Ahmad, "The Scope of Self-Defence: A Comparative Study of Islamic and Modern International Law," *Islamic Studies* 49, no. 2 (2010): 155–94.

[99] Zaman, "Pluralism, Democracy, and the 'Ulama," 68.

3.4.2 Toward a Consensus View?

Pakistan's Islamist parties have engaged inconsistently and inconclusively with these debates about enforcing shariah and the necessary conditions for rebellion against the state. Perhaps the most interesting areas of debate, described in greater detail in the case study chapters that follow, have less to do with dramatic scenarios of rebellion against state authority, and more to do with what I have elsewhere called "vigilante Islamism": the permissibility of a non-state actor to take unilateral action, through violence if necessary, to enforce shariah apart from the hand of the state.[100] This is not an abstract concern in the Pakistani context. A representative field survey conducted in 2010 "asked respondents who they believe can use military force to protect a Muslim country or Muslim Ummah in the name of jihad be it a Muslim state/government, individuals and non-state organizations or both." Forty-two percent believed that non-state actors could invoke jihad.[101] But are there commonly held views among the various Islamic communities about the conditions under which that is acceptable?

In the abstract, representatives of Pakistan's major interpretive traditions, including Islamist party leaders, hold strikingly similar views regarding shariah enforcement, and tend to be deferential to the Pakistani state. That deference if anything became more explicit after the tumultuous decade of internal violence undertaken by TTP and other anti-state militant groups. Beginning in 2017, the Islamic Research Institute of International Islamic University in Islamabad crafted, under the auspices of the government, a joint declaration and fatwa that addressed a number of questions regarding vigilantism, rebellion, and violence.[102] The documents were endorsed by leading scholars in consultation with the five major madrassah associations: Wafaq ul-Madaris al-Arabiyyah (Deobandi), Tanzim ul-Madaris Ahl-e-Sunnat (Barelvi), Wafaq ul-Madaris al-Salfiyyah (Ahl-e-Hadith), Wafaq ul-Madaris al-Shia (Shia), and Rabitat ul-Madaris Pakistan (Jamaat-e-Islami).

As befits its provenance, *Paigham-e-Pakistan* (Message of Pakistan) is replete with nationalistic bromides about Pakistan's founding and the achievements of its government. The document is most unequivocal in its rejection of violence against the state itself, declaring that "the use of force, armed escalation against the state, terrorist activities and all forms of anarchy,

[100] Joshua T. White, "Vigilante Islamism in Pakistan: Religious Party Responses to the Lal Masjid Crisis," *Current Trends in Islamist Ideology* 7 (Autumn 2008): 50.

[101] Fair, Malhotra, and Shapiro, "Islam, Militancy, and Politics in Pakistan," 509.

[102] Islamic Research Institute, *Paigham-e-Pakistan*, trans. Muhammad Ahmad Munir (Islamabad: Islamic Research Institute, International Islamic University, 2018).

that our country is facing, are strictly prohibited in *Shari'ah* and considered rebellion."[103] The joint declaration later notes that "[n]egligence in acting upon any part of the Constitution of Pakistan in no way justifies denial of Islamic identity and Islamic basis of Pakistan" and declares the fatwa that Pakistan "without any doubt, is an Islamic State and merely due to some functional issues, declaring the country, its government or its armed forces as infidel is not permissible, rather it is a sin."[104] By dismissing any state "negligence" in enacting shariah as merely a "functional issue," the fatwa rejects those who commit takfir against the state or it functionaries.

The documents also condemn, though with somewhat less precision, vigilantism in the name of shariah enforcement. The prefatory language notes that only the state has the right to "implement punishments on citizens and regulate their characters in accordance with law" and the joint declaration denounces "[u]se of force in the garb of implementation of *Shari'ah*."[105] And the fatwa explicitly reserves for the state the prerogative to declare jihad "involving physical combat and waging war."[106] Even though the main thrust of the fatwa is in denouncing violence against the state, it does nod generally to the idea that the use of force "to impose *Shari'ah* in Pakistan" is forbidden.[107] The consensus appears most tenuous on sectarian matters. The section on "Sectarianism and Trends of Declaring Infidels" is exceedingly vague and, the title notwithstanding, does not address the practice of takfir directed against other sects. Neither is this addressed in the joint statement or the fatwa.

Paigham-e-Pakistan was a landmark project and reflected a broad consensus of views across the various interpretive traditions. But some caveats are in order. The first is that one cannot directly map the signatories to the Islamist parties themselves. JUI-F leader Maulana Fazl ur-Rahman, for example, attended the launch ceremony at the presidential palace, and we can presume that JUI-F leaders would be deferential to the views of Deobandi clerics who signed the joint declaration and fatwa, but the party itself was not a signatory.[108] Second, some of the language in the documents was plainly inconsistent with the historic practices of the state and of the parties themselves. The Pakistani military has for decades sponsored militant groups in

[103] Islamic Research Institute, *Paigham-e-Pakistan*, 26.
[104] Islamic Research Institute, *Paigham-e-Pakistan*, 42, 55.
[105] Islamic Research Institute, *Paigham-e-Pakistan*, 36, 49.
[106] Islamic Research Institute, *Paigham-e-Pakistan*, 67.
[107] Islamic Research Institute, *Paigham-e-Pakistan*, 66.
[108] International Islamic University, Islamabad, "IIUI's Paigham e Pakistan Initiative Launched," January 16, 2018, https://web.archive.org/web/20240918200054/https://www.iiu.edu.pk/iiuis-paigham-e-pakistan-initiative-launched/.

India and Afghanistan, including those that employ suicide tactics of the kind denounced in the fatwa. Many of these groups have, as explored in Chapter 5, been affiliated with or endorsed by Islamist parties. The documents' language on sectarianism is also inconsistent with the Pakistani government's treatment of the Ahmadis, as well as the longstanding efforts of the Islamist parties to demonize the sect.

Although most of these contradictions were left unspoken, one in particular prompted awkward questions from Islamist parties. Noting that the fatwa reserves for the state alone the right to declare jihad, some prominent Islamist party leaders pointedly asked why the Pakistani state had not officially done so in Kashmir.[109] Others insisted that it formally declare a jihad in Kashmir. This line of inquiry underscored the parties' generally cautious views on the use of violence *within* the state's borders, and more permissive approach to the use of violence in neighboring states.

3.4.3 Islamist Party Perspectives

Pakistan's Islamist parties have rarely addressed in any direct manner these ideological questions about vigilantism, violence, and rebellion. But we can gain some insight from the debates that have taken place within their respective masalik, and which occasionally appear in their official writings.

The Barelvi parties, following Hanafi fiqh, typically take a dim view of violence against the state. The most important debates about violence within their ranks, as detailed in Chapter 10, have to do with the legitimacy of vigilantism and extra-judicial killing of those accused of blasphemy against the prophet Muhammad. The majority view in Hanafi fiqh holds that Muslims who blaspheme against God or the prophet commit apostasy, and that that sin is grave but does not have a fixed hudud punishment and is pardonable. Views among some prominent Pakistani ulama (both Barelvis and Deobandis) appeared to harden on this question after Salman Taseer's assassination in 2011, and some clerics changed their views on the applicability of pardon to the offense.[110] The consensus Hanafi view also held that non-Muslims who blasphemed should not be considered apostates, and thus their sin was pardonable and not subject to penalty of death.[111] Views on this question

[109] Kunwar Khuldune Shahid, "Jihad Decree Triggers Demands for Holy War on Kashmir," *Asia Times*, January 30, 2018, https://web.archive.org/web/20230323104232/https://asiatimes.com/2018/01/jihad-decree-triggers-demands-holy-war-kashmir/.

[110] Arafat Mazhar, "Why Blasphemy Remains Unpardonable in Pakistan," *Dawn*, February 19, 2015.

[111] Arafat Mazhar, "Blasphemy and the Death Penalty: Misconceptions Explained," *Dawn*, November 2, 2015.

also hardened after several high-profile cases of apostasy, most notably the accusation against the Christian woman Asia Bibi who was arrested in 2010.

During this same period, fringe elements within the Barelvi community took the logic of blasphemy even further, arguing that those who defended the rights of individuals accused of blasphemy were themselves guilty of apostasy and worthy of death.[112] Here are echoes of the takfiri logic of apostatizing those who hold competing interpretations of shariah. There is indeed some historical precedent for the use of takfir in the Barelvi tradition. The maslak's founder, Ahmed Raza Khan Barelvi, delivered a famous fatwa in 1906, "The Sword of the Haramain [Two Sanctuaries] at the Throat of *Kufr* and Falsehood." In the fatwa he declared Mirza Ghulam Ahmad of Qadian (the founder of the Ahmadi sect) to be an infidel, but did not stop there—he also indicted a number of leading Deobandi and Shia ulama.[113]

Even as the Deobandi ulama and Islamist parties have become more conservative on issues such as blasphemy, they have remained relatively cautious about endorsing vigilante efforts at enforcing shariah. In its own publications (read principally by its own clerical members), the JUI-F has repeatedly affirmed that nonviolence was a foundational principle of the party, and that only the state can legitimately enforce Islamic law.[114] Drawing on the tradition of the Jamiat Ulama-e-Hind and, more widely, on the mores of the Deobandi ulama of the subcontinent, the JUI-F has argued that its mission was primarily focused on bringing reform and revolution at the "individual and societal" levels rather than engaging in political revolution.[115] Even in the months following September 11, 2001, when the JUI-F was seeking to gain maximum political leverage from the American military intervention in Afghanistan, the party's leadership counseled its followers to adopt a political path rather than one of armed struggle against the Pakistani state; speaking of the Afghan Taliban, Maulana Fazl ur-Rahman explained that "our target is the same but we will adopt a democratic path" in pursuing shariah.[116]

When asked about anti-state violence perpetrated by groups claiming to enforce shariah, the JUI-F has often denounced violence, but in the same

[112] See Mashal Saif, *The 'Ulama in Contemporary Pakistan: Contesting and Cultivating an Islamic Republic* (Cambridge, UK: Cambridge University Press, 2020), 116–18.

[113] Tahir Kamran, "Unpacking the Myth of Barelvi Eclecticism: A Historical Appraisal," in *Rethinking Pakistan: A 21st Century Perspective*, ed. Bilal Zahoor and Raza Rumi (London: Anthem Press, 2020), 33.

[114] See, for example, "jam'iyat 'ulamā'-e islām ko voṭ kyūṅ kiyā jā'e! [Why Vote for Jamiat Ulama-e Islam!]," *al-Jam'iyat* 9, no. 2 (December 2007): 8–10.

[115] Ṣāḥibzādah 'Āmir Maḥmūd, "apnā farẓ pahcāni'e: jam'iyat 'ulamā'-e islām ke dast o bāzū bani'e [Recognize Your Duty: Become the Hand and Arm of Jamiat Ulama-e Islam]," *al-Jam'iyat* 12, no. 3 (December 2010): 22–24.

[116] Maulānā Faẓl ur-Raḥmān, "maiṅ mulk ko bacānā cāhtā hūṅ aur fauj is ko toṛnā cāhtī hai [I Want to Save the Country and the Army Wants to Tear It Up]," *al-Jam'iyat* 2, no. 2 (November 2001): 5–8.

breath encouraged dialogue between anti-state groups and the government.[117] The JUI-F's attempt to discredit vigilante Islamism while continuing to affirm the validity of jihad found its simplest expression in the phrase of one Baloch party leader: "The JUI," he summarized, "does not support calling jihad as evil, and it does not favor terming evil as jihad."[118] Jihad, in other words, is not a legitimate excuse for attacking the Pakistani state, but neither is the presence of an Islamic state an excuse for abandoning the principle of jihad (particularly as it is practiced in places outside of Pakistan).

JUI-F leaders have equivocated in other ways. The party's writings contain occasional and subtle intimations that the party may at some future point challenge the state in its pursuit of its religio-political agenda. It is important to remember that the tradition from which the JUI emerged is one in which nonviolence was praised—but primarily for its tactical benefits. Prominent leaders among the nineteenth century political ulama flirted with both violent and nonviolent resistance to British rule, and concluded that nonviolence was favorable when conditions precluded successful, violent struggle.[119]

This tradition helps to set into context statements like the one by party leader Gul Nasib Khan in which, after complaining about how differences in strategy between violent and nonviolent Islamist organizations are harming the cause of Islam in Pakistan, said that he "does not favor armed struggle in these circumstances," but that "if changing circumstances demand change in the policy" then the JUI-F will declare its new position after consultation with the ulama.[120] Former Chief Minister Akram Khan Durrani made a statement in 2003 that was even more suggestive of the party's tactical view of nonviolence; responding to concerns that the MMA government in NWFP might model itself on the Afghan Taliban, he said:

> We will try our best to make the entire system congenial with Islamic notions but will not propel or force anyone . . . . What the Taliban did was true according to their environment and culture *because they were powerful enough to impose it by force.*[121]

[117] See, for example, Tayyab Ali Shah, "The Deobandi Debate Terrorist Tactics in Afghanistan and Pakistan," *Jamestown Terrorism Monitor* 8, no. 21 (May 28, 2010); Maulānā Faẓl ur-Raḥmān, "qaumī siyāsat meṅ jam'iyat kā kirdār [The Role of the Jamiat in National Politics]," *al-Jam'iyat* 10, no. 6 (March 2009): 8–10.

[118] World News Connection, trans., "Calling Jihad Evil Is Crime, Contempt of Jihad: Hafiz Hamdullah," *Intikhab*, May 21, 2011.

[119] Yohanan Friedmann, "The Attitude of the Jam'iyyat-i 'Ulama'-i Hind to the Indian National Movement and the Establishment of Pakistan," *Asian and African Studies* 7 (1971): 157–80.

[120] Maulānā Gul Nasīb Khān, "maujūdah ḥālāt meṅ je yū ā'e musalaḥ jidd o jahd kī ḥāmī nahīṅ [In the Current Situation, JUI Is Not in Favor of an Armed Struggle]," *al-Jam'iyat* 10, no. 11–12 (December 2009): 10–11.

[121] Akram Khān Durrānī, "bīūrokrīsī meṅ diyānatdār logoṅ kī kamī nahīṅ [There is No Lack of Honest People in the Bureaucracy]," *al-Jam'iyat* 3, no. 5 (January 2003): 4–6. Emphasis added.

There is a sense in statements like these that the JUI-F, following in the tradition of the political Deobandi ulama, chooses to defer to state authority as a matter of longstanding policy and practical benefit, but not as a product of unalterable political or religious conviction. Party leaders have, on occasion, made indirect threats of violence—suggesting, for example, that if the state does not enforce shariah, "then people will be forced to take guns in their hands"—but have avoided openly embracing the enforcement of shariah apart from the hand of the state.[122]

Although the Jamaat-e-Islami's discourse on violence has been, if anything, less equivocal than that of the JUI parties, its public views on violence were not always so clear cut. Maulana Maududi was adamant that Muslims have a right to protest unjust governments.[123] And his early speeches and writings were replete with fiery calls for revolution against the British colonial order in India. Speaking in 1939, two years before the founding of the party, he concluded:

> Hence there is no other way left for this party but to capture power, for an evil system takes roots [sic] and flourishes under the patronage of an evil government and a righteous culture can never be established without wresting power and authority from the wicked and the corrupt and vesting it into the reformers.[124]

He also rejected the distinction between offensive and defensive jihads, arguing that jihad is "offensive because the followers of Islam assault the rule and authority of the opposing ideology," but it is defensive because Muslims "are constrained to capture and retain power to implement their revolutionary ideology."[125]

These abstractions were put to the test in 1948, when Maududi rejected the legitimacy of Pakistan's jihad in Kashmir. The party was heavily criticized for that position, and subsequently embraced the state's sponsorship of militancy in India and Afghanistan.[126] In the decades that followed, it

[122] Maulānā Faẓl ur-Raḥmān, "mere hāthon jamhūriyat ko k͟haṭrah nahīṅ: āp ke hāthoṅ sharīʿat ko k͟haṭrah hai! [My Hand Does Not Threaten Democracy: Your Hand Does Threaten Shariah!]," *al-Jamʿiyat* 12, no. 4 (January 2011): 5–7.

[123] Sayyid Abul A'la Maududi, *Human Rights in Islam*, trans. Khurshid Ahmad (Lahore: Islamic Publications, 1995), 27.

[124] Sayyid Abul A'la Maududi, *Jihad in Islam*, trans. Abdul Waheed Khan (Lahore: Islamic Publications, 1962), 17. See also Abu'l A'lā Maūdūdi, "The Necessity of Divine Government for the Elimination of Oppression and Injustice," in *Muslim Self-Statement in India and Pakistan 1857–1968*, ed. Aziz Ahmad and Gustave E. Von Grunebaum, trans. Charles J. Adams (Wiesbaden: Otto Harrassowitz, 1970), 156–57.

[125] Maududi, *Jihad in Islam*, 23–24. For more on Maududi's views of jihad, see Tariq Rahman, *Interpretations of Jihad in South Asia: An Intellectual History*, 2nd ed. (Berlin: De Gruyter, 2020), 167ff, https://doi.org/10.1515/9783110716986.

[126] Vali Nasr, *International Relations of an Islamist Movement: The Case of the Jama'at-i Islami of Pakistan* (New York: Council on Foreign Relations, 2000), 17.

moderated in other ways that were essentially deferential to state authority, largely dispensing with Maududi's seemingly revolutionary rhetoric in favor of gradual democratic change.[127] By 1969, Maududi had proposed a code of political ethics—summarily ignored by the other political parties at the time—that "called on the government to ban those political parties aiming to bring about change by undemocratic and revolutionary methods."[128] He also developed a greater appreciation for the benefits of procedural justice, which, Mumtaz Ahmad drolly notes, "could partly be explained by his own experience of periodic jail terms, 'preventive detention,' and censoring of his writings and speeches by various regimes in Pakistan."[129]

There have been, however, two principal ways in which the party has legitimated violence. The first is through its support and justification of the vigilante violence conducted largely by its student wings and affiliated groups against individuals and institutions that do not conform to the party's views of Islamic practice. This is explored in greater depth in Chapter 5. Maududi rejected takfirism, and thus this violence has not been justified by the party as taking action against apostates, but rather as a means of pressuring Muslim individuals and state institutions to abide by certain ostensibly Islamic norms.[130] Party leaders, both in the press and in interviews, have underscored that "shariah can only be enforced by the state. No one can impose it unilaterally," but have also excused, justified, or downplayed vigilante violence justified on the basis of enforcing shariah.[131]

Second, the party has been outspoken in defending violence by Muslims in locations *other than Pakistan*. In these cases, the party's view of violence has been significantly less categorical. Party leaders openly embraced the jihad in Afghanistan in the 1980s and in Kashmir in the 1990s. They also, at times, justified anti-state violence by Muslim activists in Egypt and Chechnya. In doing so, party leaders have explained the JI's embrace of the democratic process as a choice based on the Pakistani context rather than transcendent Islamic political values.

[127] Notwithstanding Maududi's anti-colonial discourse, his concept of "revolution" arguably always presumed some measure of gradualism. See Jan-Peter Hartung, *A System of Life: Mawdudi and the Ideologisation of Islam, A System of Life* (London: Hurst & Company, 2013), chap. 4.

[128] M. Rafique Afzal, *Political Parties in Pakistan: 1969–1971*, 1st ed., vol. 3 (Islamabad: National Institute of Historical and Cultural Research, 1998), 63.

[129] Ahmad, "Islamic Fundamentalism," 489.

[130] Sayyid Abul A'la Mawdudi, *Let Us Be Muslims*, ed. Khurram Murad (Leicestershire, UK: Islamic Foundation, 2008), 114–18; 130.

[131] Mumtaz Ahmad, ed., *Toward Revisiting the Debate on Shari'a: Prospects and Challenges for Pakistan* (Islamabad: Iqbal International Institute for Research and Dialogue, International Islamic University Islamabad, 2010), 28; Chaudhry Aslam Salimi, interview by Joshua White, Urdu and English, trans. Shuja Malik, February 24, 2011.

Asked in 1995 to discuss the party's views on whether violence was an appropriate means by which to come to power, Khurshid Ahmad—the party's leading intellectual—gave a highly contextualized answer, worth quoting at some length:

> [The] Islamic movement in the Indo-Pakistan subcontinent has been part and parcel of the democratic process. The electoral door was opened, providing the opportunity for Islamic parties to take part. It is true that sometimes some movements resorted to violence, yet the democratic channels were there, and solutions were negotiated. The Islamic movement in Egypt (the Muslim Brotherhood), for instance, found itself in a different situation than that of the Jamaat. . . . I think that the whole issue of violence is a complex one. In this context, I would very much submit that the Islamic movements have desired change through persuasion, *da'wah*, and democratic means. Where these means were denied to them, and where they were forced to the wall, resort to violence was inevitable . . . . So I think that the question of violence cannot be, in any way, tied to a particular time period.[132]

This answer, pointedly descriptive rather than normative, captures well the party's contextual view of political violence, as it appears throughout party publications and interviews. The party presents itself as firmly committed to the democratic process in Pakistan, but that commitment is not necessarily a deeply held ideological stance applicable to all times and places.

Pakistan's Ahl-e-Hadith community holds a diversity of views on questions related to jihad and democratic participation. Although the Markazi Jamiat Ahl-e-Hadith is only a minor player in public debates on these issues, the views of the broader Ahl-e-Hadith are important because of the prominence of Lashkar-e-Taiba and its "charitable" affiliate Jamaat ud-Dawa, and the emergence of its political party affiliate the Milli Muslim League in the 2018 general elections.

Lashkar-e-Taiba's views on jihad have been analyzed in depth by C. Christine Fair and other scholars. Lashkar-e-Taiba (LeT) figures underscore that participation in jihad is an obligation of all believers, even if only a subset of the community joins the fight on a battlefield.[133] Supporting jihad is viewed as a means of purification, and an instrument by which the community can winnow the true believers from the hypocrites.[134] Even more than that, writes

[132] Ibrahim M. Abu-Rabi', ed., *Islamic Resurgence: Challenges, Directions & Future Perspectives. A Roundtable with Prof. Khurshid Ahmad* (Islamabad: Institute of Policy Studies, 1995), 115–117.

[133] See Fair, *In Their Own Words*, 168–72.

[134] Joshua T. White, "A Cooperative Jihad? The Religious Logic of Hafiz Muhammad Saeed and the Limits of Pan-Sunni Cooperation in Pakistan," in *Pakistan's Enduring Challenges*, ed. C. Christine Fair and Sarah J. Watson (Philadelphia: University of Pennsylvania Press, 2015), 61.

LeT founder Hafiz Saeed, it reveals who among the believers are "patient, resolute, and steadfast."[135] Instead of dwelling on the traditional distinctions between defensive and offensive jihads, LeT polemicists have proposed an expansive array of objectives for jihad, which include freeing land held by infidels, defending persecuted Muslims, and securing the dominance of Islam around the world.[136] This is, by design, a recipe for perpetual jihad.[137]

Perhaps the most striking aspect of LeT's ideology—and one shared by the MJAH and other Ahl-e-Hadith parties—is the way in which it carefully exempts the Pakistani state from becoming the object of jihad. It does so by crafting a distinction between infidels and hypocrites, and judging that even if Pakistan's Muslim leaders are corrupt, weak in their faith, or tyrannical, they deserve brotherly correction rather than the sword.[138] States led by non-Muslims, notably India, are viewed by LeT as the proper objects of jihad.

In one sense, this is unsurprising, as LeT and its affiliates have long benefited from, and served as instruments of, the military and security services. In another sense, this highly deferential view toward the state puts LeT and parties like MJAH and MML at odds with a vocal faction of the global Salafi community that embraces takfir against the state—a segment that are often labeled, following Quintan Wiktorowicz, as Salafi-Jihadis, but which Shiraz Maher more aptly labels violent rejectionists.[139] Such groups, including al-Qaeda and the Islamic State, "are irreconcilably estranged from the state, regarding it as a heretical and artificial unit."[140] Pakistan's Ahl-e-Hadith community largely rejects this view, and has instead cultivated a close relationship with the Pakistani state with whom it has prioritized mobilization for jihad against India.

[135] Hafiz Muhammad Saeed, *Tafseer Surah At-Taubah*, trans. M. Saleem Ahsan (Lahore: Dar-ul-Andalus, n.d.), 213–14.

[136] Fair, *In Their Own Words*, 161–62.

[137] See C. Christine Fair, "'Why We Are Waging Jihad': A Critical Translation of Lashkar-e-Tayyaba's Foundational Document," *Current Trends in Islamist Ideology* 33 (October 2023): 5–33.

[138] White, "A Cooperative Jihad?," 61–64; Samina Yasmeen, *Jihad and Dawah: Evolving Narratives of Lashkar-e-Taiba and Jamat ud Dawah* (London: Hurst & Company, 2017), 65; Fair, *In Their Own Words*, 172–74.

[139] Quintan Wiktorowicz, "Anatomy of the Salafi Movement," *Studies in Conflict & Terrorism* 29, no. 3 (2006): 207–39, https://doi.org/10.1080/10576100500497004; Shiraz Maher, *Salafi-Jihadism: The History of an Idea*, Kindle (Oxford: Oxford University Press, 2016).

[140] Maher, *Salafi-Jihadism*, Kindle location 403.

4
The Structural Roots of Islamist Party Behavior
Party Organization and Affiliate Relationships

4.1 Introduction

This chapter and the next explore the structural determinants of Islamist party behavior. They examine the ways in which, quite apart from the sincerity or insincerity of their various ideological positions, the parties' postures toward religiously justified anti-state violence are shaped by their own organizational structures and their relationships with constituents, competitors, and the state. These chapters in particular draw on political science literatures on political party linkage patterns and the instrumental uses of political violence, and on social movement theory's insights into the ways in which organizations take advantage of political and social opportunity structures.

The two principal hypotheses that are being tested in this book, described in detail in Chapter 1, both focus on the implications of parties' structural vulnerabilities. Hypothesis 1 proposes that an Islamist party's willingness to enable anti-state violence in the name of advancing Islamic law is principally a function of its structural vulnerabilities to the state and to anti-state movements, rather than a function of its ideological commitments. Hypotheses 2a and 2b propose specific structural conditions (clientelist party linkages and weak party institutionalization, respectively) that contribute to those structural vulnerabilities.

These paired chapters address four dimensions of the parties' structural dynamics, and focus heavily on Pakistan's largest and most influential Islamist parties—the JI and JUI-F—while also examining where relevant smaller Islamist parties such as the JUI-S and TLP and providing comparative perspectives on the ways in which Islamist party structures are similar to or different from those of mainstream and ethnic parties. The first section examines the organizational coherence and institutionalization of the Islamist parties.

Vigilante Islamists. Joshua T. White, Oxford University Press. © Oxford University Press (2025).
DOI: 10.1093/9780197814178.003.0004

The second explores their relationships with their constituents, and with affiliate groups including student wings and madrassah organizations. The third, beginning in Chapter 5, maps the parties' relationships with militant organizations. The final section evaluates the parties' respective relationships with the state, and their vulnerabilities to state influence and institutions.

These four dimensions of a party's structure and relationships are often inter-related; the nature of a party's primary electoral competitors are, for example, shaped by that parties' organizational resilience and priorities, by constituent pressures, and by state policies. And each of these factors influence the party's decision-making with respect to its strategies for participating in, or responding to, anti-state violence.

These two chapters, with their examination of the structural determinants of party decision-making regarding the use of violence, engage the broader literature on parties and political violence, some of which is referenced here later. In particular, these chapters should also be read in dialogue with Niloufer Siddiqui's groundbreaking work on political parties and violence in Pakistan.[1] In certain respects, the arguments of this book complement Siddiqui's analytical framework: both place a similar emphasis on the structural incentives and determinants of party decision-making regarding violence; seek to measure organizational cohesion or institutionalization as means of evaluating those incentives; consider the costs that parties incur from engaging in violence; and explore the conditions under which parties outsource violence or seek deniable partnerships with militant organizations.

In other respects, however, the frameworks are somewhat different. This book examines Islamist parties as its principal *subjects*, rather than so-called mainstream or ethnic parties that often have more compelling electoral prospects or at least a broader support base. Moreover, this book considers cases in which the *object* of violence is the state itself; this is a narrowly construed but important and high stakes form of violence, but one that does not capture the wider forms of decision-making that parties under Siddiqui's framework consider when engaging in violence for a diverse array of electoral, clientelistic, or economic reasons.

There is another notable difference as well. On account of this book's focus on anti-state violence, the measures of a party's organizational capacity—described in some detail later—are used primarily to assess its *vulnerabilities* to the state and to anti-state organizations, while in Siddiqui's framework,

[1] Niloufer A. Siddiqui, *Under the Gun: Political Parties and Violence in Pakistan* (Cambridge: Cambridge University Press, 2023), https://doi.org/10.1017/9781009242530.

which considers wider forms of political and electoral violence, these measures of party capacity are used in large part to assess the party's *ability to exercise* violence and the strategies that it will therefore choose to employ.

These differences notwithstanding, Siddiqui's framework is indeed helpful in the context of this book's analysis of Islamist party decision-making. In particular, it illuminates the ways in which an Islamist party's organizational structures and the nature of its support base shape might shape its choices about whether to engage in violence directly, or outsource violence to what Siddiqui calls "violence specialists." I will draw on this dimension of Siddiqui's analysis in evaluating Islamist party behavior in several of the cases that follow, particularly those cases in which the parties are faced with incentives to engage in anti-state violence rather than merely endorse or tolerate it.

4.2 Party Organization

4.2.1 Organizational Dynamics

Nearly every attempt by political scientists to categorize political parties by type includes some measure of "the nature of the formal organization" as a key variable. Often this is framed as a distinction between parties that are "organizationally thin," that is, rely on personal and particularistic networks for decision-making, and those that are "thick," and tend to be mass-membership parties with well-developed, formal organizational structures.[2] These categories are typically too general to be useful. Political parties are essentially political systems in miniature, with structured ways of dealing with internal competition, coalition-building, and patronage.[3] Islamist parties are no exception. In assessing the role of party organization on Islamist party decision-making, we will focus in particular on three organizational dynamics.[4]

First, we can consider the party's organizational and bureaucratic coherence, measured by the sophistication of its staff and offices, the presence or absence of an efficient central administrative apparatus, the scope and

[2] See, for example, Richard Gunther and Larry Diamond, "Species of Political Parties," *Party Politics* 9, no. 2 (March 2003): 171.

[3] See Rosa Mulé, "Explaining the Party-Policy Link," *Party Politics* 3, no. 4 (October 1997): 501; Kay Lawson, "Political Parties: Inside and Out," *Comparative Politics* 23, no. 1 (October 1990): 105–19.

[4] Many of these metrics of institutionalization are drawn from Angelo Panebianco, *Political Parties: Organization and Power*, trans. Marc Silver, Cambridge Studies in Modern Political Economies (Cambridge, UK: Cambridge University Press, 1988).

frequency of its communications to members, the number of functional duties covered by party officers versus volunteers, the level of record-keeping on its affairs, and the frequency of training for its cadres. Here we will also appraise the role of internal procedures in party decision-making. Accessible measures include the proportion of leaders in senior decision-making bodies who are elected, constitutional authorities provided to the party leader and/or the apex decision-making body, the presence of a written constitution, demonstrated observance of a written constitution, structured procedures for making and recording decisions, and procedures or guidelines regarding the level of authority (local, provincial, central, etc.) at which decisions must be made.[5]

Second, we can evaluate the nature of party funding. The key measure here is the estimated percentage of funds for party operations raised from party members or other sustainable domestic sources. These data are typically not in the public domain, but we can make limited inferences from available information about party fundraising patterns and strategies.

Third, we can look at the level of control that the party exerts over its members. The classic measure used by political scientists to study party discipline is derived from roll-call records of parliamentary votes. These data are difficult to come by in Pakistan, and also largely irrelevant given the patchwork of legislative and constitutional limitations that prohibit voting across party lines.[6] Instead, we can look to the party's qualifications for induction into (and maintenance of) membership, its use of sanctions against members who do not adopt the party line, and its influence over member finances and donor behavior. In addition, we can examine the degree to which the central party leadership exercises influence over the programmatic, financial, and policy decision-making of provincial, district, and subdistrict party units.

4.2.2 Organizational and Bureaucratic Coherence

The Jamaat-e-Islami is the model of a highly coherent political party in Pakistan. Along with the MQM in Karachi, it is widely recognized as the most organizationally sophisticated and procedure-driven party operation in the country. Its centralized and institutionalized bureaucracy was born out

[5] Panebianco notes that although decentralization of *administrative* action can be an attribute of a strong bureaucracy, well-institutionalized parties will typically not have a highly decentralized system of decision-making on *policy* matters. Panebianco, *Political Parties*, 226.

[6] So-called "floor crossing" has been intermittently sanctioned by constitutional measures. See "The Law and Politics of Floor Crossing," *Dawn*, March 13, 2011.

of Maududi's vision of political change, in which an Islamic vanguard would shape society as a result of its disciplined and virtuous leadership. He wrote, brimming with confidence, that

> if leadership and the power of command are vested in God-fearing and righteous people, then it is inevitable that the entire system of life should proceed in terms of fear of God, goodness, and righteousness.[7]

Maududi's vision for this mechanism of social change borrowed heavily from fascism and communism, and as an organizational strategy, adopted "the principle of democratic centralism as a rationalized and modern command structure suited to projecting power in the political arena."[8] Over the decades since its founding in 1941, the JI has built a remarkably efficient bureaucracy. Its national headquarters outside of Lahore is perhaps the best managed central party office in the country.[9] Its record-keeping, while tightly controlled, is detailed. (According to one local party leader in Lahore, the JI maintains records of the blood types of its members, so that it can contact them when the need arises from a local hospital.[10]) This author's experience is that the central party bureaucracy is quite accustomed to dealing with foreign journalists and researchers, and also provides extensive advisory and training services to provincial and local party leaders from across the country.

One explanation for the party's tightly managed organization is its restrictive membership regime. Although it has been tempered somewhat by former leader Qazi Hussain's populist approach begun in the 1980s, Maududi's vision of an elite cadre organization continues to influence the party's structure and operations. According to internal party documents dated 2009, the JI claims an overall membership of over 4 million.[11] Most of these members belong to the loosest membership tier, while very few qualify as full members (*rukn*, pl. *ārkān*). Figure 4.1 shows the membership distribution by province. Figure 4.2 illustrates the membership composition by type.

[7] Abu'l A'lā Maudūdī, "The Moral Foundations of the Islamic Movement," in *Muslim Self-Statement in India and Pakistan 1857–1968*, ed. Aziz Ahmad and Gustave E. Von Grunebaum, trans. Charles J. Adams (Wiesbaden: Otto Harrassowitz, 1970), 158.

[8] Seyyed Vali Reza Nasr, "'Organization' in Islamic Movements," in *Pakistan: 1995*, ed. Charles H. Kennedy and Rasul Bakhsh Rais (Lahore: Vanguard, 1995), 67. See also Charles J. Adams, "Mawdudi and the Islamic State," in *Voices of Resurgent Islam*, ed. John L. Esposito (New York: Oxford University Press, 1983), 371–97.

[9] Sohail Mahmood, *Islamic Fundamentalism in Pakistan, Egypt and Iran* (Lahore: Vanguard, 1995), 295.

[10] Zulfiqar, interview by Joshua White, Urdu, trans. Shuja Malik, May 20, 2011.

[11] Jamā'at-e Islāmī Pākistān, "afrādī quvat jamā'at-e islāmī pākistān [Personnel Strength of Jamaat-e Islami Pakistan]" (Jamā'at-e Islāmī Pākistān, October 2009).

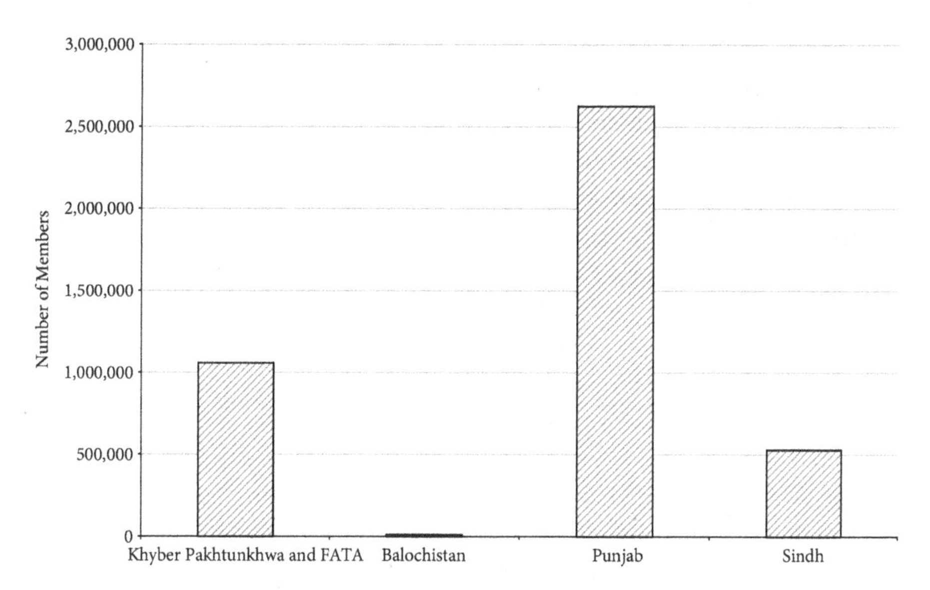

Figure 4.1 JI Membership Distribution by Province.

Source: Author's analysis of internal JI 2009–2010 membership documents. Figures include all classes of members.

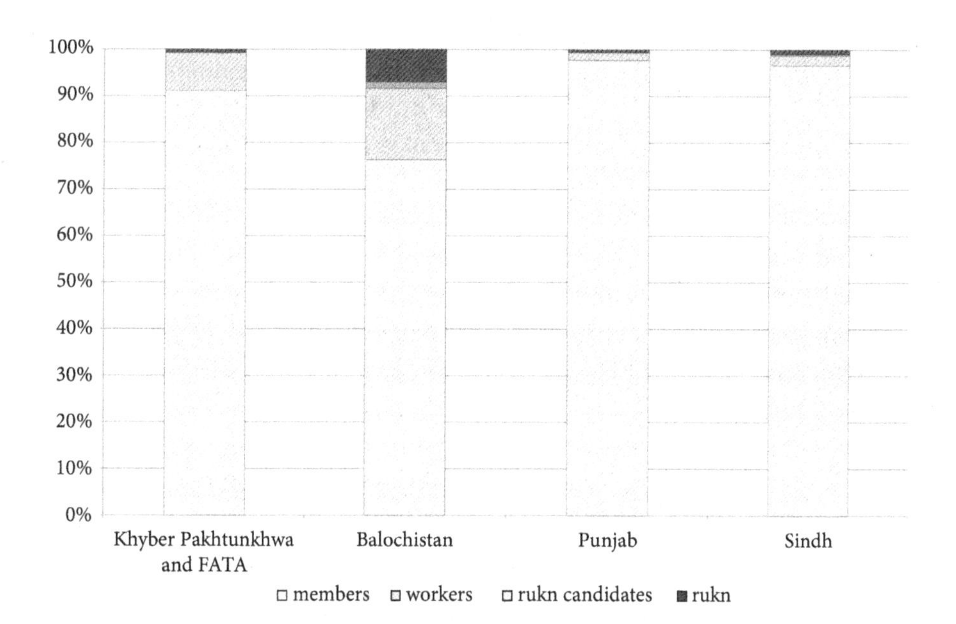

Figure 4.2 JI Membership Composition by Province.

Source: Author's analysis of internal JI 2009–2010 membership documents.

Less than half of 1 percent of total JI members are full members. The percentage of elite members is somewhat higher in Balochistan, but the party's membership in that province is negligible. In the other provinces, only a small elite achieve the status of rukn.

The party's ninety-two-page constitution outlines a detailed set of procedures for internal party elections and decision-making—processes that actually appear to be followed with some consistency—leading many observers to conclude that the JI is the most internally democratic party in Pakistan.[12] Decision-making power is concentrated in the office of an elected amir, who leads the markazi majlis-e-shura, which is about sixty members.[13] The party also has a *qayyām* (secretary general) who acts as the "custodian" of the party's organization and procedures, and allows for multiple deputy amirs and qayyams, who are chosen through a consultative process that is neither an election nor an appointment per se.[14] The shura meetings are often quite contentious, but if and when the amir holds a strong opinion, the members of the shura typically defer to his authority.[15] The shura, rather than the amir, holds the final say on matters pertaining to party policy.[16]

Although the records of party discussions within the shura are kept strictly confidential, interviews with members of the shura reveal a highly structured and formalized decision-making process. The shura typically meets quarterly at Mansurah near Lahore. An agenda is circulated to the members in advance of the meeting, and topics of debate are fixed beforehand. There are usually "fiery speeches," recalled one member, "but once a decision is made, we all must be on board."[17] Furthermore, in a procedural detail that most students of South Asian politics would consider quite atypical of parties in the subcontinent, the member continued: "If I want to speak" at the shura meeting, he said, "I put my name on the list beforehand, and I am put in the queue." The shura procedures are in this sense democratic, but also deferential to the amir's authority and structured according to the procedures of the party's constitution.

Interviews and documents suggest that this procedural rigor extends to the party's communications. That the JI produces a high volume of documents

[12] Jamā'at-e Islāmī Pākistān, "dastūr jamā'at-e islāmī pākistān [Constitution of the Jamaat-e Islami Pakistan]" (Lahore: Jamaat-e Islami Pakistan, January 2002). Other parties, such as the ANP and MQM, have reasonably strong records of internal democracy, but the JI seems to stands apart in this regard.

[13] See also International Crisis Group, "Islamic Parties in Pakistan," Asia Report 216 (Islamabad: International Crisis Group, December 12, 2011), 9ff.

[14] Khalid Rehman, interview by Joshua White, English and Urdu, trans. Shuja Malik, February 23, 2011.

[15] Farid Paracha, interview by Joshua White, English and Urdu, trans. Shuja Malik, March 8, 2011.

[16] Chaudhry Aslam Salimi, interview by Joshua White, Urdu and English, trans. Shuja Malik, February 24, 2011.

[17] Asif Luqman Qazi, interview by Joshua White, English, May 25, 2011.

should not come as a surprise to anyone who has studied its history; Maududi himself was, according to one early historian, "a prolific pamphleteer."[18] One local party leader in Lahore reported receiving one to two circulars per week, providing policy guidance and information about party events. A more senior leader reported receiving two to three such missives *per day*.[19] (Munawar Hasan, elected amir in 2009, reportedly increased the number and formality of directives, as compared to his predecessor Qazi Hussain Ahmad.) In addition to attending required weekly local meetings on matters of party organization, higher-level subnational party organizations are required to make annual plans, such as the detailed twenty-one-page action plan prepared and printed by the JI's Lahore office.[20]

Apart from the circulars, the party uses a number of means to communicate with its members. It publishes a weekly from Karachi, *Haft Rozah Aishyā* (Weekly Asia), and an intellectual monthly journal, *Tarjumān al-Qur'ān*. Senior party members purport that these publications are read by party members even in far-flung parts of Khyber Pakhtunkhwa province, but there is no independent confirmation of that assertion. The party also deputizes volunteers to set up SMS distribution networks to propagate party directives and information. In Lahore, one such volunteer reported that he regularly sends messages on behalf of the party to over 600 members, who then distribute the SMS content more widely.[21] The party was quick to embrace new media platforms, setting up a sophisticated media cell at the Mansurah headquarters. When this author visited in 2011, the cell had a team of young party members monitoring and digitally recording television coverage of the party on seven flat screens, and another team promoting the party's messages on Facebook and Twitter—all the while working to screen potential malign actors (they were particularly worried about Ahmadi "infiltration") from presenting themselves as JI members.[22]

Compared to the Jamaat-e-Islami, the JUI-F is an altogether different kind of party. Less centralized and more loosely structured than the JI, it has its roots in the Deobandi clerical tradition, which is in turn institutionally

[18] Khalid B. Sayeed, "The Jama'at-i-Islami Movement in Pakistan," *Pacific Affairs* 30, no. 1 (March 1957): 62.

[19] Zulfiqar, interview; Amir ul-Azim, interview by Joshua White, English and Urdu, trans. Shuja Malik, May 18, 2011. Some of these circulars, such as those obtained by the author, outline a monthly program for a particular constituency. 'Abd al-Ḥafiẓ Aḥmad, "khaṭ banām arkān: progrām barā'e janvarī 2011 [Letter to Members: Program for January 2011]" (jamā'at-e islāmī ḥalqah en ae 126 lāhaur [Jamaat-e Islami Constituency NA-126 Lahore], December 28, 2010).

[20] Jamā'at-e Islāmī Lāhaur, *sālānah manṣūbah-e 'amal 2011 [Annual Plan of Action 2011]* (Lahore: Jamā'at-e Islāmī Lāhaur, 2011).

[21] Amir ul-Azim, interview.

[22] Shamsuddin Amjad, interview by Joshua White, Urdu, trans. Shuja Malik, May 20, 2011.

anchored in the madaris system. Every three years, the party conducts a membership drive and signs up new members using a simple membership form. (Copies of the form are restricted to the party election officials, to discourage inflation of membership numbers from local constituencies.[23]) The party members in a union council—Pakistan's lowest division of government—form a *ḥalqah*, or party unit, and go on to elect the majlis-e-umumi (general council) for that area, on the basis of one representative for every thirty members.[24] The union council majlis-e-umumi in turn selects representatives to the next-highest majlis-e-umumi, at the district level, on the basis of a system of proportional representation. Functioning as an electoral college, these councils eventually form the markazi majlis-e-umumi at the central level, which has one representative for every 3,000 party members. The markazi majlis-e-umumi has responsibility for matters pertaining to the party constitution and elections and meets at least annually. (The district and provincial majlis-e-umumi bodies typically meet twice a year.)

Once the markazi majlis-e-umumi selects an amir and general secretary, they then select the other party office-holders, who make up the markazi majlis-e-amalah (action committee). These senior party office-holders, who number about fifteen, are charged with putting the party's policies into effect. Finally, the majlis-e-amalah selects the majlis-e-shura, which numbers around sixty, plus about fifteen honorary members. (The majlis-e-amalah remains a subset of the majlis-e-shura.) The majlis-e-shura is the main consultative body of the party and takes up all major decisions regarding alliance and coalition participation.

Although this structure may appear elaborate on paper, the procedures for decision-making within the shura are somewhat unclear—even to senior party figures. Party functionaries close to the amir suggested that he must only "take under advisement" the position of the shura when making a decision.[25] Rationalized one official: "The power of decision rests with the amir . . . this is the sunnah of the Prophet."[26] Another senior figure explained it somewhat differently; that is, that on matters of great import, the shura's decisions are made by consensus, and on all other matters, by majority. If there is a divided vote or if the shura cannot reach agreement, in this view, the decision is made by the amir.[27]

[23] Muftī as-Sayad Muḥammad Manẓhar As'adī, "k͟huṣūṣī hidāyat barā'e rukniyat sāzī [Special Instruction Relating to Recruitment]," *al-Jam'iyat* 6, no. 7 (April 2006): 37.

[24] The following explanation of JUI-F structure draws from party documents and interviews with multiple party officials.

[25] Mufti Ibrar and Lutf ur-Rahman, interview by Joshua White, Urdu, trans. Shuja Malik, May 27, 2011.

[26] Jalaluddin Khan, interview by Joshua White, Urdu, May 12, 2011.

[27] Gul Nasib Khan, interview by Joshua White and Niloufer Siddiqui, Urdu, May 26, 2011.

The ambiguity about decision-making procedures is in keeping with the party's informal character and long-standing deference to the authority of the amir. Admitted one JUI-F official, after recounting a litany of procedural weaknesses in the party: "We have no proper organization."[28] The lack of an efficient centralized bureaucracy quickly became evident to the author while conducting field research on the party. The party frequently utilizes space from mosques and madaris, including government mosques, to run its operations. It had small offices in Lahore and Quetta, and a large building on the outskirts of Peshawar that was built during the MMA period. (The JUI-F central and provincial leadership has at times used Peshawar's Dar ul-Ulum Sarhad as home for its secretariat.[29]) Most of the actual party operations and record-keeping appeared to follow the office-holders themselves, and thus could be found in whichever mosque or madrassah they happened to hold a position.

In the course of field work, this author discovered that some critical party records were being kept in a dank mosque closet on the property of a government primary school in Lahore. Others were at a madrassah in Rawalpindi. When asked where one might acquire a copy of the party's official leadership directory—designed to be used exclusively by party leaders—one well-connected JUI-F functionary thought for a moment, and eventually suggested inquiring at a small bookshop in an old Peshawar bazaar run by a "thuggish" local party worker. Compared with the JI headquarters, which has entire units devoted to record-keeping and publications, the JUI-F organization is decidedly ad hoc.

The party had made efforts to rationalize its organization and procedures. It published an article in late 2010 on organizational matters, in which it announced that the central leadership had mandated that provincial party offices put in place phone, fax, and email capabilities.[30] That at least one of the four provincial party units was apparently operating without basic communication facilities is perhaps more striking than the announcement itself. Aside from its two main publications, party monthly *al-Jam'iyat* and youth monthly *'Azm-e-Nau*, the JUI-F issues occasional party circulars, none of which appear to be published in a timely manner.[31] (When asked how they learn of the key decisions of the markazi majlis-e-shura, most senior party officials answered,

[28] Jalaluddin Khan, interview by Joshua White, English, March 4, 2011.

[29] Imtiaz Gul, *The Unholy Nexus: Pak-Afghan Relations Under the Taliban* (Lahore: Vanguard Books, 2002), 90.

[30] Maulānā Muḥammad Aḥmad K͟hān, "mulkī pālīsiyāṅ 'avāmī umangoṅ ke muṭābiq tashkīl dī jā'eṅ [National Policy Should Be Framed According to People's Wishes]," *al-Jam'iyat* 12, no. 2 (November 2010): 26–27.

[31] Fatahullah Sajjad, interview by Joshua White, Urdu, trans. Shuja Malik, March 6, 2011.

"on TV.") The party has increased the use of digital messaging apps to communicate with lower-level leaders. Befitting its overall level of organizational coherence, the party's SMS and digital messaging distribution is often inconsistent, and party leaders gave mixed opinions about whether the distributor was operating in an official or unofficial capacity.[32] The party's website has often lagged behind that of the JI in content and sophistication, and was largely offline for nearly eight years after the MMA website stopped working sometime in 2003.

Although the JUI-F does not publicly report its membership or leadership demographics, I was able to draw some conclusions about its leadership from analyzing the party's internal leadership directory from 2011 (the most recent edition I was able to acquire).

As seen in Figure 4.3, nearly three-quarters of the membership hails from Khyber Pakhtunkhwa, the former FATA, and Balochistan. Given the nature of the party's electoral system, the membership of the markazi majlis-e-umumi will accurately represent the distribution of members by province. The elite

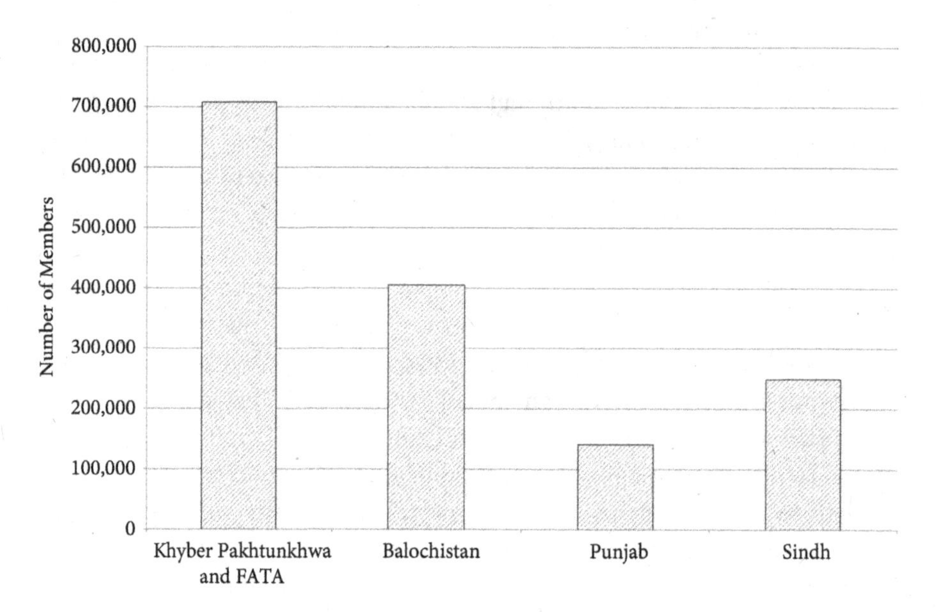

Figure 4.3 JUI-F Membership Distribution by Province.
Source: Author's analysis of internal JUI-F 2011 leadership directory.

[32] There are also reports of provincial party leaders using SMS to coordinate with local workers for events and to counter anti-JUI-F propaganda. Muḥḥabat 'Alī Khoṛū, "taḥafaẓ-e nāmūs-e risālat railī kā ānkhoṅ dekhā aḥavāl [An Eyewitness Account of the Rally for the Protection of the Defamation of Prophets (Bill)]," *al-Jam'iyat* 12, no. 4 (January 2011): 10–12.

markazi majlis-e-shura, selected through a less deterministic process, need not accurately reflect the provincial distribution of members. Indeed, analysis of party leadership data suggests that it does not. Figure 4.4, below, shows that the party has—by choice or merely by practice—made the provincial representation in the markazi majlis-e-shura substantially more representative than actual membership distributions would dictate. Several party members, when interviewed, said that the party uses shura appointments to balance out constituencies that are poorly represented by a strictly proportional process; these data may thus point to an intentional policy by the JUI-F to retain a national leadership profile and appeal to more than simply the Pashtun ethnic demographic.

The profile of the JUI-F's leadership class has rightly been assumed to be clerical and predominantly Pashtun. The importance of the clerical linkages to the JUI-F will be explored in greater detail later. Until now, however, even the most basic data on party leadership demographics for the JUI-F have been unavailable. To what extent *is* the party's leadership dominated by clerics? A thorough analysis of the party's 2011 leadership directory sheds light on this question. The directory was assiduous in listing the full name and

Figure 4.4 JUI-F Provincial Representation in Markazi Majlis-e-Shura Shura Relative to Provincial Party Membership.

Source: Author's analysis of internal JUI-F 2011 leadership directory. A negative number indicates that the province is under-represented on the shura relative to its party membership. "Other" includes Islamabad, Pakistani Kashmir, FATA, and Gilgit-Baltistan.

title of every member of the markazi majlis-e-umumi—the largest and most representative leadership body. By systematically coding the personal (i.e., non-party) titles of the members, it was possible to gather insights about the composition of the JUI-F's leading figures.

Figures 4.5 shows the results of this analysis, which distinguishes among three categories of titles: earned religious titles, of the kind that one would be granted from a formal religious education from an accredited madrassah; honorary religious titles, of the kind that would be granted on the basis of lineage or performance of hajj; and professional titles, of the kind that one would be granted upon entry to a nonreligious vocation. The percentage of earned religious titles ranged from 55 percent in Punjab, to 78 percent in Sindh, with the percentage in KP/FATA and Balochistan hovering just under 70 percent. Overall, 69 percent of members in the markazi majlis-e-umumi had earned religious titles, and only 2 percent had professional titles. Unless a large number of earned religious titles were simply omitted from the directory listing (which is unlikely, given that many entries included multiple *honorary* titles) we can conclude that, somewhat unexpectedly for a clerical party, only about

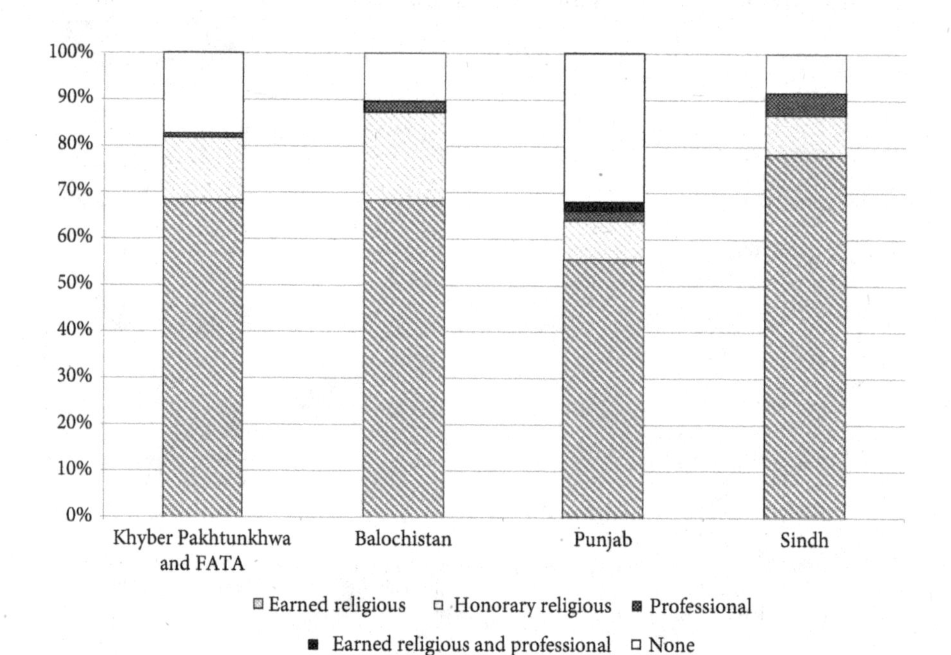

Figure 4.5 Personal Titles of JUI-F Markazi Majlis-e-Umumi Members by Province.

Source: Author's analysis of internal JUI-F 2011 leadership directory. Earned religious titles include hafiz, maulana, maulvi, mufti, qari, qazi, and shaikh. Honorary religious titles include haji, pir, and sayyid. Professional titles include advocate, doctor, and engineer. Where a member had both an earned and honorary religious title, he was credited for the former. N=501.

70 percent of the top-tier leadership are actually ulama. Moreover, unlike the JI—which research has shown to have many professionals in its upper ranks—the JUI-F has only ten out of 501 members of the majlis-e-umumi with titles suggesting a nonreligious vocation.[33]

An analysis of the elite markazi majlis-e-shura, comprising fifty-seven regular members and fifteen honorary members, yielded similar patterns.

As Figure 4.6 shows, a somewhat higher percentage of the majlis-e-shura, compared with the majlis-e-umumi, was comprised of those with earned religious titles. This again reinforces the observation that the party, while dominated by clerics, is not exclusively run by those with a madrassah background. Somewhere between one-fifth and one-quarter of the JUI-F's senior leadership ranks appear to have been filled by party functionaries who did not have a religious educational qualification from the madaris. According to party leaders and historians, the presence of prominent non-ulama members in the JUI dates to the 1970s. Although "the overall complexion

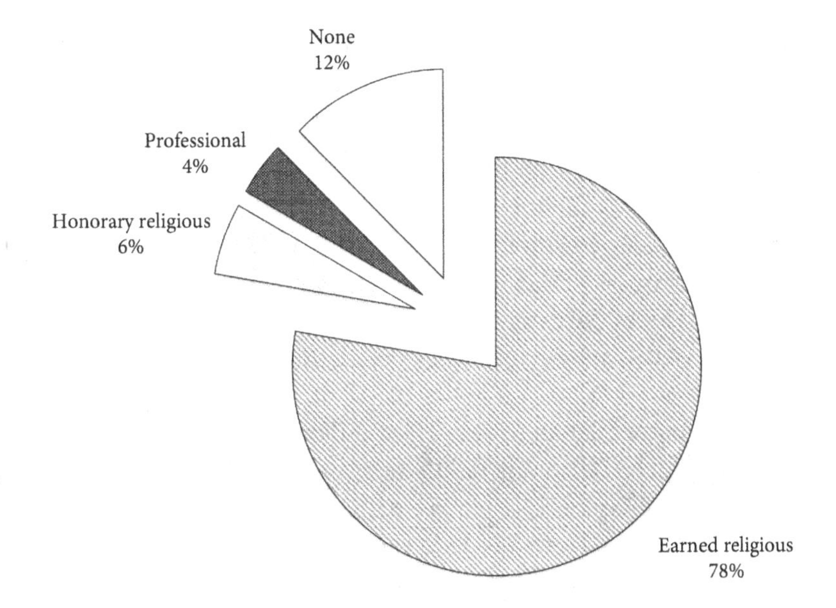

Figure 4.6 Personal Titles of JUI-F Markazi Majlis-e-Shura Members.

Source: Author's analysis of internal JUI-F 2011 leadership directory. Earned religious titles include hafiz, maulana, maulvi, mufti, qari, qazi, and shaikh. Honorary religious titles include haji, pir, and sayyid. Professional titles include advocate, doctor, and engineer. Where a member had both an earned and honorary religious title, he was credited for the former. N=72

[33] Mumtaz Ahmad, "Islamic Fundamentalism in South Asia: The Jamaat-i-Islami and the Tablighi Jamaat of South Asia," in *Fundamentalisms Observed*, ed. Martin E. Marty and R. Scott Appleby (Chicago: University of Chicago Press, 1991), 496.

[of the party] is still with the ulama," there have been efforts over the last fifteen to twenty years to make the party more balanced, and include wealthy businessmen and other non-ulama within the senior ranks.[34]

Along with its character as a clerical party, the JUI-F has developed a reputation for highly personalistic decision-making. As politician Aftab Sherpao noted dismissively, the "JUI-F is a floating sort of a party" that operates "at the will and whim of Maulana Fazl ur-Rahman."[35] This assessment of the JUI-F's decision-making is largely accurate, but applies to most Pakistani political parties. (Indeed, Sherpao has led a personalistic party named after himself: the Pakistan Peoples Party–Sherpao.) All major Pakistani parties have cultivated personality cults, and many mainstream and ethnic parties have encouraged dynastic rule. (Both the JI and JUI-F have repeatedly put forward wives, sisters, and sisters-in-law of party leaders for the reserved women's seats in the assemblies.) The JUI-F is typical in this regard. Maulana Fazl ur-Rahman is the son of the previous leader, Maulana Mufti Mahmud. His two brothers, Lutf ur-Rahman and Atta ur-Rahman, have both been active in the party, and have at times been given prominent positions.[36]

The extreme level of attention given by the party to the JUI-F's top echelon of leaders is on display in *al-Jam'iyat*. The most prominent half-dozen clerics are regularly referred to with the high honorific *madd ẓillah*, which roughly translates to, "May his shadow be extended." Following the JUI-F decision to quit the government coalition in December 2010, the party monthly in its January 2011 issue was filled with no fewer than forty-nine separate advertisements, paid for by party members, personally congratulating the amir Fazl ur-Rahman (and, in smaller print, his deputy Abdul Ghaffur Haidri) on his decision.

Organizational information was more difficult to obtain for the smaller Islamist parties. The JUI-S was rightly seen as "synonymous" with its leader, Sami ul-Haq, until his assassination in 2018, at which point the party leadership passed to his son, Hamid ul-Haq Haqqani.[37] When interviewed in 2011 about the party's decision-making, both Sami ul-Haq and other members of his leadership team were impatient with questions about party processes,

[34] Sayyid A. S. Pirzada, interview by Joshua White, English, May 14, 2011; Mahbub ur-Rahman Qureshi, interview by Joshua White, Urdu, trans. Shuja Malik, May 24, 2011; Mufti Ibrar, interview by Joshua White, Urdu, trans. Shuja Malik, February 14, 2011.

[35] Aftab Sherpao, interview by Joshua White, English, February 17, 2011.

[36] Rahimullah Yusufzai, "True to Form, Maulana Fazlur Rehman Assured Ministry for Brother," *The News*, January 27, 2009.

[37] International Crisis Group, "Islamic Parties in Pakistan," 13.

and did not contradict suggestions that party authority was effectively concentrated in the hands of one person.[38] The party's influence comes through the long-standing leadership of the family that has led Dar ul-Ulum Haqqania, which retains extensive contacts with both Afghan and Pakistani Taliban groups, and publishes the monthly *al-Ḥaq*, which reportedly has a circulation of about 6,500 copies per month.[39]

The JUP parties, as noted in Chapter 2, have been highly fragmented and electorally unsuccessful. Both of the leading factions, JUP-Imam Noorani (JUP-IN) and JUP-Noorani (JUP-N) are thinly organized and highly personalistic. The TLP, which is explored in greater depth in Chapter 10, was founded in 2015. It has had looser institutional links to the Barelvi shrine and madrassah networks than the JUP parties, but to date little is known about its internal organizational dynamics. It is notable that, despite the party having been in existence only three years, it was able to field a huge number of candidates in the 2018 general election—in 182 National Assembly constituencies, and 387 Provincial Assembly constituencies—suggesting that it had built a reasonably robust bureaucratic apparatus.[40] After the death of Khadim Hussain Rizvi, the party's founder, in 2020, his son Saad Hussain Rizvi was appointed as the party's chief.

The Milli Muslim League is the most recent Islamist party, created in 2017 by Hafiz Saeed, the founder of Lashkar-e-Taiba.[41] It performed poorly in the 2018 elections under the name Allah-o-Akbar Tahrik. Little is known about its internal and organizational dynamics. Its founding leader was a close associate of Saeed, and its website in 2017 listed seven members of the party's Central Body.[42] All seven of those members were later designated by the U.S. Department of the Treasury as Specially Designated Global Terrorists "for acting for on behalf of LeT."[43] All previously served in LeT or one of its affiliates or front organizations. The MML presumably could draw on LeT's robust organizational infrastructure, funding sources, and links to the Pakistani security services in future electoral contests.

[38] Sami ul-Haq, interview by Joshua White, Urdu, trans. Shuja Malik, February 19, 2011.

[39] Author interview with JUI-S official, March 11, 2011.

[40] "List of All TLP Candidates for General Election 2018," *The News*, 2018.

[41] C. Christine Fair, "The Milli Muslim League: The Domestic Politics of Pakistan's Lashkar-e-Taiba," *Current Trends in Islamist Ideology*, June 3, 2018; C. Christine Fair, *In Their Own Words: Understanding Lashkar-e-Tayyaba* (London: Hurst & Co., 2018), 102–6.

[42] "Milli Muslim League," November 23, 2017, https://web.archive.org/web/20171123120423/http://millimuslimleague.org/.

[43] U.S. Department of the Treasury, "Treasury Targets Terrorist Group Lashkar-e Tayyiba's Political Party," April 2, 2018. https://web.archive.org/web/20240918185542/https://home.treasury.gov/news/press-releases/sm0335.

4.2.3 Nature of Party Funding

There have been no systematic studies of political party funding in Pakistan. Funding mechanisms for mainstream and ethnic parties are opaque, and these parties are presumed to rely heavily on politicians to self-finance their campaigns and on wealthy donors to subsidize party operations. The Election Commission of Pakistan has placed limits on candidate spending, but these are routinely ignored.[44] Pakistani laws also prohibit foreign funding of political parties, but these are loosely enforced.

Funding mechanisms of the Islamist parties are similarly opaque. The JI, as an urban and middle class party, is well positioned to fundraise from its own party base. Local party cells keep records on the self-reported incomes of their full members (arkan), and they expect that the members will donate their obligatory zakat consistently to the party or its charitable affiliates.[45] Most members do not give exclusively to the JI, and local party leaders are forced to make fundraising calls on prominent businessmen and wealthy philanthropists. In order to supplement donations from its members and supporters, the party has cultivated other sources of income. It receives a funding stream from sales of Maududi's works and other JI publications, and it may draw some funds from affiliate hospitals.[46]

On a grander scale, the party has pursued investment opportunities with the blessing of its central shura. For a party that has railed against the corrupting influences of cable television, it is remarkable that one of its major investments was Pakistan On Line, an internet service provider that was structured as a joint venture between the party and "like-minded" businessmen.[47] The business eventually went under. Following that, in the late 1980s, the party established Kisan (Farmer) Supply Services, which began as a welfare project working in flood-affected areas of Pakistan. Eventually it was converted into a business with the approval of the central shura, which raised capital (on an Islamic-compliant, noninterest basis) from JI members in the form of equity. That business, too, eventually folded after several years.

In 2002, led by then-amir Qazi Hussain Ahmad, the party invested heavily in a development it labeled the Qurtaba Housing Project near Rawalpindi. (Its board of directors is a who's who of JI leaders.) It bought a large tract of land, over 3.5 square kilometers, and planned housing developments,

[44] Afshan Subohi, "Gains and the Gainers," *Dawn*, July 25, 2018.
[45] Amir ul-Azim, interview.
[46] International Crisis Group, "Pakistan: The Mullahs and the Military," Asia Report 49 (Islamabad: International Crisis Group, March 20, 2003), 10; Mahmood, *Islamic Fundamentalism in Pakistan, Egypt and Iran*, 295.
[47] Amir ul-Azim, interview.

educational institutions, a "separate markets for ladies," and an enormous mosque on the site.[48] The project foundered when Pervez Musharraf refused to grant the necessary permissions for the development of the land, and it was not until after his tenure that the development resumed. General sales of plots began in 2010 (with discounts provided to JI members), and construction was continuing as of 2021.[49] The JI has not yet realized profits from the venture, but has begun using it as a site for party training.[50]

Although JI leaders have complained about their ability to fundraise from members, it appears that the party has extensive procedures in place to both gather and solicit donations, as well as a (not entirely successful) track record of using the party itself as a vehicle by which to make large-scale investments. The party also benefits from a strong culture of volunteerism. Even at the Mansurah headquarters, nearly all of the staff work on a volunteer basis, and the provincial and district offices are staffed entirely by volunteer labor.

In comparison with the JI, the JUI-F is at a disadvantage in fundraising from its own ranks. The party's constituent base is, on the whole, smaller, poorer, and more rural. In interviews, JUI-F leaders complained frequently about the lack of funds available for party operations. The party has received some monies from member donations, but in general considers it impermissible for members to give zakat funds for political purposes. Reportedly, it has been attempting to fundraise among the urban trader community in places such as Lahore, but as this is not its natural constituency or a region in which it has strong electoral prospects, the returns are presumed to be limited.[51] The party does have deep linkages with the madaris that it could attempt to exploit, but close observers of the party agree that in practice the JUI-F does not raise many funds from the madaris themselves.[52]

Another source is the triennial membership drive, in which each member gives twenty rupees to join the party. Spread over four years, this produces upwards of Rs. 10 million per year.[53] Much of this money stays local;

[48] See "Qurtaba City," Qurtaba City, February 25, 2011, https://web.archive.org/web/20110225135359/http://www.bestgtaagent.com/qurtabacity/; "Qurtaba City: City of Peace and Knowledge" (Madinaul Ilm, n.d.); "Qurtaba City," Pillar Group, February 24, 2020, https://web.archive.org/web/20200224052802/http://qurtabacity.ukpillar.com/.

[49] "1 Kanal Residential Plot Qurtaba City Chakri Interchange Rawalpindi—Qurtaba City Block A," Lamudi.pk, 2021, https://web.archive.org/web/20210819182656/https://www.lamudi.pk/property/qurtaba-city-block-a-1-kanal-residential-plot-qurtaba-city-chakri-interchange-rawalpindi-22205789.htm.

[50] "JI to Field Candidates from All Constituencies of Rawalpindi," *The News*, April 12, 2017.

[51] Muhammad Amir Rana, interview by Joshua White, English, February 14, 2011.

[52] Islamuddin Sajid, interview by Joshua White, English and Urdu, trans. Shuja Malik, February 18, 2011; Qibla Ayaz, interview by Joshua White, English, February 10, 2011; Sayyid A. S. Pirzada, interview.

[53] Jalaluddin Khan, interview, May 12, 2011; Abu al-Fateh Muhammad Yousuf, interview by Joshua White, Urdu, trans. Shuja Malik, March 1, 2011. The scale of these numbers are similar to those reported in 2019 press reports. Zahid Gishkori, "Fazl's Azadi March: Where Is the Money Coming From?," *The News*, November 17, 2019.

15 percent is passed upward from each level of the party to the next-highest tier, leaving most of the funds for grassroots operations.[54] Central party financial resources are so meager that members of the markazi majlis-e-umumi are not only required to pay their own way to attend the regular meetings, but are required to contribute about Rs. 200 to cover the shared cost of the gathering.[55]

The party supplements these meager funds by recruiting wealthy politicians into its fold, to whom it can provide a competitive election ticket in exchange for donations to the party; making special appeals to its larger list of "registered workers," which it claims is about 3.5 million in number; and fundraising from business elites.[56] These special appeals have coincided with the party's major rallies, such as the 2019 Azadi March on the federal capital that reportedly cost nearly Rs. 1 billion.

No JUI-F party leader would admit to receiving funds from abroad. Party members did, however, acknowledge the party's close relationship with the Libyan government under the late Muammar Qaddafi. The Libyan government offered scholarships for JUI-F clerics to study Arabic in Tripoli, and the party was frequently outspoken in its support for Qaddafi.[57] Several party members noted that Saif Qaddafi, the late son of Muammar Qaddafi, was present during the MMA government's tenure in the former NWFP for the groundbreaking of the JUI-F provincial headquarters outside of Peshawar. Others claimed, though it could not be independently confirmed, that Qaddafi helped to finance the facility. Further evidence that the party has received funds from Libya, and perhaps Saudi Arabia as well, came in a cryptic exchange in a closed-door session of parliament between Shuja Pasha, Director General of the Inter-Services Intelligence directorate, and Maulana Atta ur-Rahman, brother of the JUI-F amir. Responding to sharp criticism of the army from Atta ur-Rahman, Pasha reportedly said, "If we will discuss it, then things will go very far and everyone will come to know who has been receiving dollars from Saudi Arabia and Libya."[58] The issue arose again in public in 2021, when former senior party figure Hafiz Hussain Ahmad claimed that the party had received funds from Libya

[54] Gul Nasib Khan, interview.

[55] Mufti Ibrar, interview.

[56] Gishkori, "Fazl's Azadi March."

[57] For just one example of the party's praise of Qaddafi, see Abu Salmān Shāh, "ār jī es ṭī bil, maulānā sherānī kā taqarar aur je yū ā'e ke bāre meṅ z̲arāi' ablāg̲h̲ munfī kirdār [RGST Bill, Maulana Sherani's Appointment, and the Media's Negative Role Regarding the JUI]," *al-Jam'iyat* 12, no. 3 (December 2010): 12–13.

[58] Usman Manzoor, "Did Saudis, Libyans Pay Dollars to JUI-F? Pasha Hinted So," *The News*, May 14, 2011.

and Iraq, prompting the ruling PTI to file a petition for inquiry by the Election Commission of Pakistan.[59]

These reports, and interviews with party workers, paint a picture of a party with loose financial controls, meager indigenous resources, links to foreign funders, and constant pressures to recruit wealthy politicians to endow its ongoing operations. A 2005 article in *al-Jam'iyat* called for the establishment of a finance department for the party (suggesting that one did not already exist).[60] Five years later, in late 2010, another article set out a series of basic financial controls, explaining that the central party will conduct regular audits; that district and provincial party bodies must report income to central party authorities; and that oversight of the financial record-keeping will be delegated to the party's charity, Al-Khair Trust, which in turn is run by a committee of senior JUI-F leaders.[61]

Information on party funding for the smaller Islamist parties is also fragmentary. The JUI-S, unlike the JUI-F, has been proud of its funding from Gulf states (though its leaders have not explicitly differentiated between funding to the party and to the madrassah at Akora Khattak) and in fact published an entire prospectus in Arabic.[62] The Milli Muslim League is presumed to receive financial support from LeT and its affiliates, and the other Ahl-e-Hadith parties from Saudi Arabia and other Gulf states. The IJT (then TNFJ) established a special welfare fund in the late 1990s, and told party workers it was their duty to contribute to it if they had not already paid khums and zakat (types of obligatory taxes) to clerics in their respective areas. The party has claimed that it runs its operations from these funds, but it is believed to fundraise from Iranian sources as well.[63]

4.2.4 Party Discipline

The third and final aspect of party organization with which we will concern ourselves pertains to the central party leadership's mechanisms of control over members and subordinate units. Parties that have robust mechanisms

[59] Iftikhar A. Khan, "PTI Files Foreign Funding Case Against JUI-F," *Dawn*, January 27, 2021.

[60] Ḥāfiẓ Naṣīr Aḥmad Aḥrār, "kārkun kī tarbīat: kyūṅ aur kaise? [Worker's Training: Why and How?]," *al-Jam'iyat* 5, no. 8 (May 2005): 25–27.

[61] K͟hān, "mulkī pālīsiyāṅ 'avāmī umangoṅ ke muṭābiq tashkīl dī jā'eṅ [National Policy Should be Framed According to People's Wishes]."

[62] Maulānā Samī' al-Ḥaq, *jam'iyat 'ulamā'-e islām pākistān tārīk͟hhā o ahadāfhā [History and Objectives of Jamiat Ulama-e Islam]* (Peshawar: Jām'iyah Ḥaqqāniyah, n.d.).

[63] Andreas Rieck, *The Shias of Pakistan: An Assertive and Beleaguered Minority* (Oxford: Oxford University Press, 2015), 247–49.

of control have a greater ability to make decisions coherently without the fear of internal fragmentation or cadre defection, and are therefore in principle more resilient and less vulnerable to pressures from anti-state organizations or from state institutions. This section examines party members and subordinate units; the subsequent part of the chapter explores parties' control over affiliate organizations such as youth wings, student wings, labor wings, and madrassah organizations.

One of the notable features of Pakistan's political party system is, in the words of scholar Mariam Mufti, "rampant factionalism and indiscipline."[64] Most Pakistani parties are highly personalistic and oriented around dynastic politics. They exhibit varying degrees of messaging discipline and internal coherence, though most are characterized by frequent factionalization and infighting. The two most prominent exceptions to this general trend are the MQM and the Jamaat-e-Islami, both of which have had small electoral footprints and have drawn from similar middle-class urban social strata. As Paul Staniland observes, the MQM emerged in the 1980s "with a tight organizational structure rooted in student mobilization, which Altaf Hussain dominated and was not dependent on state patronage or resources."[65] The party developed a reputation for disciplined decision-making, and a willingness to use violence to enforce its writ among members and in territories it effectively controlled.[66]

In contrast, the Jamaat-e-Islami has developed a less personalistic style of leadership and instituted more legalistic mechanisms of accountability for its members in positions of leadership. The party's process for initiation into the ranks of arkan—a level that only about 0.6 percent of members achieve, and is necessary for most leadership roles—is rigorous, and does not stop when one becomes a rukn.[67] Prospective candidates need to fill out forms, undergo interviews, and demonstrate a knowledge of the Quran and the core ideological works of the party, especially those of Maududi.[68] Once they are members,

[64] Mariam Mufti, "Factionalism and Indiscipline in Pakistan's Party Political System," in *State and Nation-Building in Pakistan: Beyond Islam and Security*, ed. Roger D. Long et al. (Abingdon, UK and New York, NY: Routledge, 2016), 60.

[65] Paul Staniland, "Armed Groups and Militarized Elections," *International Studies Quarterly* 59, no. 4 (December 2015): 700, https://doi.org/10.1111/isqu.12195.

[66] See Laurent Gayer, *Karachi: Ordered Disorder and the Struggle for the City* (New York: Oxford University Press, 2014), 104–21.

[67] Jamā'at-e Islāmī Pākistān, "afrādī quvat jamā'at-e islāmī pākistān [Personnel Strength of Jamaat-e Islami Pakistan]."

[68] See Jamā'at-e Islāmī Pākistān, "niṣāb barā'e ummīdvār rukniyat [Curriculum for Membership Applicant]" (Jamaat-e Islami Pakistan, January 10, 2005); Jamā'at-e Islāmī Pākistān, "jamā'at-e islāmī pākistān umīdvāran-e rukniyat se ẓarūrī savālāt [Necessary Questions for Jamaat-e Islami Pakistan Membership Candidates]" (Jamaat-e Islami Pakistan, n.d.); Jamā'at-e Islāmī Pākistān, "goshvārah rukniyat jamā'at-e islāmī pākistān [Jamaat-e Islami Pakistan Membership Register]" (Jamaat-e Islami Pakistan, n.d.); Jamā'at-e Islāmī Pākistān, "'ahad-e rukniyat jamā'at-e islāmī pākistān [Jamaat-e Islami Pakistan Membership Oath]" (Jamaat-e Islami Pakistan, n.d.).

the local leadership will continue to provide oversight of their business activities, character, and reputation, so as to ensure that they are following party guidelines.[69]

The party is concerned not only with formal adherence to party principles, but also with its reputation: "People's perceptions matter," explained one member of the markazi shura. "If a rukn watches a movie in a cinema, whether or not the movie is bad, it is *perceived* as bad . . . . We have to take account of what is Islamic, but also of people's perceptions."[70] For leaders, the party has developed mechanisms of accountability; if a prominent member acts inappropriately or speaks against party policy, he can expect to be held accountable by a special committee of the central shura, which will decide on penalties or even expulsion. Such formal mechanisms, together with the high levels of participation and indoctrination required for rukn membership, have created a party with high levels of discipline, in which "no one can make a faction" or speak out against the leadership without reasonable fear of official retribution.[71] These mechanisms of control, it should be noted, do not necessarily translate into electoral success. In the case of the JI, they may have made the party less competitive by making it difficult to cultivate candidates who are wealthy or have already established a substantial constituency.

The JI has also demonstrated high levels of control over provincial party policies, and a willingness to devolve certain organizational decisions to local party offices. National party officials are active in traveling the country to meet with, and advise, provincial and local party units.[72] Local offices are granted the freedom to make local policy, but also must submit detailed action plans to higher-level units for approval in order to ensure that their policies are in alignment with the party at large.[73] For example, local JI officials reportedly do not need higher-headquarters permission to meet with leaders of another political party in their area, but typically do need permission to participate in joint rallies, press conferences, or other events.[74]

The party appears to have instituted particularly strict lines of control between the central and provincial leadership bodies. JI leaders at the provincial level are adamant that they must obey the central shura, and it appears that provincial amirs have little discretion to diverge from party policy

[69] Zulfiqar, interview.
[70] Asif Luqman Qazi, interview.
[71] Islamuddin Sajid, interview.
[72] Khalid Rehman, interview.
[73] Zulfiqar, interview; Syed Belal, interview by Joshua White, English, February 18, 2011; Jamā'at-e Islāmī Lāhaur, *sālānah manṣūbah-e 'amal 2011 [Annual Plan of Action 2011]*.
[74] Amir ul-Azim, interview.

within their jurisdictions.[75] Local and provincial JI officials play a role in selecting candidates for party tickets, but all candidates for Provincial or National Assembly seats must then be approved by special JI parliamentary boards. Mansurah keeps tight control over the provincial party offices, effectively placing candidate selection under the thumb of the central party shura.[76]

The JI system is thus one in which the central party apparatus exerts control over the provincial offices, and permits modest devolution of authority to the local level. Such an arrangement means that interprovincial party differences must be resolved at the level of the central shura. Most of the time this presents few challenges, but the geographically dispersed nature of the party membership is such that on occasion deep differences emerge between provincial party offices. Interprovincial tensions flared within the party before and after the 2008 elections, which the JI central shura boycotted against wishes of some prominent leaders from the erstwhile NWFP. Provincial party offices also clashed over issues such as the Kalabagh Dam, which was a heated matter of public debate in Pakistan. Responding to these tensions, after 2008, the party instituted a new system of standing committees within the markazi majlis-e-shura. There are multiple committees, the most powerful of which is the political committee, originally led by Liaquat Baloch.[77] The purpose of these committees, according to one prominent party leader, was to allow for more diverse provincial party input at the central shura level. Reading between the lines, the underlying objective was to provide fora for airing interprovincial debates *within* the central shura, so that those debates did not play out *between* the provincial shuras themselves. It was, in other words, an adaptation to facilitate the central shura's ongoing policy control of the provincial party offices.

The JUI-F has developed similar mechanisms of party accountability, but they do not function as well as those of the JI. The party leadership has shown the willingness to disassociate itself from highly contentious factions, as it did with the JUI-Nazryati (ideological) bloc in Balochistan beginning in 2007, or with four senior leaders in late 2020, but its accountability system is haphazard.[78] In theory, the party has rules about who is allowed to speak on its behalf,

[75] 'Abd uṣ-Ṣamad Ṣāfī, "sherpā'o ḥukūmat ne mālākanḍ ke 'avām se frāḍ kiyā hai: sābiq amīr jamā'at-e islāmī ṣūbah sarḥad aur mumtāz 'ālim-e dīn maulānā gohar raḥmān se khaṣūṣī bāt cīt [The Sherpao Government has Defrauded the People of Malakand. A Special Conversation with the Former NWFP Provincial Amir of Jamaat-e Islami, and Renowned Religious Scholar Gohar Rahman]," *Haft Rozah Aishyā (Asia)* 43, no. 24 (June 13, 1994): 9–10.

[76] Amir ul-Azim, interview.

[77] Farid Paracha, interview.

[78] Mufti Ibrar and Lutf ur-Rahman, interview; International Crisis Group, "Islamic Parties in Pakistan," 13; Zia Ur Rehman, "The F and N of JUI," *The News*, February 28, 2016; Kalbe Ali, "JUI-F Expels Disgruntled Sherani, Three Others," *Dawn*, December 26, 2020.

and the amir at every level of party governance is empowered to issue a show cause notice against members who do not hew to party policy.[79] In practice, as the TNSM case of Chapter 6 makes clear, the party's message discipline is often very poor—even bordering on chaotic. It is telling that the party monthly contains repeated admonitions to JUI-F workers not to speak against their leaders in public.[80] There is evidence that the party requires written assurances from candidates contesting on a JUI-F (or MMA) ticket that they will follow party policy, but in reality, the loose requirements for membership and dispersed party organization preclude strict accountability.[81]

Within the JUI-F system, considerable power is devolved to provincial party officials. Members of the central party leadership were both open and proud of this fact. They described how a decentralized structure resulted in fewer requirements for a national secretariat, and how it conveniently allowed the party to serve in a pro-government role in one province while adopting an anti-government role in Islamabad (as was the case during part of the Musharraf government).[82] The provincial party offices typically hold a final say on nominations for candidates for the Senate, and for a number of other electoral positions as well.[83] When the MMA returned a majority in the former NWFP in the 2002 general elections, the JUI-F central shura chose Akram Khan Durrani as the Chief Minister, but delegated the selection of JUI-F cabinet members to the provincial shura.[84]

On most matters, provincial party leaders are permitted to speak about policy without receiving formal permission from the markazi shura.[85] Typically, they are able to meet with leaders from other political parties, or take out rallies, after obtaining permission from the provincial shura.[86] The provincial shura's role also appears to be critical to the process of candidate selection. In advance of the 2005 local bodies elections, *al-Jam'iyat* ran an article explaining the process to party workers. It described the markazi shura as having provided the overall decision for the party to participate in the polls, but the provincial shuras as the bodies which would approve candidates for the election.[87]

[79] Gul Nasib Khan, interview.
[80] See Maulānā Gul Nasīb K͟hān, "jamā'atī zindagī kyūṅ ẓarūrī hai? [Why is a Party Lifestyle Necessary?]," *al-Jam'iyat* 7, no. 7 (April 2007): 12–13; Aḥrār, "kārkun kī tarbīat: kyūṅ aur kaise? [Worker's Training: Why and How?]."
[81] Muḥammad Iqbāl A'vān, "baladyātī intik͟hābāt kā ma'rkah kaise sar kyā jā'e? [How Should We Conquer the Local Bodies Election?]," *al-Jam'iyat* 5, no. 6 (March 2005): 7–8.
[82] Mufti Ibrar and Lutf ur-Rahman, interview; Qibla Ayaz, interview.
[83] Muhammad Riaz Durrani, interview by Joshua White and Shuja Malik, Urdu, February 25, 2011.
[84] Mufti Ibrar and Lutf ur-Rahman, interview.
[85] Gul Nasib Khan, interview.
[86] Muhammad Abu Bakar, interview by Joshua White, Urdu, trans. Shuja Malik, May 19, 2011.
[87] A'vān, "baladyātī intik͟hābāt kā ma'rkah kaise sar kyā jā'e? [How Should We Conquer the Local Bodies Election?]."

The JUI-F, in sum, appears to use the markazi shura as the central body for high-level policymaking and as an occasional arbiter for disputes that arise between provincial shuras. In this way, it devolves greater authorities to the provincial level than the JI. This arrangement provides the central party leadership with a lower level of directive control over subordinate units, but in return, allows for greater flexibility and ambiguity in policymaking. For a party that has historically experienced high levels of factionalism and open conflict about whether to participate in various alliances and coalitions, flexibility and ambiguity provide substantial benefits, and may even contribute to the party's ability to avoid debilitating fragmentation.[88] But it also makes the party particularly vulnerable to manipulation by the state.

4.3 Relationships with Constituents and Affiliates

4.3.1 Constituent Profiles

This section explores the Islamist parties' relationships with their constituents and affiliate organizations, and compares these patterns of interaction with those of other political parties in Pakistan, including so-called mainstream parties as well as regional and ethnic parties.

Like all parties, Pakistan's Islamist parties have, over time, built distinct constituent profiles that can be described with respect to geography, ethnicity, language, class, sectarian affiliation, and other characteristics. Although there is often a strong path dependency to these profiles, they are not static. Islamist parties compete with mainstream and ethnic parties for workers and voters.

The Jamaat-e-Islami began as a party dominated by Urdu-speaking migrants known as Muhajirs who settled in urban Sindh and Punjab in Pakistan's early years. As Vali Nasr has noted, this constituency dominated the party into the 1980s, and their "loyalty can be attributed in part to the extensive relief work the party undertook among the refugees in Karachi and Lahore after partition."[89] The party's vote banks in Sindh and Punjab did not last long, however. The rise of the MQM in the late 1980s, which competed for the same urban Muhajir vote banks in and around Karachi, severely eroded the JI's influence in Sindh.[90] In the 1970 general election, the JI received 10.3

[88] For more on the history of factionalism within the JUI, see Sayyid A. S. Pirzada, *The Politics of the Jamiat-i-Ulema-i-Islam Pakistan 1971–1977* (Karachi: Oxford University Press, 2000).

[89] Seyyed Vali Reza Nasr, *The Vanguard of the Islamic Revolution: The Jama'at-i Islami of Pakistan* (Berkeley: University of California Press, 1994), 88.

[90] Seyyed Vali Reza Nasr, "Islamic Opposition to the Islamic State: The Jamaat-i Islami, 1977–88," *International Journal of Middle East Studies* 25, no. 2 (May 1993): 275–76.

percent of the votes cast for Provincial Assembly seats in Sindh, and won two of the twenty-seven seats.[91] By the 1988 election, the party's base had eroded such that it could win no National or Provincial Assembly seats in the province.[92] It continued to perform very poorly in both Sindh and Punjab in subsequent elections.

During the 1970s, the party broadened its base of support to focus more heavily on Punjab and the erstwhile NWFP. The former amir Qazi Hussain Ahmad, a Pashtun from Nowshera district in present-day Khyber Pakhtunkhwa, was instrumental in expanding the party's reach into the Frontier during the 1980s, as part of a populist campaign.[93] At the same time that the party was reaching out to non-Muhajir ethnic groups, it was also broadening its base from urban areas to include peri-urban and rural regions.[94]

This strategy helped the party to build a small electoral stronghold in some of the most remote northern districts of present-day KP—specifically, the administrative area known as Malakand Division that was formed from the princely states of Chitral, Dir, and Swat. As shown in Figure 4.7, the JI for three decades secured almost all of its NWFP/KP provincial seats from this northern and highly rural area of the province. Indeed, though the party's electoral successes have been episodic and its overall electoral profile across the country has been shrinking, most of its seats in recent elections have come from Malakand Division.

This geographic and demographic shift—from a Muhajir base in Sindh and Punjab, to a more diverse constituency in which rural Pashtun areas provide most of the party's electoral victories—makes it difficult to generalize about the party's constituent profile. The party's headquarters and organizational apparatus are centered in Punjab, and according to the most recent data available, the majority of the party's members reside in Punjab (with the second-highest concentration in Khyber Pakhtunkhwa, followed by Sindh; see Figure 4.1). Scholarly literature on the party has long emphasized its lower-middle class profile, and its efforts to recruit educated workers into its ranks.[95] Humeira Iqtidar, who conducted detailed fieldwork on the party circa 2005, wrote that most members of the party today belong to "the aspiring

[91] Hasan-Askari Rizvi and Ijaz Shafi Gilani, "The First 10 General Elections of Pakistan: A Story of Pakistan's Transition from Democracy Above Rule of Law to Democracy Under Rule of Law: 1970–2013" (Islamabad: Pakistan Institute of Legislative Development and Transparency, August 2013), 49–50.

[92] Nasr, *Vanguard*, 208–9.

[93] Khalid Masud, interview by Joshua White and Niloufer Siddiqui, English, July 16, 2009.

[94] Nasr, *Vanguard*, 91–92.

[95] Ahmad, "Islamic Fundamentalism," 496–499; Sayeed, "The Jama'at-i-Islami Movement in Pakistan," 63.

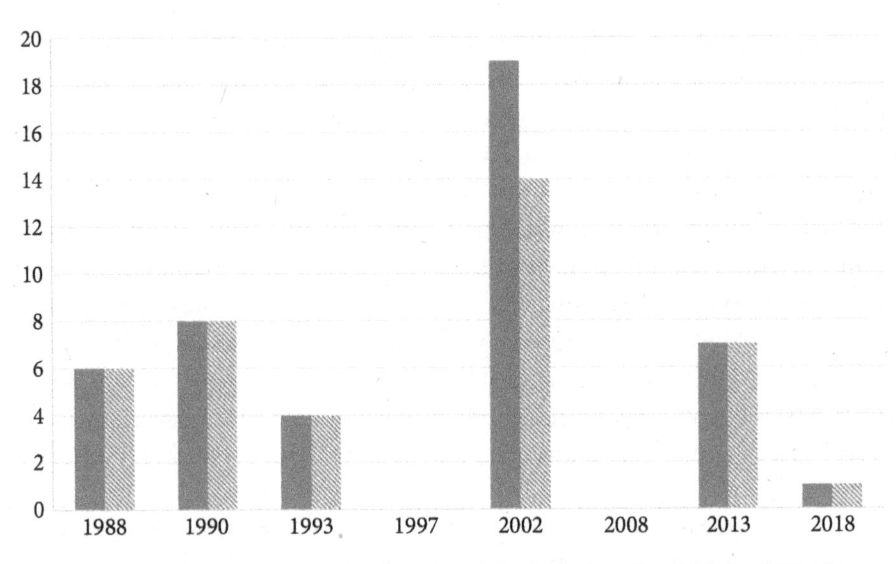

Figure 4.7 Jamaat-e-Islami Provincial Assembly Seats Won in NWFP/KP.

Note: JI boycotted the elections in 1997 and 2008. Present-day Malakand Division includes districts in Buner, Dir, Chitral, Malakand, Shangla, and Swat.

middle class," and that the current leadership "comprises predominantly first generation university and college graduates who have, over the last 30 years, moved up the social ladder . . . mostly through state sponsored schools, colleges and universities."[96] With its roots in what one scholar called "small-scale trade and industry," the JI's membership demographic appears to mirror that of other urban Islamist parties around the world, such as the Muslim Brotherhood in Egypt.[97]

This narrative largely tracks with the available data about the party's leadership, but does not fully account for the ways in which the party has become more Pashtun and rural since the 1980s, even as Pakistan as a whole has become more urbanized.[98] Party members spoke of increasingly pronounced regional differences between urban and rural members. One young JI functionary who worked at the party's headquarters in Mansurah explained, for

[96] Humeira Iqtidar, "Secularism Beyond the State: The 'State' and the 'Market' in Islamist Imagination," *Modern Asian Studies* 45, no. 3 (2011): 557, https://doi.org/10.1017/S0026749X11000217.

[97] Abdul Rashid Moten, "Mawdudi and the Transformation of Jamaat-e-Islam in Pakistan," *The Muslim World* 93, no. 3–4 (July 2003): 401, https://doi.org/10.1111/1478-1913.00029; Janine Clark, "Social Movement Theory and Patron-Clientelism," *Comparative Political Studies* 37, no. 8 (October 2004): 943.

[98] In interviews, some party figures were optimistic that, over the long run, a more urbanized, educated population would be more likely to embrace the JI's platform and candidates. Farid Paracha, interview; Amir ul-Azim, interview.

example, that party members in his home district of Charsadda in Khyber Pakhtunkhwa were mostly farmers, whereas those in Lahore were shopkeepers and small businessmen.[99] The JI party cadres in Malakand Division were frequently described by Karachi- and Punjab-based party workers as being "atypical" and poorly educated compared to the traditionally urban worker that the party cultivated in its first few decades. Some JI leaders also alluded to regionally based policy divisions within the party. Luqman Qazi, son of the former amir and a figure in the party's national politics, observed that the Pashtun members of the party in KP are "more conscious of shariah and the role of clergy," whereas the Punjabi party workers care more deeply about "political principles like supremacy of [the] constitution and democracy."[100]

Party workers also described the JI's efforts, beginning in earnest in the 1980s, to court ulama into the party's ranks.[101] The party established an Ulama Academy in 1976, which reportedly provides free three-to-six-month training courses to clerics in Quranic studies and the relationship between Islam and modern subject such as banking, science, and technology.[102] The party claims that a substantial portion of the ulama who complete the program decide to join the JI. The party's affiliated madrassah organization, the Jamiat Talaba Arabia (JTA), introduces clerics-in-training to the JI ideology and provides a mechanism for them to join the party after they graduate, but most observers of the party describe these efforts to recruit ulama to be small-scale.[103]

For the JUI-F, by contrast, the rural Pashtun madrassah worker represents the archetypal constituent. Limited data are available regarding the party's constituent profile. Survey data from 2009 suggests that, compared to other political parties, the JUI-F may have a relatively high percentage of poor voters.[104] The data also suggest that, compared to other political parties, a relatively high percentage of those who identify with the party have completed matriculation or more advanced levels of education, though it is unclear

[99] Sami ul-Haq, interview by Joshua White, Urdu, trans. Shuja Malik, May 21, 2011.

[100] Asif Luqman Qazi, interview.

[101] Farid Paracha, interview.

[102] Farid Paracha, interview.

[103] Muhammad Rashid, interview by Joshua White, English, March 6, 2011; Abdul Malik, interview by Joshua White, Urdu, trans. Shuja Malik, May 18, 2011. Technically, the JTA is independent from the JI, but it coordinates closely with the party, and encourages interlocking leadership between the respective shuras.

[104] Of those respondents who identified with the JUI-F, approximately 12 percent reported their monthly household income to be less than Rs 3,000 per month. This figure was considerably lower for those who identified with MQM (1%), PML-N (5%), PTI (5%), and ANP (6%). It was, however, comparable or lower than figures reported by respondents who identified with PML-Q (13%) and PPP (18%). These data might not accurately reflect views of the JUI-F, given that some respondents listed MMA—which effectively disbanded in 2008, and which included the JUI-F—as the party that best represents their views. Graeme Blair et al., "Poverty and Support for Militant Politics: Evidence from Pakistan," *American Journal of Political Science* 57, no. 1 (2012): 30–48. See crosstab, D12 and Q290.

whether respondents would have considered madrassah equivalents to the matriculation degree level.[105] District-level membership figures compiled by the author, together with qualitative data from interviews, point strongly toward a core constituent base that is ethnically Pashtun, lower and lower-middle class, concentrated heavily in Khyber Pakhtunkhwa and northern Balochistan, Deobandi Sunni by sect, and linked to—or highly sympathetic to—madrassah institutions.[106]

We will explore in greater detail the nature of the party's interaction with the madaris later in this chapter, but at this point it suffices to say that there is, in the words of one party leader, a resilient "natural bond" between the madaris and the party.[107] Important party positions are reserved for clerics, and leaders regularly cite the protection of madaris as a key party objective.[108] As shown in Figure 4.6, over three-quarters of the markazi majlis-e-shura members have earned religious titles. The class profile of the JUI-F appears to be solidly lower and lower-middle class, as judged from the candidates that the party puts forward (many of whom are themselves clerics), and the party's populist rhetoric.[109] Writing in *al-Jam'iyat* in 2006, the party's provincial information secretary blasted Pakistan's political parties for being "completely helpless before landlords, capitalists and nawabs [princes]"—excepting only the MMA parties from his critique.[110] An editorial the following year said that the party considered "landlords and industrialists [to be] the actual reason behind the political demise" of Pakistan, and harshly criticized the landlord class.[111]

Analysis of district-level membership figures, shown in Figures 4.8 and 4.9, suggest that the party's core geographic base is in the southern and northern districts of KP (that is, outside the densely populated central Peshawar valley) and the northern districts of Balochistan province, which are predominantly ethnically Pashtun. This is consistent with electoral data; at its high-water mark in the 2002 general elections, the party secured most of its seats from these regions.

[105] Approximately 48 percent of respondents who identified with JUI-F reported educational attainment at the level of matriculation or higher. This was higher than the other parties, with the exception of the ANP (56%) and the MQM (86%). Blair et al., "Poverty and Support for Militant Politics: Evidence from Pakistan." See crosstab, D11 and Q290.

[106] Some 100 percent of respondents who identified with JUI-F reported that they were Sunni. Blair et al., "Poverty and Support for Militant Politics: Evidence from Pakistan." See crosstab, D19 and Q290.

[107] Mahbub ur-Rahman Qureshi, interview.

[108] Mufti Ibrar and Lutf ur-Rahman, interview.

[109] For more on the JUI-F's "Islamic populism" under the MMA government, see Joshua T. White, *Pakistan's Islamist Frontier: Islamic Politics and U.S. Policy in Pakistan's North-West Frontier*, Religion & Security Monograph Series 1 (Arlington, VA: Center on Faith & International Affairs, 2008), 63–65.

[110] 'Abd al-Jalīl Jān, "siyāsī jamā'atoṅ ke andar jamhūriyat: ek taqābulī jā'izah [Democracy Inside Political Parties: A Comparative Analysis]," *al-Jam'iyat* 6, no. 10 (August 2006): 26–27.

[111] "jam'iyat 'ulamā'-e islām ko voṭ kyūṅ kiyā jā'e! [Why Vote for Jamiat Ulama-e Islam!]," *al-Jam'iyat* 9, no. 2 (December 2007): 8–10.

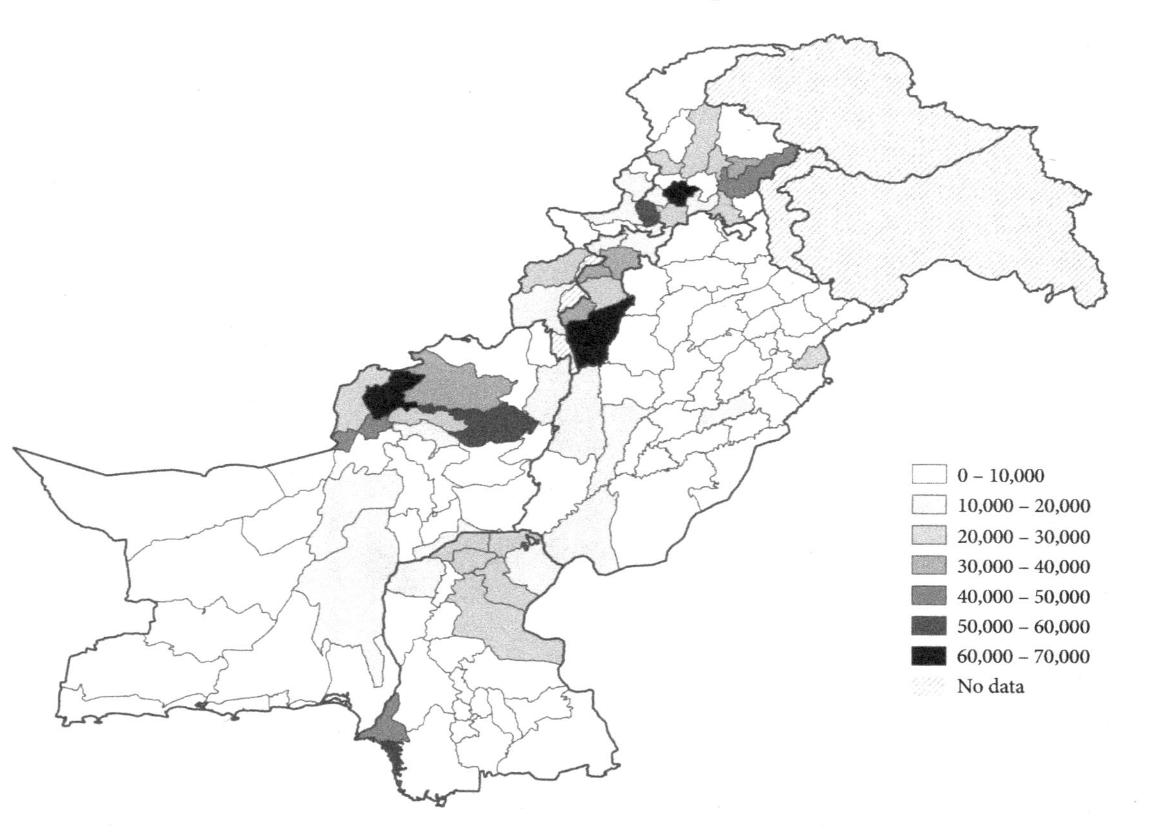

Figure 4.8 JUI-F Estimated Membership by District.

Source: Estimated minimum party membership based on author's analysis of 2011 district-level markazi majlis-e-umumi party elector data.

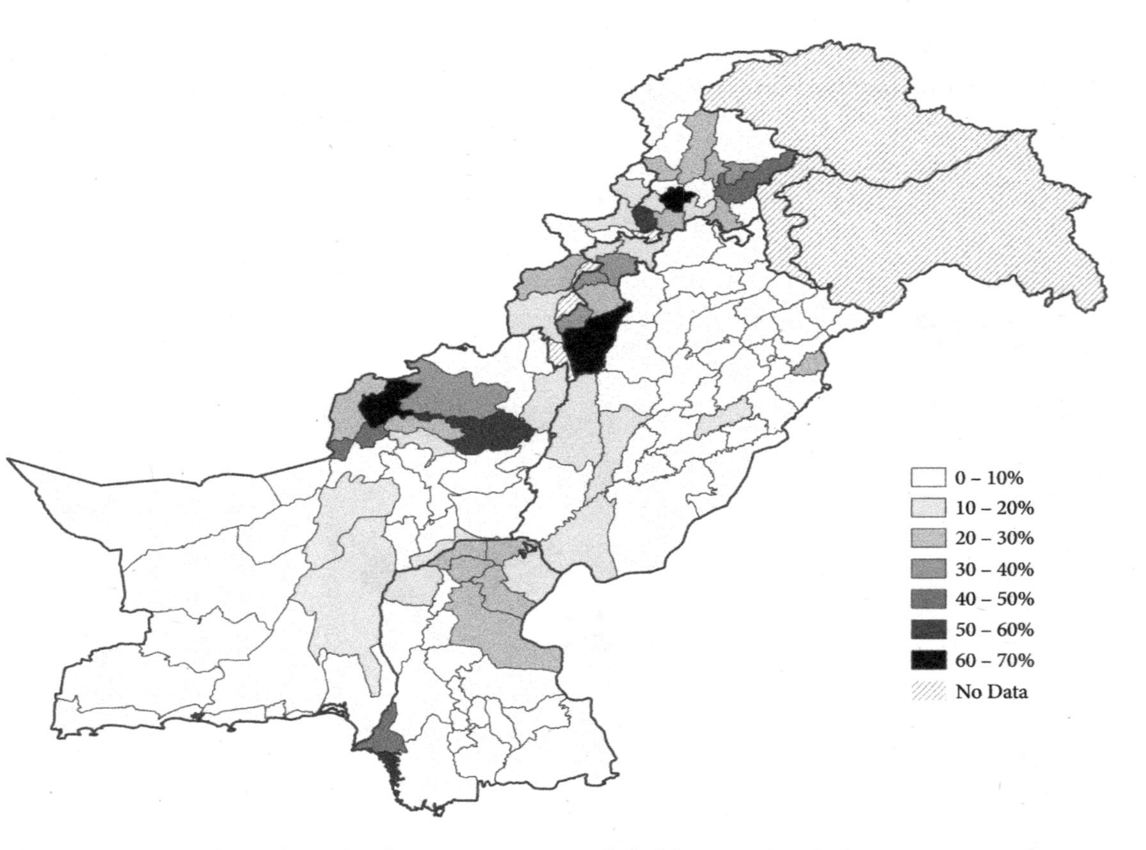

Figure 4.9 JUI-F Estimated Membership as a Percentage of Eligible Voters by District.

Source: Estimated minimum party membership based on author's analysis of 2011 district-level markazi majlis-e-umumi party elector data, standardized against registered voter figures from the Election Commission of Pakistan's Draft Electoral Rolls (2011).

Although the JUI-F is dominated by Pashtuns, it has since the 1970s kept its distance from Pashtun nationalist movements. When it was governing then-NWFP province under the MMA alliance, it pointedly denounced the Awami National Party's claims that "Urdu is not the national language," and made no efforts to promote the public use of the Pashto language.[112] Its position in Balochistan degraded somewhat after 2008 with the emergence of a rival JUI faction, the JUI-Nazryati (ideological) group, known as JUI-N, which was more supportive of the anti-state TTP and less amenable to making concessions to the government.[113]

In Punjab, the party has small pockets of support in Lahore and Gujranwala in the east, and portions of the Seraiki belt in the south.[114] By and large in Punjab, writes political scientist Mohammad Waseem, "the appeal of Deobandis has been limited to some lower middle class sections of the population," but there, too, they face competition from leftist parties such as the PPP.[115] In Sindh, the party presence is strongest in the Seraiki areas in the north, and in Karachi, but in both cases its overall electoral returns have been meager. Its two main levers of influence in Sindh are its linkages with the powerful Deobandi madaris in Karachi, and its proven ability to stage rallies that far outstrip its electoral or membership profile.[116]

There is comparatively less information available regarding the constituent demographics of the smaller Islamist parties, in part because these parties have had a minuscule electoral profile relative to the JI and JUI-F. In the 2002 general elections, which represented the historic electoral high-water mark for the Islamist parties, the JUP (Noorani) won a single Provincial Assembly seat from Gujranwala in Punjab, and one from Hyderabad in Sindh; and scored an upset against a leading MQM figure in a National Assembly race in Hyderabad.[117] The JUI-S, led by its then-amir Maulana Sami ul-Haq, won three National Assembly seats—two in NWFP (one of which went to Sami ul-Haq's son Hamid ul-Haq) and one in Karachi—and two seats in the NWFP Assembly. A Shia party led by Sajid Naqvi, Tahrik Millat-e-Islami

[112] "Bilour Claims Urdu Not National Language, NWFP Opp Protests," *Daily Times*, February 27, 2010.
[113] "Balochistan: Extremism In Making...," *Frontier Post*, August 8, 2008.
[114] Muhammad Abu Bakar, interview.
[115] Mohammad Waseem, "Origins and Growth Patterns of Islamic Organizations in Pakistan," in *Religious Radicalism and Security in South Asia*, ed. Satu P. Limaye, Mohan Malik, and Robert Wirsing (Honolulu, HI: Asia-Pacific Center for Security Studies, 2004), 25.
[116] See Saba Imtiaz, "'We Will Make Pakistan an Islamic Welfare State': JUI-F Chief Maulana Fazlur Rehman," *Express Tribune*, January 27, 2012; Ahsan I. Butt, "Street Power: Friday Prayers, Islamist Protests, and Islamization in Pakistan," *Politics & Religion* 9, no. 1 (March 2016): 1–28, http://dx.doi.org/10.1017/S1755048316000031.
[117] Rahimullah Yusufzai, "JUI, JI Leaders Dominate MMA," *Gulf News*, October 17, 2002.

Pakistan, won one Provincial Assembly seat in Punjab as part of the MMA alliance.[118] And the Jamiat Ahl-e-Hadith of Sajid Mir won a single Provincial Assembly seat, in Peshawar, but pulled out of the MMA alliance prior to the elections.[119]

With respect to two more recently formed Islamist parties, the MML and the TLP, we can look to 2018 electoral data for insights into the parties' target constituencies. As noted in Chapter 2, the MML's party registration was rejected by the Election Commission of Pakistan, after which the party chose to effectively contest the election under the Allah-o-Akbar Tahrik (AAT) party name. It won no seats. An analysis of National Assembly seat electoral returns reveals that there were only ten constituencies in which the AAT garnered 2 percent or more of the vote. Eight of those ten constituencies were in the Faisalabad or Gujranwala districts in Punjab; one was in Sargodha in Punjab, in which LeT founder Hafiz Saeed's son lost; and one was in Balochistan.

The TLP had a considerably better showing than the MML in the 2018 general elections. It won no National Assembly seats but secured the fifth-highest number of votes cast across the country. An analysis of its electoral returns shows that its voters were geographically dispersed. This can be seen in Figure 4.10.[120] The party fared relatively well in northern and central Punjab, particularly around Rawalpindi, Jhang, Sargodha, and Faisalabad. The party's other area of strength was in Karachi, where it won two Provincial Assembly seats, and exceeded a 10 percent share of votes in twenty separate Provincial Assembly constituencies.

Exit polls conducted by Gallup Pakistan suggest that the average TLP voter was slightly more likely than the average voter to be urban and male, and have somewhat lower self-reported income.[121] Nearly half of TLP voters (48%) had voted for the PML-N in the 2013 general election, with the next percentage (9%) having voted for the MQM.[122] Gallup Pakistan identified nineteen National Assembly constituencies, all but three in Punjab, in which a PML-N candidate would have won if they had received the votes cast for the TLP candidate. One cannot reliably estimate with high confidence how

[118] This party is the renamed incarnation of Tahrik-e-Jafariah Pakistan, which was previously banned by the government.

[119] Yusufzai, "JUI, JI Leaders Dominate MMA."

[120] The data in Figure 4.10 are drawn from Colin Cookman, "Provisional Election Results Data for Pakistan's 2018 General Elections," September 5, 2018, https://github.com/colincookman/pakistan_election_results_2018.

[121] Gilani Research Foundation, "Pakistan's 11th General Election 2018: Who Voted for Whom and Why" (Islamabad: Gallup Pakistan, March 2019), 107. Urban/rural (+11% urban), gender (+13% male), self-reported income (−16% of average).

[122] Gilani Research Foundation, "Pakistan's 11th General Election 2018: Who Voted for Whom and Why," 108.

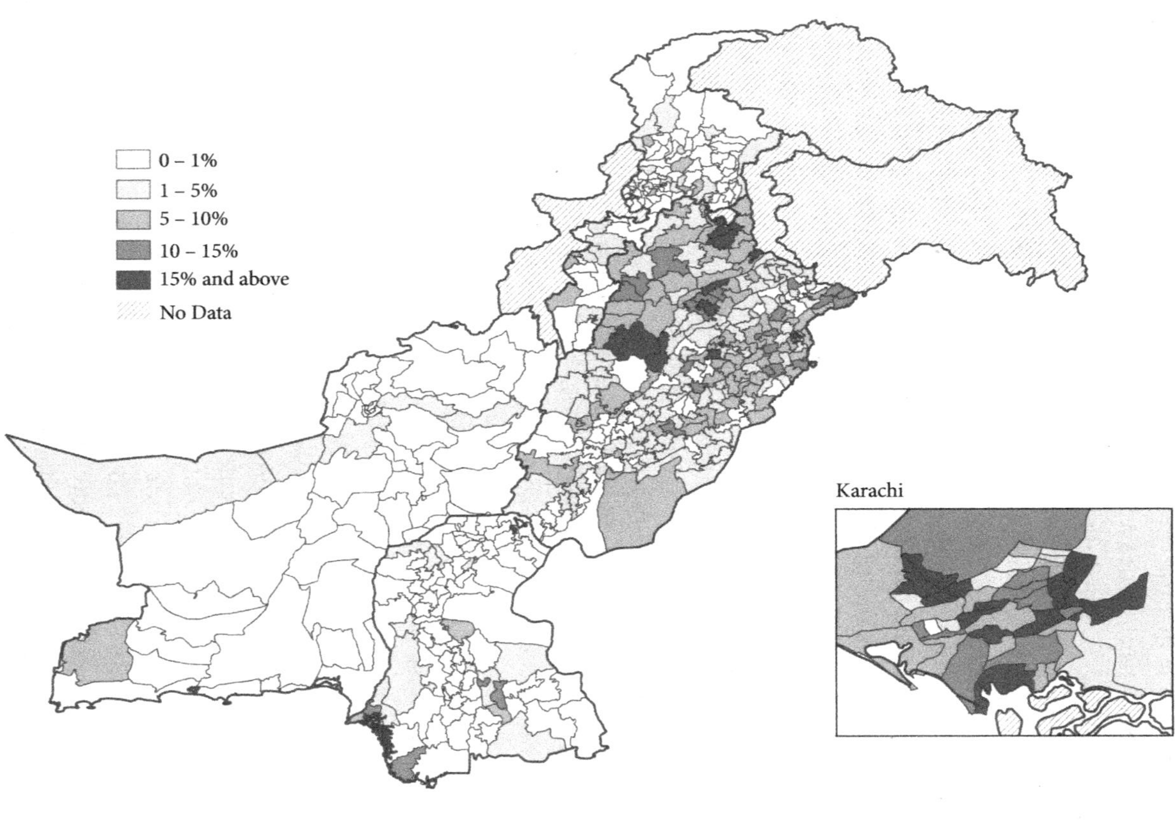

Figure 4.10 TLP Share of Votes by Provincial Constituency, 2018.
Source: Provisional 2018 election data compiled by Colin Cookman.

votes cast for TLP candidates would have been distributed to other parties if the TLP had not contested, but it is fair to conclude that the TLP likely cost PML-N a number of Provincial and National Assembly seats in Punjab.

Two tentative conclusions can be drawn from the constituency data presented here. One is that the three most prominent Islamist parties—the JI, JUI-F, and TLP—have, to use Angelo Panebianco's phrase, distinct electoral "hunting domains" in which they compete.[123] That is, there are few locales where the parties consistently compete head-to-head for the same voters. JI and JUI-F compete to some extent in the Peshawar valley and occasionally in parts of KP's Malakand Division; and JI and TLP competed in 2018 in certain areas of Karachi.[124] More frequently, however, the Islamist parties are competing with mainstream parties such as the PPP, PML-N, and PTI; and with ethnic parties such as the ANP (in KP), and the MQM and its factions (in Karachi).

The disjoint nature of these parties' potential electoral domains helps to explain why, for example, the JI and JUI-F have been able to form electoral pre-election alliances such as the MMA. It also suggests that the Islamist parties' sometimes divergent postures toward anti-state movements is not likely to be explained by electoral competition among the Islamist parties themselves. Certainly, these parties might endorse or reject anti-state movements as a means of differentiating themselves from mainstream or ethnic parties, but typically not because they are competing against other Islamist parties for votes.

Second, we can observe that the JI draws three-quarters of its members from the two most populous provinces, whereas the JUI-F draws three-quarters of its members from the two least populous provinces.[125] (The TLP does not appear to have a robust formal membership process but, like the JI, its electoral ambitions are clearly focused on Punjab and Sindh.) One might suspect that the JUI-F, dependent on votes from KP and Balochistan, would be more sympathetic with arguments in favor of provincial autonomy; critical of the central government's outsized role in Pakistan's federal system; and more intransigent in its posture toward the central government. In one respect, this appears to be true: The JUI-F leadership has, more than that of other Islamist parties, repeatedly made arguments in favor of providing more funds to KP and Balochistan. But the party's disproportionate political investment in Pakistan's marginalized provinces also means that it must rely

[123] Panebianco, *Political Parties*, 13.

[124] Author's review of Cookman, "Provisional Election Results Data for Pakistan's 2018 General Elections."

[125] Author's calculations derived from Jamā'at-e Islāmī Pākistān, "afrādī quvat jamā'at-e islāmī pākistān [Personnel Strength of Jamaat-e Islami Pakistan]"; Maulānā Maḥbūb ur-Raḥmān Qureshī, ed., *ḍā'irekṭrī jami'yat 'ulamā'-e islām pākistān 2011 tā 2013* (Rawalpindi: Ṣadā'e Qur'ān Publīkeshanz, 2011).

on the fiscal generosity of the central government to fund the provinces—monies which then indirectly support the party's elected officials. As argued later in this chapter, this exacerbates the JUI-F's structural vulnerabilities to the state.

4.3.2 Linkage Patterns

If political parties are to be electorally successful, they must establish some kind of relationship with their constituents. The nature of these party-constituent relationships has been the subject of a small branch of political science theory known as "linkage politics."[126] Linkage politics is germane to the study of Islamist parties in Pakistan because it highlights the ways in which constituent pressures "from below" shape political decision-making "from above" by party leaders. Party linkages represent the patterns by which a party connects its organizational structures with its constituent profile and ambitions and, conversely, by which political activists shape and constrain the behavior of political institutions.[127]

There are four dominant forms of political party linkages.[128] The first are linkages based on "programs," defined as "joint preference ranking[s] supported by multiple politicians" that can be articulated by parties, and then used by voters to "infer a party's position on a range of issues from basic programmatic cues and then choose between the alternatives in an intelligent fashion."[129] In the public domain, programmatic parties sell themselves on the basis of a policy agenda, and make promises to potential voters that they will be *indirectly* compensated through the vehicle of future policy decisions.[130] In their internal workings, programmatic parties tend to be reasonably well institutionalized, given that they often benefit from developing intraparty mechanisms devoted to consensus-building, policy formation, and the maintenance of ideological discipline.

[126] See, for example, Kay Lawson, ed., *Political Parties and Linkage: A Comparative Perspective* (New Haven, CT: Yale University Press, 1980); Andrea Römmele, David M. Farrell, and Piero Ignazi, eds., *Political Parties and Political Systems: The Concept of Linkage Revisited* (Westport, CT: Praeger Publishing, 2005).

[127] See, for example, A. J. McGann, "The Advantages of Ideological Cohesion: A Model of Constituency Representation and Electoral Competition in Multi-Party Democracies," *Journal of Theoretical Politics* 14, no. 1 (January 2002): 37–70.

[128] These draw from the work of Herbert Kitschelt, but add a category for ethnic- or kinship-based linkages.

[129] Herbert Kitschelt, "Linkages Between Citizens and Politicians in Democratic Polities," *Comparative Political Studies* 33, no. 6 (2000): 848.

[130] See Herbert Kitschelt et al., *Post-Communist Party Systems: Competition, Representation, and Inter-Party Cooperation* (Cambridge, UK: Cambridge University Press, 1999), 48.

The second type of linkages are oriented around identity. These draw on voters' sense of ethnic identity, kinship networks, or what in Pakistan are often called *birādarīs* (brotherhood or clan). Some parties are defined explicitly in ethnic terms, or recruit voters only among particular groups. Other parties that have a broader geographic or ethnic base will allot tickets to members of particular ethnic groups or subgroups so that those candidates will, in turn, "garner the support of local leaders in their constituencies that are from the same or related biraderis."[131]

A third type of linkages are clientelist in nature. Clientelism refers to a political exchange between a patron and a client based on *direct* forms of compensation. One simple definition has clientelism as "the proffering of material goods in return for electoral support, where the criterion of distribution that the patron uses is simply: Did you (will you) support me?"[132] This definition is fairly standard and has the advantage of clarity, but can be expanded even further to include the proffering of protection by the patron, instead of simply material goods; and the reciprocity of general support by the client, instead of specifically electoral support.[133]

Clientelism, which is sometimes used synonymously with "patronage" (though the latter typically refers more specifically to the provision of public jobs), represents a complex form of political exchange. As Kitschelt and Wilkinson have argued, the crux of clientelism is not that goods are promised to a particular political subgroup, nor that goods are actually delivered. Clientelism, rather, rests on what they call "contingent direct exchange," that is, the ability of the patron to not only target the delivery of goods, but to do so contingent on some kind of reciprocity by the client.[134] This, in turn, demands a measure of predictability about voters' behavior and their willingness to engage in a clientelist transaction; as well as some mechanism for monitoring and enforcement of the implicit "deal," which inevitably is easier on the group level than on an individual basis.[135]

[131] Shandana Khan Mohmand, "Losing the Connection: Party-Voter Linkages in Pakistan," *Commonwealth & Comparative Politics* 52, no. 1 (January 2, 2014): 16–17, https://doi.org/10.1080/14662043.2013.867687.

[132] Susan C. Stokes, "Political Clientelism," in *Oxford Handbook of Comparative Politics*, ed. Carles Boix and Susan C. Stokes (Oxford: Oxford University Press, 2007), 605.

[133] James Scott, "Patron-Client Politics and Political Change in Southeast Asia," *American Political Science Review* 66 (1972): 1142–58.

[134] Herbert Kitschelt and Steven Wilkinson, "Citizen-Politician Linkages: An Introduction," in *Patrons, Clients, and Policies: Patterns of Democratic Accountability and Political Competition*, ed. Herbert Kitschelt and Steven Wilkinson (Cambridge, UK: Cambridge University Press, 2007), 10ff.

[135] For examples of this kind of transactional clientelist exchange in Pakistan, see Azam Chaudhry and Kate Vyborny, "Patronage in Rural Punjab: Evidence from a New Household Survey Dataset," *The Lahore Journal of Economics* 18, no. Special Edition (September 1, 2013): 183–209, https://doi.org/10.35536/lje.2013.v18.isp.a8; Hassan Javid, "Democracy and Patronage in Pakistan," in *New Perspectives on Pakistan's Political Economy*, ed. Matthew McCartney and S. Akbar Zaidi (Cambridge: Cambridge University Press, 2020), 221, https://doi.org/10.1017/9781108761154.012.

The fourth type of linkage pattern is based on a charismatic relationship between a party leader and his or her constituents.[136] This type of leadership, what Atul Kohli calls "rule by theatrics," is often improvisational and lightly institutionalized.[137] Max Weber famously observed that charismatic authority is difficult to sustain in the absence of bureaucratic institutionalization.[138] This is a longstanding challenge for charismatic party leaders. Parties based on charismatic linkages typically downplay the importance of consistent and structured policies, as well as broad-based clientelist programs, so that they can "maintain maximum personal discretion over the strategy of their party vehicle."[139] Scholars have spent relatively little time examining charismatic parties; indeed, most parties that at first blush seem to have strong charismatic influence are, upon deeper examination, actually primarily programmatic or clientelistic in nature.

These four linkage patterns can exist alongside one another in a particular party, but each privileges a particular type of appeal and creates particular incentives for parties that make use of that pattern. Scholars have posited that programmatic parties—or those that layer policy discourse onto their clientelist or kinship appeals—have more ways of differentiating themselves from the competition than parties that are exclusively clientelist or kinship-oriented. Clientelist parties, for example, appeal to "valence competition," in which they differentiate themselves by delivering the most value or quantity of a universally desired good, such as political access or material favors.[140] Programmatic parties, on the other hand, have a wider array of appeal strategies to which they can resort. They can choose to engage in valence competition ("we can deliver the most of what you want, and do so reliably"), but also positional competition ("we have superior policies that deliver superior outcomes").

As a practical matter, researchers cannot inquire directly of party workers about their linkage preferences, because clientelist and charismatic linkages are widely viewed with opprobrium, even in environments such as Pakistan in which they are widespread. As Herbert Kitschelt observed from his field research in Russia, engaging in programmatic competition is itself a valence issue among politicians: Everyone wants to be seen as being policy-oriented,

[136] Kitschelt, "Linkages Between Citizens and Politicians," 849.

[137] Atul Kohli, *Democracy and Discontent* (Cambridge: Cambridge University Press, 1990), 191.

[138] Max Weber, *Economy and Society: An Outline of Interpretive Sociology* (Berkeley: University of California Press, 1978).

[139] Kitschelt, "Linkages Between Citizens and Politicians," 849.

[140] As Kitschelt notes, "In clientelistic politics, parties compete for votes by advertising themselves as suppliers of the most copious, reliable, and expediently delivered targeted benefits." Herbert Kitschelt, "Party Systems," in *Oxford Handbook of Comparative Politics*, ed. Carles Boix and Susan C. Stokes (Oxford: Oxford University Press, 2007), 528. See also Donald E. Stokes, "Spatial Models of Party Competition," *American Political Science Review* 57, no. 2 (June 1963): 368–77.

even when they are not.[141] How then can one hope to measure such linkages? Common markers of programmatic linkages include evidence of "intraparty programmatic cohesion" widely shared by both leaders and members; signs that opposing politicians hold a coherent view of the party's positions that are consistent with the party's stated policies; and indicators that the party is serious about enforcing policy discipline among its members who freelance as independent entrepreneurs.[142]

By contrast, clientelist linkage markers include evidence that the party provides or directs material support or political protection to its members in the form of private or so-called semiprivate "club goods"; that it targets the delivery of goods or protection, and does so contingent on some kind of reciprocity by its voting base; or that it suffers from a lack of cohesive policies or absence of discipline in roll-call votes.[143] Beyond these metrics, we will attempt to examine cases in which political parties face competing pressures between providing indirect constituent benefits, such as an ideological line consistent with their stated beliefs, and direct benefits, such as patronage, political access, or political protection. It is in these circumstances that we may be able to discern whether a party privileges one set of linkage patterns over another.

Pakistani political parties exhibit a variety of linkage patterns. Many mainstream parties, including the PPP and PML parties along with their various antecedents and splinter groups, have historically relied on various forms of clientelist relationships. These include the so-called "feudal" mode of politics in which large landholders, particularly in Punjab and Sindh, use their control over land and livelihoods to influence, or direct, voters' electoral choices.[144] (S. Akbar Zaidi has persuasively argued that this does not constitute a feudal economic system in the classic sense, but reflects remnants of feudal economic and social relations.[145]) Another variation is candidature clientelism, in which "clientelistic parties raise 'private' resources from asset-rich, but vote-poor clients in exchange for favors and in order to dole them out to asset-poor, but vote-rich other client groups."[146] In this case, the

[141] Kitschelt, "Linkages Between Citizens and Politicians," 869.

[142] Kitschelt, "Linkages Between Citizens and Politicians," 869; Richard S. Katz, *A Theory of Parties and Electoral Systems* (Baltimore, MD: John Hopkins University Press, 1980), 6.

[143] Club goods exist in a middle ground between public and private goods; they "provide benefits for subsets of citizens and impose costs on other subsets." Kitschelt and Wilkinson, "Citizen-Politician Linkages," 11; Kitschelt, "Linkages Between Citizens and Politicians," 870.

[144] Umair Javed, "Profit, Protest and Power: Bazaar Politics in Urban Pakistan," in *Routledge Handbook of Contemporary Pakistan*, ed. Aparna Pande (New York: Routledge, 2018), 148–59.

[145] S. Akbar Zaidi, "Is Pakistan Feudal? A Historical Account of the Development of Agriculture in Pakistan," in *Issues in Pakistan's Economy*, 2nd ed. (Karachi: Oxford University Press, 2005), 12–27.

[146] Kitschelt and Wilkinson, "Citizen-Politician Linkages," 24.

patron remains the party itself, but the client is no longer the voter, but (typically) a wealthy supporter intent on procuring from the party an electoral ticket.[147]

There is also ample evidence of ethnic and kinship-based appeals. Some parties, such as the ANP and its antecedents, have made explicit appeals based on ethnic identity.[148] Others, such as the MQM, were founded to exploit ethnic solidarity but later attempted to expand beyond ethnic categories. And although they tend to deny it, a wide variety of Pakistani parties have built their electoral strategies at the provincial and local levels around targeting biraderis.[149] For parties such as the PML-N in Punjab, or the PPP in Sindh, these kinship-based linkage strategies are often a matter of open discussion, and party candidates are sometimes explicitly identified by biraderi. (The highly fragmented geography of biraderis in places such as Punjab make it difficult, however, to assess how much power kinship-based explanations have in predicting party strategies.[150]) For other parties, kinship appeals are more subtle. Pashtun-dominated parties such as the ANP and JUI-F account for tribe and *khel* (clan) politics when awarding party tickets, but are reluctant to discuss this dimension of their decision-making.[151]

Some Pakistani parties' linkage patterns are particularly difficult to characterize. The ANP makes explicit ethnic appeals to Pashtun voters, but—operating largely in a province that is dominated by ethnic Pashtuns—also has campaigned with a detailed programmatic agenda. The party's 2018 manifesto ran to twenty-seven pages and, in addition to outlining policy platforms on federalism, health, security, and other major topics, made specific pledges on the party's commitment to student-teacher ratios in primary schools, and the precise routing of Chinese-funded rail networks.[152] The MQM's success in Sindh has similarly depended on ethnic appeals, but the party has also articulated detailed policy platforms (programmatic linkages); encouraged a cult of personality around its founder, Altaf Hussain (charismatic linkages); and used the promise of both service delivery and physical protection as tools

[147] Candidature clientelism works particularly well in a country like Pakistan, in which party tickets are often decided upon and distributed by a small clique of party elites rather than a wider nominating process.
[148] Javid, "Democracy and Patronage in Pakistan," 232.
[149] See, for example, Ian Talbot, *Pakistan: A Modern History* (New York: St. Martin's Press, 1998); Andrew R. Wilder, *The Pakistani Voter: Electoral Politics and Voting Behaviour in the Punjab* (Karachi: Oxford University Press, 1999); Mohammad Waseem, *Democratization in Pakistan: A Study of the 2002 Elections* (Oxford: Oxford University Press, 2006).
[150] Mohmand, "Losing the Connection," 18.
[151] Author's conversations with ANP and JUI-F party officials, 2006–2010.
[152] Awami National Party, "Election Manifesto 2018," 2018.

to secure votes (clientelist appeals).[153] The PTI, too, defies easy characterization. Despite preparing a detailed manifesto in 2018 (which included, inter alia, a policy position favoring the development of tilapia aquaculture) the party, following its electoral victory, proved to be highly personalistic in its governance style, poorly institutionalized, and haphazard in its attention to policy matters.[154]

What of the Islamist parties' linkage patterns? Some are comparatively easier to discern. The JI fits, almost paradigmatically, the definition of a party that employs programmatic linkages, providing nonmaterial and ideological benefits to its constituents. People largely vote for the JI because they believe in its ideology and its program, and the party's outreach focuses heavily on policy themes. As noted earlier, the party leadership spends extensive time on matters of public policy rather than patronage. It funds and staffs a leading think tank in Islamabad, the Institute for Policy Studies, which produces multiple publications in English and Urdu; is active in public policy debates; and has a robust program of member indoctrination in order to promote ideological consistency and uniform policy opinions. The party's interest in policy issues is highlighted by its famously aggressive interventions in the parliament. During a three-year period, from March 2008 to March 2011, the JI had three sitting senators in Pakistan's upper house of parliament. The Islamabad-based think-tank PILDAT conducted an analysis of the use of "Calling Attention Notices," which according to the Senate rules are restricted to matters of "urgent public importance" and cannot be issued more than once in a single sitting.[155] According to PILDAT:

> Among the members who presented the highest number of Calling Attention Notices, Senator Prof. Khurshid Ahmed (KP, JIP [Jamaat-e-Islami Pakistan]) tops the list with 153 Calling Attention Notices followed by Senator Prof. Muhammad Ibrahim Khan (KP, JIP) with 71 Calling Attention Notices and Senator Afia Zia (KP, JIP) who presented 64 Notices.[156]

In other words, the three most active users of the Calling Attention Notice in the Senate were the JI's three senators, who commonly used the intervention

[153] See Farhat Haq, "Rise of the MQM in Pakistan: Politics of Ethnic Mobilization," *Asian Survey* 35, no. 11 (November 1995): 990–1004; Mohammad Waseem, "The MQM of Pakistan: Between Political Party and Ethnic Movement," in *Political Parties in South Asia*, ed. Subrata Kumar Mitra, Mike Enskat, and Clemens Spieß, Political Parties in Context (Westport, CT: Praeger, 2004); Muttahida Qaumi Movement, "Empowered Pakistan: Election Manifesto 2018," 2018.

[154] Pakistan Tahrik-e-Insaf, "The Road to Naya Pakistan: PTI Manifesto 2018," 2018.

[155] Senate of Pakistan, "Rules of Procedure and Conduct of Business in the Senate" (Islamabad: Senate of Pakistan, 2012), chap. IX.

[156] Pakistan Institute of Legislative Development and Transparency, "Score Card: Performance of the Senate of Pakistan: Three Years March 12, 2008–March 11, 2011" (Islamabad: PILDAT, December 2011), 8.

to press the government to pursue actions in line with the party's Islamist agenda. This is clearly the behavior of a party that prioritizes policy matters.

The JI displays high levels of "intraparty programmatic cohesion"; one can observe a coherent view of party policies that is widely held by party leaders and members alike. The party's policy worldview is shaped by the standardized curriculum for membership, the wide distribution of party publications, and the systems of accountability that keep members in line. Numerous interviews with members of other political parties, including Islamist parties, strongly suggest that opposing politicians *also* hold consistent views of the JI's policy positions, and ones that are congruent with the party's self-perceptions.[157]

Traditional forms of clientelism appear to play a secondary role in the party's linkages with its constituents. Does the party provide material support or political protection to members in the form of public or club goods? The answer is yes, insofar as all political parties in Pakistan must provide constituent services in order to survive. Numerous JI elected officials described in interviews the ways in which their constituents regularly came to them for petty favors.[158] Particularly in urban Punjab, the JI once had a reputation for providing protection and political access to the small shopkeepers who formed its constituent base. In Khyber Pakhtunkhwa, the party runs a vast network of private schools which, while not particularly vulnerable to state interference, can only be helped by the presence of sympathetic JI elected officials.[159]

These instances of minor clientelism notwithstanding, the JI is not structured to provide an exchange of goods-for-votes or protection-for-votes as befits a truly clientelist party. There is also little evidence of candidature clientelism—the selection of party candidates on the basis of their ability to fund not only their own campaign, but contribute to party coffers. JI candidates, however much disliked by opposing politicians, often have a reputation for fiscal probity. Moreover, while the party is deferential to its senior leadership, it places less emphasis on charismatic leadership and the cult of personality than do most other parties in Pakistan.

The most compelling argument for the JI as a programmatic party is not that it is weakly clientelistic, but that it is strongly ideological. It is by its own account "an ideological party which believes in complete, all-embracing and comprehensive Islamic way of life and wishes to implement it in every

[157] Author's interviews, 2006–2012.
[158] Asif Luqman Qazi, interview.
[159] Husnul Amin, interview by Joshua White, English, February 21, 2011.

sphere of life."[160] Explained one observer of the party, "For JI, the revolution is the prime objective.... It conceives of a complete change. This is the offer" that the party provides to voters.[161] From its earliest days, the party has focused more on maintaining its distinctive ideological core than on the work of broadening its electoral political base. In 1941, Maududi reportedly told the party's shura that "we desire no demonstrations or agitations, no flag waving, slogans, or the like.... [For us] such display of uncontrolled emotions will prove deadly."[162] Such political austerity did not, of course, survive contact with Pakistan's competitive political arena. Today the party campaigns vigorously and can organize high-profile and disruptive demonstrations. But the basic good on offer has not changed. The party still sees itself as a vanguard of a social and political revolution, and promotes itself to the electorate on those terms.

The JUI-F, too, appears at first blush to be a programmatic party. It is, from its name to its constitution to its party platform, ideological in nature. It supports an Islamist agenda, including but not limited to the expansion of shariah's place in the legal system, a higher profile political role for religious scholars and experts, and closer ties with other Muslim countries. Indeed, though its election manifestos are considerably more vague than those of the JI, ANP, and other electoral competitors, they advance positions that would likely poll well with Pashtun voters in KP and Balochistan: greater provincial autonomy, federal subventions to poorer provinces, investments in the tribal areas, and policies to reduce the cost of remittances that affect Pashtun families with relatives working in the Gulf states.[163] Others would look at the cult of personality that surrounds the amir, and his high degree of control over decision-making, and conclude that the JUI-F fits the classic definition of a party organized around charismatic linkages.

Each of these arguments have merit. But they fail to capture the essential characteristic of the party's relationship with its constituent base. That relationship is anchored not in the promise of ideological benefits as such, nor in a charismatic linkage inseparable from the personal authority of the leader, nor in a classic clientelism of provision in which the party delivers targeted baskets of material goods in exchange for votes. (The party is chronically

[160] Jamaat-e-Islami Pakistan, "Manifesto Jamaat-e-Islami Pakistan" (Mansoorah Lahore: Department of Public Relations, Jamaat-e-Islami Pakistan, 2013), 7.

[161] Muhammad Amir Rana, interview.

[162] Seyyed Vali Reza Nasr, *Mawdudi and the Making of Islamic Revivalism* (Oxford: Oxford University Press, 1996), 71.

[163] Jamiat Ulama-e-Islam, Pakistan, "Manifesto for Election 2013," 2013. I reviewed the 2013 manifesto because it represented a recent instance in which the party contested the elections independently rather than as part of the MMA.

short of funds, and lacks the basic organizational infrastructure necessary to both collect and deliver funds under a targeted system of distributive patronage.) Rather, the party linkage is defined by what one might call a "clientelism of protection," in which, in exchange for votes and the promise of voter mobilization, the party provides targeted benefits to the Deobandi madaris.

This impetus is partly organizational. As an ulama-dominant party, the JUI-F has structural incentives to protect its affiliated institutions. With 70 percent to 80 percent of the JUI-F leadership holding earned religious degrees, the majority of party elites have a personal stake in protecting madaris. The party frequently gives party election tickets to prominent madrassah directors, who in turn consider protection of the madaris to be a core political objective.

This is evident from the ways in which the party employs a discourse that focuses on threats to religious institutions. When addressing public audiences, leaders of the JUI-F often expand the purview of their discussion to include threats faced by "madrassahs and mosques." Data show that less than 1 percent of children across Pakistan are enrolled in a madrassah, and that even along the Afghan border the number does not exceed 7.5 percent.[164] Thus we should not expect—and the JUI-F certainly does not expect—that protection of the madaris constitutes a highly salient political issue for the wider electorate, even in KP and the former tribal areas. Nonetheless, by highlighting an ostensible threat to religious institutions writ large, to include mosques, the party can get more political mileage from its core message.[165]

The party's focus on mosques and madrassahs is not merely one-sided. In emphasizing the madaris the JUI-F effectuates an exchange of value that lies at the heart of clientelist politics: it gets something in return. As explored later in this chapter, the Deobandi madaris are the locus of the party's efforts at political mobilization and fundraising.[166]

One madrassah student who requested anonymity described how madaris friendly to the JUI-F would send home their students prior to an election with instructions about how to promote the party. Often, madrassah students returning to their home villages would be honored with delivering the Friday sermon at the mosque, and they would use that platform to expound on the religious virtues of voting for the JUI-F. Tactics such as these recall

[164] Tahir Andrabi et al., "Religious School Enrollment in Pakistan: A Look at the Data," John F. Kennedy School of Government Faculty Research Papers Series, March 2005.

[165] Adnan Aurangzeb, interview by Joshua White, English, May 13, 2011.

[166] For some background on the relationship between the madaris and the ulama parties, see Vali R. Nasr, "The Rise of Sunni Militancy in Pakistan: The Changing Role of Islamism and the Ulama in Society and Politics," *Modern Asian Studies* 34, no. 1 (February 2000): 153–54.

the operations of another party that took advantage of a clientelism of protection: Italy's Christian Democratic (DC) party in the postwar decades of the 1940s and 1950s. Like the JUI-F, the DC party was not large enough to be a mass movement, but found its niche in a clientelism closely linked to religious authority—in its case, the Catholic Church. Writes one scholar, in language that closely mirrors the behavior of Pakistan's Deobandi institutions: "The Church and its lay organizations threw their weight behind the DC, exploiting the social authority of the priesthood to deliver votes, and filling the gaps in the DC's territorial party infrastructure."[167] The madaris adeptly play this role for the JUI-F, "exploiting the social authority" of the clergy to deliver a religious imprimatur to the party, and providing a vast organizational infrastructure that would otherwise be too expensive and unwieldy to maintain.

The linkage patterns of Pakistan's newer Islamist parties are not as clearly defined as those of the JI and JUI-F. The Milli Muslim League does not appear to have developed a coherent formula to organize its linkages with potential constituents. Its programmatic agenda, as outlined in its minimalist 2018 manifesto, is vague and nonsectarian. (The only unusual policy element is its specific denunciation of takfiri ideology, presumably referring to ideologues opposing the Pakistani state.[168]) It does not rely on charismatic leadership, given that none of its party leaders have a meaningful public profile outside of the Lashar-e-Taiba and Jamaat ud-Dawa organizations.[169] And there is no evidence to suggest that the party pursued clientelist linkages with potential groups of voters, or focused on contingent exchange of services. For these reasons, the MML has been seen principally as an instrumental vehicle of the Pakistani military and intelligence services to further legitimize LeT and JuD in domestic politics, and to provide a platform to discredit anti-state ideologues.

The TLP exhibited both charismatic and programmatic linkage patterns in the run-up to the 2018 general election. The party relied heavily on the personal appeal and public profile of its leader, Khadim Hussain Rizvi, who led the party's major rallies and dominated its online outreach. A charismatic leader, Rizvi bolstered and sustained Barelvi activism and used his influence to draw on Barelvi madrassah networks to support his party's aims. The TLP was also narrowly programmatic, in that it campaigned on what was virtually

[167] Jonathan Hopkin, "Paying for Party Response: Parties of the Centre-Right in Post-War Italy," in *How Political Parties Respond: Interest Aggregation Revisited*, ed. Kay Lawson and Thomas Poguntke, Routledge Research in Comparative Politics 9 (London: Routledge, 2004), 183.

[168] Milli Muslim League, "Manifesto," 2018, https://web.archive.org/web/20180729030337/http://www.millimuslimleague.org/english/manifesto/.

[169] See "Milli Muslim League."

a one-point agenda to safeguard the honor of the prophet Muhammad by ensuring that no leniency was given to those accused of blasphemy. Indeed, the TLP's manifesto highlights the protection of the "place of the prophet" and the "honor of the prophet" as among the party's leading objectives, and does so in a more explicit and prominent manner than any other major party manifesto, including the Barelvi JUP.[170]

4.3.3 Affiliate Organizations

One final but important dimension of Islamist parties' relationships with their constituents relates to affiliate organizations. Parties use affiliate organizations to reinforce key constituent linkage patterns (e.g., promote a party's ideology, sustain devotion to a charismatic leader, or engage in clientelistic exchanges), exercise control over party members, and engage in deniable forms of violence. Here we will examine principally the affiliates of two of the oldest and institutionalized Islamist parties, the JI and the JUI-F. In the next section we will consider parties' interactions with unaffiliated militant organizations and competitor groups.

The JI has a wide array of affiliate organizations. The most prominent of these are the party's youth wing, Shabab-e-Milli; the male collegiate organization, Islami Jamiat-e-Talaba (IJT); the female collegiate organization, Islami Jamiat-e-Talibat; the madrassah student organization, Jamiat Talaba Arabia (JTA); and various professional affiliates for doctors, teachers, farmers, and other groups. It also has a robust and active women's wing, Halqah-e-Khavatin, that reports to the JI amir but "operates as a separate, sovereign entity within the Jamaat's larger organizational structure."[171] With the exception of the women's wing and the Shabab-e-Milli, these affiliates are not under the formal or direct control of the party. (The Shabab-e-Milli is managed by the party, and its headquarters is co-located on the Mansurah campus.)

All of the party's affiliates support in principle the party's mission, but in practice occasionally deviate from stated party policies. The Shabab-e-Milli,

[170] See Tahrik-e-Labbaik Pakistan, "manshūr [Manifesto]," 2021, https://web.archive.org/web/20210227092541/https://tlyp.org.pk/ur/manifesto.php. The English version is even more explicit on these points: Tahrik-e-Labbaik Pakistan, "Manifesto," 2021, https://web.archive.org/web/20210227103049/https://tlyp.org.pk/manifesto.php. Compare to Jamiat Ulama-e-Pakistan Noorani, "manshūr (jam'iyat 'ulamā'-e pākistān nūrānī) [Manifesto (Jamiat Ulama-e-Pakistan Noorani]," n.d., https://web.archive.org/web/20201017204125/https://www.jamiat.net/category-%D9%85%D9%86%D8%B4%D9%88%D8%B1/. Author reviewed publicly available manifestos, including those for JI, JUI-F, MMA, and mainstream and ethnic parties.

[171] Niloufer Siddiqui, "Gender Ideology and the Jamaat-e-Islami," *Current Trends in Islamist Ideology* 10 (August 2010): 180.

for example, vandalized billboards in Peshawar during the MMA's tenure, an activity that embarrassed the provincial government and elicited warnings from the central government about vigilantism.[172]

The male collegiate organization, the IJT, also has a long history of behaving in ways that contradict stated JI policies. The organization is arguably Pakistan's most powerful campus organization, and it has at times completely dominated public-sector institutions such as Punjab University.[173] The IJT's membership structure mirrors that of the JI, with multiple levels of membership and a reading list that is heavy on Maududi.[174] About a quarter of IJT members reportedly go on to participate in the JI after they graduate, and the organization functions as an effective feeder into JI party leadership.[175] As of 2011, the IJT had a secretariat in Lahore staffed by about twenty volunteers and comprising eighteen separate departments. Since 1964, it has published a journal, *Hamqadam*, which has a monthly print run of about 10,000 copies.[176]

For all its influence and myriad links to the Jamaat-e-Islami, the IJT has not always acted at the direction of its patron. It has a well-deserved reputation for engaging in low-level violence, vigilantism, and thuggery on campuses around Pakistan, and IJT militias were directly implicated in supporting Pakistan Army efforts to put down Bengali protests in East Pakistan in 1971.[177] At some of the country's largest public universities, the IJT has long been feared—even by senior administrators. This reputation dates to the 1960s, but crystalized in the late 1970s and 1980s, when campus politics in Pakistan became more contentious and more violent, and student leaders began to face assassinations from rival groups.[178]

The IJT is by no means the only youth or collegiate party affiliate in Pakistan that engages in violence. The All Pakistan Muttahida Students Organization (affiliated with the MQM), the Pashtun Students Federation (affiliated with the ANP), the Jamiat Ahle Hadith Youth Force (affiliated with the JAH), and

[172] Mohammad Shehzad, "MMA-Islamabad Preparing to Slug It Out?," *Friday Times*, June 6, 2003; Anita M. Weiss, "A Provincial Islamist Victory in Pakistan: The Social Reform Agenda of the Muttahida Majlis-i-Amal," in *Asian Islam in the 21st Century*, ed. John L. Esposito, John O. Voll, and Osman Bakar (Oxford: Oxford University Press, 2008), 155.

[173] See Seyyed Vali Reza Nasr, "Students, Islam, and Politics: Islami Jami'at-i Tulaba in Pakistan," *Middle East Journal* 46, no. 1 (Winter 1992): 59–76; Matthew J. Nelson, "Embracing the Ummah: Student Politics Beyond State Power in Pakistan," *Modern Asian Studies* 45, no. 3 (2011): 565–96, https://doi.org/10.1017/S0026749X11000242; International Crisis Group, "Islamic Parties in Pakistan," 28ff; Aryn Baker, "The Battle for Punjab U.," *Time*, October 8, 2006.

[174] For details on IJT structure, see Wajid Mehmood, "Consensual and Conflictual Political Culture in Pakistan: A Comparative Analysis of Jamaat-i-Islami and Jamiat Ulema-i-Islam Socialization Process" (PhD, Peshawar, University of Peshawar, 2017), 172–76.

[175] Yasir Riaz, interview by Joshua White, English, May 12, 2011.

[176] Qaisar Sharif, interview by Joshua White, Urdu, trans. Shuja Malik, May 19, 2011.

[177] Nasr, *Vanguard*, 171–82.

[178] Nasr, "Students, Islam, and Politics: Islami Jami'at-i Tulaba in Pakistan," 68ff.

other similar organizations have engaged in violence against political and sectarian opponents in ways that their respective parties can disavow.[179] But none of these party affiliates have been as influential or arguably as overtly coercive as the IJT.

Although the JI officially disavows violence, some observers of the party privately speculate that it tolerates and even encourages the behavior of the IJT as a way of pressuring rival parties and building strong membership networks among college-educated youth. This raises the prospect that the party finds it useful to leverage the vigilantism of the IJT and other affiliates in ways that are publicly deniable. (One party leader admitted as much, saying that the vigilante campaign of the Shabab-e-Milli in then-NWFP was "symbolic [to show that the JUI-F] chief minister was supposed to pay attention" to the slow pace of Islamization that was frustrating the JI.[180])

The organizational separation between the JI and IJT has at times made it difficult for the former to control the latter, particularly in the face of substantive policy disagreements. In the early years of Zia ul-Haq's government, for example, the two groups were on opposite sides of the political divide: Zia had enticed the JI into his government with promises of cabinet positions, but he had made an enemy of the IJT through his policies that crippled student campus politics.[181] Again under Pervez Musharraf, the two groups diverged, with the IJT fiercely opposed to the government's establishment of the Aga Khan University Examination Board, and the JI taking a more moderate tack.[182]

The party's relationships with the IJT and the professional affiliates are marked by considerable frustrations. The IJT is independent and influential in its own right, and acts accordingly. "Sometimes we try to pull them into JI activities," complained one party leader, "but they're always busy! They always come and ask for things, like boys come to their parents."[183] The party has just as much trouble trying to mobilize the professional affiliates to participate in rallies and party activities. Some of them have become a "burden," and the party leadership has considered absorbing them into the formal party apparatus.

[179] See, for example, Khaled Ahmed, "The Power of the Ahle Hadith," *The Friday Times*, July 18, 2002, https://web.archive.org/web/20221219165153/http://www.indianet.nl/indpak87.html; Nelson, "Embracing the Ummah: Student Politics Beyond State Power in Pakistan"; Nadeem F. Paracha, "Smokers' Corner: Politics on Campus," *Dawn*, February 4, 2018; Fair, *In Their Own Words*, 70.

[180] Asif Luqman Qazi, interview.

[181] Yasir Riaz, interview; Qaisar Sharif, interview; Nasr, "Islamic Opposition to the Islamic State: The Jamaat-i Islami, 1977–88," 269ff; Christophe Jaffrelot, "From Jinnah's Secularism to Zia's Islamisation Policy," in *The Pakistan Paradox: Instability and Resilience* (New York: Oxford University Press, 2015), 476.

[182] See Khaled Ahmed, "Madrassa Versus Enlightenment," *Daily Times*, May 10, 2009.

[183] Amir ul-Azim, interview.

Despite these tensions, what the Shabab-e-Milli and IJT provide the JI are channels for the party to mobilize workers and voters, and disrupt public life in ways that draw attention to the party's demands. By cultivating affiliates that are adept in the use of deniable violence, the JI reduces its vulnerabilities to competitors and generates some leverage against attempts by the state to constrain its influence and activities.

For the JUI-F, links with the madaris are paramount. The party's leadership draws from madrassah-educated graduates; its policy priorities include the protection and independence of the Deobandi madaris; and its political muscle depends upon its ability to mobilize clerics and madrassah students.[184] Estimates of the number of Deobandi madrassahs and the number of students enrolled in those institutions varies wildly. As C. Christine Fair has noted, "there is no central database of registered madaris," and registration records are likely not kept up-to-date.[185] Neither are reliable enrollment data available. A detailed study funded by the World Bank in 2005 found that madrassahs accounted for less than 1 percent of overall enrollment; and the available data suggest that many students attend religious studies part-time.[186] But although the thousands of Deobandi madaris in Pakistan educate only a small fraction of the country's student population, they loom large as important hubs for social, political, and militant mobilization.

Institutionally, the party has two key madrassah-related affiliates—one formal, the other informal. The most important formal affiliate is the JUI-F's madrassah student organization, the Jamiat Talaba Islam (JTI), which operates as a subordinate branch of the party. The JTI is ostensibly not directly involved in electoral politics, but it wields considerable influence in JUI-affiliated madaris, and provides the party with ligaments of control into the madrassah system.[187] The JTI organizes events, distributes flyers throughout madaris, and serves as a conduit for announcements from the JUI-F to

[184] The party acknowledges that it retains an armed group called *Ansar ul-Islam* (supporters of Islam) that provides security to its senior officials and at rallies, but there is no indication that this group operates independently from the party mandate, or proactively against the party's adversaries. See Jamiat Ulama-e-Islam, "Daf'ah Numbar 26 (Tanẓīm Anṣār al-Islām) [Section Number 26: Organization of Ansar al-Islam]," accessed March 30, 2022, https://bit.ly/3JpJTqU; "Mufti Mehmood Conference Today," *Nation*, October 23, 2011; Saba Imtiaz, "When Thousands Show Up to a Rally, It's Change Fazlur Rehman Wants You to Believe In," *Express Tribune*, January 28, 2012; "JUI-F Moves IHC Against Ban on Ansarul Islam Wing," *Dawn*, October 27, 2019.

[185] C. Christine Fair, "The Madrassah Challenge: Militancy and Religious Education in Pakistan" (Washington, DC: U.S. Institute of Peace, March 2008), 50.

[186] Andrabi et al., "Religious School Enrollment in Pakistan: A Look at the Data"; Fair, "The Madrassah Challenge: Militancy and Religious Education in Pakistan"; C. Christine Fair, "The Enduring Madrasa Myth," *Current History* 111, no. 744 (April 2012): 135–40, https://doi.org/10.1525/curh.2012.111.744.135.

[187] See, for example, Mehmood, "Consensual and Conflictual Political Culture in Pakistan: A Comparative Analysis of Jamaat-i-Islami and Jamiat Ulema-i-Islam Socialization Process," 193ff.

interested students. One JTI leader suggested that the group's role was to provide "educational politics" to madrassah students that conditions them for political activism.[188] According to some JTI leaders, the vast majority of JTI members remain active supporters of the JUI-F, whereas about half contribute actively to the party's cause after they complete their madrassah studies. Interviews and a review of JUI-F and JTI party documents did not reveal any obvious conflicts between the party and its affiliate on matters of policy.[189]

The party also has informal but much more consequential links with the nationwide Deobandi madrassah association, the Wafaq ul-Madaris al-Arabia, headquartered in Multan. As noted in Chapter 3, this organization is one of five such associations representing, respectively, the five major interpretive traditions. All of these associations are part of a wider federation, the Ittihad-e-Tanzimat Madaris Pakistan (ITMP), and they perform administrative and oversight functions for madrassah curriculum, examinations, and the issuance of degrees. Although the senior leaders of the Wafaq ul-Madaris al-Arabia generally take care not to engage overtly in electoral politics, the JUI-F—and, to a much lesser extent, the JUI-S—has deep and mutually beneficial ties with the association.

The JUI-F has a mutually beneficial relationship with the Deobandi madaris and the Wafaq-ul Madaris al-Arabia. There are several dimensions to this exchange. In the first place, the party provides political protection to the madaris. JUI-F leaders regularly stage rallies, write articles, organize conferences, and raise parliamentary questions in defense of the madrassah system. Party publications and public speeches are replete with references to the threats faced by the madaris, and the JUI-F's critical role in protecting them.[190] In an interview with a Karachi-based Urdu newspaper, for example, party leader Hafiz Hussain Ahmad bragged that the party had resisted the government's "conspiracy" to change madrassah curriculum and syllabi, and to identify seminaries with terrorism.[191] In cases in which madrassah students face harassment by local officials, the party has been known to step in and

[188] Fatahullah Sajjad, interview.

[189] Syed Hidayatullah Shah, interview by Joshua White and Niloufer Siddiqui, Urdu, trans. Shuja Malik, March 2, 2011.

[190] See, for example, K͟hān, "jamā'atī zindagī kyūṅ ẓarūrī hai? [Why is a Party Lifestyle Necessary?]"; Maulānā Gul Nasīb K͟hān, "svāt āpareshun aur madāris o masājid ko lāḥaq k͟haṭrāt [The Swat Operation and the Dangers Befalling the Madaris and Masjids]," *al-Jam'iyat* 10, no. 12–13 (October 2009): 11–14; Ḥāfiẓ 'Azīz ur-Raḥmān 'Azīzī, "dīnī madāris par manḍalāte k͟haṭrāt [The Dangers Hovering Upon Dini Madaris]," *al-Jam'iyat* 10, no. 12–13 (October 2009): 15–16; Maulānā 'Abd al-G͟hafūr Ḥaidrī, "'ulamā' o madāris g͟hair maḥfūẓ kyūṅ? [Why are the Ulama and the Madaris Unsafe?]," *al-Jam'iyat* 10, no. 12–13 (October 2009): 6, 56.

[191] Muhammad Abdullah Sajid, "'President and Interior Minister May Also Be Involved in Killing of Usama Bin Ladin': Interview with Maulana Hafiz Hussain Ahmad," *Islam*, June 6, 2011.

raise the matter with higher-level officials to whom they have access.[192] On a more systemic level, the party has consistently resisted pressures by the government to reform the madaris in the 1960s, 1970s, 1980s, and again under Pervez Musharraf's government. Acting as "the custodian of the madrassahs' interests in the democratic framework," the party gives the religious institutions a valuable veto gate in the political process, through which they can slow the advance of undesirable state policies.[193]

At times the party has been able to provide other benefits to the madaris, including certain kinds of state funds that do not give the government undue leverage over religious institutions. Deobandi madrassah leaders in Pakistan have historically been reticent to accept long-term government funding to their institutions, lest they become beholden to the state. The propensity of the JUI-F to consider government support to be corrupting can be seen in the reaction of the ITMD to terminate the affiliation of 125 seminaries in then-NWFP that agreed in February 2007 to receive government funds under the Madrassah Reforms Project. Expressing the consensus opinion of the party, ITMD central leader Maulana Hanif Jalandhri argued at the time that "financial aid would provide the government an excuse to interfere in the affairs of the seminaries."[194] In interviews conducted by the author, party leaders frequently echoed this concern.

The party's resistance to long-term government funding of madaris has not, however, extended to other less contingent forms of funding. Students enrolled in Pakistani madaris are eligible for specially designated education stipends that are drawn from government-collected zakat funds and disbursed by provincial and local zakat departments in cooperation with madrassah administrators.[195] Even as the JUI-F has warned the government not to take over the madaris, and warned the madaris not to be lured into taking state funds, its leaders have supported these kind of zakat subventions to madrassa students.[196] In an interview in 2004, JUI-F leader Fazl ur-Rahman claimed to have encouraged the government to provide other kinds of *in-kind benefits* to the madaris, such as electricity, gas, and water subsidies.[197]

[192] See, for example, the report of JUI-F intervention in Punjab in Abūbakar Shaikh, "dīnī madāris ke ṭulabā kā maqām aur zimah dāriyāṅ [The Place and Responsibilities of Dini Madaris Students]," *al-Jam'iyat* 11, no. 7 (April 2010): 25.

[193] Muhammad Amir Rana, interview.

[194] Zulfiqar Ali, "25 Seminaries Agree to Receive Govt Aid," *Dawn*, February 23, 2007.

[195] See, for example, Zakat & Ushr Department, Government of Punjab, "Education Stipends (Deeni Madris)," accessed November 10, 2021, https://web.archive.org/web/20240725123319/https://zakat.punjab.gov.pk/education-stipends-deeni-madris.

[196] Nasr, "The Rise of Sunni Militancy in Pakistan," 154.

[197] Maulānā Faẓl ur-Raḥmān, "dīnī madāris kā sṛukcar tabdīl nahīṅ kareṅge [We Will Not Change the Structure of the Religious Madaris]," *al-Jam'iyat* 4, no. 5 (February 2004): 4–6.

Under the MMA government in then-NWFP, the party adopted this approach. It pushed for modest increases to the official Auqaf funds earmarked for mosques and seminaries. Principally, however, it chose to direct state funds to the madaris through development channels and in-kind grants rather than outright transfers.[198] To provide but one of dozens of similar examples from the confidential NWFP Chief Minister Directives database that I obtained, JUI-F party leader and Chief Minister Akram Khan Durrani issued a nonpublic order to the provincial Local Government and Rural Development department on April 22, 2003, to provide in perpetuity for the "Exemption from water Bill [sic] all the Deni Madrassas and Mosque" in district Karak.[199]

Analysis of the database shows that from December 2002 to July 2007, the Chief Minister directed Rs 61 million to individual madaris through confidential directives not publicly reported. This figure does not include funds channeled to the madaris through other mechanisms, including funds allocated to party MPAs and MNAs. (On occasion, the MPA funds are routed to the madaris in curious ways: A leading JUI-F parliamentarian in Balochistan confessed to "extorting money from MPAs and confirmed that he had collected a total of Rs 90 million from them . . . for building a seminary in his constituency in Qila Saifullah."[200])

A third source of support that the JUI-F has been able to provide to the Deobandi madaris has been its advocacy for the creation of government jobs for madrassah graduates, who otherwise face limited employment prospects. The JUI-F has consistently maintained that a madrassah certificate should, in the eyes of the state, be considered equivalent to a bachelors degree. As documented in Chapter 7, the JUI-F also undertook efforts to enact a law in then-NWFP that would establish dozens of new positions designated for ulama. In quieter ways, too, the party has worked to put more clerics on the public payroll, defend the interest of the petty ulama class, and promote the idea that religious authority is properly found in those leaders who have completed formal madrassah training and not in parties such as the JI that eschew the traditional institutions and curriculum.

These examples make it clear that the JUI-F delivers a number of "services" to the madaris. What, if anything, might it expect in return? The party provides these services for several reasons. The impetus is in part ideological. The JUI-F is the successor movement to the JUH, which was formed as an

[198] White, *Pakistan's Islamist Frontier*, 56–58.

[199] Chief Minister's Secretariat, "NWFP Chief Minister Directives Database" (Peshawar: Chief Minister's Secretariat, Government of NWFP, August 2007).

[200] Mohammad Zafar, "Minister Confesses to 'Extortion of Money,'" *Daily Times*, February 5, 2011.

advocacy organization for the Deobandi ulama in pre-Partition India. Even superficial conversation with JUI-F leaders reveals a deeply held belief in the value of the Deobandi educational project. Far more than the JI, the JUI-F has a "from below" view of political change that is grounded in social and educational reform. The madaris are central to that mission.

More concretely, it is evident from interviews that the party also taps its madaris networks for discreet and indirect fundraising, by soliciting donations to a madrassah in exchange for political favors that are at the party's disposal. (Reportedly, the party sometimes even issues receipts for these donations.[201]) The party also uses its connections in the madaris to organize Friday protests at the grassroots, or larger rallies that can draw tens of thousands of demonstrators.[202] Sometimes this mobilization happens through the activities of a JTI chapter within the madrassah, but just as often it takes place through a personal relationship between the madrassah leadership and local JUI-F politicians.

Taken together, these patterns suggest that the JUI-F operates using loose clientelist linkages in which modes of protection and political advocacy rather than material goods constitute the primary mode of exchange between the party and its constituents. Leonard Binder, one of the earliest and most prescient scholars of religion in Pakistan, penned in 1958 an analysis of the ulama's perception of its own agenda. He wrote:

> Thus, the ulama appear as an interest group, seeking two ill-distinguished ends: (1) the recognition of their own institution, and (2) the supremacy of the shari'a. In their own minds the ulama do not seem to distinguish between these two ends because of their conviction of their own special competence in regard to the latter. Ideal and self-interest neatly coincide.[203]

What Binder attributed to the Pakistani ulama of his day might well be attributed to the JUI-F today: a belief that the protection of the madaris and the promotion of the shariah are synonymous. Thus, while the party follows certain ideological principles, the roots of its bargain with its constituents is tied up in the promise to protect the Deobandi ulama's educational institutions, both from sectarian competitors and from interference by the state.

[201] Sikandar Sherpao, interview by Joshua White, English, July 11, 2007.

[202] See Butt, "Street Power"; "How Many People Are Participating in Fazlur Rehman's Azadi March?," *The News*, November 2, 2019.

[203] Leonard Binder, "Problems of Islamic Political Thought in the Light of Recent Developments in Pakistan," *The Journal of Politics* 20, no. 4 (November 1958): 667.

5
The Structural Roots of Islamist Party Behavior

Relationships with Militants and the State

5.1 Relationships with Militant Groups

Building on the previous chapter, this chapter continues to explore the structural drivers of Islamist party behavior. This first section examines the parties' relationships with militant organizations. The second section that follows evaluates the parties' relationships with the state, and their vulnerabilities to state influence and institutions.

At the heart of this book is a puzzle: What explains Islamist parties' decisions to enable religiously justified anti-state violence, particularly when doing so could undermine their standing as legitimate political actors or the benefits that they accrue from political participation? We cannot answer this question without exploring the Islamist parties' relationships with external militant groups that justify violence on religious grounds. The five case studies in the chapters that follow provide a wealth of detailed examples of interactions between Islamist parties and militant groups over nearly three decades. This section sets the context for those case studies by describing the parties' historical relationships with militant actors and the underlying dynamics that they face.

The data on these relationships are fragmentary at best. Both parties and militant groups typically wish to keep their interactions with one another out of the public eye. Mapping these relationships is, however, important. Chapter 1 of this book proposes that Islamist parties' structural vulnerabilities often play a decisive role in shaping their behavior toward groups that advocate or conduct anti-state violence. To that end, this section will give particular attention to the parties' incentives to *partner* with militant groups, and their *vulnerabilities* to those groups.

Vigilante Islamists. Joshua T. White, Oxford University Press. © Oxford University Press (2025).
DOI: 10.1093/9780197814178.003.0005

Nearly all Pakistani political parties interact with violent actors. For some of these parties, their principal strategy involves cultivating internal capabilities to employ violence for the purpose of ensuring organizational cohesion or degrading political competitors. The MQM has long pursued this approach in Karachi, at times with the support of the Pakistani military. The party has used violence to consolidate its standing among the ethnic Muhajir community, extract rents from local businesses, coerce voters in advance of elections, intimidate local politicians from rival parties such as the PPP and ANP, and challenge rival factions such as the MQM Haqiqi (MQM-H).[1]

Other Pakistani parties have largely forgone building an internal capacity for violence, and have chosen instead to secure relationships with groups that regularly employ violence. The PPP, which casts itself as a "progressive" party opposed to the "extremist mindset" of militant groups, forged deep ties in the 1990s with the militant anti-Shia group Sipah-e-Sahabah Pakistan (SSP), which helped the party solidify its control over electorally competitive areas of Punjab province.[2] More recently, the PML-N was criticized for its ties to violent sectarian groups after Rana Sanaullah, a senior member of the party and provincial law minister in Punjab, repeatedly campaigned with the head of the SSP, and newspapers reported that the PML-N provincial government was providing a monthly stipend to the family of Lashkar-e-Jhangvi leader Malik Ishaq.[3]

Why do parties forge links with militant groups? As I posit in Chapter 1, political parties build and sustain such links—even if they enable anti-state violence, and sometimes complicate the parties' relationships with the government—for three reasons.[4] First, these links can result from parties' ideological sympathy to militant groups. In the Pakistani context, political

[1] See Farhat Haq, "Rise of the MQM in Pakistan: Politics of Ethnic Mobilization," *Asian Survey* 35, no. 11 (November 1995): 990–1004; Mohammad Waseem, "The MQM of Pakistan: Between Political Party and Ethnic Movement," in *Political Parties in South Asia*, ed. Subrata Kumar Mitra, Mike Enskat, and Clemens Spieß, Political Parties in Context (Westport, CT: Praeger, 2004), 184; Huma Yusuf, "Conflict Dynamics in Karachi," PeaceWorks (Washington, DC: U.S. Institute of Peace, October 2012); Paul Staniland, "Armed Groups and Militarized Elections," *International Studies Quarterly* 59, no. 4 (December 2015): 699ff, https://doi.org/10.1111/isqu.12195; Oskar Verkaaik, *Migrants and Militants: Fun and Urban Violence in Pakistan* (Princeton, NJ: Princeton University Press, 2018), chap. 2.

[2] Pakistan Peoples Party Parliamentarians, "Manifesto 2013," 2013; Frédéric Grare, "The Evolution of Sectarian Conflicts in Pakistan and the Ever-Changing Face of Islamic Violence," *South Asia: Journal of South Asian Studies* 30, no. 1 (April 1, 2007): 127–43; Andreas Rieck, *The Shias of Pakistan: An Assertive and Beleaguered Minority* (Oxford: Oxford University Press, 2015), 257–58.

[3] Chris Allbritton, "Pakistan's Punjab 'In Denial' Over Local Militants," *Reuters*, June 8, 2010; Asad Kharal, "LeJ's Malik Received Monthly Stipend from Punjab Govt," *Express Tribune*, July 16, 2011.

[4] This typology differs somewhat from the one proposed by Niloufer Siddiqui, who describes Islamist parties' incentives to utilize violence as relating to policy advocacy, ideology, and electoral advantage. Niloufer Siddiqui, "Strategic Violence Among Religious Parties in Pakistan," in *Oxford Research Encyclopedia of Politics* (New York: Oxford University Press, March 2019).

leaders may be sympathetic to Islamic militants' stated objective of furthering the Islamic character of the Pakistani state, even if they do not condone the means by which that "Islamization" takes place. More narrowly, political party leaders might sympathize with the sectarian prejudices of militants, such as the anti-Shia agitation of groups such as SSP and LeJ, or the anti-blasphemy polemics of radical Barelvi groups.

Second, parties may derive advantages from establishing symbiotic and deniable relationships with militant groups, on whom they rely to carry out targeted violence against opponents, and to whom they might provide in exchange some measure of political protection. Parties can leverage militant proxies to intimidate opponents and create electoral advantages. As Paul Staniland observes, "The electoral value of an armed group varies by context, but includes the ability to directly deliver votes, to act as a coalition partner, and/or to use plausibly 'deniable' violence against the government's electoral opponents. Governments are most likely to collude with electoral armed groups that are ideologically compatible and able to deliver electoral benefits."[5] What is true for governments is equally true for political parties contesting elections. And while governments are best positioned to provide political protection to militant groups, the Pakistani political system provides numerous pathways by which politicians—even unelected ones—can intervene with security officials and judicial authorities to protect militant groups with whom they have a productive relationship.

Third and lastly, political parties may sustain ties with militant groups in order to manage competition with those, and similar, groups. Fearing defection of their own party cadres to more radical or militant organizations, they may decide to publicly or privately support those organizations rather than risk challenging them. The leadership of the PML-N, for example, has often been wary of taking on sectarian militants in southern Punjab, lest it lose votes and party workers who are sympathetic to groups carrying out anti-Shia violence.

All Pakistani political parties may at times face these three incentives for engaging with militant groups. But for Islamist parties these incentives may be felt more acutely: they are, for example, likely to have closer ideological proximity to Islamic militant groups, and be at greater risk of losing party workers and adherents. We will explore these dynamics, beginning with the JI's relationship with militant groups, and proceeding to the Deobandi parties, followed by the Shia, Ahl-e-Hadith, and Barelvi parties.

[5] Staniland, "Armed Groups and Militarized Elections," 696.

5.1.1 The Jamaat-e-Islami

The Jamaat-e-Islami has had ties to various militant groups. During the anti-Soviet jihad in the 1980s, the JI directly supported several mujahidin groups with funding and recruits, most notably the Hizb-e-Islami of Gulbuddin Hekmatyar, and the Jamiat-e-Islami led by Burhanuddin Rabbani.[6] The party also provided, through its copius publications and public rallies, the intellectual architecture that helped justify armed resistance against the Soviets.

After the Afghan jihad, the JI retained ties with Hekmatyar and Rabbani, but turned its attention to Kashmir, where the Pakistani intelligence services were beginning to orchestrate a new and more vigorous militant front against India. The JI's most notable contribution to the anti-India jihad in the 1990s was its support for the Hizb ul-Mujahidin (HM), which operated as an armed affiliate of the Jamaat-e-Islami Jammu and Kashmir (JIJK). HM was founded in 1989 in Indian-administered Kashmir, and although it is unclear whether it was created at the behest of the intelligence services—which sought to cultivate a more Pakistan-sympathetic alternative to the Jammu and Kashmir Liberation Front—or merely operated in support of the military's objectives, the group developed robust capabilities and focused its efforts on attacking military targets in India.[7]

The precise nature of the relationship between JI and HM remains opaque.[8] Amélie Blom has noted that the HM has described JI Pakistan as its "mother organization" and, drawing on familial ties between JI party workers and HM fighters, has relied on the party and its collegiate affiliate IJT for recruits.[9] We know that HM has recruited heavily in both Indian- and Pakistani-administered Kashmir, but also in Pakistani Punjab, and that its relatively well-educated base of recruits can perhaps be explained by its ties with the JI.[10] It has also been reported that HM operated in Afghanistan in the mid-1990s alongside Hizb-i-Islami Gulbuddin (HIG), a relationship that may have been facilitated by each group's respective relationship with JI.[11]

[6] Husain Haqqani, "The Ideologies of South Asian Jihadi Groups," *Current Trends in Islamist Ideology* 1 (2005): 17–18.

[7] Haqqani, "The Ideologies of South Asian Jihadi Groups," 18; C. Christine Fair, "Insights from a Database of Lashkar-e-Taiba and Hizb-ul-Mujahideen Militants," *Journal of Strategic Studies* 37, no. 2 (February 23, 2014): 264, https://doi.org/10.1080/01402390.2013.811647; C. Christine Fair, *In Their Own Words: Understanding Lashkar-e-Tayyaba* (London: Hurst & Co., 2018), 62.

[8] For a deeper narrative about JIJK's history in Kashmir, see Yoginder Sikand, "The Emergence and Development of the Jama'at-i-Islami of Jammu and Kashmir (1940s–1990)," *Modern Asian Studies* 36, no. 3 (2002): 705–51.

[9] Amélie Blom, "A Patron-Client Perspective on Militia-State Relations: The Case of the Hizb-ul-Mujahidin of Kashmir," in *Armed Militias of South Asia: Fundamentalists, Maoists and Separatists*, ed. Laurent Gayer and Christophe Jaffrelot, trans. Cynthia Schoch, Gregory Elliott, and Roger Leverdier (New York: Columbia University Press, 2009), 143–46.

[10] See Fair, "Insights from a Database of Lashkar-e-Taiba and Hizb-ul-Mujahideen Militants."

[11] U.S. Department of State, "Patterns of Global Terrorism 2003" (Washington, DC, April 2004), 147.

Recognizing after the attacks on September 11, 2001 that it might incur reputational risks for its links to HM, the JI instructed its leaders—down to the district level—to keep their distance from the group.[12] When a reporter noted in 2003 that many HM offices in Pakistan were being run by JI workers, the party leader attributed this to sympathizers within the party, and reportedly asked HM to relocate out of JI properties and directed JI officials to remove HM materials from those properties.[13] (The directive appears not to have been consistently carried out. I discovered in 2011 a large cache of 1990s-era HM propaganda posters for sale at the official bookshop of JI's Mansurah headquarters outside Lahore.)

Public attention on JI links with HM proved inconvenient for the party, but was ultimately not overly troublesome, given that HM—like the Afghanistan-focused jihadi groups that JI supported in the 1980s—was operating in accord with the policies and priorities of the Pakistani military. JI's relationship with al-Qaeda (AQ), by contrast, has been considerably more opaque, and potentially more problematic for the party given the Pakistani state's own complex relationship with AQ's leadership. The Pakistani military adamantly denies that it knew about Osama bin Laden's compound in Abbottabad, which was raided by U.S. forces in 2011, but commentators continue to speculate that the Pakistani intelligence services may have protected the AQ leader.

Since 2001, there have been scattered reports of al-Qaeda operatives captured at houses affiliated with JI or IJT members including, most prominently, senior AQ planner Khalid Sheikh Muhammad in 2003.[14] Some years later, in 2010, there was a report suggesting that a large number of IJT-affiliated students traveled from Karachi to North Waziristan to join AQ training camps.[15] At a minimum, these accounts suggest that some lower-level party operatives may be sympathetic to the movement. One of the demographic segments most inclined to join groups such as al-Qaeda—"educated strivers who come from the lower middle class," in the words of one journalist—maps closely to the profile of a typical JI member.[16]

[12] Islamuddin Sajid, interview by Joshua White, English and Urdu, trans. Shuja Malik, February 18, 2011.

[13] Abdullah Iqbal, "Jamaat-e-Islami Denies Links with Hizbul Mujahideen," *Gulf News*, May 29, 2003.

[14] See, for example, B. Raman, "Jamaat-e-Islami, Hizbul Mujahideen & Al Qaeda" (South Asia Analysis Group, March 29, 2003), https://web.archive.org/web/20110507084010/http://www.southasiaanalysis.org/papers7/paper699.html; "A Timely Arrest," *The Economist*, March 8, 2003; Asad Kharal and Ali Usman, "Punjab University: Consensus Against IJT Grew from Al Qaeda Man's Arrest," *Express Tribune*, December 3, 2013.

[15] Syed Saleem Shahzad, "Pakistani Students Prefer Guns to Books," *Asia Times Online*, July 27, 2010, https://web.archive.org/web/20130209110616/http://www.atimes.com/atimes/South_Asia/LG27Df01.html.

[16] See, for example, Sabrina Tavernise and Waqar Gillani, "Generation of Frustrated Strivers Wages Jihad on Pakistan," *New York Times*, February 27, 2010.

The JI leadership has gone to great lengths since 2001 to distance itself from any association with AQ. When asked in interviews about the intellectual arc connecting Maududi to Syed Qutb, party leaders did not even wait to hear the end of the question before preemptively rebutting the accusation that Maududi's thought had anything to do with Qutb and—by extension—al-Qaeda.[17] They pointed as well to the party's explicit denunciation of Ayman al-Zawahiri's treatise against the Pakistani state.[18]

As the case studies in subsequent chapters will highlight, the JI has been largely successful at minimizing its vulnerabilities to militant groups. It has consistently adopted a militant-sympathetic discourse, and even though it did not praise AQ it often echoed and amplified the movement's critiques of the West and the Pakistani state. The JI leadership, insulated somewhat due to its lack of a notable constituent base near the southern tribal areas and Balochistan, was generally critical of the Pakistani military's forays into the tribal areas to combat TTP and other anti-state groups, and thus did not invite antagonism from those groups in the way that the JUI-F did. And the party, as noted above, has maintained good relations with militant groups that have been used by the Pakistani military in Afghanistan and India, and indeed sponsored some of those groups directly. (One senior JI official wryly explained the party's inclination to support the intelligence services' shifting priorities in Afghanistan, and then Kashmir, and then Afghanistan again, with a Pashto proverb: "If the oven is hot, everyone will come and cook chapatis"[19])

5.1.2 The JUI Parties

The Deobandi parties have had significantly more numerous and complex relationships with militant groups than the JI. Members of the JUI-F and JUI-S sometimes have overlapping membership with other organizations in the Deobandi universe, including sectarian groups, Kashmir-focused militant groups, the Afghan Taliban, and the TTP, and share with them common networks of madaris and masajid.[20]

The first strand of these relationships involve the JUI parties' links with anti-Shia sectarian organizations, most notably Sipah-e-Sahabah Pakistan

[17] Author interviews with JI leaders, 2006–2012.

[18] See Anjum Rasheed, "Zawahiri's Viewpoint—A Challenge to Pak Institutions," *The News*, June 25, 2011; Michael W. S. Ryan, "The Jamestown Foundation: Al-Qaeda on Pakistan: Dr. Ayman al-Zawahiri's Morning and the Lamp," *Jamestown Terrorism Monitor* 8, no. 11 (March 19, 2010): 6–8.

[19] Interview with JI leader, Lahore, 2011.

[20] C. Christine Fair, "Explaining Support for Sectarian Terrorism in Pakistan: Piety, Maslak and Sharia," *Religions* 6, no. 4 (September 25, 2015): 1142.

(SSP) and Lashkar-e-Jhangvi (LeJ). The parties' interactions with these organizations have been particularly tumultuous. In the late 1980s and early 1990s, the SSP practically operated as a wing of the JUI, with SSP candidates contesting elections on JUI tickets.[21] The early leaders of the organization were senior figures of the JUI, were patronized by the party, and were given party tickets.[22] In spite of these links, writes Mariam Abou Zahab, "the SSP has always maintained ambiguous relations with the JUI, skillfully playing off the rivalry between the Maulana Fazlur Rahman and Maulana Sami ul Haq factions . . . . The links with the JUI have never been broken; the party's leaders claim to agree with the SSP's ideas, but differ as to its methods."[23]

As the SSP's tactics became more radical—and its methods less politically palatable—the JUI-F in particular began to create distance between itself and the sectarian radicals. In 2005, the JUI-F found itself marginalized by the SSP in Sindh, which chose to ally with the JUI-S and against the JUI-F in the local bodies elections.[24] Later, JUI-F party leaders condemned the SSP for its tactics, and for taking an "emotional" approach to carrying out its agenda.[25] The reluctance by the JUI-F to be closely identified with the SSP and its successors may, as Arif Rafiq has speculated, be related to JUI-F Maulana Fazl ur-Rahman's efforts to court Shia votes in his home constituency of Dera Ismail Khan and his longstanding relationship with Shia politicians such as Sajid Naqvi.[26]

Part of the JUI-F's public shift with respect to the SSP and other sectarian organizations may also have been a response to pressure after the attacks of September 11, 2001. As late as 2000, advertisements for radical Deobandi organizations were being published in the party's flagship *al-Jam'iyat*; the May 2000 issue, for example, included an advertisement for a bookshop in Sargodha that stocked materials supportive of sectarian groups, the Afghan

[21] See Seyyed Vali Reza Nasr, "Islam, the State and the Rise of Sectarian Militancy in Pakistan," in *Pakistan: Nationalism Without a Nation?*, ed. Christophe Jaffrelot (New York: Zed Books, 2002). For more on the rise of the SSP, see Muhammad Qasim Zaman, *The Ulama in Contemporary Islam: Custodians of Change*, Princeton Studies in Muslim Politics (Princeton, NJ: Princeton University Press, 2002), 118–31; Mariam Abou Zahab, *A Kaleidoscope of Islam* (New York: Oxford University Press, 2020), 73–74.

[22] Hassan Abbas, "Shiism and Sectarian Conflict in Pakistan: Identity Politics, Iranian Influence, and Tit-for-Tat Violence," Occasional Paper Series (West Point, NY: Combatting Terrorism Center at West Point, September 22, 2010), 35.

[23] Mariam Abou Zahab, "The SSP: Herald of Militant Sunni Islam in Pakistan," in *Armed Militias of South Asia: Fundamentalists, Maoists and Separatists*, ed. Laurent Gayer and Christophe Jaffrelot, trans. Cynthia Schoch, Gregory Elliott, and Roger Leverdier (New York: Columbia University Press, 2009), 161.

[24] Hasan Mansoor, "Sipah-e-Sahaba to Participate in LB Polls," *Friday Times*, March 11, 2005.

[25] Maulānā Gul Nasīb K̲h̲ān, "svāt āpareshun aur madāris o masājid ko lāḥaq k̲h̲aṭrāt [The Swat Operation and the Dangers Befalling the Madaris and Masjids]," *al-Jam'iyat* 10, no. 12–13 (October 2009): 11–14.

[26] Arif Rafiq, "Sunni Deobandi-Shi'i Sectarian Violence in Pakistan: Explaining the Resurgence Since 2007" (Washington, DC: Middle East Institute, December 2014), 25–26.

Taliban, Harkat ul-Mujahidin, and Harkat al-Jihad al-Islami (HuJI).[27] Even after the change in public posture after 2001, however, the party did not abandoned its outreach to SSP and its successors. In March 2011 the JUI-F, JUI-S, and JI all sent representatives to the SSP's annual conference in honor of martyrs in the army-controlled cantonment area of Wah (though the JUI-F was represented by a more junior leader than the other two parties), and the JUI parties both explored electoral alliances with ASWJ-backed candidates in 2018.[28]

The second strand of these relationships involves the parties' links with Kashmir-oriented militant organizations. These include an array of Deobandi groups that Don Rassler has collectively labeled the Pakistani Harakat Movement: Harakat ul-Jihad Islami (HuJI), Harakat ul-Mujahidin (HuM), Harakat ul-Ansar (HuA), and Jaish-e-Muhammad (JeM). (LeT shares with these groups a common focus on attacking the Indian state, and ties with the Pakistani intelligence services, but as an Ahl-e-Hadith organization is of a different character ideologically and has limited links with the JUI parties.)

These Deobandi groups share a common but complex genealogy, tracing their roots to the Afghan jihad in the 1980s where they mixed with Pakistan-backed jihadi groups, al-Qaeda, and others.[29] With substantial support from the Inter-Services Intelligence directorate, they rose to prominence in the Kashmir jihad in the 1990s, and forged wide-ranging ties with militants within Pakistan, including sectarian militants described above, and in other locales as far away as Bosnia and the Philippines.

The JUI parties have longstanding links with these Kashmir-oriented Deobandi militant organizations. Mariam Abu Zahab notes that the HuA's office in Peshawar was inaugurated in 1997 by Maulana Sami ul-Haq of the JUI-S.[30] In the late 1990s, *Jane's Intelligence Review* quoted one Western intelligence analyst who described the HuA as "essentially the armed wing" of the JUI-F, and noted that the U.S. government believed that the party had active links and influence with the militant group.[31] That view was confirmed by a

[27] Publication of such advertisements may have continued after September 2001, but a cursory review of the publication from 1999 to 2011 suggests that implicit endorsements of radical Deobandi organizations fell off after that date.

[28] "[Annual Conference in Memory of Martyrs To Uphold the Sanctity of Prophet's Companions]," *Islam*, March 23, 2011; Kalbe Ali, "Banned ASWJ Faces Isolation, Plans to Contest Polls Under New Name," *Dawn*, March 12, 2018.

[29] Mariam Mufti, "Religion and Militancy in Pakistan and Afghanistan: A Literature Review" (Washington, DC: Center for Strategic and International Studies, June 2012), 32ff; Don Rassler, "Al-Qaida and the Pakistani Harakat Movement: Reflections and Questions about the Pre-2001 Period," *Perspectives on Terrorism* 11, no. 6 (December 2017): 39–41.

[30] Mariam Abou Zahab, "The Regional Dimension of Sectarian Conflicts in Pakistan," in *Pakistan: Nationalism Without a Nation?*, ed. Christophe Jaffrelot (New York: Zed Books, 2002), 120.

[31] Roger Howard, "Wrath of Islam: The HUA Analysed," *Jane's Intelligence Review*, October 1, 1997.

secret U.S. State Department cable from 1995, since redacted and declassified, in which the U.S. Embassy in Karachi reported that the JUI-F appeared to have operational and financial links with HuA.[32]

Although parties such as the JUI-F and JUI-S became more careful after 2001 to obscure their links with Kashmir-oriented militants, the thick Deobandi madaris-based relational networks between the Harakat Movement and the JUI likely remained robust. One prominent example of these linkages was Mufti Nizamuddin Shamzai, who led the Jamiat ul-Ulum Islamiyah, Binori Town in Karachi. Shamzai had close ties with Osama bin Laden, and was named chief patron of the JeM.[33] He also sat on the JUI-F's apex council, the majlis-e-shura, and actively advised the MMA government in then-NWFP.[34] When he was assassinated by unknown assailants in 2004, he was lauded by the party, and senior JUI-F officials attended his funeral in Karachi.

The third, and most prominent, aspect of the JUI parties' relationships with militant groups involves the Afghan Taliban. The JUI has a long, open, and well-documented history of support for the Taliban's activities in Afghanistan. It has assisted the Afghan Taliban—with rhetoric, recruits, rallies, and presumably funding—in ways that have been consistent with the interests of the Pakistani security services' unstated policy of "strategic depth," which sought to foment insurgency in Afghanistan so as to deny political influence to Tajiks and other ethnic groups that it viewed as being sympathetic to India.[35]

The JUI is widely seen as the intellectual forebearer and political benefactor of the Afghan Taliban.[36] Sami ul-Haq, who ran a prominent madrassah in KP at which Mullah Omar and other senior Taliban figures studied, relished the fact that he was known as "Father of the Taliban." (He regaled this author, and presumably many visitors before him, with a bound volume of over two decades of press clippings highlighting his links to the Taliban movement.[37])

[32] U.S. Consulate Karachi, "The Harakat Ul Ansar—The Pakistan Dimension [Excised]" (KARACHI 01617 (SECRET), March 29, 1995), Declassified under FOIA request by the National Security Archive, https://nsarchive.gwu.edu/document/24670-document-1-karachi-01617-us-consulate-karachi-cable-harakat-ul-ansar-pakistan.

[33] Farhan Zahid, "Deconstructing Thoughts and Worldviews of Militant Ideologue Mufti Nizamuddin Shamzai," *Counter Terrorist Trends and Analyses* 10, no. 7 (July 2018): 10–11.

[34] Rahimullah Yusufzai, "Mufti Nizamudin Shamzai," Khyber.org, September 16, 2005, https://web.archive.org/web/20170712181653/http://www.khyber.org/people/a/Mufti_Nizamudin_Shamzai.shtml.

[35] S. Paul Kapur and Sumit Ganguly, "The Jihad Paradox: Pakistan and Islamist Militancy in South Asia," *International Security* 37, no. 1 (Summer 2012): 111–41.

[36] Ahmed Rashid, *Taliban: Militant Islam, Oil, and Fundamentalism in Central Asia* (New Haven, CT: Yale University Press, 2000), 88–94; Sana Haroon, "The Rise of Deobandi Islam in the North-West Frontier Province and Its Implications in Colonial India and Pakistan 1914–1996," *Journal of the Royal Asiatic Society*, 3, 18, no. 1 (2008): 66–69.

[37] Sami ul-Haq, interview by Joshua White, Urdu, trans. Shuja Malik, February 19, 2011.

Even in November 2001, as the United States was beginning a campaign to topple the Taliban government, a senior JUI-F leader wrote that the party "is with Taliban government and Afghan people."[38]

Throughout the two decade interregnum in which the Taliban was out of power, 2001 through 2021, the JUI parties continued their public criticism of the U.S.- and coalition-led government in Kabul, and their support for the Taliban's efforts at regaining power. This support was overt, and the JUI parties used it to emphasize their commitment to Pashtuns, to critique Pakistani civilian leaders for their pace of Islamization, and to suggest (as they did many times to this author) that they were well-positioned to serve as "intermediaries" between the Taliban and the Government of Pakistan to advance "solutions" to the conflict in Afghanistan. When the Taliban recaptured Kabul in 2021, the JUI parties—and indeed, all of the Sunni Islamist parties—were therefore not shy about exulting in the outcome. The JUI-S leader, son of Sami ul-Haq, reportedly described the Taliban's victory as a fulfillment of his father's dream.[39] And JUI-F leader Maulana Fazl ur-Rahman sent a public letter to Taliban leader Maulana Hibatullah Akhundzada congratulating him on the movement's success.[40]

If the JUI parties' relationships with the Afghan Taliban were overt and positive in tenor, their relationships with the Pakistani Taliban were considerably more fraught and ambivalent. This is examined in greater detail in Chapter 9, which explores the rise of the Tahrik-e-Taliban Pakistan (TTP) and the ways in which the Islamist parties responded to it. Broadly speaking, the JUI-S was more proactive and public than the JUI-F about maintaining constructive ties with the TTP, while continuing to sustain links with Pakistan's intelligence services.[41] As late as 2011, as the TTP were carrying out attacks across Pakistan, Maulana Sami ul-Haq refused to formally acknowledge the existence of a "Pakistani Taliban."[42]

For reasons explored in the case study later in this volume, the JUI-F was not able to finesse its relationship with the TTP while simultaneously protecting its interests and access to the Pakistani security services. At least as early as 2006, newspaper accounts and other documents indicated that the party was feeling pressure from the rising influence of the Pakistani Taliban

[38] Maulānā 'Abd al-G̲h̲afūr Ḥaidrī, "kārkun jihād kī tayārī kareṅ [Workers, Prepare for Jihad]," *al-Jam'iyat* 2, no. 2 (November 2001): 23–24.

[39] See, for example, "JUI-S Greets Afghan Taliban on Capturing Kabul," *The News*, August 17, 2021.

[40] "JUI F Chief Tries to Take Credit for Taliban Mujaddin Victory in Afghanistan," *Times of Islamabad*, August 16, 2021.

[41] Vali R. Nasr, "The Rise of Sunni Militancy in Pakistan: The Changing Role of Islamism and the Ulama in Society and Politics," *Modern Asian Studies* 34, no. 1 (February 2000): 139–80; Imtiaz Ali, "Interview with Maulana Sami Ul-Haq," *Jamestown Spotlight on Terror* 4, no. 2 (May 23, 2007).

[42] Tariq Jamal, "['The Taliban Do Not Exist in Pakistan': Interview with Sami Ul-Haq]," *Ausaf*, April 5, 2011.

(which had not yet organized formally as the TTP) in what was then the tribal areas bordering Afghanistan.[43] In 2008, the party faced opposition by the TTP to some of its general election campaigns, and threats of boycotts in others. It also suffered, following the elections, a string of attacks on its leadership in which dozens of leaders were killed.[44] Most stunning to the party was a wave of attempted attacks on Fazl ur-Rahman himself that began in 2011. Although several months later Rahman was ostensibly "pardoned" by the unidentified Pakistani Taliban elements that had targeted him, the message to the party leadership was clear: The anti-state TTP considered the JUI-F to be an adjunct to the government, and therefore a legitimate target in its campaign to forcibly Islamize the state.[45]

In summary, the JUI parties have maintained close ties with a wide range of Deobandi militant organizations. Both parties, but particularly the JUI-F, have generally taken positions consistent with those of the Pakistani intelligence services: tolerating or encouraging the activities of anti-Shia sectarian organizations, and endorsing or sponsoring Deobandi militants operating in Afghanistan and Kashmir. Where the Pakistani services were ambivalent or antagonistic—such as toward al-Qaeda and TTP—we find that the JUI-F tended to respond similarly.

Like the JI, the JUI-F has sought to distance itself from al-Qaeda. In interviews, party leaders gave one of two responses to questions about the organization: either they strongly denounced it and its tactics, or they questioned its very existence. Osama bin Laden appears to have had some support among the lower party ranks—in the days after his death in an American raid, JUI-F workers in Quetta organized a rally in which they chanted "Long Live Osama" and burnt an American flag—but the party leadership was not eager to endorse bin Laden or his anti-state violence.[46] Even JUI-F leader Hafiz Hussain Ahmad, who often praised the Pakistani Taliban, responded ambivalently when asked about bin Laden in June 2011, saying that AQ leader "had his own viewpoint, his own targets and his own style. The JUI-F and other religious movements here have their own style. I said in the beginning that while following in the footsteps of our elders, we kept our movement on the constitutional and legal course."[47]

[43] "2006: JUI-F Felt Threatened by Rising Taliban Influence," *Dawn*, May 27, 2011; Nicholas Schmidle, "Next-Gen Taliban," *New York Times Magazine*, January 6, 2008; Joshua T. White, *Pakistan's Islamist Frontier: Islamic Politics and U.S. Policy in Pakistan's North-West Frontier*, Religion & Security Monograph Series 1 (Arlington, VA: Center on Faith & International Affairs, 2008).

[44] Zia Ur Rehman, "Militants Turn Against Pakistan's JUI-F Islamist Party," *CTC Sentinel* 5, no. 4 (April 2012): 15–17.

[45] Mazhar Tufail, "Maulana Fazl Pardoned by Taliban," *The News*, October 17, 2011.

[46] "JUI Rally Pays Homage to 'Martyred' Bin Laden," *Agence France-Presse*, May 6, 2011.

[47] Muhammad Abdullah Sajid, "'President and Interior Minister May Also Be Involved in Killing of Usama Bin Ladin': Interview with Maulana Hafiz Hussain Ahmad," *Islam*, June 6, 2011.

The JUI-F also faced internal turmoil over its ambiguous position on al-Qaeda and its decision not to endorse the Pakistani Taliban. A dissident faction, the JUI-N, broke away in 2008, taking with it a number of prominent party members from Balochistan. The faction largely reintegrated in 2016, when pressure from the TTP on Pakistan's Islamist parties had notably diminished.[48]

5.1.3 Other Islamist Parties

Pakistan's other Islamist parties have also cultivated ties with militant organizations. The TNFJ and its successor Shia parties—the TJP, and later the ITP—have generally tried to "maintain a discreet distance" from militant groups such as Sipah-e-Muhammad Pakistan (SMP), but often share common cause with the group's desire not to leave anti-Shia violence unanswered.[49] As sectarian violence rose in the 1990s, the TNFJ had itself sought out ways to protect its vulnerable Shia constituents, and although the party did not publicly support the SMP's militancy, it was widely believed that many of the SMP's ranks were initially drawn from TNFJ's younger ranks.[50] Since that time, the party has reportedly "restricted itself to providing legal aid to arrested SMP cadres."[51]

The Ahl-e-Hadith parties are presumed to have ideological affinities with Ahl-e-Hadith militant groups, but such ties are opaque. The MJAH has been linked to the Tahrik-e-Mujahidin, a jihadi group that has trained in Afghanistan and fought in Indian-administered Kashmir.[52] It has likely entertained informal relations with Lashkar-e-Taiba and its various front organizations, though some reports suggest that MJAH leaders have "condemn[ed] the behaviour of some of the LeT recruits who loot banks, make money out of jihad and embezzle huge sums of money collected under the name of jihad."[53] The party likely uses its influence over the Ahl-e-Hadith madaris networks to facilitate recruiting and possibly operations by Tahrik-e-Mujahidin.[54] Little is

[48] Zia Ur Rehman, "The F and N of JUI," *The News*, February 28, 2016.
[49] Muhammad Qasim Zaman, "Sectarianism in Pakistan: The Radicalization of Shi'i and Sunni Identities," *Modern Asian Studies* 32, no. 3 (July 1998): 698.
[50] Rieck, *The Shias of Pakistan*, 244, 252; "Sipah-e-Mohammed Pakistan, Terrorist Group of Pakistan," South Asia Terrorism Portal, 2014, https://web.archive.org/web/20230812121210/https://www.satp.org/satporgtp/countries/pakistan/terroristoutfits/smp.htm; Zaman, *The Ulama in Contemporary Islam*, 117–18.
[51] "Sipah-e-Mohammed Pakistan, Terrorist Group of Pakistan."
[52] Mariam Abou Zahab, "Salafism In Pakistan: The Ahl-e Hadith Movement," in *Global Salafism: Islam's New Religious Movement*, ed. Roel Meijer (New York: Oxford University Press, 2014), 137.
[53] Zahab, "Salafism In Pakistan," 137.
[54] Zahab, "Salafism In Pakistan," 133.

known about the other Ahl-e-Hadith party discussed in this volume, the Milli Muslim League, but its leadership roster demonstrates that it is closely linked to, if not operationally controlled by, LeT.

Like their sectarian competitors, the Barelvi parties, too, have at times found it useful to sustain ties with militant groups. The JUP parties have typically been careful about making such ties overt, though they are believed to have links with Sunni Tahrik. More interesting is the TLP. As explored in detail in Chapter 10, the party itself helped to mobilize vigilante violence, and at times violence against government security forces; rather than forming a militant proxy organization that might insulate the party from pressure by the state, the TLP chose to organize violence from within its own ranks. The important implications of that decision for the party are explored later in this book.

5.2 Relationships with the State

The last, but certainly not least, of the important structural dynamics that shape Islamist party behavior involves the parties' relationships with the Pakistani state. These relationships have the potential to be mutually beneficial, and indeed Islamist parties have rightly been seen in general terms as collaborators with the state.[55]

The drivers of this collaboration are not difficult to discern. Military and elected leaders in Pakistan have an interest in supporting political and religious figures who will buttress the regime's Islamic legitimacy; who can be useful in advancing the state's foreign policy objectives in India and Afghanistan by recruiting and facilitating militants operating in those theaters; and who can at times serve as spoilers to complicate democratic politics or disrupt establishment politicians, thus easing the work of the security services to manipulate electoral outcomes.[56]

For their part, Islamist parties have often found relationship with the state to be a useful source of influence, providing them with channels to advance their policy goals, to procure both direct and indirect sources of funding, and to protect not only their parties but affiliated institutions such as the

[55] See Husain Haqqani, *Pakistan: Between Mosque and Military* (Washington, DC: Carnegie Endowment for International Peace, 2005).

[56] For an analysis of Pakistan's segmented approach to facilitating militant groups, see Stephen Tankel, "Beyond the Double Game: Lessons from Pakistan's Approach to Islamist Militancy," *Journal of Strategic Studies* 41, no. 4 (2018): 545–75, https://doi.org/10.1080/01402390.2016.1174114.

madaris.[57] As chronicled in Chapter 2, however, certain Islamist parties have also at times been dissenters, unwilling or unable to collaborate with the state. This has occurred when the parties have chosen to oppose military rule, or be openly critical about the pace or nature of the state's Islamization program—sometimes as a result of genuine ideological conviction, and sometimes as a strategy to distinguish themselves from the state or out-bid other non-state competitors.

One of this book's central hypotheses, presented in Chapter 1, is that the Islamist parties' structural vulnerabilities profoundly shape their decision-making with respect to religiously justified anti-state violence. Namely, parties that are vulnerable to the state are more likely to be cautious about publicly endorsing anti-state violence by party members, affiliates, and outside movements. We examined earlier in this chapter the benefits that Islamist parties can receive through patronage—that is, some of their positive incentives for collaboration with the state. In this section, we will focus on the nature of the parties' other incentives and vulnerabilities vis-à-vis the state. The section begins with a discussion of "the state" in Pakistan, and the tools available to state institutions to influence the behavior of Islamist parties. It then examines in particular the vulnerabilities of the JI, JUI-F and—to a lesser extent—the TLP, for whom there is an as-yet-ill-defined relationship with state authority. Less attention is given here to the smaller Islamist parties, which due to their size are highly vulnerable to state influence; and to the MML, which has operated as a front for a militant group with close ties to the intelligence services.

The military's influence over politics in Pakistan is undeniable. Led by the Chief of Army Staff, the military has directly governed the country for over three decades of its history, and its manipulation of electoral politics under nominally civilian regimes is well established.[58] It has brooked little interference in, and virtually no oversight over, defense-related budgeting or operations. It is widely believed to exercise almost unfettered control over foreign policy-making with respect to India and Afghanistan; and substantial control over relations with the United States, China, international financial institutions, and other major interlocutors.

[57] Quinn Mecham, "Islamist Parties as Strategic Actors: Electoral Participation and Its Consequences," in *Islamist Parties and Political Normalization in the Muslim World*, ed. Quinn Mecham and Julie Chernov Hwang (Philadelphia: University of Pennsylvania Press, 2014), 24–25.

[58] See Stephen P. Cohen, *The Pakistan Army* (Karachi: Oxford University Press, 1998); Shuja Nawaz, *Crossed Swords: Pakistan, Its Army, and the Wars Within* (Karachi: Oxford University Press, 2008); C. Christine Fair, *Fighting to the End: The Pakistan Army's Way of War* (New York: Oxford University Press, 2014); Aqil Shah, *The Army and Democracy: Military Politics in Pakistan* (Cambridge, MA: Harvard University Press, 2014).

The powerful Inter-Services Intelligence (ISI) directorate, along with Military Intelligence (MI) and various specialized security services, have a long track record of intimidating and blackmailing politicians, harassing journalists, and actively shaping media reporting, particularly in the vernacular press.[59] Civilian security agencies, notably the Intelligence Bureau (IB) and Special Branch (SB), which are nominally under the control of elected civilian officials, are in practice highly deferential to, and at times co-opted by, the military. This pattern of military dominance has been sustained during both periods of direct military rule, and during periods of civilian leadership.

Given the preponderant influence of the military, I use "security services" to refer principally to the army leadership and the ISI directorate; and secondarily, to the other military and civilian intelligence agencies (e.g., MI, IB, SB) that liaise with, pressure, and at times support Islamist parties. To be sure, even the powerful military and its penumbra of security agencies do not always operate as a unitary actor. The various military services compete for promotions, funding, and influence, and the military and civilian intelligence agencies can act at cross-purposes to each other when the chief of army staff's perceived interests are at odds with those of the prime minister. But on the whole, the military's tools of political influence are so expansive as to overshadow those of elected civilians or bureaucrats.

What kinds of pressures can the Pakistani security services exert over political parties—and Islamist parties in particular? The security services have a substantial repertoire of techniques, many of which were borrowed from established British colonial methods of political control.[60] These agencies can, in the first place, ban or substantively limit the operations of a political party, or encourage the party to believe that it may be subject to restrictions. It is, for example, not uncommon for states in Asia, Europe, and the Middle East to ban or severely restrict religious parties.[61] And the Pakistani government has occasionally done so through the Election Commission, at times in response to foreign pressures.

[59] The military holds a clear edge over civilians in intelligence-gathering. Hasan-Askari Rizvi, *Military, State and Society in Pakistan* (New York: St. Martin's Press, 2000), 193.

[60] This list draws in part from Kenneth Janda, *Political Parties: A Cross-National Survey* (New York: Free Press, 1980), 31–32. See also Rizvi, *Military, State and Society in Pakistan*, 79. For a comparative examination of how these processes of continuity functioned in neighboring India, see Sudipta Kaviraj, "A State of Contradictions: The Post-Colonial State in India," in *States and Citizens: History, Theory, Prospects*, ed. Quentin Skinner and Bo Strath (Cambridge, UK: Cambridge University Press, 2003), 145–67.

[61] For further discussion on this point, see, for example, Suzie Navot's work, which examines the difficulties that states face in deciding whether or not parties in a democracy should be banned on the basis of their goals and ideology, or their actual political actions. Suzie Navot, "Fighting Terrorism in the Political Arena: The Banning of Political Parties," *Party Politics* 14, no. 6 (November 2008): 745–62, https://doi.org/10.1177/1354068808093409.

Somewhat less overtly, the security services can disqualify party officeholders or preclude politicians from contesting elections, or use threats of violence or blackmail to prevent them from doing so. Here state institutions have demonstrated an expansive repertoire, from instituting formal educational requirements for parliamentary seats, to more contingent forms of disqualification, such as the use of anticorruption committees to target contenders for public office. Looking beyond party leaders themselves, the security services have sometimes pressured parties by exerting—or threatening—control over party- or constituent-linked institutions, such as schools, housing developments, offices, places of worship, affiliate membership organizations, and madaris. Targeting party affiliates can be an effective and deniable method by which state agents can exercise indirect leverage over a party, or intimidate party elites.

A final form of leverage available to the security services is financial. The state can try to restrict the present and prospective financial resources available to parties. Sometimes this involves direct forms of resource capture, such as seizure of accounts or property. Other times the pressures are indirect, such as efforts by the security services to discourage parties' domestic and foreign funders.

It is important to note that each of these forms of leverage is subject to some inherent limitations upon the state. Political scientists have often observed that more repression by the state can lead to more resistance by the affected organization.[62] This dynamic can make states and their security agencies reluctant to actually carry out threats against internal challengers or problematic parties, and instead leave those threats implicit. Public opinion provides another check on the state's ability to carry out threats against Islamist parties that do not hew to the state's policy. Pakistani politician Aftab Sherpao, who for decades interacted with Pakistan's Islamist parties—including in his role as Interior Minister responsible for domestic security under the Musharraf government—explained in an interview that when the religious parties took to the streets, "tear-gassing them . . .that option isn't there. You can disperse them on a given occasion" but, he observed, they have sufficient public support that they cannot easily be shut down.[63] As Quinn Mecham has noted, states also have to

[62] See, for example, A. Nizar Hamzeh, "Lebanon's Islamists and Local Politics: A New Reality," *Third World Quarterly* 21, no. 5 (October 2000): 739–59; Mohammed M. Hafez, *Why Muslims Rebel: Repression and Resistance in the Islamic World* (Boulder, CO: Lynne Rienner Publishers, 2003), 28.

[63] Aftab Sherpao, interview by Joshua White, English, February 17, 2011. See also Ahsan Butt's work on how the Islamist parties leverage their street mobilizations. Ahsan I. Butt, "Street Power: Friday Prayers, Islamist Protests, and Islamization in Pakistan," *Politics & Religion* 9, no. 1 (March 2016): 1–28, http://dx.doi.org/10.1017/S1755048316000031.

worry that heavy-handed actions against Islamist parties might "extend a party's popularity and make it a focal point for the political opposition" and can reinforce the party's argument that the state is acting against Islamic norms.[64]

5.2.1 The Jamaat-e-Islami

We begin with an examination of the Jamaat-e-Islami's relationship with the state, and its vulnerability to state pressure. The JI is no stranger to influence and intimidation. Maududi himself was imprisoned by the government in 1948 for opposing the war in Kashmir, and the JI "was charged with sedition, a charge hitherto leveled only against Communist organizations."[65] He later recanted and was released, but the incident left the party wary of government interference in its activities. Several years later, after the vicious anti-Ahmadi agitations in 1953–1954, Maududi was again detained. This time he was sentenced to death, a charge which eventually was dropped. This episode, in hindsight, had a particularly notable impact on the IJT, which saw itself as a "soldier's brigade" that could undertake activities on behalf of a threatened party.[66]

The party fared relatively well during the martial law period, 1958–1962, during which time political parties were outlawed. Centrally organized and well-prepared for its eventual reinstatement, the JI "claimed the distinction of being the first party to revive its activities" in 1962 and, despite ongoing prohibitions against government officials from associating with the party, "started functioning without much difficulty."[67] It was not long before the party entered into fierce political conflict with Ayub Khan over a host of domestic and foreign policy issues. In January 1964, the government took the surprising step of banning the party, confiscating its funds, sealing its offices, discontinuing its publications, and arresting its senior leaders. The crackdown did not last long, as the government's legal case was weak, and by October of that year the ban had been overturned and the leaders released.[68] Nonetheless, the episode demonstrated the party's vulnerability to targeted

[64] Mecham, "Islamist Parties as Strategic Actors: Electoral Participation and Its Consequences," 22.
[65] Seyyed Vali Reza Nasr, *Mawdudi and the Making of Islamic Revivalism* (Oxford: Oxford University Press, 1996), 42; S. M. M. Qureshi, "Religion and Party Politics in Pakistan," *Contributions to Asian Studies* 2 (July 1971): 40.
[66] Seyyed Vali Reza Nasr, "Students, Islam, and Politics: Islami Jami'at-i Tulaba in Pakistan," *Middle East Journal* 46, no. 1 (Winter 1992): 63.
[67] M. Rafique Afzal, *Political Parties in Pakistan: 1958–1969*, 3rd ed., vol. 2 (Islamabad: National Institute of Historical and Cultural Research, 2000), 148.
[68] Afzal, *Political Parties in Pakistan: 1958–1969*, 2:152–57.

pressure by the state, along with its organizational resilience to long-term or existential threats to its activities.

Although the party did not again face outright and targeted bans by the government, the Zia ul-Haq years provided a new set of challenges. As documented earlier, the JI had a tumultuous relationship with the Zia government. It was, in the words of one historian, "an organization under great strain" during the early 1980s, as it fell in and out of favor with the martial government and began losing influence in Karachi to the MQM.[69] It also lost credibility among its own constituent base when Zia ul-Haq failed to pursue structural Islamization measures favored by the party, and reneged on his promise to maintain the sovereignty of the National Assembly.[70]

In light of this history, how does the JI leadership perceive its vulnerability to state pressure? In the first place, party leaders seem to expect—and prepare for—state interference in their operations. Well acquainted with state pressure, they recall that the party has been subjected to it under a wide variety of governments. More than one party leader explained in interviews that the JI had made active preparations for continuing its operations if it were banned by the government. "You can ban the skeleton," explained one senior official with a shrug, "but not the philosophy."[71]

Among the party leaders, it was practically a matter of dogma that the party did not need to be worried about state pressure. Party elites believed that the JI leadership provided little in the way of blackmail material to the security services; that they had few if any assets or affiliate organizations that would not survive a shutdown order by the government; and that the state, even under martial governments, had weak legal grounds for closing the party. One researcher speculated that, because many JI members have close family links with the army, the party is vulnerable to influence by the military.[72] But even if that were the case, the party elite have shown a willingness over time to sacrifice individual leaders for the good of the party as a whole. In interviews, government elites and outside observers held a similarly dismissive view of the state's ability to sway the JI. The party was viewed as difficult to blackmail, and obstinate in its negotiations with the government. "The JI is not vulnerable," recounted Aftab Sherpao. "You'd talk to them for three hours

[69] Humeira Iqtidar, "Secularism Beyond the State: The 'State' and the 'Market' in Islamist Imagination," *Modern Asian Studies* 45, no. 3 (2011): 543, https://doi.org/10.1017/S0026749X11000217; Verkaaik, *Migrants and Militants*, chap. 2.

[70] Seyyed Vali Reza Nasr, "Islamic Opposition to the Islamic State: The Jamaat-i Islami, 1977–88," *International Journal of Middle East Studies* 25, no. 2 (May 1993): 266–70.

[71] Abdul Ghaffar Aziz, interview by Joshua White, English, May 18, 2011.

[72] Muhammad Amir Rana, interview by Joshua White, English, February 14, 2011.

and in the end they'd just repeat what they said [at the outset] . . . . They're hard bargainers."[73]

The Jamaat-e-Islami has always lived with a peculiar paradox. Its ideology is deeply rooted in the idea of state authority and shaping government institutions so as to create an Islamic society from the top down. At the same time, the party has often challenged the state, its institutions, and its legitimacy. Khalid Masud, former chairman of the CII, explained how the party has historically navigated this paradox: "The JI will challenge the state until it is Islamic . . . . It's not the institution of the state they challenge, but its irreligosity."[74] To some, particularly in the government, this has sounded like a distinction without a difference. But both the party and the state elite know that the JI, with its organizational resilience, indigenous funding, ideologically based linkages, and demonstrated willingness to boycott elections for perceived longer-term political gains, is not nearly as vulnerable to state influence as are most parties in Pakistan's political system.[75]

5.2.2 The JUI Parties

States throughout the Muslim-majority world have for centuries sought to co-opt and marginalize the ulama. One scholarly study of the ulama lays out the state's ideal method in six simple steps: (a) marginalize Islamic law by relegating the ulama to family law; (b) make the leading ulama state bureaucrats subject to official policy; (c) regulate training; (d) control or even nationalize mosques; (e) control religious education in schools; and (f) control auqaf and other religious establishments.[76] Pakistan has not pursued this course explicitly, but it has done so substantially—co-opting ulama through many of these same methods. The JUI parties, like the ulama writ large, have been subject to unique and pervasive forms of state influence, and that vulnerability is arguably what makes state elites willing—when it suits them—to include the parties in positions of governance at the provincial or federal levels.

Although in certain narrow respects the JUI-F has proven to be less susceptible to state pressure than the JI, overall it has more serious vulnerabilities.

[73] Aftab Sherpao, interview.

[74] Khalid Masud, interview by Joshua White, English, February 22, 2011.

[75] If anything, the JI has felt increased political pressure from pro-state jihadi groups, which have the potential to encroach on the party's public reputation as the leading voice for the Islamization of Pakistani society. See Saba Imtiaz and Noman Ahmed, "Paradigm Shift: In Political Vacuum, JI Stands at Crossroads," *Express Tribune*, February 27, 2012.

[76] Abdullah Saeed, "The Official Ulema and Religious Legitimacy of the Modern Nation State," in *Islam and Political Legitimacy* (London: RoutledgeCurzon, 2003), 19–26.

Prevalent among the Pakistani urban elite and some foreign commentators is the notion that the JUI-F is entirely co-opted, or even "controlled," by the security services.[77] Such a view overstates the degree of influence held by the state over the party, and understates the agency available to party leaders to choose their posture vis-à-vis state institutions. Can the state easily ban the party? In fact, the JUI-F has proven to be adept at maintaining its party operations in restrictive environments. Its status as an ulama party makes it uniquely resistant to outright bans by the government, given that its activities are distributed across mosques and madaris. Under the cover of the Nizam al-Ulama (System of Clerics) movement, for example, the party was able to function rather well during Ayub Khan's martial law.[78]

Some years later, when the JUI began strongly challenging the state in the late 1960s to demand an Islamic constitution, it did so from the cover of the mosques. As M. Rafique Afzal, the leading historian of Pakistan's political parties, recounts:

> Mosques, where no preventive law could be invoked, served as good covers for their increasingly strident campaign against the government. In desperation, the government arrested Maulana Hazarvi, a virulent critic of government policies, under the West Pakistan Public Order Ordinance, on September 24, 1968. This did not restrain other JUI leaders. In fact, they became more aggressive and stepped up their propaganda; and soon, on October 2, the government was forced to release Maulana Hazarvi on bail.[79]

However inefficient and occasionally incoherent the party's decentralized decision-making has been, this incoherence has had the benefit of protecting it against formal government attempts to limit religious party influence. The JUI-F's mosque- and madrassah-based mobilization also played to its advantage in the former FATA, where until the passage of the Political Parties Act in 2011, political party activity was legally prohibited. By running unofficial campaigns from mosques and madaris, the party was able to consistently win support for its preferred National Assembly candidates, who formally ran as independents.

If the state cannot easily ban the party, can it restrict its financial resources? Here again, the state has only modest leverage over the party. The JUI-F, as

[77] See, for example, Frédéric Grare, "Islam, Militarism, and the 2007–2008 Elections in Pakistan," Carnegie Papers 70 (Washington, DC: Carnegie Endowment for International Peace, July 2006), 8.
[78] Afzal, *Political Parties in Pakistan: 1958–1969*, 2:136.
[79] Afzal, *Political Parties in Pakistan: 1958–1969*, 2:144.

documented earlier in this volume, does not operate an expensive bureaucracy. It survives on minimal resources, and looks to foreign funding and candidature clientelism to raise funds for electoral campaigns. If the central government wished to pressure the JUI-F, it could conduct a high-profile investigation into the party's foreign donors, or merely hint that it would do so, as it did in 2005 and again in 2011.[80] With the fall of the Qaddafi regime, the party's main sources of external support likely shifted to Saudi Arabia and the United Arab Emirates, both countries with which Pakistan has very strong bilateral relations and intelligence-sharing arrangements.

Can the state easily disqualify JUI-F officeholders? It has, in fact, done so, and the threat of disqualification stands as one of the JUI-F's most obvious and serious vulnerabilities vis-à-vis state agencies. The qualification for political office—typically, a bachelor's degree—was interpreted for the 2002 elections in such a way as to include candidates with equivalent madrassah degrees. But in 2005 and later, there were cases in which clerics with the very same madrassah degrees were disqualified. Interviews with JUI-F workers indicate that the party leadership was very sensitive to this vulnerability, and knew that an unfavorable Supreme Court ruling at the national level (prompted, perhaps, at the behest of the security services) could at once disqualify almost all of its potential candidates.[81] Even in June 2003, just months following the MMA's October 2002 victory, Maulana Fazl ur-Rahman was complaining in the Provincial Assembly that the federal government was putting pressure on the party by threatening to disqualify madaris-educated politicians.[82]

Even if elements of the state decided against directly targeting party members through candidate qualification standards, they have indirect tools at their disposal: regulation of the madaris. We have examined at length the ways in which the JUI-F is linked to the Deobandi madrassah system. Government pressure on the madaris does not directly threaten the standing of the party, but any policies that erode madrassah influence would negatively affect the JUI-F. Even threats of action against the madaris would be a means by which the state could ensure policy compliance by the party.

The madaris—and by extension, the JUI-F—have clear vulnerabilities to the state. The Deobandi ulama have long been wary of accepting state

[80] Mazhar Abbas, "Will Musharraf Ban the Jama'at and JUI?," *Friday Times*, August 26, 2005; Usman Manzoor, "Did Saudis, Libyans Pay Dollars to JUI-F? Pasha Hinted So," *The News*, May 14, 2011.

[81] Muhammad Riaz Durrani, interview by Joshua White and Shuja Malik, Urdu, February 25, 2011.

[82] Maulānā Ḥāfiẓ Momin Khān 'Uṣmānī, ed., *khuṭbāt-e qā'id jam'iyat [Speeches of the Jamiat Leader]*, vol. 2 (Lahore: Dār ul-Kitāb, 2007), 164–65.

funds for the madaris, and on those grounds Mufti Mahmud convinced JUI-affiliated institutions not to take federal zakat funds.[83] But while the state cannot entirely control the supply side of the clerical market, it nearly monopolizes the demand side. Vali Nasr has written eloquently about the state's role, beginning in the 1980s, in supporting the creation of a class of "Islamic bureaucrats" who would serve state educational and political institutions.[84] In 1982, in exchange for requiring some reforms to the madrassah curriculum, the government began to accept madrassah certificates as equivalent to formal school certificates, thus opening the door to the "bureaucratization" of the petty ulama class. Many JUI-F clerics are today employed by schools and government agencies.

Whenever the government has attempted to institute further reforms to the madaris, either in the form of registration requirements or curricular reforms, the JUI-F has protested vigorously. Pervez Musharraf's proposed reforms, presented under the rubric of "Enlightened Moderation," were opposed with particular vitriol by the ulama, who accused the government of attempting to Westernize the madaris. (The reforms that the ulama most feared—ones in which the state would have dictated curriculum, or even taken over madaris—were successfully stymied by the JUI-F and the ulama themselves.) In interviews, party elites regularly expressed anxiety about new attempts to regulate the madaris, and expressed their view that pressure on the madaris is in fact the principal means by which the state intentionally pressures the JUI-F.

The madaris, and thus the JUI-F, are also vulnerable because of the many linkages between the madrassah system and militant groups, some which were described in the previous section. One of Musharraf's few successful madrassah reforms was a ban on foreign students, which he justified on national security grounds. The JUI-F leadership is highly sensitive to the accusation that madaris are breeding grounds for terrorism. Even before September 2001, the monthly party publication was full of commentary bemoaning the ways in which terrorism creates an excuse for the state to raid the madaris.[85] After the 9/11 attacks, the party monthly contained an inconsistent mix of arguments praising the anti-American

[83] Nasr, "The Rise of Sunni Militancy in Pakistan," 154.

[84] Nasr, "The Rise of Sunni Militancy in Pakistan," 146ff.

[85] See, for example, Maulānā 'Abd al-G̲h̲afūr Ḥaidrī, "dīnī madāris ke taḥafuẓ keli'e jān kī bāzī lagā denge [We Will Put Our Lives on the Line for the Protection of the Religious Madaris]," *al-Jam'iyat*, November 1999, 8. Two volumes of collected speeches of Fazl ur-Rahman are also replete with references to this theme. See especially Maulānā Ḥāfiẓ Momin K̲h̲ān 'Uṣmānī, ed., *k̲h̲uṭbāt-e qā'id jam'iyat [Speeches of the Jamiat Leader]*, vol. 1 (Lahore: Dār ul-Kitāb, 2002), 170–234; 'Uṣmānī, *k̲h̲uṭbāt-e qā'id jam'iyat [Speeches of the Jamiat Leader]*, 2007, 2: 373–92.

activities of the Afghan Taliban, while lamenting the ways in which the "carelessness" of the ulama has given the government a reason to impinge on the freedom of the madaris.[86] Similarly, following the Red Mosque crisis described in Chapter 8, party leader Abdul Ghaffur Haidri spoke on the floor of the National Assembly, worrying aloud that although the Red Mosque administration clerics were not in the right, the incident might give the government a reason to close madaris, thus depriving students and their families of the free education that the religious schools provide.[87]

Some scholars have suggested that the social immobility of the ulama class is a major contributor to the emergence of radicalism among madaris graduates.[88] Madrassah students who complete the standard degree course graduate with limited employment options, most of which are in the public sector. Some leaders in the JUI-F have publicly made a case for self-reflection among the ulama, urging them to revisit and modernize the madaris curriculum before the state takes it upon itself to do so.[89] Nonetheless, as a protector but not manager of the madaris, the party itself has only limited influence among the wider Deobandi community on matters such as curriculum and religious institutions' linkages with militant groups. It therefore remains indirectly susceptible to state pressure due to the vulnerability of its primary constituent base.

The security services can also offer numerous inducements, which have been effective in co-opting the JUI-F. Since the 1970s, the party has generally been disposed to participating in coalition politics, and most observers believe that the state has effectively co-opted the party by providing electoral and other favors in Khyber Pakhtunkhwa and Balochistan in return for political support in Islamabad. There is truth to this analysis. One JUI-F leader described the process by which the "agencies" would visit party notables during the 1990s, and using inducements, try to convince them to join various

[86] Maulānā 'Abd al-G̲h̲afūr Ḥaidrī, "madāris ke dafā' keli'e k̲h̲ūn kā āk̲h̲irī qaṭrah tak bahā deṅge [We Will Give the Last Drop of our Blood to Defend the Madaris]," *al-Jam'iyat* 4, no. 10 (September 2004): 6–7.

[87] "National Assembly of Pakistan Debates: Official Report," 2007, vol. 42, no. 2 (Islamabad, July 31, 2007).

[88] Dietrich Reetz, *Islam in the Public Sphere: Religious Groups in India, 1900–1947* (New Delhi: Oxford University Press, 2006), 310.

[89] Maulānā Muḥammad K̲h̲ān Sherānī, "shāndār māẓī kī bāz yāfat aur ahl-e madāris z̲imah dāryān [Recovery of the Glorious Past and Responsibilities of the People of the Madaris]," *al-Jam'iyat* 10, no. 12–13 (October 2009): 7–10. It is not inconceivable that the party would push for curricular reforms. One commentator writing in the JUI-F's student magazine admitted that the party changed the syllabus for its affiliate organization JTI after communism was shown to be a failure following the collapse of the Soviet Union. Ḥāfiẓ G̲h̲aẓunfar 'Azīz, "jam'īatah ṭalabā'-e islām kā tarbīatī niẓām [Jamiat Talaba-e Islam's System of Training]," *'Āzm-e Nau* 22, no. 2 (February 2008): 26.

alliances or coalitions.[90] Others leaders recalled the ways in which the central government occasionally threw up roadblocks to Mufti Mahmud's attempt in the early 1970s to obtain state funding for a new university in his home district of Dera Ismail Khan; the lesson, they said, was that cooperation would be well rewarded.[91] (It was eventually established as Gomal University.) At least according to Aftab Sherpao—who, as Musharraf's interior minister, would be in a position to know—the inducements rarely needed to be offered beyond the party leader's immediate family: "The JUI is totally vulnerable [to the government], there is no doubt about that. You [merely] have to appease Maulana Fazl ur-Rahman and his brothers."[92]

It is impossible to know how heavily the state's financial inducements have weighed on the JUI-F leadership. Two brief examples, however, paint a picture of the opportunities that state patronage provide to the party. The first is a remarkable aside from a 2010 newspaper article on the party's standing in Balochistan: "All of 10 [sic] JUI MPAs in the Balochistan Assembly are either ministers or advisers to the chief minister and will firmly oppose any move resulting in their ouster from power."[93] That is, even after the party's relatively poor performance in the 2008 elections, *every single JUI-F MPA* in Balochistan was given a ministerial-level appointment, complete with perquisites and "development fund" allocations. As the article underscores, this is almost certain to create a cadre of elected officials highly resistant to challenging the state.

The second example is drawn from the MMA period in the former NWFP province. Figure 5.1 shows the results of a district-wise analysis of the confidential Chief Minister Directives database. Out of 4,438 directives issued between December 2002 and July 2007, 335 (or about 7.5%) were identified on the basis of the directive description as providing benefit to a mosque or madrassah. The figure distinguishes between funds given through auqaf channels, which are typically publicly accountable direct grants, and in-kind channels, such as grants for construction, water or power services, or utility subsidies. The results are striking in that they suggest a high degree of correspondence between key JUI-F electoral districts, and districts in which mosques and madaris were made the beneficiaries of state monies. (The Chief Minister was from Bannu, and Maulana Fazl ur-Rahman hailed from Dera Ismail Khan.)

[90] Abu al-Fateh Muhammad Yousuf, interview by Joshua White, Urdu, trans. Shuja Malik, March 1, 2011.
[91] Sayyid A. S. Pirzada, interview by Joshua White, English, May 14, 2011.
[92] Aftab Sherpao, interview.
[93] Tariq Butt, "Is Sherani the Weak Link in Maulana JUI's Strategy?," *The News*, December 19, 2010.

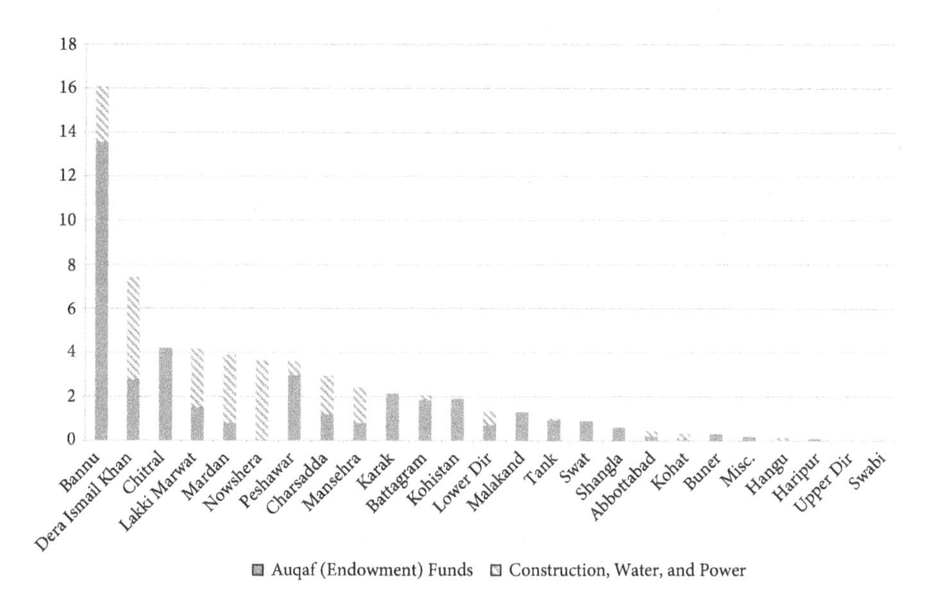

Figure 5.1 Rupees (Millions) Provided to Mosques and Madaris in Direct Transfers and Government Services through NWFP Chief Minister Directives from December 2002 through July 2007, by District.
Source: Author's analysis of confidential Chief Minister Directives database

These results help to explain why, for example, the JUI-F leadership was—even as late as the summer of 2007—reluctant to give up the party's place in the governing coalitions in NWFP and Balochistan.

And what of the state's ability to shape the political environment in which the party operated? In the 2002 general elections, the government tipped the scales in favor of the religious parties. The Musharraf government restricted most kinds of political rallies, but the JUI-F was able to skirt this prohibition by campaigning in mosques and madaris.[94] The government also, in the words of JUI-F leader Hafiz Hussain Ahmad, "showed kindness [to] us" by giving the MMA the election symbol of the book, which they represented to the voting population as the Quran.[95] The state's ability to create an unfavorable political environment for a party or parties of its choosing has similarly been demonstrated, most visibly during the widespread manipulations of the political process by the army during the so-called decade of democracy between 1988 and 1999.

[94] Grare, "Islam, Militarism, and the 2007–2008 Elections in Pakistan," 6.
[95] Sajid, "'President and Interior Minister May Also Be Involved in Killing of Usama Bin Ladin': Interview with Maulana Hafiz Hussain Ahmad."

The last item in this litany of JUI-F vulnerabilities is also the most difficult to evaluate: the party's susceptibility to blackmail. The consensus of party officials and outside observers, when interviewed, was that the JUI-F was far more vulnerable to quiet manipulation by the state than the JI. In part this is because the party is believed to be more corrupt than the famously austere JI. The apex leadership of the party has been implicated in a number of scandals. Maulana Fazl ur-Rahman became known as "Maulana Diesel" in some circles "because of his reputed involvement in fuel smuggling" in the 1990s.[96] More recently, Rahman was implicated in a scam in which he and other party leaders quietly received grants of land from the army, presumably in exchange for the party's acquiescence to the Legal Framework Order which legitimized Musharraf's military government.[97] In a country in which official retribution against former political opponents is practically a matter of state policy, it is impossible to judiciously evaluate the claims against the party and compare them to charges against, say, the PPP or PML-N. But credible charges have been brought against JUI-F party leaders, and credible sources suggest that there is plenty of material available for future use by the state.[98]

In conclusion, the JUI-F faces substantially higher and more varied exposure to state pressure than the JI. Although it is inoculated against some forms of legal sanction by virtue of its operations in the mosques and madaris, on almost every other count it is vulnerable to pressure from state agencies. Moreover, the party's clientelist linkage pattern incentivizes its leadership to be particularly wary of having to pay the opportunity cost of confronting the state.

5.2.3 The TLP

The third and final party that we will examine here is the TLP. The party has been able to attract a mass following and obtain a substantial tally of votes. It has episodically challenged the state through its endorsements of vigilante violence (including its praise of the killing of Governor Taseer), and disruptive rallies. At the same time, despite its public profile, it has clear vulnerabilities: as established earlier in this chapter, the TLP is thinly organized and highly personalistic, led by a small cadre of high-profile leaders.

[96] Barbara D. Metcalf, *'Traditionalist' Islamic Activism: Deoband, Tablighis, and Talibs* (Leiden: ISIM, 2002), 13.

[97] "Partymen Stunned: 'Fazl in Land Scam,'" *Dawn*, November 3, 2008.

[98] Ansar Abbasi, "Maulana JUI Back in NAB Focus," *The News*, December 17, 2010.

Like the Deobandi JUI parties, the TLP can draw to some extent on the Barelvi madaris for its street mobilizations, but is not yet as well organized as the Deobandis for this purpose.

The party, as chronicled in Chapter 10, has had a tumultuous relationship with government authorities. The government at various times threatened to ban the party, and arrested a number of its senior leaders. The provincial government of Punjab in 2021 conducted an investigation into the party's funding, which had been opaque to outside observers, and traced 328 domestic financiers, many of whom were from urban areas, with a particular concentration in southern Punjab.[99] The combination of the party's poor organizational infrastructure, small leadership cadre, and vulnerability to state interference with its fundraising would suggest that the party is highly vulnerable to manipulation by the security services.

At the same time, however, numerous reports suggest that the TLP cultivated a deep base of support within key security organizations. Recordings circulated on social media of a serving army general handing out envelopes of cash at a TLP rally in 2017 reinforced the public perception that the TLP had close ties with the army leadership, and was possibly being used as a tool to pressure Imran Khan's elected government.[100] Other anecdotal reporting suggested that the TLP had a significant well of support among the Punjab police and some paramilitary organizations. These relationships presumably served to some extent to insulate the party from state pressure; the government banned the TLP in April 2021 but negotiated an agreement to lift the ban later that year. As discussed in the TLP case study, both the party and the security services appear to have misjudged each other.

[99] Asif Chaudhry, "Punjab CTD Set to Act Against Banned TLP's Financiers," *Dawn*, May 7, 2021.
[100] "Why Was Pakistan General Giving Money to Protesters?," *BBC News*, November 29, 2017, https://web.archive.org/web/20240910033457/https://www.bbc.com/news/world-asia-42149535.

PART 2

6
Early Uprisings
TNSM in Malakand

6.1 Introduction

This chapter will examine a foundational case of violent opposition to the Pakistani state on religious grounds, and one to which Pakistan's Islamist parties were forced to respond. In the early 1990s in the former NWFP, the Tahrik-e-Nifaz-e-Shariat-e-Muhammadi (TNSM) clashed with government authorities in a dispute that arose over the role of shariah in local governance. The TNSM's agitation began with peaceful protests, such as blocking highways, and then evolved into violent confrontations. These confrontations culminated in late 1994 when the movement overtook government facilities, attacked security forces with rocket propelled grenades, seized a key regional airport, and took elected officials, judges, and civil servants hostage. The TNSM and the government eventually agreed to a cessation of hostilities, and the crisis dissipated.

The movement garnered further attention a decade later when a reconstituted TNSM, allied with anti-state militants in the southern tribal agencies of Waziristan that later formed into the TTP, mounted a renewed and violent challenge to the state—and later again in 2013 when a TNSM leader acceded to the leadership of the TTP.

At no point was the TNSM a particularly powerful movement. It did not present an existential threat to the Pakistani state. But the events of 1994 posed one of the highest profile internal challenges to the state's authority since the 1971 war, and represented a prominent attack on the state's religious legitimacy. The movement had clear antecedents from colonial times, in particular the nineteenth century mujahidin movements (which the British dubbed the "Hindustani fanatics") that used the language of jihad to rally public support,

Vigilante Islamists. Joshua T. White, Oxford University Press. © Oxford University Press (2025).
DOI: 10.1093/9780197814178.003.0006

and violently challenged the colonial government in the frontier, including in the mountains of Swat.[1]

The fact that the TNSM's agitation took place in Malakand Division, a peripheral region in which the state historically exercised more limited control, has led some commentators to write off the incidents as unimportant.[2] That would be a mistake. For one, the early TNSM agitations foreshadowed a number of clashes between religiously justified anti-state movements and the Pakistani government that unfolded along very similar lines: not only the rebirth of the TNSM a decade later, but the Red Mosque crisis detailed in Chapter 8, and the state's wider confrontation with the Tahrik-e-Taliban Pakistan movement across the tribal areas described in Chapter 9.

Second, Pakistan's periphery was precisely where violent anti-state movements found the most opportunities for political expansion, and encountered the least resistance from civil and military authorities. Armed, religiously justified challenges to state authority in Pakistan's far-flung regions, which seemed anomalous in 1994, would become, in just over a decade, a common feature of the political scene.

And third, the 1994 TNSM case, critically, has analytical utility for our examination of Islamist party decision-making. The uprising took place in a region that had a strong presence of the Jamaat-e-Islami, and in which the Deobandi ulama were influential as well. Both the JI and the JUI parties were forced to confront the new movement and reconcile its demands for shariah—with which they largely agreed—with its confrontational posture and use of violence toward the state.

6.2 Background to the Case

The regions comprising Malakand Division have a unique place in Pakistan's history. Following the partition of India in 1947, three princely states acceded to Pakistan: Dir, Swat, and Chitral. These states were nominally governed by local sovereigns—the Nawab of Dir, the Wali of Swat, and the Mehtar of Chitral—and were indirectly administered by the Pakistani government as part of its Malakand Agency. In 1969, the three states were

[1] See Magnus Marsden and Benjamin D. Hopkins, "Sitana and Swat: Patterns of Revolt Along the Frontier," in *Fragments of the Afghan Frontier* (New York: Columbia University Press, 2011), 75–100.

[2] The provincial government of Khyber Pakhtunkhwa no longer uses the division as a significant unit of administration; the major subprovincial tier of government is the district. Divisions, which historically constituted a higher-level tier comprising several districts, are still technically in use, however, and it is common practice to use the label "Malakand Division" to refer to the districts of Buner, Chitral, Dir (split in 1996 into Lower and Upper Dir), Malakand, Shangla, and Swat.

fully merged into Pakistan, but their legal and judicial systems remained anomalous.[3] The federal government chose not to fully "settle" the newly integrated territories, but instead to allow the continuation of certain types of customary law. Tribal *jirgas* rather than district courts continued to be used to settle most disputes. Levy forces were raised from the population in place of a regular standing police force. The regions received representation in the Provincial Assembly, but were exempt from most taxes. The civil and criminal codes did not fully apply, and government civil officers were given extraordinary powers to decide cases, or refer them to jirgas.

This unusual system bred discontent. When the highly personalistic—and at times, authoritarian—rule of the princes was abolished in 1969, the government of Pakistan did not create alternate modes of dispute resolution that were efficient or equitable. Eventually in 1976, the government formalized its indirect rule by designating the area as a Provincially Administered Tribal Area (PATA), but this did little more than reify the status quo. Under the PATA regime, wealthy tribal leaders "enjoyed judicial powers through the jirga system," and often exercised those powers unchecked.[4] One twenty-eight-year-old was quoted in 1994 complaining, "I have not seen a single case being decided by the courts of this area in my entire life."[5]

The PATA regulations were eventually challenged by Malakand lawyers on the basis that they violated the "fundamental rights" and "equality of citizens" provisions of the constitution.[6] During the first of Benazir Bhutto's terms as prime minister, in February 1990, the Peshawar High Court unexpectedly sided with the lawyers, declaring the regulations to be unconstitutional. The provincial government appealed, and in February 1994 the Supreme Court ruled decisively in favor of the plaintiffs, and declared the PATA regulations to be null and void. This decision forced the provincial government to confront a quite unwelcome set of alternative legal regimes that might be established in place of the PATA regulations, and brought to the forefront those activists who had been calling for the legal system to be re-architected around shariah.

[3] For more on this history, see Sultan-i-Rome, *Swat State (1915–1969): From Genesis to Merger: An Analysis of Political, Administrative, Socio-Political, and Economic Developments* (Karachi: Oxford University Press, 2008); Sultan-i-Rome, "Swat: A Critical Analysis," IPCS Research Papers 18 (New Delhi: Institute of Peace and Conflict Studies, January 2009), 7ff.

[4] Adnan Adil, "Unholy Alliance Provokes Swat Uprising," *Friday Times*, November 10, 1994.

[5] Tahir Mehdi, "Malakand's Holy War," *Newsline*, November 1994, 28.

[6] Muhammad Amir Rana, "Backgrounder: Shariah Movement in Malakand" (Pakistan Institute for Peace Studies, April 29, 2008); Sultan-i-Rome, "Swat: A Critical Analysis," 13.

6.2.1 The Rise of TNSM

The emergence of the TNSM roughly coincided with this period in the early 1990s when the legal status of Malakand was being actively disputed. The movement was founded in 1989 by Maulana Sufi Muhammad.[7] Little is known about Sufi Muhammad's life prior to this date. He hailed from Maidan, a town in district Lower Dir, and studied, by most accounts, at the seminary in Swabi district run by Maulana Tahir—a connection that we will examine in greater detail below.[8] He was for several years associated with the Jamaat-e-Islami in Dir, but curtailed that affiliation sometime between 1989 and 1992.

A Pashto-language account by a compatriot of Sufi Muhammad suggests that the TNSM was founded when elders in Dir who favored shariah convened members from several major parties—ANP, JI, JUI-F, and PPP—and sought the creation of a unifying movement for Islamic law. Sufi Muhammad was appointed the first leader of the movement, though it is unclear whether he had direct influence in its creation.[9] Sufi Muhammad's first recorded public demonstrations after the founding of the TNSM came in May 1990, when the movement set up a protest camp in Dir to demand shariah.[10] The government paid them little attention, but in the wake of these protests the TNSM set up their own qazi courts in Dir to decide cases quickly and ostensibly in conformity with shariah.[11] Reports indicate that in 1992, feeling relatively satisfied with the operation of the qazi courts in Dir, Sufi Muhammad moved to neighboring Swat and established a madrassah there.[12] The Taliban movement was, at about this same time, gaining strength in Afghanistan, and Sufi Muhammad mobilized members of his madrassah and the surrounding community to participate in the Taliban's consolidation of power.[13] In

[7] Fazal-ur-Rahim Khan Marwat and Parvez Khan Toru, *Talibanization of Pakistan: A Case Study of TNSM* (Peshawar: Pakistan Study Centre, University of Peshawar, 2005), 10; A. S. Yousufi, "Malakand: Leaders Not Sincere," *Dawn*, May 19, 1994; Pakistan Institute for Peace Studies, "TNSM: A Taliban-Like Movement" (Islamabad: PIPS, August 15, 2007).

[8] Navid Iqbal Khan, "Tehreek-i-Nifaz-i-Shariat-i-Muhammadi in Malakand Division (Khyber Pakhtunkhwa): A Case Study of the Process of 'State Inversion,'" *Pakistan Journal of History and Culture* 31, no. 1 (2010): 140–41.

[9] Maulana Syed Ali Shah, *De Shariat Karwan, Manzal ba Manzal [The Shariat Caravan, Step by Step]* (Lahore: Muktar Ahmed Khan Swati, 1995), chap. 1.

[10] Marwat and Toru, *Talibanization of Pakistan*, 21.

[11] Rana, "Backgrounder: Shariah Movement in Malakand."

[12] Shah, *De Shariat Karwan*, chap. 2.

[13] Umer Farooq, "Profile: Maulana Sufi Muhammad," *Asharq Al-Awsat*, May 1, 2009, https://web.archive.org/web/20240925165011/https://eng-archive.aawsat.com/theaawsat/features/profiles/profile-maulana-sufi-muhammad. Sufi Muhammad maintained a good relationship with the Taliban government. After September 11, 2001, but before the U.S. military action against the Taliban, Sufi Muhammad led a group of approximately 10,000 volunteers to Afghanistan; they were squarely defeated, and returned

May 1993, continuing its expansion outside of Dir, the TNSM held its first large public gathering in Swat, pressing for the enforcement of shariah; and in July, a public rally in Chitral.[14] This rally gave the TNSM's leadership the impetus to establish a more robust organizational structure in Swat.[15] Nonetheless, the movement remained rather disorganized, with devolved authorities, and lacking "defined method of enforcing discipline in party ranks."[16] It was a weakness that would soon prove to be a liability for the movement.

The TNSM's most significant early confrontation with the state came in the spring of 1994, shortly after the Supreme Court judgment. In April, the movement set a deadline of early May for the government to enforce shariah.[17] When it failed to do so, Sufi Muhammad launched a sit-in in the Malakand city of Batkhela. With crowds reportedly upward of 25,000, Sufi Muhammad's followers blocked the main highway leading to Swat and demanded the establishment of qazi courts across Malakand Division.[18] They also took the opportunity to declare that driving on the left-hand side of the road was un-Islamic, and mandated that people switch to right-hand drive, a change that resulted in a number of traffic accidents across the Malakand region.[19]

The conflict came to a head when paramilitary forces fired on a TNSM rally in Buner district of Malakand on May 16, killing ten and wounding over two dozen activists.[20] Fearing that the conflict might spiral out of control, the governor of NWFP announced the enforcement of shariah, and through a "meaningless notification" managed to diffuse the situation and temporarily appease Sufi Muhammad and his followers.[21] Sufi Muhammad and the government entered into negotiations, the crowds dispersed, and the government was granted a temporary reprieve from the protests.

suffering heavy losses. Iqbal Khattak, "Attempts on Musharraf's Life Are Terrorism but What I Did in Malakand and Afghanistan Was in Line with Shariah . . . . " *Friday Times*, February 11, 2005.

[14] Azizullah Khan, "'Malakand Incident—Extension of Afghan War,'" *Frontier Post*, November 6, 1994; Shah, *De Shariat Karwan*, chap. 4.

[15] Shah, *De Shariat Karwan*, chap. 2.

[16] Mehdi, "Malakand's Holy War," 27.

[17] Mazhar Zaidi and Behroz Khan, "Holy Law," *Newsline*, May 1994, 44.

[18] Zaffar Abbas, "Showdown in Malakand," *Herald*, May 1994; Ayaz Qazi, "Malakand People Demand Shariat Laws Implemented," *Dawn*, May 13, 1994; "Malakand Rally Disrupts Life," *Dawn*, May 14, 1994.

[19] "'Right-Hand Drive Is Islamic,'" *Dawn*, May 16, 1994.

[20] Ahmad Hassan, "10 Die as Militia Fire on Malakand Rally," *Dawn*, May 17, 1994.

[21] I.A. Rehman, "The Lessons of Malakand," *Newsline*, November 1994, 38.

6.2.2 Sufi Muhammad Confronts the State

The reprieve would not last. In early November 1994, the TNSM launched a major offensive against the government. The TNSM's takeover was swift and stunning.[22] Members of the movement took local judges, a member of the National Assembly, and dozens of government functionaries hostage. In what one security official described as "utter chaos" and "open rebellion," they quickly overtook government facilities.[23] They killed a member of the Provincial Assembly. They attacked government security forces with rocket propelled grenades. They blocked major roads, including the Karakoram Highway connecting Pakistan to China, and captured the Saidu Sharif airport—thereby controlling the main transportation links between Malakand and the rest of the province.[24] They fought fiercely, and were well equipped with ammunition, machine guns, and guerrilla war booklets in Urdu and Pashto.[25] "Within one day of the uprising," a local journalist recounted, "the militant group's flag was seen fluttering atop most government buildings from Mingora to Matta, and Khwazakhela to Ammandarra. This was nothing short of an insurgency."[26]

Sufi Muhammad was quick to express his displeasure with the militancy of his subordinates within the TNSM: "To take up arms against an Islamic government is stupidity... I have never called for such an action."[27] But this was a post facto rationalization: His rhetoric from the preceding months was both confrontational and full of references of a jihad for shariah in Malakand.[28] Sufi Muhammad at first refused to negotiate with the provincial chief minister Aftab Sherpao, but eventually accepted a cease-fire and the government's shariah proposal on November 6. This followed several days of intensive paramilitary operations against the TNSM insurgents in which many were

[22] Shah, *De Shariat Karwan*, chap. 21; Zaffar Abbas, "Turban Guerrillas," *Herald*, November 1994; Adnan Adil, "Seven Days That Shook Swat," *Friday Times*, November 10, 1994.

[23] U.S. Consulate Peshawar, "Shariat Activists Kill MPA, Occupy Airport in Swat" (PESHAWAR 1031 (CONFIDENTIAL), November 4, 1994), Declassified under FOIA request by the author.

[24] "MNA, Several Others Taken Hostage," *Dawn*, November 5, 1994; A.S. Yousufi and Intikhab Amir, "14 Killed as Army Cracks Down on TNSM Men," *Dawn*, November 6, 1994; Adil, "Seven Days That Shook Swat"; U.S. Consulate Peshawar, "TNSM Activists Resist Government Forces in Bajaur, Politicians Worried, Karakoram Highway Remains Blocked" (PESHAWAR 1058 (CONFIDENTIAL), November 14, 1994), Declassified under FOIA request by the author.

[25] Muhammad Ihtesham Khan, interview by Joshua White, English, March 3, 2011.

[26] Abbas, "Turban Guerrillas."

[27] Rahimullah Yusufzai and Tahir Mehdi, "The Way of the Sufi," *Newsline*, November 1994; Intikhab Amir, "Shariat Enforced in Malakand Div and Kohistan," *Dawn*, November 4, 1994.

[28] "TNSM Chief Has Changed His Stand," *Dawn*, November 15, 1994.

killed and captured.[29] The combination of Sufi Muhammad's pleas for a cessation of fighting and the government's robust paramilitary response led the TNSM to release their hostages and capitulate by November 9.[30]

Even as the crisis was winding down in Swat, it flared up in neighboring Bajaur, where the paramilitary forces were engaged in flanking maneuvers to regain control of the major road leading into Swat.[31] Here, the TNSM cadres fought with unusual intensity, with both sides using heavy weapons and taking casualties.[32] The TNSM fighters in Bajaur were apparently armed with Russian-made weapons, including mortars, and were seen by government officials as being "more TNSM than the TNSM [in Swat]."[33] A confidential cable sent from the U.S. Consulate in Peshawar reported that "equipped with light cannons, rocket launchers, and AK-47s, an estimated 200 TNSM members reportedly were digging in at strategic locations in the [Bajaur] agency."[34] The fighting in Bajaur may have been fed by the participation of Afghan militant groups, including those linked to the Taliban, but also may have owed its longevity to economic factors; according to one government official, "no less than 80,000 logs were smuggled from the Dir district to Bajaur Agency and elsewhere in the tribal area" during the uprising, suggesting that many local figures had incentives to prolong the conflict.[35]

Although the conflict between the TNSM and the government in Malakand Division continued intermittently into the middle of 1995—when, for example, Sufi Muhammad and a crowd of his followers in June again occupied government offices in Swat—by December 1994 the insurgency had largely burned out. In part this was due to the paramilitary operations,

[29] A. S. Yousufi and Intikhab Amir, "Swat Airport Recaptured," *Dawn*, November 7, 1994; M. Zahid and Fazle Subhan, "TNSM Frees 60 Hostages: Normalcy Returns to Malakand," *Frontier Post*, November 9, 1994.

[30] Intikhab Amir, "Militants Release Hostages: Life Normal," *Dawn*, November 9, 1994; Adil, "Seven Days That Shook Swat."

[31] Aftab Sherpao, interview by Joshua White, English, February 17, 2011.

[32] Ahmad Hassan, "Bajaur Crisis Continues," *Dawn*, November 11, 1994; "Militants, Security Forces Clash in Bajaur," *Dawn*, November 12, 1994; A. S. Yousufi, "Mopping Up Operation Begins in Bajaur," *Dawn*, November 17, 1994; "Destruction, Release of Hostages and Arrest of Militants in Bajaur Agency," *Dawn*, November 18, 1994.

[33] Intikhab Amir and Ahmad Hassan, "Situation in Bajaur Still Fluid," *Dawn*, November 15, 1994; Ijaz Rahim, interview by Joshua White, English, February 15, 2011.

[34] U.S. Consulate Peshawar, "Troops Move In as Malakand Crisis Takes Toll in Lives and Credibility of NWFP Government" (PESHAWAR 1036 (CONFIDENTIAL), November 6, 1994), Declassified under FOIA request by the author. A cable sent the next day reported that "according to government sources, the 'civil compound' in the Bajaur agency administration center of Khar was 'under siege' by scores, possibly hundreds, of TNSM supporters . . . . " U.S. Consulate Peshawar, "Government 'Clean-Up' Operation in Malakand Division Area Begins to Take Hold; Another ANP MPA Joins Sherpao's Frontier Government" (PESHAWAR 1043 (CONFIDENTIAL), November 7, 1994), Declassified under FOIA request by the author.

[35] Mehdi, "Malakand's Holy War," 32.

and in part to the political shrewdness of the provincial government, which mollified protesters with a new and largely procedural shariah ordinance called the Nifaz-e-Nizam-e-Shariah (Enforcement of the System of Shariah) Regulation.

6.2.3 Explaining the TNSM

The historiography of the TNSM uprising remains unsettled. Some commentators have focused on the lack of an efficient judicial system as a key driver of social discontent. Others have suggested that the TNSM leveraged existing tribal and class conflicts to attract dispossessed farmers and peasants to the movement.[36] Still other scholars, most notably Sultan-i-Rome, have argued persuasively that the TNSM in fact attracted a significant following of large landholders who were principally concerned about the prospect of losing the tax advantages that accrued to them, first under the princely states and later under the PATA regulations.[37] Similarly, timber traders and smugglers were said to be worried that changes to the legal regime would be disadvantageous to their interests and historic prerogatives.[38] Regardless, however, of which of these factors was most significant, it was clear that the TNSM was able to benefit from multiple vectors of social, economic, and political discontent and draw together religious figures, large landholders, timber smugglers, tenant farmers, and opportunistic political opponents of the newly installed provincial government.

The movement was also influenced by the ideology of its leaders, who were decidedly ambiguous about what shariah demanded but consistently critical of democracy. Sufi Muhammad was perhaps the most famous alumnus of the Deobandi Panjpiri school of thought, a relatively obscure movement founded by Maulana Muhammad Tahir Panjpiri that became influential among the religious elite of district Swabi, parts of Malakand Division, and the Badakhshan, Kunar, and Nuristan provinces of Afghanistan.[39]

[36] Sartaj Khan, "Behind the Crisis in Swat," *The News*, November 27, 2008, https://web.archive.org/web/20141016085712/http://www.thenews.com.pk/PrintEdition.aspx?ID=149242&Cat=9&dt=11/27/2008; Sartaj Khan, "Imperialism, Religion and Class in Swat," *International Socialism*, no. 123 (June 24, 2009), https://isj.org.uk/imperialism-religion-and-class-in-swat/; Robert Nichols, "Class, State, and Power in Swat Conflict," in *Beyond Swat: History, Society and Economy Along the Afghanistan-Pakistan Frontier*, ed. Magnus Marsden and Benjamin Hopkins (Oxford: Oxford University Press, 2012), 140.

[37] See Sultan-i-Rome, "The 'Class War' Dimension of the Swat Crises," *Journal of Pakistan Historical Society* 63, no. 1 (2015): 49–76.

[38] See Rana, "Backgrounder: Shariah Movement in Malakand"; Sultan-i-Rome, "Forest Governance in Transition: From the Princely State of Swat, and Kalam to the State of Pakistan," WP2/IP6 Working Paper No. 9 (National Centre of Competence in Research North-South, 2008).

[39] Olivier Roy, "The Taliban: A Strategic Tool for Pakistan," in *Pakistan: Nationalism Without a Nation?*, ed. Christophe Jaffrelot (New York: Zed Books, 2002), 153–54.

Maulana Tahir followed a curious intellectual path. He studied at the famous Dar ul-Ulum Deoband madrassah in modern-day Uttar Pradesh and, like many early Deobandis, took an oath in the Naqshbandi Sufi order.[40] He later traveled to Arabia in 1938 for Hajj, and stayed on to study in Mecca and Medina. There he became enamored with Wahhabi teachings, which he brought back to India when he established his own madrassah in Panjpir. His emphasis from that time forward was fixated on opposing innovation in religious practice, and veneration of saints and of the prophet Muhammad. The Panjpiris came to be known as the Wahhabis of the Deobandi movement, and to this day remain focused on opposing certain practices—such as, apparently, the use of collared shirts—which they consider to be modern and un-Islamic.[41]

One of Maulana Tahir's key preoccupations was the inadequacy of modern democracy. According to one biographer, he "was deadly against the political system of the Western type," and urged his followers not to take part in Western-style politics.[42] As a young man, he had actively participated in the jihad of Haji Sahib Turangzai in Dir against the British in the 1930s (for which he was arrested and kept in detention for four months) and, later, had written in support of the anti-British agitator the Faqir of Ipi in the 1940s.[43] After Pakistan's independence, however, he adopted a certain political quietism, cautioning that Muslims should keep a distance from politics.[44] He wrote fiercely against Maulana Maududi, founder of the Jamaat-e-Islami, dedicating an entire book to refuting his views on political participation, and comparing him to the Shia and the Jews.[45] He also wrote against, inter alia, Maulana Abdul Haq, the father of Sami ul-Haq of the JUI-S, and Maulana Hassan Jan, a leading Deobandi cleric in Peshawar long affiliated with the JUI-F.[46] In this respect, the Panjpiri movement provided an ideological foundation for opposition in Malakand to democratic institutions, but also more specifically to the Jamaat-e-Islami and the JUI parties. Sufi Muhammad's affiliation with the Panjpiris also explains in part his eventual split with the JI, chronicled later in this chapter.[47]

[40] Muhammad Muttahir, "The Religious Thought of Maulana Muhammad Tahir Panjpiri" (M. A. Thesis, Peshawar, Pakistan Study Centre, University of Peshawar, 1991), 20.

[41] Husnul Amin, interview by Joshua White, English, February 21, 2011.

[42] Muttahir, "The Religious Thought of Maulana Muhammad Tahir Panjpiri," 119–22.

[43] Muttahir, "The Religious Thought of Maulana Muhammad Tahir Panjpiri," 37–39.

[44] Muhammad Amir Rana, interview by Joshua White, English, February 14, 2011.

[45] Muttahir, "The Religious Thought of Maulana Muhammad Tahir Panjpiri," 67–68.

[46] Saleem Safi, interview by Joshua White, English, March 2, 2011.

[47] Panjpiri influence on the events of 1994 extended even beyond these ideological factors. The Panjpiris founded a movement, *Jamā'at Ishā'at at-Tauḥīd o Sunnah* (Group for the Propagation of the Oneness of God and the Traditions of the Prophet), which was led by Maulana Tahir's son, Maulana Tayyab, who took over the main madrassah upon his father's death. Tayyab, according to some reports, "played an instigatory role contributing to the militancy" of the TNSM. Equally significant was the role played by Tayyab's brother, Major Muhammad Amir, a former ISI officer who gained some infamy for his involvement in

The TNSM was clear from the outset that it took a dim view of democracy and was not a political party.[48] One of the three principles on which it was founded was "boycott" (the others being "unity" and "jihad").[49] Initially, the movement was not strictly opposed to elections, but at some point that changed. According to reporting by the U.S. Consulate in Peshawar, the TNSM was "calling the elections un-Islamic and distributing pamphlets labeling voters as sinners."[50]

Syed Ali Shah, Sufi Muhammad's compatriot, devoted an entire chapter of his book describing the flaws of Western democracy.[51] He argued—in ways that, we will examine below, contrast sharply with the political ideologies of the religious parties—that Pakistan's Western-style democracy has three critical flaws. First, it weights the vote of all citizens equally. He quotes the Quran to suggest that since two women are equivalent to one man as witnesses, a similar ratio should apply in voting.[52] Second, he criticizes the majoritarian principle of modern democracy, arguing that reliance on the views of the common people will lead to evil.[53] Third, he condemns democracy for allowing un-Islamic officials to persist in public office: "People who vote in selecting these assembly members are also the shareholders in the sins these members commit . . . . In Islam, there is no tolerance for the wrongdoer to be a ruler even for a minute."[54] This last point in particular draws implicitly from the logic ascribed to Ibn Taymiyyah, whose fatawa have controversially been read to challenge the legitimacy of Muslim rulers who fail in the course of their official duties to enforce shariah.

The TNSM's opinions about shariah were equally forceful but decidedly more vague. Syed Ali Shah argued that shariah would put a stop to the ills that were plaguing Malakand, including murders, the use of interest in lending, insurance policies, alcohol, drugs, theft, robbery, bribery, and the revealing attire worn by women.[55] Sufi Muhammad was even less specific in identifying what his shariah reforms would actually look like. He proposed the establishment of religious courts, in which the local Islamic judge

the Operation Midnight Jackal scandal in 1989 that sought to topple Benazir Bhutto's PPP government. See Abbas, "Turban Guerrillas"; Shah, *De Shariat Karwan*, chap. 4; "Return of the Jackals" (Dawn News, September 2009).

[48] Marwat and Toru, *Talibanization of Pakistan*, 12.

[49] Marwat and Toru, *Talibanization of Pakistan*, 15. See also Shah, *De Shariat Karwan*, chap. 12.

[50] U.S. Consulate Peshawar, "Shariat Law Activists Take Hostages in Malakand Division" (PESHAWAR 1027 (LOU), November 3, 1994), Decontrolled under FOIA request by the author.

[51] Shah, *De Shariat Karwan*, chap. 10.

[52] The verse quoted is, ". . . get two witnesses, out of your own men, and if there are not two men, then a man and two women, such as ye choose, for witnesses . . . . " *Qur'ān*, 2:282.

[53] Here he quotes, "Wert thou to follow the common run of those on earth, they will lead thee away from the way of Allah." *Qur'ān*, 6:116.

[54] Shah, *De Shariat Karwan*, chap. 10.

[55] Shah, *De Shariat Karwan*, chap. 20.

would have near-complete powers to decide cases according to shariah—decisions that could not be appealed. But beyond this, his vision seemed ill-defined. One journalist who interviewed him in May 1994 complained that he was "unable to explain what laws he wants as he does not believe in formulating written laws and cannot identify a set of laws which he can declare Islamic."[56] Another journalist interviewing him in December of that year left similarly exasperated: Sufi Muhammad would only say that he wanted "Islamic laws which are strictly in accordance with Quran and Sunnah."

6.3 The Role of the Islamist Parties

We now consider how the Islamist parties responded to the rise of TNSM and its violent confrontation with the state. This section begins with a brief discussion of the political context in which these events took place, followed by more detailed explorations of how the JI, JUI-F, and JUI-S wrestled with the political, structural, and ideological pressures that the TNSM's violence created.

6.3.1 The Political Context

The major clashes between the TNSM and the government occurred during the year following the October 1993 general elections, the third election since the end of Zia ul-Haq's rule and the restoration of democratic politics. In 1988, Benazir Bhutto's PPP had gained a majority; in 1990, Nawaz Sharif's PML had dominated; and in 1993, the PPP again won an upper hand. The politics of the so-called decade of democracy between 1988 and 1999 were, however, messier than the top-line national election results might suggest. The 1990 elections had been marred by blatant manipulation by the Pakistani security establishment—a fact since admitted by then-Director General of the ISI, Asad Durrani.[57] Although the vote that followed, in 1993, was judged by international observers to be relatively free and fair, it did not produce a particularly decisive outcome.[58] Neither the PPP nor the PML-N garnered an outright majority; it was only after the PPP allied with Manzoor Wattoo's

[56] Zaidi and Khan, "Holy Law," 45.
[57] Salman Masood and Declan Walsh, "Pakistan's High Court Resurrects Election Tampering Case," *New York Times*, February 29, 2012.
[58] See, for example, National Democratic Institute, "The 1993 Elections in Pakistan" (Washington, DC: National Democratic Institute, 1994).

PML-J and independent politicians that it was able to form a fragile coalition government at the federal level and in Punjab.

In the NWFP, Benazir Bhutto's position was even worse. There, the PML-N had formed a coalition government with the Pashtun nationalist Awami National Party (ANP), and had installed a PML-N-supporting independent, Pir Sabir Shah, as the province's chief minister. The PPP-led coalition in Islamabad was worried about its opposition's foothold in the Frontier, and set about immediately trying to undermine the Sabir Shah government. It eventually did so in late February 1994, when it convinced a number of NWFP Provincial Assembly members—with promise of incentives from the central government—to switch sides and caucus with the PPP.[59] Far from being an organic uprising against the incumbent provincial government, this was a carefully staged parliamentary coup by Benazir's advisors: "the government ferried [the defecting MPAs] from Islamabad to Peshawar in three helicopters . . . [the] Federal Minister of Interior received them at Peshawar's Army Stadium. They were guarded and escorted by hundreds of battle-ready soldiers" to the assembly building, then returned just as quickly to Islamabad.[60] Having at last secured a majority in the assembly, the PPP appointed Aftab Sherpao as chief minister in late March 1994.

The result of this political drama in the NWFP was two-fold. It produced an unusually bitter political environment in the province. And it created ongoing incentives for the PML-N and ANP opposition to retake the assembly. Chief Minister Sherpao's margin was razor thin, so much so that even a provincial by-election (that is, a special election) for a single vacated seat would take on enormous political importance. This is precisely what happened in late 1994, just as the TNSM was gaining momentum in Malakand.

Pakistan's Islamist parties also found themselves in a changed political environment following the 1993 elections. In the 1998 and 1990 elections, the JI had participated as an active member of the IJI, an umbrella group that was fashioned by the intelligence agencies and led by the PML-N to counter the influence of the PPP. In the run-up to the 1993 polls, the party re-evaluated its participation in the IJI. Some leaders felt as though the party was losing its distinctive identity and advantages by participating in the alliance.[61] The PML-N was also becoming less enamored with the JI's contribution.[62] The

[59] Tahir Amin, "Pakistan in 1994: The Politics of Confrontation," *Asian Survey* 35, no. 2 (February 1995): 142.

[60] Eqbal Ahmed, "Parliamentary Hara-Kiri," *Dawn*, March 6, 1994.

[61] Mohammad Waseem, *The 1993 Elections in Pakistan* (Lahore: Vanguard, 1994), 105.

[62] The PML-N saw that the JI was losing ground in Karachi to the MQM. The two parties also diverged on policy toward Afghanistan; the PML-N recognized the government led by Mojaddedi, against strong opposition from the JI, which favored Rabbani. Abdul Rashid Moten, "Mawdudi and the Transformation

amir, Qazi Hussain Ahmad, steered the party to create and contest from a new alliance platform, the Pakistan Islamic Front (PIF), of which the JI was the only significant member, and adopt a more populist campaign narrative.[63]

The JI's strategy was an utter failure.[64] It was "completely routed" in the 1993 elections, winning only three seats from the eighty candidates it fielded for the National Assembly.[65] Qazi Hussain Ahmad faced recriminations from the party faithful, who could not understand what the JI gained from distancing itself from a successful alliance and creating a new, unsuccessful, brand. He resigned in January 1994, only to be re-elected with a three-quarters vote of confidence in February.[66] The result of these machinations was that, by spring 1994, the party was still smarting from a dismal electoral showing; conflicted about its leaders' new populist bent; and eager to find ways to regain its political momentum.

The JUI-F, which had contested elections under its own name in the previous two contests, decided in 1993 to form an alliance with the Barelvi Jamiat Ulama-e-Pakistan (JUP), under the name of the Islami Jamhuri Muhaz (Islamic Democratic Front). As if the religious party scene were not fragmented enough, the JUI-S decided to join a third religious alliance, along with other parties including the militantly anti-Shia Sipah-e-Sahabah Pakistan (SSP), which they called the Muttahida Dini Muhaz (United Religious Front; MDM).[67] To further complicate matters, the JUI-F entered into a seat adjustment agreement with the PPP and PML-J in the NWFP. Effectively, the PPP "bargained for more seats in the province in exchange for fewer seats in the National Assembly," because it wanted to control the Provincial Assembly.[68] This made the JUI-F a partner of sorts with the PPP, and gave the PPP an incentive following the elections to court the JUI-F as part of its plan to dethrone Shabir Shah from Peshawar.

For this and other reasons, the PPP invited the JUI-F to join the coalition government in late 1993. The deal resulted in some measure of cooperation in the NWFP, but also in a prominent appointment of the JUI-F's leader, Maulana Fazl ur-Rahman, to the chairmanship of the National Assembly's standing committee on foreign affairs. Thus it was that by spring 1994, the

of Jama'at-e-Islam in Pakistan," *The Muslim World* 93, no. 3–4 (July 2003): 403, https://doi.org/10.1111/1478-1913.00029.

[63] Nisar Osmani, "What Now That the Qazi Is Back?," *Dawn*, March 1, 1994; Vali Nasr, "Military Rule, Islamism and Democracy in Pakistan," *Middle East Journal* 58, no. 2 (Spring 2004): 198.

[64] Waseem, *The 1993 Elections in Pakistan*, 91.

[65] Rasul Bakhsh Rais, "Elections, Regime Change, and Democracy," in *State, Society and Democratic Change in Pakistan*, ed. Rasul Bakhsh Rais (Karachi: Oxford University Press, 1997), 269.

[66] "Qazi Back as Jamaat Chief," *Dawn*, February 28, 1994.

[67] Waseem, *The 1993 Elections in Pakistan*, 92.

[68] Waseem, *The 1993 Elections in Pakistan*, 174.

JUI-F was a visible member of the PPP-led government coalition, both in NWFP and at the federal level. Its role as a member of the status-quo political coalition would affect its response to the TNSM uprising over the year that followed.

6.3.2 The JI and "Fortress Dir"

The Jamaat-e-Islami had a longstanding base of support in Malakand Division, particularly in Dir and to a lesser extent in Chitral. The Nawab of Dir tolerated the party's presence, unlike in neighboring Swat, where the Wali banned them from operating. (The Wali, according to his grandson, personally ordered Qazi Hussain Ahmad, then a young JI cleric, removed when he tried to settle in Swat.[69]) During the time of the Nawab, the JI "chose a few religious families in Dir" through which to establish itself.[70] The most prominent of these was the family of Sahibzada Saifullah. In the 1970 election, Saifullah won one of the four National Assembly seats that went to the JI; and his fellow party member in Dir, a veterinarian named Dr. Yaqoob Khan, won one of the four NWFP Provincial Assembly seats that went to the party.[71]

The party faced increased competition in the early 1970s following the government's decision to constitute a Dir-Swat Land Disputes Enquiry Commission in late 1970, which gave the PPP a political advantage over the JI in the region.[72] By 1977, however, the JI was again looking strong. Saifullah won his National Assembly seat a second time, and JI party members won in Swat and Malakand Agency as well. This meant that fully a third of the party's nine seats in the National Assembly were from Malakand Division. When General Zia ul-Haq took power in a coup shortly after the 1977 elections, the JI's prospects improved even further. The party cooperated with Zia, until the partnership began to sour in 1984. The party's candidates nonetheless performed well in the 1985 nonparty general elections. Aided by the decision of leftist and center-right parties to boycott the polls, the JI won ten National Assembly seats, three of which were from Malakand Division, and five Provincial Assembly seats, three of which were from Dir alone.[73]

Dir thus represented throughout the 1970s and 1980s a disproportionately significant electoral stronghold for the JI, and they "very jealously

[69] Adnan Aurangzeb, interview by Joshua White, English, May 13, 2011.
[70] Muhammad Ihtesham Khan, interview.
[71] Asim Hussain, "Lessons from Past Failures Gave Birth to MMA," *The News*, October 1, 2002.
[72] Muhammad Ihtesham Khan, interview.
[73] Seyyed Vali Reza Nasr, *The Vanguard of the Islamic Revolution: The Jama'at-i Islami of Pakistan* (Berkeley: University of California Press, 1994), chap. 9.

guarded their fort" by attempting to preempt political competition throughout Malakand Division.[74] If anything, this imperative grew in the late 1980s as the rise of the Muhajir Qaumi Movement (MQM) party in Karachi cut deeply into the JI's middle class constituency in Sindh.[75] These dynamics, taken together, meant that by the early 1990s Malakand was critical electoral geography for the party.

The party little expected that its fiercest competition in Malakand would come from one of its own, Sufi Muhammad. Most reports claim that, in the years prior to 1990, Sufi Muhammad was a member of the party's district council in Dir, though some sources argue that he was just a regular member without any notable leadership role.[76] Regardless, it is clear that several months before the scheduled general elections in October 1990, Sufi Muhammad had a falling out with the JI, and particularly with the provincial amir, Dr. Yaqub.[77] He called for a boycott of the polls, but JI leaders received orders from their national headquarters to reject the boycott, and Yaqub narrowly won the election.[78] The next general election, in 1993, was even worse for the JI: it was a humiliating defeat on the national stage.[79] In NWFP, the JI won only four Provincial Assembly seats, and Dr. Yaqub lost his seat to the PPP, apparently on account of Sufi Muhammad's opposition.[80] In three short years, the JI's electoral fortress in Malakand had begun to crumble.

In the months preceding the violent confrontation between the TNSM and the government in early November 1994, the JI was initially supportive of the TNSM's protests. Reporters noted participation of some JI members in the protests, including party workers who had come from areas outside of Malakand to demonstrate.[81] Given the degree of institutionalization within the party, as detailed in Chapter 4, this almost certainly signals that the protests had the support of the provincial party leadership. Indeed, it appears that JI notables in Malakand saw opportunity in the TNSM's protests to advance their own Islamization agenda.[82]

[74] Asif Luqman Qazi, interview by Joshua White, English, May 25, 2011.

[75] Farhat Haq, "Rise of the MQM in Pakistan: Politics of Ethnic Mobilization," *Asian Survey* 35, no. 11 (November 1995): 998ff.

[76] Ikram Hoti, "The Crusade of Maulana Sufi Mohammad," *Friday Times*, May 19, 1994; Asif Luqman Qazi, interview.

[77] Hoti, "The Crusade of Maulana Sufi Mohammad." Some date the split to 1988. Muhammad Ibrahim Khan, interview by Joshua White, English and Urdu, trans. Shuja Malik, March 9, 2011.

[78] Shah, *De Shariat Karwan*, chap. 1. When asked whether the JI or Sufi Muhammad initiated the split, the son of the former central amir replied only, "If you are not comfortable with a friend, he is not comfortable with you." Asif Luqman Qazi, interview.

[79] Nasr, "Military Rule, Islamism and Democracy in Pakistan," 198ff.

[80] Hoti, "The Crusade of Maulana Sufi Mohammad."

[81] Abbas, "Showdown in Malakand."

[82] "Enforcement of Shariat Laws in Malakand Urged," *Dawn*, May 9, 1994.

This strategy held several advantages for the JI. It allowed the party to present the TNSM as an ally, so as to appeal to its local constituency and not create a deeper rift between the two organizations; and, at the same time, to finger the TNSM as a mercurial and potentially dangerous actor whose demands must be met lest chaos ensue. It was a nearly cost-free means of threatening the government and advancing its own agenda.[83]

After the government killed protesters in Buner, the JI sensed a new opportunity, joining the TNSM in criticizing the government (which, it claimed breathlessly, "had revived the memories of the English rulers by shedding the blood of the people").[84] The central party amir Qazi Hussain Ahmad made a point of personally meeting with Sufi Muhammad and voicing his support for the TNSM.[85] Not long after, in a pointed Friday sermon delivered at the JI headquarters in Mansurah, the amir escalated his rhetoric even further, noting a resemblance between the Buner killings and the February 1994 incident in the Palestinian West Bank in which a Jewish settler killed twenty-nine Muslim worshippers, and wounded 125, at the Cave of the Patriarchs in Al-Khalil (Hebron). Comparing the Pakistani government to Jewish extremists, he decried that it was impossible to criticize the *actual* Jews in Israel, the Serbs in Bosnia, or the Indian army in Kashmir so long as the Pakistani government was preying on Muslims in its own territory.[86]

In early October, the party made public plans for a large gathering in Peshawar and, according to one contemporary report, "threatened to wage jihad until the administration implemented shariah law in Malakand."[87] They warned the provincial government not to thwart the rally, and then made political hay of the government's threat to impose section 144 of the Code of Criminal Procedure, prohibiting "unlawful assembly."[88] When the event eventually did take place, it took on the character of an anti-PPP and anti-PML rally; again, Qazi Hussain Ahmad indirectly wielded the threat of

[83] See also "Jamaat Mounts Pressure for Shariat," *Dawn*, May 10, 1994.

[84] "JI Launching Protest Strike Today," *Dawn*, May 17, 1994. See also ʿAbd uṣ-Ṣamad Ṣāfī, "agar ḥukūmat ne mālākanḍ meṅ vāqiʿī sharīʿat nāfiẕ kar dī hai to shahudāʾe būner ko sharaʿī diyat dī jāʾe: amīr jamāʿat-e islamī ṣūbah sarḥad profesur muḥamad ibrāhīm se inṭarviū [If the Government has Truly Implemented Shariah in Malakand, then Blood Money in Accordance with Shariah Should be Given to the Martyrs of Buner. Interview with the NWFP Provincial Amir of Jamaat-e Islami, Prof Muhammad Ibrahim]," *Haft Rozah Aishyā (Asia)* 43, no. 25 (June 19, 1994): 19–22.

[85] Ahmad Hassan, "Tribesmen End Campaign, Malakand Reopened," *Dawn*, May 18, 1994.

[86] Qāẓī Ḥussain Aḥmad, "būner meṅ qatl-e ʿām ẕālimānah aur sifākānah iqdām hai [The Mass Murder in Buner is a Cruel Step]," *Haft Rozah Aishyā (Asia)* 43, no. 23 (June 5, 1994): 9.

[87] U.S. Consulate Peshawar, "Opposition Protest in Peshawar Uneventful; Some ANP-PML(N) Leaders Remain Jailed" (PESHAWAR 925 (CONFIDENTIAL), October 4, 1994), Declassified under FOIA request by the author.

[88] Malick, "NWFP Govt Warned on Shariat Moot," *Dawn*, October 6, 1994; "Shariat: Govt Not Fulfilling Its Promises: JI," *Dawn*, October 7, 1994.

TNSM violence, arguing that unless the government deals with "obscenity, vulgarity and pornography," then "people would force them to do so."[89] The party also sponsored a resolution in the Provincial Assembly, passed unanimously, that urged the federal government to implement a shariah system in Malakand Division.[90]

Direct involvement by the JI in the TNSM's activities at this stage was carefully calibrated. The party praised the TNSM's advocacy of shariah, but worked quietly to undermine the movement and minimize the fallout of its anti-electoral position. In the run-up to the Buner by-election in November, Qazi Hussain Ahmad made the case that only the JI would be able to implement the shariah in Malakand, criticizing the ability of the TNSM to deliver on its promises.[91] One government official who was present in Malakand as the events unfolded recalled watching Dr. Yaqub of the JI walk this fine line:

> Yaqub would send his people to the TNSM procession, have them leave before the lathi-charge [crowd dispersal by the police], then tell the Chief Minister to take action against Sufi Muhammad! . . . JI was taking the role of the spoiler . . . [it] wanted the government to go after Sufi Muhammad so that they would have electoral gain.[92]

The party appears to have been able to exert pressure on its local leadership to hew to this kind of quietly subversive policy, but had somewhat less success with the local party members. One young cleric from a JI-affiliated family in Dir explained that some members were indeed active in both groups. Speaking of his father, he recalled: "His oath was to JI, but he never missed a Sufi Muhammad rally."[93] In this vein, one confidential cable from the U.S. Consulate in Peshawar titled, "Who Bears the Shariat Torch in the Frontier?" recalled that:

> [D]uring the May protests, the JI leadership made repeated attempts to join in the TNSM's discussions with the government, and gain prominent positions in photo coverage of the demonstrations—those efforts were contemptuously rebuffed by the TNSM leaders who viewed the JI as talkers not doers. Many JI and Jamiat Ulema-i-Islam (JUI) members have defected to join the TNSM ranks.[94]

[89] "Islamic Revolution Within 3 Years, Says Qazi," *Dawn*, October 9, 1994.
[90] "Islamic System for Malakand Demanded," *Dawn*, October 21, 1994.
[91] Intikhab Amir, "Only Jamaat Can Enforce Shariat, Says Qazi," *Dawn*, November 3, 1994.
[92] Muhammad Ihtesham Khan, interview.
[93] Muhammad Rashid, interview by Joshua White, English, March 6, 2011.
[94] U.S. Consulate Peshawar, "Who Bears the Shariat Torch in the Frontier?" (PESHAWAR 953 (CONFIDENTIAL), October 13, 1994), Declassified under FOIA request by the author.

The party seems to have faced the prospect of its local members participating in the TNSM activities—indeed, at times they were being encouraged to do so—but this also entailed the risk of them actually defecting to the new movement.[95]

There is little information available about the JI's reactions while the events of November 1994 were actually unfolding. One journalist from Dir recounted that, during the midst of the crisis when the roads to Malakand were blocked, Sufi Muhammad met with Qazi Hussain, who counseled him not to compromise with the government. Sufi Muhammad ostensibly replied that he was now the leader of Malakand Division, and did not need to be given advice by the JI amir.[96]

This rebuff did not seem to dampen the party's enthusiasm for using the Malakand crisis to further several of its interrelated political goals: weakening the provincial government; putting itself forward as the true champion of shariah; reestablishing its electoral dominance; and using the TNSM as a foil from which to urge the "responsible" implementation of shariah. All of these themes were evident in the days immediately following the uprising. The JI blamed the government for the outbreak of violence and argued that the protesters were presenting legitimate demands for shariah.[97] Aftab Sherpao was particularly vilified by the party, which went so far as to claim that his government's chief secretary "belongs to Qadiani [Ahmadi] group" and does not want shariah implemented.[98] Even the relatively mild-mannered JI provincial amir Ibrahim Khan accused the president, prime minister, chief minister, and governor of NWFP of being "infidels" for opposing Islamic injunctions.[99]

Following the outbreak of violent protest in early November, the JI employed a fresh version of its argument indirectly threatening violence if shariah was not enforced. Whereas previously they threatened that the Malakand protests might get out of hand, they now broached the possibility that violent protest for shariah would spread throughout Pakistan, warning that "people would feel compelled to adopt methods similar to those of [TNSM]."[100] Simultaneously, JI leaders in the province criticized the army

[95] Saleem Safi, interview.

[96] Islamuddin Sajid, interview by Joshua White, English and Urdu, trans. Shuja Malik, February 18, 2011.

[97] Khan, "'Malakand Incident—Extension of Afghan War'"; "JI Leaders' Concern Over Malakand Situation," *Frontier Post*, November 7, 1994; "JI Holds Sherpao Responsible for Clash," *Dawn*, November 7, 1994.

[98] "'Sherpao Govt Responsible for Malakand Situation,'" *Frontier Post*, November 15, 1994.

[99] "Jamaat Rally Protests Action Against TNSM," *Frontier Post*, November 19, 1994.

[100] "Nine Religious Parties Call for Shariat Laws in Country," *Frontier Post*, November 6, 1994; "No Foreign Hand Behind TNSM Violence: Qazi," *Frontier Post*, November 8, 1994.

for supposedly overreacting to the crisis, and—unlike the PPP and JUI-F—expressed skepticism of the deal eventually reached between Sufi Muhammad and the government.[101]

The party continued to agitate against the government and in favor of shariah even after this deal was struck. It used the army's follow-on operations in Bajaur to justify a new wave of protests. On November 14, the "party high command . . . directed its district organizations throughout the province to hold meetings and take out protest processions in their respective districts."[102] These protests were duly organized, and took place in districts across the province.[103] (On November 17, it even held a joint rally with the JUI-S in the JUI-F stronghold of Bannu.[104]) The JI's superbly mobilized support for the vague shariah agenda of the TNSM was not, however, duly reciprocated by the movement. The TNSM leadership plainly saw the JI's intervention on behalf of shariah as being deeply linked to their own electoral interests in Malakand, and thus disconnected from the TNSM's agenda.[105]

6.3.3 The JUI Parties Respond

The JUI parties had dramatically less political influence in Malakand than the Jamaat-e-Islami. The JUI had boycotted the 1985 nonparty election held under Zia ul-Haq. In 1988, they made a strong showing, winning eight National Assembly seats, half of which were from NWFP, and twelve Provincial Assembly seats, two of which were from NWFP.[106] But the distribution of the seats in NWFP is telling. From the National Assembly, Mardan, Karak, Dera Ismail Khan, and Bannu; from the Provincial Assembly, Kohat and Kohistan. Most of these districts are in the southern part of the province, where the ulama parties have traditionally drawn their strength. Only two are near Malakand Division: Mardan abuts Malakand district from the south, and Kohistan abuts Swat from the east. Prior to the 1990 election, the JUI split into two factions, JUI-F and JUI-S. The JUI-F won six National Assembly seats, with NWFP representation in Charsadda, Mansehra, Kohistan, and

[101] Ihtashamul Haque, "Troika Discusses Malakand and Karachi Situation," *Dawn*, November 7, 1994; "Tension Brewing in Bajaur," *Frontier Post*, November 11, 1994.
[102] "NWFP JI to Observe Protest Day Tomorrow," *Frontier Post*, November 15, 1994.
[103] "JI Asks Govt to Stop Malakand Operation," *Frontier Post*, November 17, 1994; "JI Rallies Against Malakand Operations," *Dawn*, November 17, 1994.
[104] U.S. Consulate Peshawar, "NWFP Officials Meet as Deadline Approaches for Implementation of Shariah Regulations; Government Crack-Down in Bajaur Criticized" (PESHAWAR 1087 (CONFIDENTIAL), November 23, 1994), Declassified under FOIA request by the author.
[105] "TNSM Rejects Shariat Package," *Frontier Post*, November 25, 1994.
[106] Electoral tabulations drawn from data provided by the Election Commission of Pakistan, and the author's calculations.

Bannu; and two NWFP Provincial Assembly seats, in Kohistan and Bannu. In that election, in which the PML-led IJI dominated, the JUI-F did best in areas outside of its core southern constituency, with the notable exception of Bannu. The JUI-S won one National Assembly seat from Jhang (Maulana Azam Tariq, cofounder of the radical anti-Shia group Sipah-e-Sahabah). In the 1993 elections, the JUI-F's results declined even further. Contesting under the IJM banner, they won only four National Assembly seats, two of which (Swabi and Dera Ismail Khan) were in NWFP; and two Provincial Assembly seats in NWFP, in Bannu and Karak. The JUI-S once again won a single National Assembly seat from Jhang.

Neither the JUI-F nor JUI-S, therefore, had notable electoral interests in Malakand Division. They reacted to the TNSM as outsiders and not as parties trying to retain a longstanding electoral foothold. This dynamic is seen in the parties' slow and relatively muted response to the movement beginning in 1994. News reports from May of that year indicate that local JUI-F leaders joined an ulama rally criticizing the government's proposed shariah measures as inadequate, and condemning the government's use of force against protesters.[107] Even so, the "enthusiasm gap" between the JUI-F and the JI on the Malakand issue is evident from the Senate debates surrounding the Buner killings; while the JI amir Qazi Hussain Ahmad accused the government of ignoring a "burning issue," leading JUI-F Senator Hafiz Hussain Ahmad made use of his speaking time to complain about the lack of availability of chilled drinking water on the Senate floor.[108]

The JUI-S was in general more supportive of the TNSM than the JUI-F. This should not be a surprise, given that the two JUI factions split over whether or not to partner with the PPP government led by Benazir Bhutto; the JUI-S took a hard line against Bhutto, while the JUI-F was effectively acting as "sort of the PPP's ally" in NWFP in the months following the 1993 general election.[109] (The support of its two MPAs, who provisionally caucused with the PPP, was critical to Sherpao's majority in the assembly.[110]) The JUI-F was bound to be more sympathetic to the PPP and less welcoming of a movement that would challenge the Sherpao government. The JUI-S, feeling no such constraints, enthusiastically supported Sufi Muhammad. In August 1994, the flagship publication of Maulana Sami ul-Haq's

[107] "Ulema Stage Rally in Peshawar," *Dawn*, May 18, 1994.
[108] "Senate of Pakistan Debates: Official Report," 1994, vol. 4, no. 12 (Islamabad, May 19, 1994).
[109] A. S. Yousufi, "PF-63: The Most Hotly Contested By-Election," *Dawn*, November 3, 1994.
[110] U.S. Consulate Peshawar, "Troops Move In as Malakand Crisis Takes Toll in Lives and Credibility of NWFP Government."

movement, *al-Ḥaq* reported on a visit by clerics from Malakand to the madrassah. Sami ul-Haq subsequently wrote a letter to the clerics of the region, calling their movement for shariah "a very praiseworthy and daring step," pledging his support, and urging the ulama to cooperate with one another (and, presumably, the TNSM movement) for implementation of shariah.[111]

In November, an editorial in the same monthly publication lashed out at the government for its treatment of the TNSM, and praised the movement for the purity of its demands: "An apparently weak and feeble voice which was raised from the mountains of Malakand is now roaring all over the world and has rattled the edifices of Delhi, Moscow and Washington."[112] The editorial continued, situating the TNSM's actions in a world-historical frame, and labeling it a "*mujāhid* organization" under attack from the state. Although he and other JUI-S leaders in Pakistan praised the TNSM, the party does not appear to have taken any further action regarding the movement.[113]

The JUI-F, by far the larger of the ulama parties, faced a more complex set of incentives. Not only was it loosely partnering with the PPP government, but it stood to gain from the somewhat mild shariah measures that the state had proposed. Under the provincial government's offer, every district in Malakand Division would establish panels of up to thirty ulama to assist the courts in deciding both civil and criminal cases.[114] These clerics would almost certainly be drawn from JUI or JUI-affiliated ranks. Contemporaneous reporting and interviews suggest that the party leadership, free from having to consider direct electoral implications of their support, presented a "responsible" message at the senior leadership level, and otherwise took a hands-off approach.

The JUI-F amir, Maulana Fazl ur-Rahman, "disapproved of the use of force by Malakand agitators," one journalist noted, "but his views were apparently not shared by the rest of his party."[115] While, for example, the party's NWFP deputy amir warned that the unfolding violence in Malakand would "harm the cause of Islam" and that the JUI-F would support the government's efforts

[111] Shafīq ud-Dīn Fārūqī, "malākanḍ aur dīgar ejansiyoṅ ke fuẓalā' ḥaqqāniyah kī Maulānā Samī' ul-Ḥaq se mulāqāt: taḥrīk-e nifāẕ-e sharī'at kī ḥimāyat aur 'ulamā' o mashā'ikh ke nām aham peghām [Meeting of the Haqqaniyah Learned from Malakand and Other Agencies with Maulana Sami ul-Haq: An Important Message for the Ulema and Sheikhs in Support of Tahrik-e Nifaz-e Shariat]," *al-Ḥaq* 29, no. 11 (August 1994): 63–64.

[112] "malākanḍ aur bājauṛ ejansī meṅ nifāẕ-e sharī'at kī jad o jahad [The Struggle for Nifaz-e Shariat in Malakand and Bajaur Agency]," *al-Ḥaq* 30, no. 2 (November 1994): 2–8.

[113] See, for example, "Implementation of Islamic Laws Demanded," *Muslim*, November 13, 1994.

[114] "Frontier to Enforce Shariat Laws in Malakand Division," *Dawn*, November 2, 1994.

[115] Rehman, "The Lessons of Malakand."

to enforce shariah, the provincial amir in Sindh lashed out at the NWFP government, claiming that it had "deliberately" created chaos in Malakand.[116] The government's announcement that it had reached an agreement with Sufi Muhammad on a shariah plan did little to harmonize the JUI-F's messaging. On a single day, November 10, the JUI-F district amir in Karak was leading a procession in solidarity with the TNSM; JUI-F district leaders in Chitral were praising the government and passing judgment on the TNSM's behavior; and the JUI-F central amir Fazl ur-Rahman told a reporter that he had sent the TNSM leadership, "a message that the Ulema had not issued any edict for an armed struggle."[117] Message discipline was not the JUI-F's forte.

The JUI-F's rhetoric, like that of the JI, took a predictable turn in the days following the TNSM's violent uprising. As the violence spread to Buner, the JUI-F began joining the JI and other political parties in condemning the government's actions against the movement. The provincial party leadership "expressed grave concern over the bloodshed in Malakand and Bajaur," used the public's anger toward the government to push for rapid implementation of shariah, and delivered (empty) threats to leave the PPP coalition unless it carried out a new Islamic law agenda.[118]

6.4 Conclusion: The Logics of Anti-State Violence

We conclude here with two questions: What was the pattern of Islamist parties' responses to the TNSM's violent clashes with the government in 1994? And what seems to explain that pattern of responses?

The Jamaat-e-Islami adopted a complex posture toward the TNSM. It attempted to undermine the movement in private while at the same time supporting it in public. The JI's praise of the TNSM appears to have reached its peak at the moment when Sufi Muhammad's movement was most vocal and credible in its threats against the government, that is, in the days leading up to the November clashes. After the TNSM's violent confrontation with the state, the JI's rhetoric shifted to criticism of the government's actions, and more measured support of the TNSM itself. The JUI-S, by contrast,

[116] "TNSM's Extremism Harming Cause of Islam," *Frontier Post*, November 5, 1994; "JUI Blames Govt," *Dawn*, November 9, 1994.

[117] "Rally Demands Enforcement of Shariat Laws," *Frontier Post*, November 11, 1994; "Tension Brewing in Bajaur"; "Pakistan Should Concentrate on 1948 Resolution, Says Fazl," *Dawn*, November 11, 1994.

[118] "JUI-F Decry Bajaur Operation," *Frontier Post*, November 18, 1994; "JUI for Enforcement of Shariat in Malakand," *Frontier Post*, November 19, 1994; "'Govt Keen to Enforce Shariah in Malakand,'" *Frontier Post*, November 22, 1994; "'JUI(F) to Part Ways with Govt If Shariat Not Enforced,'" *Frontier Post*, November 23, 1994.

was enthusiastic in its support of the TNSM, while its larger Deobandi counterpart the JUI-F took a strikingly different posture: cautious and indisciplined.

To what extent were ideological debates central to the Islamist parties' responses to the TNSM uprising? All of the Islamist parties demonstrated some measure of ideological sympathy with the movement's demands. The JI leadership unquestionably had a more articulate vision of the kind of shariah it wanted to see in Malakand than did the TNSM. The party had, in fact, put up posters in the region detailing a twenty-three-point shariah agenda that covered the legal, educational, and financial sectors.[119] And it consistently advocated for those twenty-three points, rather than the shariah generalities of the TNSM.[120] In this sense, the JI and TNSM did not disagree about the substance of shariah, because the TNSM's objectives were too vague to discern. They did disagree publicly about the mechanism of implementation, that is, over the legitimacy of democratic process. The then-provincial amir of the JI, Muhammad Ibrahim Khan, admitted in an interview that democratic action formed the crux of the disagreement: "We had favored [Sufi Muhammad's] demand," he explained, "but he was apolitical. His basic concept was that democracy was kufr."[121]

The JUI parties were in a similar position as the JI: they agreed in general terms with the TNSM's vague advocacy for shariah reforms, but disagreed about its rejection of the democratic process. The JUI-F and JUI-S were at times unhappy with the so-called Wahhabi influence (and, by some accounts, funding) that the Panjpiris brought to Malakand, but both parties had significant ties to the Panjpiri networks.[122]

That the strikingly divergent responses by the Islamist parties do not seem to be attributable to ideological differences suggests that structural factors related to coalition politics and electoral competition, organizational coherence, and exposure to state pressure were paramount. This is particularly clear with respect to the JI, which saw the TNSM as a political danger. The party faced real and growing threats to its electoral dominance in Malakand in the early 1990s, and provincial leaders acknowledged that the TNSM's threatened boycotts negatively influenced the party's electoral prospects.[123]

[119] Ishtiaq Ahmad, "In the Killing Fields of Malakand," *Nation*, November 11, 1994.
[120] "Sherpao Criticised for Detaining Opposition Leader," *Frontier Post*, November 28, 1994.
[121] Muhammad Ibrahim Khan, interview.
[122] One former provincial official with access to intelligence reports claimed that "money started pouring in from Saudi Arabia" for the TNSM, by way of the Panjpiri madaris. Interview by the author, February 2011.
[123] Muhammad Ibrahim Khan, interview.

Its posture toward the TNSM makes sense in light of its efforts to manage this political competition.

Although the JI was not excited to see the rise of a challenger movement, it appears to have used the emergence of the TNSM as a foil with which to weaken the PPP-led provincial government, and advance the profile of its own signature issue, shariah implementation. And although the JI was not particularly effective in blunting the competitive effects of the TNSM's rise, the party's tight organizational structure both contributed to, and explains, its relatively coherent response to the challenge. The record and interviews both make clear that the party's response was directed with personal intervention by the central amir, Qazi Hussain Ahmad, with minimal public dissent from any other party leader at the provincial or district levels. For a party engaged in such a delicate balancing act with respect to new political competition—praising it in public while undermining it in private—this level of discipline is remarkable. It allowed the JI at times to ride on the TNSM's growing popularity without having to fear that the movement would entice away its own local cadres.

In this way, the JI's pattern of response is consistent with the two hypotheses described in Chapter 1. The party—bolstered by its programmatic linkages and organizational coherence—had relatively low vulnerability to the state, but relatively high vulnerability to the anti-state movement. It thus settled upon a complex strategy of praising the TNSM while undermining its activities.

The JUI-S' enthusiasm for the TNSM and its activities makes sense in light of its own position vis-à-vis the state and the anti-state movement. As a small party with a minimal electoral footprint, no meaningful history in Malakand, and no participation in the provincial coalition government, the JUI-S did not feel politically threatened by the TNSM. Its vulnerability to the state is harder to discern. The party's size suggests that it would be susceptible to state manipulation, and indeed the JUI-S has long been seen as useful to—and at times co-opted by—the ISI. At the same time, Sami ul-Haq had become well known for his early support of the Afghan Taliban, and as the movement was ascendant in 1994 he may have felt to some extent insulated from pressure by the Pakistani security services.

As for the JUI-F, its critical tenor toward the TNSM is similarly consistent with the two hypotheses from Chapter 1. Compared to the JI, the JUI-F was notably disorganized and lacked a cohesive response from the senior leadership and lower-level figures. Its loose partnership with the

PPP government made it somewhat vulnerable to the TNSM, and while it issued statements from Peshawar and elsewhere, it largely adopted the role of "silent spectator" on the ground in Malakand.[124] The senior figures in the party were, in the words of one leader, in favor of a "reconciliatory politics," but in private made it clear that they were "annoyed" with Sufi Muhammad, and they did not see a political upside to strongly supporting his movement.[125]

The JUI-F leadership seemed particularly attuned to reputational risk. Fazl ur-Rahman was, by several accounts, wary of appearing to support a movement that was openly challenging the state. One researcher who has studied both the religious parties and the clashes in Malakand noted that Fazl ur-Rahman declined in this case to bring the issue of the TNSM to his own party shuras for a decision, lest they choose to endorse Sufi Muhammad.[126]

This policy of caution was not simply the product of the JUI-F's particular political environment in 1994. When the TNSM reemerged in Malakand in force in 2007 to challenge the state, the JUI-F once again had to take a position on its activities. Writing to party loyalists in the JUI-F monthly *al-Jam'iyat* in June 2008, one of the editors recounted the party's stance in 1994. He wrote that the TNSM "had neither any relation with the Jamiat-e-Ulama nor was involved in any consultation with the party"; that the JUI-F had protested the government's actions; and that, on balance, the party "was not against this movement due to its basic objective, but could not side with it due to difference in methodology."[127] It is possible that this retrospective take on the party's policy may have been colored by the events then underway in Malakand, but the article is surprisingly forthcoming about its opposition to armed promotion of shariah, and its preference for "parliamentary politics."

Even more revealing of the JUI-F's posture was a speech given a year later by Senator Gul Nasib Khan, delivered at a party conference devoted to the protection of madaris. Not only was Gul Nasib then serving as the party's central naib amir (vice president) but, hailing from Lower Dir, he was by far the most influential central leader of the JUI-F with ties to Malakand Division.

[124] Saleem Safi, interview.

[125] Fatahullah Sajjad, interview by Joshua White, Urdu, trans. Shuja Malik, March 6, 2011; Aftab Sherpao, interview.

[126] Muhammad Amir Rana, interview.

[127] Ḥāfiẓ ʻAzīz ur-Raḥmān ʻAzīzī, "pārlīmānī siyāsat meṅ ʻulamā' kā kirdār: ifādiyat o muẓarāt [The Role of Ulama in Parliamentary Politics: Benefits and Detriments]," *al-Jam'iyat* 9, no. 9 (June 2008): 12–14.

His speech, transcribed in *al-Jam'iyat*, lamented the TNSM campaigns of 1994 and 1999, which failed in their objectives to bring about shariah. He recounted the thousands of people who were rendered homeless by the uprising and subsequent operations, and continued: "I can say categorically that if anyone had suffered any loss due to the JUI, I am liable for it. And those who diverged from the JUI's policy and got nabbed or killed—we do not take any responsibility [for them], because they violated party policy."[128] In a later interview, Gul Nasib recapitulated these themes, noting that the ulama in Dir and the JUI-F used to agree with Sufi Muhammad, but were critical of his methods of promoting shariah.[129]

If anything, these sources suggest that the JUI-F's concern about the TNSM was less related to any form of *direct* pressure—either from the movement itself, or from the JUI-F's constituents—and more related to concerns that the TNSM's activities might indirectly prompt pressures from the *state* against Islamist parties like the JUI-F, or their associated madaris.

This was, then, a case in which the JUI-F did not face significant risk of cadre defection to the TNSM, but had modest vulnerability to the movement because of the potential implications on the provincial coalition of which the JUI-F was a member. Vulnerability to the state may have been a factor in shaping the party's cautious response, but these concerns during the 1994 episode are merely anecdotal. The party's cautious but muddled response toward the TNSM is consistent with the rubric of Islamist party strategies in Figure 1.1, but as it was not a major player in this event, we should not read too much into its behavior.

In summary, this is a case in which structural rather than ideological factors appear to have played a leading role in shaping the Islamist parties' decision-making with respect to anti-state violence. None of these parties initiated the violence, although some had members participate in it. Neither did these parties appear to strategize at the outset about challenging the state, or using the TNSM as a means to "outsource" violence, although some eventually found it convenient to do so.

Rather, this episode—like several of the cases that follow—reveals the Islamist parties grappling with the risks and opportunities that arise from engaging with groups that use violence against the state and justify it on religious grounds. In Malakand the Islamist parties could simply not afford to

[128] Maulānā Gul Nasīb K͟hān, "svāt āpareshun aur madāris o masājid ko lāḥaq k͟haṭrāt [The Swat Operation and the Dangers Befalling the Madaris and Masjids]," *al-Jam'iyat* 10, no. 12–13 (October 2009): 11–14.

[129] Gul Nasib Khan, interview by Joshua White and Niloufer Siddiqui, Urdu, May 26, 2011.

oppose such a movement, but each in its own way perceived risks to meaningfully endorsing it. The situation forced them to balance competing concerns regarding their electoral interests, their anxieties about losing control over party workers, and the risks they might invite by clashing with the powerful security services.

7

Islamic Governance and the Allure of Vigilantism

The MMA in the Frontier

7.1 Introduction

The tenure of the MMA alliance in the former NWFP and Balochistan (where it governed in coalition) from 2002 to 2007 represented the first sustained example of governance by Islamist parties in Pakistan's history. The Islamists' victory, which emerged from an unusually favorable political environment and with clear support from the martial government of Pervez Musharraf, was something of a perfect storm of opportunity for the Islamists' political ambitions. The MMA's tenure represents a fascinating case study into the pressures that Islamist parties face when they find themselves in roles in which they must do the unglamorous work of governing and are accountable to the public.[1]

This case chapter is different from the preceding one and from those that follow. It does not trace the Islamist parties' responses to a new movement that used religiously justified violence against the state. Rather, it explores in brief how the Islamist parties themselves, while in power at the provincial level, wrestled with the questions of whether and how to use their own authorities to enable and legitimize the use of force to implement shariah. In particular, this case examines two episodes in the MMA's tenure in NWFP that brought this issue to the forefront. The first was the use of vigilante violence and vandalism by members of the alliance to intimidate members of the public into acting in ways that the MMA believed to be in conformance with shariah. The second was a legal effort by the MMA to pass the Hisbah bill, an Islamization measure that—its critics feared—would empower a "virtue-and-vice squad" that would act at the command of the Islamist parties to enforce their vision of shariah in the province.

[1] Portions of this chapter are drawn from Joshua T. White, *Pakistan's Islamist Frontier: Islamic Politics and U.S. Policy in Pakistan's North-West Frontier*, Religion & Security Monograph Series 1 (Arlington, VA: Center on Faith & International Affairs, 2008).

Vigilante Islamists. Joshua T. White, Oxford University Press. © Oxford University Press (2025).
DOI: 10.1093/9780197814178.003.0007

Although this case is unique, it is important because it sheds light on the Islamist parties' views of religiously justified violence, and provides a lens for examining the structural relationship between the Islamist parties and the state, and the ways in which the parties' vulnerabilities to state pressure are affected by their role in governance. It also provides a means of examining the constituent pressures that these parties face on matters of shariah, and the extent to which they may be willing to challenge the state in order to pursue policy objectives or appease constituents.

7.2 Background to the Case

7.2.1 Rise of the MMA

In retrospect it appears natural that, following the American invasion of Afghanistan in late 2001, the JUI-F, JUI-S, and JI would coalesce into an alliance opposing American intervention. But in fact, the parties had a long history of dysfunctional interaction, and had never before formed a broad-based Islamist alliance.[2] In the year preceding the 9/11 attacks there were signs that such an alliance was increasingly possible, but it seems to have taken prodding from former ISI chief Hamid Gul to coalesce the Islamists into a Pak-Afghan Defense Council, which in 2002 became the basis for the MMA electoral alliance.[3] The six-party alliance brought together the Pashtun-dominated JUI-F and JUI-S; the Jamaat-e-Islami; the Jamiat Ulama-e-Pakistan (JUP), a Barelvi party then led by Shah Ahmad Noorani; the Jamiat Ahl-e-Hadith (JAH), a Saudi-influenced party led by Sajid Mir; and the Islami Tahrik-e-Pakistan (ITP), a Shia party formerly known as Tahrik-e-Jafariah Pakistan (TJP) and led by Allama Sajid Naqvi.[4] The formation of this broad-based alliance served the interests of the Pakistani state by stoking pro-Taliban

[2] Religious parties had come together before for other purposes, such as in 1995 when a group of parties formed the Milli Yakjehti Council (MYC) to address sectarian conflicts. The MYC was not, however, able to coalesce as an electoral alliance for the 1997 polls.

[3] See, for example, M. Ilyas Khan, "Inside the MMA," *Herald*, November 2002. Hamid Gul was later described as a "strategic advisor" to the MMA, and in 2006 was involved in an unsuccessful attempt to create a more hardline Islamist alliance, which would include organizations of a more militant character than the JI and JUI-F. Arnaud de Borchgrave, "Gulled by Gul," *Washington Times*, December 2, 2004; Hasan Mansoor, "New Religious Alliance in the Offing? JUI-S Takes Fight to the Next Level," *Daily Times*, March 11, 2006. Some have also suggested that the massive JUI-organized Deoband conference in Peshawar in May 2001 served as a catalyzing force for developing a common platform among the religious parties. See Behroz Khan, "Assembly of Faith," *Newsline*, May 2001. Ahmed Rashid plausibly claims that this conference was in fact funded by the ISI. Ahmed Rashid, *Descent Into Chaos: The United States and the Failure of Nation Building in Pakistan, Afghanistan, and Central Asia* (New York: Viking, 2008), 53.

[4] Note that the ITP was also referred to as Pakistan Islami Tahrik. The four smaller parties of the alliance played a quite minor role in the MMA's policymaking and its governance in then-NWFP and Balochistan. For an insightful window into the JUP's place in the alliance, see Alix Philippon, *Soufisme et Politique au*

sentiment in the Pakistan–Afghanistan border areas, but also by fostering the perception (not least to the Americans) that Islamism was on the rise in Pakistan's frontier areas, and that only a strong military-executive power in Islamabad could properly check this emergent danger.

The domestic situation was also advantageous to the Islamists.[5] President Musharraf had instituted Governor's Rule in the NWFP after his 1999 coup, and the 2002 polls were to be the first general elections since 1997. Two parties that had traditionally been dominant in Pakistan's frontier areas—the PPP and the Pashtun nationalist Awami National Party—were both weak, fragmented, and demoralized. The MMA found it especially easy to impugn the credibility of the nationalists, who had supported Musharraf's post-9/11 "capitulation" to the Americans.[6]

The MMA alliance also benefited from support by the security services, which recognized that the Islamists could serve as a useful proxy by which the Musharraf government could decapitate its chief political rivals in the NWFP. Musharraf's own PML-Q faced grim prospects outside of the non-Pashtun Hazara Division in the eastern part of the province and the isolated PML bastion of Lakki Marwat in the south, and the Islamists therefore presented a second-best solution to the ruling party's political quandary in the NWFP. Particularly in those areas in which representatives of the central government and security services could not convince local power-brokers to support a weak PML-Q candidate, they often asked them to throw their weight instead behind the religious parties.[7]

The role of the Pakistani security services in the 2002 NWFP elections has been disputed. Some commentators suggested in retrospect that the Islamists' victory was entirely engineered by the ISI; in reality it is more likely that the manipulation was significant but subtle. Rather than engaging in large-scale electoral manipulation, the services chose instead to stifle the mainstream

Pakistan: Le Mouvement Barelwi à L'heure de "La Guerre Contre Le Terrorisme" (Paris: Éditions Karthala and Sciences Po Aix, 2011), 218–22.

[5] For more on the rise of the MMA, see Anita M. Weiss, "A Provincial Islamist Victory in Pakistan: The Social Reform Agenda of the Muttahida Majlis-i-Amal," in *Asian Islam in the 21st Century*, ed. John L. Esposito, John O. Voll, and Osman Bakar (Oxford: Oxford University Press, 2008), 145–73.

[6] The Peoples Party in the NWFP had seen its political organization atrophy since its period of dominance in the 1990s and had been weakened by the defection of Aftab Sherpao in 1999, which drained the party of its base in the politically important Charsadda district. The ANP was similarly contesting the elections from a position of internal weakness. The Pashtun nationalist movement, which traces its political heritage to the "Frontier Gandhi" Khan Abdul Ghaffar Khan, had fragmented in the 1990s. By 2002, the nationalists were in disarray and party workers were despondent. Author interviews with ANP party workers, July 2007, Peshawar.

[7] Khan, "Inside the MMA," 45–46. MMA President Maulana Shah Ahmad Noorani (of the Barelvi JUP) later acknowledged that "the government propaganda against the PPP and PML-N" also contributed to the alliance's success in 2002. "Noorani—A Binding Force," *Dawn*, December 12, 2003.

parties while allowing religious leaders a free hand in capitalizing on the wave of anti-American sentiment.[8]

The government's assistance to the religious alliance took several forms. First, the mainstream and nationalist parties were given only a narrow window of time before the elections in which to campaign and counter the MMA's electoral rhetoric. This restriction, perhaps more than anything else, played to the advantage of the Islamists, who were able to organize blatantly political "religious gatherings" in mosques and madaris throughout the province, beginning weeks and even months before the official start of the campaign season. The result was the creation of an organizational vacuum that the MMA was easily able to fill.

Second, the election commission further boosted the prospects of the MMA by "arbitrarily" assigning to it the official electoral symbol of the book, which the religious parties had themselves pressed for.[9] The alliance's leadership wasted no time in playing up the religious significance of the symbol, claiming the book to be the Quran and making the MMA out to be a party of piety. Third, federal electoral statutes holding that candidates must possess certain educational qualifications (typically, a bachelors degree) were interpreted by the federal government so as not to disqualify candidates who held certificates from the madaris. This was a great boon to the JUI parties, many of whose members did not have degrees from accredited institutions. And finally, some MMA candidates were reportedly aided by the quiet withdrawal of criminal cases against them in advance of their nomination papers being scrutinized. This process was well-documented in the case of MMA leaders in Balochistan, and there is good reason to believe that the same process took place in the NWFP.

By late 2002, the conflict in Afghanistan had given the MMA a potent political issue and electoral momentum. Not only did the ruling elites in Islamabad find it unnecessary to use blunt instruments of electoral manipulation in support of the MMA, but doing so would have posed special challenges: Unlike the politics of Punjab and Sindh in which large landholders often held sway, Pashtun politics in NWFP was more egalitarian, and the security services have historically found it more challenging to engage in wholesale vote-buying and intimidation in the NWFP than in the other provinces.[10] It appears that the extent of the MMA's success proved surprising even to

[8] See "Government Helped MMA Leaders Contest Elections," *Daily Times*, November 8, 2002; Frédéric Grare, "Islam, Militarism, and the 2007–2008 Elections in Pakistan," Carnegie Papers 70 (Washington, DC: Carnegie Endowment for International Peace, July 2006); Rashid, *Descent into Chaos*, 156.

[9] Vali Nasr, "Military Rule, Islamism and Democracy in Pakistan," *Middle East Journal* 58, no. 2 (Spring 2004): 202.

[10] Author interview with a senior NWFP provincial official, July 2007, Peshawar.

those agencies charged with facilitating its victory; many in the security services reportedly underestimated the extent of the MMA's popularity in the Peshawar valley and Malakand areas.[11]

7.2.2 The MMA's Agenda

The MMA alliance was originally formed around a relatively narrow, Afghanistan-focused agenda. As it began campaigning in 2002, however, the MMA gradually adopted a more robust platform. Unlike the mainstream parties, which relied on charismatic party leadership, or the ethno-nationalist parties, which relied on a set of ethnically charged historical grievances, the JUI-F and the JI brought complementary methods of mobilization to the alliance's campaign strategy. The JUI-F drew on its madaris network for mass-mobilization, and the JI, under the leadership of Qazi Hussain Ahmad, was able to tap a burgeoning network of Pashtun political workers who could leverage the party's famously disciplined bureaucracy. What began as a proto-political movement oriented against Western military action in Afghanistan became over the course of the campaign a fairly robust alliance. However vague or unrealistic its promises may have been, the MMA was arguably the electoral bloc that articulated the most forceful "pro-change" agenda of any party contesting the elections.[12]

This change agenda was not only reactive, but also sweepingly proactive. The MMA promised the institution of a true Islamic system in the NWFP and Balochistan, including the prohibition of "obscene" material on cable television, the provision of Islamic banking, and the conversion of the NWFP Provincial Assembly into an "Islamic jirga."[13] Other pledges were considerably more vague, such as the curtailing of un-Islamic work by nongovernmental organizations (NGOs) and foreign elements, the enforcement of "Islamic justice," the imposition of the shariah into the provincial framework of law, and the promotion of policies designed to encourage the use of head coverings. Much as Mufti Mahmud had done in 1970, the MMA wove this Islamic reform agenda together with a rhetoric of populist governance, an approach

[11] It was reportedly analysts from the police service's Special Branch who most accurately predicted the MMA's overwhelming electoral gains. Author interviews with federal and provincial officials, 2007, Islamabad and Peshawar.

[12] See Mohammad Waseem, *Democratization in Pakistan: A Study of the 2002 Elections* (Oxford: Oxford University Press, 2006), 129. Note also that the MMA's campaign promises were much more extensive than its formal manifesto, which was "critically devoid of specifics" and did not even address Pakistan's relations with the United States. Pakistan Institute of Legislative Development and Transparency, "Election 2002: A Comparative Study of Election Manifestos of Major Political Parties" (Islamabad: PILDAT, October 2002), 34.

[13] Quotation by Qazi Hussain Ahmad, from *Mashriq*, October 20, 2002.

which in many ways echoed the language of the PPP.[14] Drawing on its lower- and middle-class roots, the religious alliance put forward a strikingly populist campaign that equated Islamic political reforms with a pro-poor agenda.[15] The MMA's plan for its first hundred days promised the creation of a half-million new jobs, free education through the secondary level, interest-free loans for low-cost housing, cheap medications, and old-age allowances.[16]

It was not surprising that the JUI-F would prove successful in the conservative southern districts bordering Afghanistan, or that the JI would gain solid support in outlying areas such as district Dir. What surprised analysts was the MMA's success in making inroads into areas that had previously been almost off-limits to Islamist politics, such as the Pashtun agricultural heartland of the Peshawar valley, regions like Malakand Division in which ANP and PPP had traditionally held sway, and even PML strongholds such as Hazara Division. Capturing a remarkable forty-eight of ninety-nine Provincial Assembly seats, and twenty-nine of thirty-five National Assembly seats from the NWFP, the MMA's victory in 2002 was a dramatic realignment of the provincial electoral map away from virtually all of the established parties such as the PPP, the ANP, and the PML factions, and toward a group of mostly unknown, politically inexperienced religious leaders and party operatives.[17]

Having won against the expectations of most political observers, the MMA's governance from 2002 to 2007, particularly in the NWFP, was characterized by a hybrid of Islamist and populist themes. The alliance attempted to push through a number of shariah initiatives; pressed the central government for greater provincial autonomy and fiscal transfers; and, in most respects, governed in a manner relatively consistent with its predecessors. Although the literature on the MMA's tenure has naturally been quite critical of the alliance's Islamist initiatives, the reality of the MMA's tenure was actually quite complex.[18] The Islamists were unable to implement the most controversial

[14] See, for example, Rahimullah Yusufzai, "Durrani Follows Mufti Mahmud," *The News*, November 30, 2002.

[15] Ironically, exit polling conducted during the 2002 elections showed that those who voted for the MMA tended to be richer and more educated than those who voted for the mainstream parties. But neither the alliance's platform nor its program of governance specifically appealed to educated or upper-class voters. Pakistan Institute of Legislative Development and Transparency, "Election 2002: Who Voted for Whom? Findings from an Exit Poll Survey" (Islamabad: PILDAT, October 2002).

[16] "MMA's Plan for First 100 Days in Power," *Dawn*, October 10, 2002.

[17] Figures from the Election Commission of Pakistan. The MMA's final party position, including reserved seats, accounted for 68 out of 124. Waseem Ahmad Shah, "MMA Tally in NWFP PA Rises to 68: Names for Reserved Seats Notified," *Dawn*, November 3, 2002. For detailed studies of the 2002 elections, see Waseem, *Democratization in Pakistan*; Andrew Wilder, "Elections 2002: Legitimizing the Status Quo," in *Pakistan on the Brink: Politics, Economics, and Society*, ed. Craig Baxter (Maryland: Lexington Books, 2004).

[18] Representative of this genre are International Crisis Group, "Pakistan: The Mullahs and the Military," Asia Report 49 (Islamabad: International Crisis Group, March 20, 2003); Ashutosh Misra, "The Rise of Religious Parties in Pakistan: Causes and Prospects," *Strategic Analysis* 27, no. 2 (June 2003): 186–215; Nazish Brohi, "The MMA Offensive: Three Years in Power: 2003–2005" (Islamabad: ActionAid, 2006);

aspects of their shariah plans, but at the same time seemed content to get political mileage from the proposals, demonstrate their independence from the political establishment, and gain the experiential and financial benefits of a first-ever sustained tenure in government.[19]

7.2.3 Political Pressures

The political context in which the MMA governed during this period imposed a number of constraints on its Islamist ambitions. From the moment that the MMA alliance secured its victories in NWFP and Balochistan, it began a difficult balancing act with the Musharraf government. Musharraf had paved the way for the MMA's success by marginalizing mainstream parties, and it quickly became clear that, in return, he expected the Islamist parties to provide legitimacy for his military government. Musharraf first proposed in the summer of 2002, just prior to the general elections, a Legal Framework Order (LFO) designed to solidify and legally substantiate his dual role as President and Chief of Army Staff.[20] The opposition parties, under the umbrella of the Alliance for the Restoration of Democracy (ARD), fiercely opposed the LFO, and the MMA's early reaction was similarly critical. Musharraf continued to court the Islamist alliance over the year that followed, and began engaging its leadership again in the summer of 2003, pressing for a deal.

The MMA eventually capitulated, and the LFO was approved as the seventeenth amendment to the constitution and signed on December 31, 2003. The amendment solidified Musharraf's position by electing him to a five-year term, reaffirming his ability to appoint key judicial and military officials, and establishing a military-dominated National Security Council (NSC). Most critically, it retained the infamous article 58(2)(b), which allowed the president to dissolve parliament. The government did not make explicit the terms of the MMA's assent to the LFO in late 2003, but many commentators

Grare, "Islam, Militarism, and the 2007–2008 Elections in Pakistan"; Ashutosh Misra, "MMA-Democracy Interface in Pakistan: From Natural Confrontation to Co-Habitation?," *Strategic Analysis* 30, no. 2 (June 2006): 377–88. More sophisticated analyses include Weiss, "A Provincial Islamist Victory in Pakistan"; Mohammed Waseem and Mariam Mufti, "Religion, Politics and Governance in Pakistan," Religions and Development Working Paper 27 (Birmingham, UK: University of Birmingham, 2009).

[19] For earlier treatments of the MMA's tenure by the author, see White, *Pakistan's Islamist Frontier*; Joshua T. White, "Beyond Moderation: Dynamics of Political Islam in Pakistan," *Contemporary South Asia* 20, no. 2 (June 2012): 179–94.

[20] Misra, "The Rise of Religious Parties in Pakistan," 378.

presumed that the Islamists' continued governance in NWFP and Balochistan was contingent on its support to the military leader.[21]

The MMA's embrace of the LFO in 2003 severely damaged its relationship with the ARD opposition alliance. The Musharraf government let the MMA take on the role of parliamentary opposition even though it represented a smaller opposition bloc than the ARD—under the argument that the ARD was not a formal electoral alliance—and Fazl ur-Rahman was named in May 2004 as leader of the opposition in the National Assembly.[22] Having lost credibility through its support of the LFO, the MMA looked for opportunities to tack back toward the ARD and demonstrate its opposition bona fides. It found such an opportunity in September 2004 when Musharraf reneged on his promise to remove his army uniform by December 31st of that year. This time, a "politically betrayed MMA took a firm position against General Musharraf," and the alliance sided decisively with the ARD's demands.[23]

The MMA's uneasy relationship with the Musharraf government did not end with the uniform issue. When Musharraf established a National Security Council, as authorized by the seventeenth amendment, the MMA opposed it. But once the NSC was established, MMA leaders were torn about whether to participate.[24] The JI elements of the MMA were opposed, while the JUI-F leadership was conflicted. NWFP Chief Minister Akram Khan Durrani eventually, in late 2005, received a green light from Maulana Fazl ur-Rahman to participate in NSC meetings, ostensibly to advance the party's interests in the province, but the move was controversial within the MMA and the chief minister's participation was discontinued.

These issues—the LFO, Musharraf's uniform, the NSC—together highlight the contentious nature of center–provincial relations from 2003 to 2004, and the MMA's reactions to the central government's attempts to solidify Musharraf's martial rule. In general, during the early years of the MMA's tenure, the alliance adopted a dual-track approach to dealing with its precarious position in the NWFP. It capitulated on most structural matters pertaining to center–provincial relations, with the hope that a conciliatory policy toward Musharraf would secure its tenure in the NWFP and Balochistan and would give it the opportunity to exploit—financially and politically—its unprecedented position in provincial governance. At the same time, as

[21] Waseem and Mufti, "Religion, Politics and Governance in Pakistan," 42; Khaled Ahmed, "Musharraf and the Mullahs," *Friday Times*, April 15, 2005.
[22] Misra, "The Rise of Religious Parties in Pakistan," 380.
[23] Misra, "The Rise of Religious Parties in Pakistan," 382.
[24] Grare, "Islam, Militarism, and the 2007–2008 Elections in Pakistan," 10.

explored below, leaders and affiliates of the MMA constituent parties pushed the boundaries of what the central government was willing to tolerate, both in terms of policy and agitation.

7.3 The Role of the Islamist Parties

The MMA entered government ambitious and inexperienced. Two notable challenges that it faced had their origins in the alliance's Islamization agenda. The first was the unofficial use of vigilante violence and vandalism by members of the MMA parties, and the second was the official effort by party leaders to pass the Hisbah bill to enforce ostensibly Islamic behavior in the province.

7.3.1 Vigilantism

In the first several years of the MMA's tenure, young vigilantes vandalized billboards that displayed pictures of women's faces, and burned music shops in Peshawar and other cities.[25] Many of these vigilantes had low-level connections to the youth organizations of the MMA parties, and while the Islamist government occasionally criticized these incidents, it did not vigorously investigate them.[26] Some of these were members of the JI's youth wing, Shabab-e-Milli. (Unlike the JI's collegiate affiliate, the Islami Jamiat-e-Talaba, the Shabab-e-Milli operates under the direct control of the party, and is subject to party discipline.[27])

At the time that these events occurred, the provincial government was proposing a haphazard array of Islamization measures, such as bans on public music performances and edicts requiring that senior government officials attend mosque for Friday prayers.[28] Some of these measures were formalized as cabinet decisions or official government orders, but many others were merely announced, with the expectation that the opacity of local government

[25] "'Offensive' Billboards to Get the Boot Again in the NWFP," *Herald*, March 2005.

[26] Author interviews, 2005–2007, Peshawar. See also, for example, "Vigilante Action Against Cable Operators Continues in Peshawar," *Daily Times*, January 11, 2003; "Editorial: Talibanisation of NWFP," *Daily Times*, May 25, 2003; Iqbal Khattak, "Police Warns MMA Against Taking Law in Own Hands," *Daily Times*, December 29, 2003; Amy Waldman, "In One Pakistan Province, Reality Tempers Ideology," *The New York Times*, January 18, 2004.

[27] Asif Luqman Qazi, interview by Joshua White, English, May 25, 2011.

[28] See, for example, Weiss, "A Provincial Islamist Victory in Pakistan," 160; Government of NWFP, "The Achievements of the Provincial Government of Muthahida Majlis-e-Amal (MMA) (since 30th November, 2002 till Date)" (Cabinet Wing, Establishment Department, n.d.); Misra, "MMA-Democracy Interface in Pakistan," 389ff.

decision-making would render them effective whether or not they were legally codified.[29]

Understandably, these activities were troubling to both domestic and foreign observers. Even outside of NWFP and Balochistan, the MMA's vigilantism was drawing fire. The alliance, to give just one example, came under "tremendous pressure after the government disclosed intelligence reports before the National Assembly confirming rumors that that MMA brought in armed supporters from the NWFP to disrupt a mini-marathon scheduled for April 2 in Gujranwala."[30] Although Fazl ur-Rahman argued unpersuasively that the armed MMA activists were actually local JUI-F madrassah students, incidents like these caused the ARD opposition parties to further distance themselves from the MMA.

The central government, too, grew concerned. On the one hand, it was useful to Musharraf to be able to point to the MMA government in NWFP as a way of warning his Western counterparts about the nascent danger of Islamic radicalism within Pakistan's borders. On the other hand, Islamabad had to worry about the reputational damage that a vigilante MMA might inflict on Musharraf's government over the long-term. The security services had reportedly reached out to ARD politicians in NWFP in 2004 to give them tips on how they might topple the MMA provincial government.[31] As early as the middle of 2003, the press was reporting discussions by the federal government about ways that it might find a pretext for imposing Governor's Rule, effectively dismissing the MMA in the Frontier.[32]

7.3.2 The Hisbah Bill

The Hisbah bill was the second major initiative to come out of the MMA's Nifaz-e-Shariat Council, a consultative body established as a kind of think-tank for developing legislative policy for the alliance. The Council consisted of twenty-one members, and was chaired by Mufi Ghulam ur-Rahman, principal of Jamia Usmania in Nothia, Peshawar, and a cleric closely linked to the JUI-F.[33] The Council's first proposal to be implemented by the MMA

[29] For a somewhat lengthier discussion of "governance by perception" in the MMA government, see White, *Pakistan's Islamist Frontier*, 54–55.

[30] M. R. Klasra, "MMA Brought in Activists from NWFP to Attack Race," *Friday Times*, April 15, 2005. A JUI-F Member of the National Assembly had stirred up trouble in Gujranwala several years earlier after he led an attack on a circus show. Adnan Adil, "The Obscene Obsession," *Newsline*, July 2003.

[31] Iqbal Khattak, "JI-JUIF Gulf Widens on the Uniform Campaign," *Friday Times*, December 31, 2005.

[32] Mohammad Shehzad, "MMA-Islamabad Preparing to Slug It Out?," *Friday Times*, June 6, 2003.

[33] Rifatullah Orakzai, "Who's Who: Islamic Ideological Council NWFP," Khyber.org, n.d., https://web.archive.org/web/20050802081054/http://www.khyber.org/articles/2004/WhosWho-IslamicIdeological

government in NWFP was the Shariah Bill, which was adopted unanimously by the Provincial Assembly on June 2, 2003, and came into force as the NWFP Shariah Act of 2003. The NWFP Shariah Act was a close replica of the 1991 Enforcement of Shariah Act, adopted by the National Assembly under the PML-N government of Nawaz Sharif.[34] The Shariah Act of 2003 was considered a political success, but it was not substantive, given that it did not alter the courts' existing jurisdictions or change their standards of interpretation.[35] By mimicking the 1991 federal act, the MMA was admitting that the legislation was effectively remedial in nature. The Council needed to follow up the 2003 act with something concrete, and it chose Hisbah as its first signature initiative.[36]

What *was* the Hisbah bill, and why was it so controversial? The concept of *ḥisbah,* or accountability, in Islamic law hearkens to the idea of commanding the right and forbidding the wrong. This idea, while present in the Quran, figures only peripherally in Sunni jurisprudence.[37] And while the Islamist parties did make hisbah a central pillar of their Islamization program, they did not embrace the vigilante or "rebellion" paradigms of confronting the state violently for its failure to command the good. Instead, they drew upon a correlate of the hisbah concept: the idea of the muhtasib.

Muhtasibs, or ombudsmen, date at least to the Abbasid period. (The NWFP Minister for Religious Affairs, a JUI-F cleric, insisted during the Provincial Assembly debates on Hisbah that it dates much earlier, to Muhammad himself.[38]) Historically, muhtasibs were officials tasked with promoting good behavior and correcting public displays of sinful conduct. In practice, the job was rather prosaic: Muhtasibs, according to one scholar, "heard disputes mainly in three domains: (1) foul play with respect to weights and measures in the marketplace; (2) fraud in the sale and pricing of merchandise; (3) refusal to pay back debts when the debtor was solvent."[39] The muhtasib was charged,

Coun.shtml. Ghulam ur-Rahman was once a student of Maulana Sami ul-Haq, but after the split in the JUI, sided with the Fazl ur-Rahman faction. Sami ul-Haq, interview by Joshua White, Urdu, trans. Shuja Malik, February 19, 2011.

[34] Shaheen Sardar Ali, "'Sigh of the Oppressed'? 'Islamisation' of Laws in Pakistan under Muttahida Majlis-e-Amal: The Case of the North West Frontier Province," ed. Eugene Cotran and Martin Lau, *Yearbook of Islamic and Middle Eastern Law* 10 (2006): 111–14.

[35] Charles H. Kennedy, "Repugnancy to Islam: Who Decides? Islam and Legal Reform in Pakistan," *The International and Comparative Law Quarterly* 41, no. 4 (October 1992): 779.

[36] Gul Nasib Khan, interview by Joshua White and Niloufer Siddiqui, Urdu, May 26, 2011.

[37] *Qur'ān*, 3:104; Michael Cook, *Commanding Right and Forbidding Wrong in Islamic Thought* (Cambridge, UK: Cambridge University Press, 2000).

[38] Maulana Amanullah Haqqani, "NWFP Provincial Assembly Debates," Session 17 (Peshawar, July 14, 2005).

[39] Wael B. Hallaq, *An Introduction to Islamic Law* (Cambridge, UK: Cambridge University Press, 2009), 75.

in the words of one scholar of Islamic political philosophy, to serve as "the eye of the law on both state and society."[40]

But whereas the scholar considered the muhtasib as the eye of the law, the MMA leadership wished him to be the hand: A quick perusal of the original Hisbah bill text makes it clear that the MMA envisioned a muhtasib with vague but sweeping powers.[41] The bill would establish the office of muhtasib, a "qualified religious scholar" serving as an ombudsman, to which citizens could refer complaints about the presence of "un-Islamic" behavior in the province.[42] He also had the authority to take up complaints himself on the basis of unchecked *suo moto* powers. The muhtasib was empowered to inquire into "allegations of mal-administration"; to "protect/watch the Islamic values and etiquettes" in the province; and to "forbid persons, agencies and authorities . . . [from acting] against shariah and to guide them to good governance."[43] He was also given a specific list of authorities, which ranged from discouraging beggary, to preventing cruelty to animals, to discouraging "un-Islamic and inhuman customs," to eradicating sorcery, to eliminating "un-Islamic traditions which effect the rights of women."[44] In order to carry out this sweeping mandate, the muhtasib was given the legal authorities of a civil court judge, including subpoena powers, and the ability to appoint subordinate muhtasibs at the district and subdistrict levels. Moreover, "defiance" of the muhtasib's orders was to be recognized as a punishable, criminal offense.

The Hisbah bill received intense scrutiny and public criticism. Critics took particular exception to the bill's designation of a "Hisbah Force," which they feared would become a sort of partisan "gestapo" modeled along the lines of the Afghan Taliban's arbitrary "virtue and vice" courts.[45] The government of NWFP referred the draft bill to the governor and the Council of Islamic Ideology in late 2003, and the latter, an advisory body, issued a stinging report nearly a year later regarding the bill's contents following a meeting of the

[40] Hasan Hanafi, "Alternative Conceptions of Civil Society: A Reflective Islamic Approach," in *Islamic Political Ethics: Civil Society, Pluralism, and Conflict*, ed. Sohail H. Hashmi (Princeton, NJ: Princeton University Press, 2002), 60.

[41] In an interview, one of the bill's key drafters did not appear to understand the implications of the legal language. Malik Zafar Azam, interview by Joshua White, English and Urdu, trans. Shuja Malik, March 8, 2011.

[42] "Text of Hasba Bill," *Dawn*, July 16, 2005.

[43] Law Department, Government of NWFP, *Hisbah Bill* (Peshawar: Government of NWFP, 2005), sec. 10.

[44] Law Department, Government of NWFP, *Hisbah Bill*, sec. 23.

[45] See, for example, Zakir Hassnain, "Opposition Calls Hisbah 'Martial Law of Mullas,'" *Daily Times*, August 27, 2003; Ali, "'Sigh of the Oppressed'?"; Khalid Masud, interview by Joshua White, English, February 22, 2011.

council in August 2004.[46] The governor also criticized the bill, along with NGOs, bar associations, and other civil society organizations. Despite these criticisms, reviewed in greater detail later, the MMA made no significant modifications to the bill, and it passed the assembly on July 14, 2005.[47]

The government in Islamabad wasted little time in taking aim at the new legislation. One day after its passage, President Musharraf filed a reference with the Supreme Court seeking an opinion under its advisory jurisdiction. The court, in short order, rejected the Hisbah bill's most substantive articles. Ruling on August 4, 2005, it recommended to the governor of NWFP to reject the bill as passed. In an authoritative rebuke, the court dismissed the bill for reasons of it being "vague, overbroad, unreasonable, based on excessive delegation of jurisdiction, denying the right of access to justice to the citizens and attempting to set up a parallel judicial system."[48]

Just days after the Supreme Court released its full opinion, the MMA government tabled a revised version of the Hisbah bill in the Provincial Assembly.[49] This time, it was not the courts that intervened to prevent its passage, but the devastating earthquake of October 8, 2005, which hit NWFP hardest of the four provinces and quickly absorbed the entire attentions of the MMA provincial leadership. Remarkably, the revised bill was briefly tabled on October 31, but after the MMA leadership was met with strong opposition and accusations of trying to divert attention from its mishandling of the earthquake relief efforts, it decided to postpone further action on the legislation until after the crisis.[50] It was not until over a year later, November 13, 2006, that the assembly got around to passing the revised version of the bill.[51] And once again, with little delay, the Supreme Court took up a challenge to the legislation. It issued a stay order on December 15, 2006, and about three months later a Supreme Court bench led by Chief Justice Iftikhar Muhammad Chaudhry issued a short order, upholding almost all of the revised bill, except for two provisions "which [appear] to have escaped the notice of the provincial legislature, [and] which now may be given due

[46] Council of Islamic Ideology, *Summary Annual Report (2004–05)*, ed. Muhammad Ilyas Khan (Islamabad: Council of Islamic Ideology, 2006).

[47] Assembly Secretariat, *Assembly Activities Between 2002 and 2007* (Peshawar: Provincial Assembly, Government of NWFP, 2008).

[48] Supreme Court of Pakistan, "Opinion of the Supreme Court in Reference No. 2 of 2005 (PLD 2005 SC 873) [Hisba Bill Case]" (Supreme Court of Pakistan, August 4, 2005).

[49] Assembly Secretariat, *Assembly Activities Between 2002 and 2007*.

[50] Law Department, Government of NWFP, "idārah-e ḥisbah kā qayām [Establishment of the Hisbah Department]" (Peshawar: Provincial Assembly, NWFP, October 31, 2005); ʻAbd ur-Raḥmān, "suprīm korṭ ke faiṣle kī roshnī meṅ ḥasbah bil meṅ tarāmīm: tarmīmī musavadah asamblī meṅ pesh kar diyā giyā [Amendments in the Hisbah Bill in Light of the Supreme Court's Decision: Amended Package Presented in the Assembly]," *Haft Rozah Aishyā (Asia)* 54, no. 47 (November 17, 2005): 22–27.

[51] Mohammed Riaz, "Govt to Table Hisba Bill on Monday," *Dawn*, November 12, 2006.

consideration" by the provincial government.[52] Although the court effectively upheld the bill, the ruling was interpreted as another defeat for the MMA's Islamization agenda. Throughout the summer of 2007 the provincial government vowed to pass yet another version of the bill, but, as its five-year tenure wound down, the MMA simply let the bill die, relegating it to a symbol of failed Islamization and fruitless confrontation with the Musharraf government. In the 2008 elections that followed, the Islamist parties were swept out of power in the Frontier on a wave of anti-incumbency sentiment, as well as public disillusionment with their perceived failure to deliver on their agenda.

7.4 Conclusion: The Logics of Anti-State Violence

How should we make sense of the MMA's flirtations with vigilante violence, and its decision to pursue legislation that would have given it sweeping powers to impose its vision of shariah? Unlike the TLP's decisions, explored in Chapter 10, to actively endorse and justify vigilante and anti-state violence, the MMA's decisions represented merely oblique challenges to central government authority. But they are a valuable subject of study precisely because they illuminate the structural pressures on the Islamist parties, and the ways in which those pressures may become more acute when the parties are themselves in positions of government authority.

Both of the major parties in the MMA—the JI and the JUI-F—had ideological reasons to support Islamization measures. Both parties had campaigned pledging to advance shariah, and had made clear their displeasure over social ills, including so-called vulgarity in music shops and venues, and on billboards and cable television. Both parties had also advocated for more structural Islamist reforms in the areas of finance and law. But even when there was debate among the parties about whether to speak out against vigilantism that targeted social ills, or pursue legislation that could have imposed stricter rules on citizens they perceived as deviant, the disagreements were largely about means rather than ends.

Although they were for the most part ideologically aligned about the shariah outcomes they sought, the JI and JUI-F adopted divergent tactics and strategies for pursuing Islamization when they shared power in NWFP. This case illustrates the ways in which structural pressures—in particular, political

[52] Iftikhar Muhammad Chaudhry, "Short Order of the Honorable Chief Justice of Pakistan, Opinion on Hisbah Bill, 2006" (Supreme Court of Pakistan, February 20, 2007); Iftikhar A. Khan, "SC Upholds Most Parts of Hasba," *Dawn*, February 21, 2007.

and patronage incentives generated from within the alliance, and vulnerability to pressure from the security services outside of it—influenced Islamist party decision-making.

7.4.1 Political Incentives

From its earliest days, the MMA was an alliance fraught with internal divisions. These fractures played out differently at the local, provincial, and national levels. At the local level the differences between the two dominant parties were not related to strategic objectives so much as jostling for influence. It was to the benefit of the MMA as an alliance that such tensions were, in 2002, somewhat obviated by the NWFP's political geography. The power bases of the JUI-F and the JI were largely geographically disjoint, with the former dominant in the southern districts and the latter in the northern Malakand Division. The major parties did not avoid electoral tension altogether, but the historic weakness of Islamist parties in the province made it such that neither party had a strong bench of experienced candidates, particularly for those regions outside their traditional spheres of influence.

At the provincial level, disputes predictably centered around the distribution of patronage, including cabinet positions, in which the JI and especially the smaller parties in the alliance felt excluded.[53] Somewhat less expected was that the pace of the MMA's Islamization agenda would also prove to be a point of provincial-level contention within the alliance. The MMA faced a nearly constant tension between those leaders who were in a governing role, such as members of the provincial cabinet, and those who were not, such as party workers and activists. The former group had a strong incentive to demonstrate the government's credentials as a responsible party committed to the rule of law, while the latter remained primarily focused on appeasing their party's political base.

When, for example, JI cadres were publicly linked to vigilante actions in the summer of 2003—defacing billboards and burning music shops—the chief minister, who belonged to the JUI-F, spoke out against the action, precipitating a feud within the alliance. It was but one of many: The "governing" leadership of the MMA consistently demonstrated greater concern for

[53] The JUI-F was the undisputed leader of the alliance in NWFP and received the chief minister slot, while the JI received the senior minister and speaker of the assembly positions. The year 2006 saw the formation of a "forward block" (dissenting faction) within the MMA opposed to the actions of the chief minister; tellingly, the JUI-F was able to appease the dissidents at minimal cost, bringing them back into the fold with promises of more equitable distribution of funds.

procedure, for the public reputation of the alliance, and for a gradual reform path than did those without such obligations.

At the national level, the forces acting upon the constituent parties were in some sense reversed from those at the local level. Here the JI and JUI-F shared relatively less in the way of overall objectives, and saw the relationship between the MMA and the state through starkly different lenses. While the JUI-F sought to establish itself as a dominant status quo political force in the Pashtun areas of NWFP and Balochistan (even if that meant compromising with the Musharraf government), the JI sought to act on a broader agenda that included structural Islamist reforms—changes which necessitated opposition to Musharraf's regime and its philosophy of "enlightened moderation." The vigilante actions of its party cadres thus represented an ultimately ineffective effort at sparking deniable acts of violence to weaken the position of the central government.

In the end, the JUI-F's more pragmatic orientation toward the central government prevailed. The JI amir Qazi Hussain Ahmad threatened frequently to resign from the National Assembly in protest of martial rule, but the JUI-F—seeing a large downside in the potential loss of the NWFP government, and an uncertain upside at the national level—refused to go along, and reluctantly signed on to the Legal Framework Order in late 2003 that gave legal validation to the martial regime. (Ahmad resigned only in August 2007, long after it had ceased to matter.) When Chief Minister and JUI-F leader Akram Khan Durrani was asked how he managed to work with President Musharraf, he reportedly joked, "Don't ask me about Musharraf. Give me credit for being able to work with the Jamaat-e-Islami."[54] This internal fragmentation, which was felt at all levels of the MMA's governance, helps to explain the JUI-F's comparative reluctance relative to the JI to sanction violent or vigilante efforts at Islamization, and to minimize the leverage and rationale that the military might have to dismiss the MMA government.

7.4.2 The Politics of Patronage

Critics saw the MMA's Hisbah bill as a blatant attempt to create an unaccountable security force, managed by the elected Islamists, to impose shariah on the population of NWFP. That was the vision of at least some MMA leaders. But they also saw the bill through the lens of patronage.

[54] International Crisis Group, "Islamic Parties in Pakistan," Asia Report 216 (Islamabad: International Crisis Group, December 12, 2011), 7.

The JI was never particularly enthusiastic about championing the Hisbah bill as the MMA's flagship legislative effort.[55] The party's leaders had long privileged structural Islamization reforms, and its think-tank, the Institute for Policy Studies in Islamabad, had produced considerable work on reforms to the banking and education sectors. The JI preferred to focus on those issues, but the MMA's Nifaz-e-Shariat Council was dominated by the JUI-F and those (such as members of the JUI-S and JUI-N; and a non-Muslim parliamentarian who owed his seat to the JUI-F) who were sympathetic to the ulama party's priorities.[56] A JI leader later admitted that Hisbah "was not proposed because it was necessary, but because it was a doable thing" at the time given the political environment and the internal politics of the MMA.[57] The Hisbah bill also resonated with the MMA's populist discourse. In the JUI-F's publications, written for members, they framed the bill as a means of redressing abuses of power by political officials, and often couched the legislation in the language of human rights.[58] The JUI-F also saw the bill as an opportunity to appease hardline elements that might be inclined to take to the streets if their demands for shariah were not being met through the political process.[59]

Within the MMA, however, there was a conflict over the details of the Hisbah bill—one that speaks to the role of patronage in shaping the parties' Islamization agendas. Simply put, the JUI-F saw the bill as a potential patronage bonanza for the ulama. The distribution of patronage benefits from Hisbah institutions became *the* focal point of conflict between the JUI-F and the JI during the drafting process. For the JUI-F, the Hisbah bill represented an ingenious jobs-creation scheme for the party's madrassa-educated cadres. The bill required that the muhtasib be a "qualified religious scholar" from a government-recognized institution. What observers often failed to note was the way in which the legislation established multiple tiers of muhtasibs at the three major levels of local government: province, district, and *tehsil* (town). The provincial muhtasib was granted the power to appoint district muhtasibs, who in turn, with the provincial muhtasib's permission, "may appoint as many Tehsil Muhtasib as the need may be."

[55] Malik Zafar Azam, interview. Remarkably, the JI's annual action plan, published in January 2005, contained not a single mention of the Hisbah bill as a party priority for the year.

[56] Orakzai, "Who's Who: Islamic Ideological Council NWFP."

[57] Khalid Rehman, interview by Joshua White, English and Urdu, trans. Shuja Malik, February 23, 2011.

[58] Muhammad Ibrahim Khan, interview by Joshua White, English and Urdu, trans. Shuja Malik, March 9, 2011; "Hasba System to Cost Rs80m a Year: CM," *Dawn*, November 17, 2006; Muftī Abū al-'Aṭā' Raḥmat Za'ī, "ḥukūmat sarḥad kā ḥisbah ekṭ [Frontier Government's Hisbah Act]," *al-Jam'iyat* 4, no. 6 (March 2004): 8–9; "Hasba Bill to Ensure Cheap Justice: Qazi," *Dawn*, August 30, 2004; Muḥammad Idrīs Upal, "ḥisbah bil: yih hangāmah ae k͟hudā kyā hai? [Hisbah Bill: O God, What Is This Ruckus?]," *al-Jam'iyat* 5, no. 11 (August 2005): 5–6, 4.

[59] Qibla Ayaz, interview by Joshua White, English, February 10, 2011.

Assuming that this permitted at least as many muhtasibs as existed jurisdictions, this would create the opportunity for the JUI-F to appoint nearly a hundred madrassah graduates from the party's political ranks into well paid, quasi-official roles throughout every region of the province. This no doubt appealed to the JUI-F elite, which—on account of the educational backgrounds of its party workers—otherwise had few ways of gaining entry into state-funded patronage. (This number does not include members of the muhtasib's staff, the size of which was left indeterminate in the bill; or the "experts and consultants" who could be retained by the muhtasib with remuneration.) The JUI-F knew that a province-wide muhtasib network of party cadres, empowered with nearly unchecked authorities and the ability to requisition government documents, could prove to be a decisive influence in future election campaigns, not to mention grassroots political mobilization.

Not surprisingly, a fierce debate erupted within the MMA leadership about the proposed qualifications of a muhtasib. In short, the JUI-F, as a largely clerical party, wanted to restrict the definition of a "religious scholar" to someone who had graduated with a "Shahadat ul-Aalmiah from any Institute recognized by the Higher Education Commission"—that is, from a madrassah—while the JI, as a largely nonclerical party, wanted a broader definition that could include religious scholars with "modern education" who had attended non-madrassah institutions.[60] Although the JI was adamant on this point, the JUI-F was able to forestall a change to the proposed text, and the definition favorable to the JUI-F was retained.[61]

7.4.3 Vulnerability to State Pressure

MMA leaders faced pressures from party members to embrace the vigilante attacks on music shops and venues, and to aggressively advance the Hisbah bill (including fighting court challenges) to create new enforcement structures for the party's shariah policies. In the end, they were cautious on both counts, most likely because they were constrained by the central government. They stood to lose important patronage opportunities, or face painful sanctions, had they chosen to escalate their Islamization agenda in ways that more obviously embraced violence and coercion, or challenged state authority. There

[60] Law Department, Government of NWFP, *Hisbah Bill*, sec. 2(q). The Shahadat ul-Aalmiah is generally recognized as a masters-level degree. The JI wanted to allow for those who held an M.A. in Islamiyat (Islamic Studies) to qualify as muhtasibs.

[61] Rifatullah Orakzai, interview by Joshua White, Urdu, Telephone, May 30, 2011; Asif Luqman Qazi, interview; Malik Zafar Azam, interview.

were three significant ways in which the martial government and the security services exerted pressure on the MMA: financial pressure, leverage over the madaris, and direct intimidation.

After its victory in 2002, the MMA leaders quickly came to appreciate the benefits of running the NWFP. And just as quickly, they realized that the provincial budget was largely a creature outside of their direct control. The province, they discovered, relied heavily upon funding from foreign donor agencies, and those agencies were, as early as 2003, already skittish about the MMA's Islamization campaign.[62] Just two weeks into his job as senior minister and minister of finance, Siraj ul-Haq of the JI acknowledged that "all planning is dependent on foreign assistance. All our projects are waiting for foreign financial assistance . . . No work is possible in the present state of affairs."[63]

The senior minister was correct. Foreign donor contributions were critical to the MMA's promises to improve basic services in NWFP. The deeper truth, which the MMA also learned early in its tenure, was that political support from Islamabad was even more indispensable. The federal arrangement on taxation effectively granted the central government powers to collect tax in the provinces, and then redistribute the income to the provinces for both operating and developmental budgets. The result was that the NWFP was dependent upon federal transfer payments for approximately 90 percent of the provincial budget. To say that the NWFP found itself in "complete reliance on the federal divisible pool" hardly captures the staggering degree of fiscal leverage exercised by the central government over the province.[64]

One of the top priorities of the MMA leadership was to secure a greater share of federal funds for the provincial exchequer. This meant lobbying the central government to revise the National Finance Commission (NFC) award that distributed federal funds, and also to resolve a long-standing dispute over NWFP's hydroelectric sales. Chief Minister Akram Khan Durrani (JUI-F) and Senior Minister Siraj ul-Haq (JI) focused intensely on these negotiations, both of which ultimately bore fruit for the provincial government. They must also have grappled with the reality that it would have been an inopportune time to defend an outbreak of vigilante violence in the province, or press too hard to secure the creation of a new bespoke shariah police force under their control. As if to make this point, an article in the JI weekly *Aishyā* in early June 2005 segued seamlessly from a discussion of the Hisbah bill to this:

[62] Shehzad, "MMA-Islamabad Preparing to Slug It Out?"
[63] Iqbal Khattak, "Haq Raises Alarm Bells on Frontier Govt," *Daily Times*, December 19, 2002.
[64] Waseem and Mufti, "Religion, Politics and Governance in Pakistan," 47.

> The MMA has to remain very determined and united, because it is facing challenges on many fronts; the NFC award is pending [as is] the royalty on electricity. If these two issues could not be solved, then presentation of the [provincial] budget would be almost impossible.[65]

In another article a few months later, the JI's leading intellectual, Professor Khurshid Ahmad, again made the point, arguing that the central government's "virtual financial blockade" was an obstacle to pursuing its "socio-economic and moral reforms."[66] The MMA leaders apparently came to the conclusion that in order not to be labeled "a disruptive force" by international donors and the Musharraf government, and risk imperiling their ability to engage in lucrative and successful expropriation of public funds, they needed to adopt relatively status-quo policies.[67]

Second, the martial government signaled its willingness to put pressure on madrassahs and madrassah-educated politicians. These moves were felt most acutely within the JUI-F and JUI-S, whose party members were drawn principally from the Deobandi madaris networks. In interviews, a number of JUI leaders spoke about their concern over the central government's restrictions on religious institutions, particularly after 2004, when Musharraf started a new drive to register the madaris nationwide.[68] Pressures on the JUI parties increased again in mid-August 2005—just as the Hisbah debate was in full swing and the local bodies elections were about to begin—when the Lahore High Court unexpectedly "barred several candidates from contesting local bodies polls on the grounds that their degrees were not equivalent to the Matriculation or Secondary School Certificates."[69] Whether or not the Court issued its judgment with the blessing of the Musharraf government is immaterial; the JUI parties saw it as a shot across the bow, and feared that challenging the central government might lead to widespread disqualifications in future elections.

The central government's ability to exert leverage over madaris may help to explain the somewhat different viewpoints on vigilante violence and Hisbah

[65] 'Abdullah K̲h̲ān, "ḥisbah bil manz̤ūrī aur bujaṭ tayārī ke marāḥil meṅ [Hisbah Bill's Passage and the Stages of Budget Preparation]," *Haft Rozah Aishyā (Asia)* 54, no. 23 (June 2, 2005): 19.

[66] K̲h̲ūrshīd Aḥmad, "ṣūbah sarḥad meṅ niz̤ām-e ḥisbah kā aḥyā: hangāmah hai kyūṅ barpā? [System of Hisbah in NWFP: Why the Ruckus Raised?]," *Tarjumān al-Qur'ān* 132, no. 8 (August 2005): 3–27. Translation by the Government of NWFP.

[67] See Waseem and Mufti, "Religion, Politics and Governance in Pakistan," 47; White, *Pakistan's Islamist Frontier*, 68–70.

[68] Misra, "MMA-Democracy Interface in Pakistan," 391.

[69] Mehreen Zahra-Malik, "JI Plans to Exploit LHC Verdict," *Friday Times*, August 12, 2005; Iftikhar Muhammad Chaudhry, "Civil Petitions for Leave to Appeal No. 1569-L, 1579-L, 1597-L, 1600-L, 1622-L and 1624-L of 2005" (Supreme Court of Pakistan, August 16, 2005).

between JI and JUI-F. As the most visible party in the NWFP provincial leadership, and the one most closely affiliated with the madaris, the JUI-F had the most to gain from the MMA's success in the province, and the most to lose if Musharraf began exerting pressure on the madrassah networks.[70] The JI, by contrast, seems to have expected a challenge from Musharraf, and was quicker than the JUI-F to welcome the confrontation as a way of bolstering its political position nationally as an opposition party.[71]

Third, MMA leaders noted in interviews that they were subject to quiet pressures from the state security services. State agencies reportedly started whisper campaigns attempting to fragment the MMA as early as 2003, which included suggestions that the JUI-F should abandon the JI as a coalition partner to ensure the success of its main legislative deliverables, including the Hisbah bill.[72] Later, in 2005, the Islamist parties complained that "the government has mischievously spread the word that religious parties may be banned the world over if their links with al-Qaeda and terror activities are proven."[73] Of course, Musharraf also stood to suffer if he pushed the MMA too far; he would lose a measure of his democratic credentials in the eyes of the international community, and would lose the ability to point to the MMA's Islamization as an internal threat against which he needed American support.

Occasionally the security services threatened the MMA more directly. Malik Zafar Azam, who led the Hisbah effort for the provincial government, recounted:

> As a minister, one time an officer came to my office. He told me that I am from a secret agency. From which department, I didn't know. And told me that I should not make an example of this bill. Very politely, I said that this law was our objective . . . that the local courts don't provide for pity cases, don't provide solutions [for the poor who need justice]. He said "fuck the poor." These are his words.[74]

Such allegations cannot be independently verified, but are not inconsistent with the author's conversations with other provincial officials who were privately pressured by intelligence agencies during the MMA's tenure.

[70] Gul Nasib Khan, interview.

[71] Asif Luqman Qazi, interview; Malik Zafar Azam, interview.

[72] See Misra, "The Rise of Religious Parties in Pakistan"; Shehzad, "MMA-Islamabad Preparing to Slug It Out?"; Muḥammad Rahīm Ḥaqqānī, "sharīʿat kī bālādastī kī manzil pāne keliʾe ḥisbah bil kī manẓūrī nāguzīr hai [To Reach the Stage of Shariah's Superiority, the Passage of Hisbah Bill is Unavoidable]," *al-Jamʿiyat* 4, no. 10 (September 2004): 17; "Differences in MMA Deepen," *Dawn*, August 31, 2005.

[73] Mazhar Abbas, "Will Musharraf Ban the Jamaʿat and JUI?," *Friday Times*, August 26, 2005.

[74] Malik Zafar Azam, interview.

7.4.4 A Rational Restraint

While the MMA was in power in NWFP it tolerated some degree of violence and vigilantism, but its behavior was essentially cautious: It did not indirectly threaten mass unrest if its demands were not met, it proved reluctant to make use of its affiliates or fringe groups to violently advance its agenda, it did not appoint its own muhtasibs to impose shariah, and it did not push beyond what it saw as the constitutional limits to legal change. Two important lessons from this case speak to the arguments from the first chapter of this volume.

The first conclusion is that while the cautious behavior exhibited by the Islamist parties in this case is consistent with their longstanding tendencies to publicly eschew violence against the state, as described in Chapter 3, it is evident that they were particularly cautious given their perceived vulnerabilities to the state. This is consistent with Corollary 1a from the first chapter, and indeed, the Islamist parties' financial and legal vulnerabilities were in fact amplified when they became elected officials rather than merely opposition gadflies.

The second conclusion is that the Islamist parties experienced differential forms of pressure from internal constituencies and from the state. The JUI-F saw its tenure, and its legal Islamization agenda, more in constituent-benefit terms than did the JI. It worried about vigilantism undercutting the longevity of its tenure, and thus its ability to make use of public funds. And it considered the Hisbah to be a valuable source of patronage to its elite constituents (via the muhtasib jobbery), and a necessary demonstration to its lower-level constituents that it was following through on its promises—particularly in the months leading up to the August 2005 local bodies elections.[75] In addition to these internal pressures, the JUI-F was unusually vulnerable to state agencies because of its ties to the madrassah networks, and its reliance on state policy to allow madrassah graduates to stand for elections.

The JI was more focused on playing out a longer-horizon competition with the martial government at the federal level, and was insulated from these particular constituent pressures.[76] This pattern is consistent with Hypotheses 2a and 2b from the first chapter, which posited that clientelist and weakly

[75] Raja Asghar, "All Not Lost for Hasba Sponsors," *Dawn*, August 5, 2005.

[76] Mumtaz Ahmad, ed., *Toward Revisiting the Debate on Shari'a: Prospects and Challenges for Pakistan* (Islamabad: Iqbal International Institute for Research and Dialogue, International Islamic University Islamabad, 2010). After the Hisbah bill was first rejected by the Supreme Court, alliance partners JI and JUI-F actually hired separate lawyers to defend the bill. One plausible explanation for such redundancy was that both parties wanted public credit for standing up to Musharraf over a matter of Islamization. Malik Zafar Azam, interview.

institutionalized parties such as the JUI parties are generally more vulnerable to the state than programmatic and strongly institutionalized parties such as the JI.

The MMA government's tenure in the Frontier raises a number of broader questions about the priorities, decision-making, and viability of Islamist coalitions that face the pressures of governance rather than merely the incentives that come with oppositional politics. Some of these implications will be addressed in the final chapter. Others I have assessed in previous publications.[77] But it is worth noting that over the course of its nearly five-year term, the MMA repeatedly chose to temper aspects of its agenda that were opposed by the central government. They reined in vigilantism, worked to assuage concerns of the World Bank and other international donors, and sought to project an image of responsible governance. Their reasons for doing so were undoubtedly varied and complex. They were looking ahead to the next election, were worried about pressures from the security services, and were aware of the risks posed by their own inexperience in providing government services. But the net result was a reluctance on the part of the MMA to sustain or institutionalize anti-state vigilantism of the kind that the movement's detractors had feared it would carry out when it gained its first sustained taste of power at the provincial level.

[77] See White, *Pakistan's Islamist Frontier*, 65–74.

8

Capital Crimes

The Red Mosque in Islamabad

8.1 Introduction

The year leading up to Pakistan's February 2008 general elections was one of the most tumultuous in the country's history. In March 2007, lawyers and their allies launched a large public protest movement challenging President Musharraf's military government and his suspension of the Chief Justice of the Supreme Court. In November 2007, Musharraf imposed emergency rule, which provided, inter alia, that "the President may, from time to time, by Order amend the Constitution, as is deemed expedient."[1] In December 2007, two-time prime minister and presumptive frontrunner for the forthcoming general elections, Benazir Bhutto, was assassinated at a public rally. Also in December of that year, a group of anti-state militants in the Pakistani tribal areas coalesced under the leadership of Baitullah Mehsud as the Tahrik-e-Taliban Pakistan (TTP).

But this was not all. One of the most important episodes of 2007 was the crisis that unfolded in the summer over the radical Red Mosque (Lal Masjid) in the heart of the capital city Islamabad—an institution whose leaders had become increasingly aggressive about undertaking vigilante violence to enforce their vision of shariah. The Pakistan Army's subsequent siege of the Red Mosque led to an upsurge in anti-state violence across the country. It also sparked debate among the country's various Islamist parties over the legitimacy and efficacy of vigilante Islamism: that is, over the permissibility of a non-state actor to take unilateral action, through violence if necessary, to enforce the shariah apart from the hand of the state.

This case is important because it speaks directly to the central question of this volume: Why, and under what conditions, do Pakistan's Islamist parties enable religiously justified anti-state violence? For this case, the JI, JUI-F, and JUI-S were the principal parties responding to the Red Mosque crisis. This

[1] "Provisional Constitutional Order," *Dawn*, November 4, 2007.

Vigilante Islamists. Joshua T. White, Oxford University Press. © Oxford University Press (2025).
DOI: 10.1093/9780197814178.003.0008

chapter begins with a review of the crisis itself, then proceeds to examine the Islamist parties' reactions to the events surrounding the Red Mosque, and concludes with an analysis of the ideological and structural drivers of those reactions.[2]

8.2 Background to the Case

The Red Mosque had not always been a symbol of anti-state agitation. The mosque's founder and former head, Maulana Muhammad Abdullah, was a beneficiary of President Zia ul-Haq's program of state-directed Islamization in the 1980s and had developed close ties to the Inter-Services Intelligence bureaucracy headquartered nearby. Abdullah was assassinated in a sectarian attack in 1998, during a period of intense Sunni–Shia conflict. He had been educated at the hardline Binori Town madrassah in Karachi, and had developed deep links with militant Deobandi organizations such as Jaish-e-Muhammad and Harkat ul-Mujahidin, along with more narrowly anti-Shia movements such as Sipah-e-Sahabah and Lashkar-e-Jhangvi.[3] The Red Mosque thus had decades of deep links to the Deobandi militant universe as well as ties to the Pakistani security services.

Following Abdullah's death, his sons Abdul Aziz and Abdur Rashid Ghazi assumed control of the state-administered mosque. Affiliated with the mosque were major male and female madaris—the Jamia Faridia and Jamia Hafsa, respectively—which drew a large number of students from the Pakistani frontier, along with other affiliate institutions beyond Islamabad. (One Islamabad official estimated that about 70% of the thousands of students that studied in the two madaris came from the North-West Frontier Province or from the adjacent tribal areas.[4]) Both Jamia Faridia and Jamia Hafsa were originally constructed on land granted from the Islamabad Capital Development Authority, but later were dramatically and illegally expanded. Up until 2007, neither local nor federal authorities had shown an interest in challenging the blatant land grabs, or confronting what appeared to be the development of an armed "state within the state" inside the walls of the two institutions.[5]

[2] Portions of this chapter are drawn from Joshua T. White, "Vigilante Islamism in Pakistan: Religious Party Responses to the Lal Masjid Crisis," *Current Trends in Islamist Ideology* 7 (Autumn 2008).

[3] Amir Mir, *The Fluttering Flag of Jehad* (Lahore: Mashal Books, 2008), 63; Khaled Ahmed, *Religious Developments in Pakistan: 1999–2008*, vol. 2, The Musharraf Years (Lahore: Vanguard, 2010), 316; Amélie Blom, "Changing Religious Leadership in Contemporary Pakistan: The Case of the Red Mosque," in *Pakistan and Its Diaspora: Multidisciplinary Approaches*, ed. Marta Bolognani and Stephen M. Lyon (New York: Palgrave Macmillan, 2011), 143ff.

[4] Umer Farooq, "Deceptively Smart," *Herald*, May 2007, 49–50.

[5] Azfar-ul-Ashfaque, "Students Trained for Suicide Attacks: MQM Report on Lal Masjid," *Dawn*, April 23, 2007.

The crisis was triggered by a series of provocations by the madrassah students that included a campaign protesting the demolition of an illegally constructed mosque in Islamabad; the takeover of a nearby children's library by heavily-armed female students; the kidnapping of alleged prostitutes from a Chinese acupuncture clinic; the abduction of police officers; the attacking of music shops; the stockpiling of weapons; and the burning of a nearby government building.[6] In addition, Abdul Aziz Ghazi established a parallel qazi court in Islamabad, and soon thereafter began issuing fatawa against local purveyors of "vulgarity," including a female federal minister whom he accused of obscenity for being photographed hugging a paragliding instructor in Paris.[7]

The Ghazi brothers appear to have decided that if the state would not act against public "indecency," then they would do so themselves.[8] Their intentions were, at the outset, seemingly limited in scope. As Faisal Devji has noted, "Their kidnappings and forcible closing of immoral businesses were attempts to court publicity that resulted not so much in the meting out of any Islamic punishments as in the almost Maoist 're-education' and subsequent release of alleged prostitutes."[9] Gradually, however, the Red Mosque leaders lost confidence in the state to carry out their vision of a complete Islamic reformation. The Ghazi brothers, drawing on their expansive links to Deobandi militant networks, had built close linkages with the Afghan Taliban and with capable militant groups such as Jaish-e-Muhammad. Combined with the Ghazis' own self-amplified cult of martyrdom, these ties likely gave them confidence in mounting a full-scale confrontation with state institutions.[10]

The religious justifications for the Red Mosque clerics' vigilantism was never entirely spelled out by the Ghazi brothers. But there are clues to their views of shariah. Consistent with their close ties with Deobandi sectarian organizations, some of their vigilantism had a pronounced anti-Shia impetus.[11] They "abducted a Shia lady in Islamabad after accusing her of running a brothel" and, according to one BBC report, "while they were dragging her family out, the Lal Masjid vigilantes had referred to the Shia sect as a 'sect of

[6] See, inter alia, Shakeel Anjum, "Lal Masjid Seizes Four Cops," *The News*, May 19, 2007; Declan Walsh, "Army Ready to Storm Mosque as Conflict Grows," *Guardian*, July 4, 2007; "Chronology of Lal Masjid Clashes," *Press Trust of India*, July 10, 2007. Some of these actions were similar to those undertaken by Jamia Faridia students in 2003, when they organized riots following the killing of anti-Shia militant Azam Tariq. Hassan Abbas, "The Road to Lal Masjid and Its Aftermath," *Jamestown Terrorism Monitor* 5, no. 14 (July 19, 2007).

[7] Syed Irfan Raza, "Fatwa Against Nilofar Issued," *Dawn*, April 9, 2007.

[8] Blom, "Changing Religious Leadership in Contemporary Pakistan: The Case of the Red Mosque," 156.

[9] Faisal Devji, "Red Mosque," *Public Culture* 20, no. 1 (Winter 2008): 20.

[10] Journalist Nicholas Schmidle, who interviewed Abdur Rashid Ghazi on multiple occasions, has noted the important catalyzing influence of more hardline militant groups like Jaish in shaping Ghazi's approach to the state. Nicholas Schmidle, interview by Joshua White, English, May 2008. See also Qandeel Siddique, "The Red Mosque Operation and Its Impact on the Growth of the Pakistani Taliban" (Kjeller, Norway: Norwegian Defence Research Establishment, October 8, 2008), 37ff.

[11] Ahmed, *Religious Developments in Pakistan: 1999–2008*, 2: 316.

prostitutes.'"[12] Mariam Abu Zahab observed that Jaish-e-Muhammad played a significant role in supporting the Red Mosque clerics and that "[t]he militants entrenched in the mosque were made to believe that the soldiers who led the assault were all Shias."[13] The Ghazi brothers had also gradually grown distant from and disillusioned with the Pakistani state. In 2004, they issued a fatwa against the Pakistan Army's military operations in the FATA. This displeased the military and security services. Abdur Rashid Ghazi recounted:

> At first, pressure was brought to bear upon us by government functionaries (including the ISI) to withdraw the fatwa. No amount of reasoning that a fatwa was not like an official notification which could be withdrawn on anyone's whims . . . and that its withdrawal meant denial of the injunctions of the Quran and Sunnah had any effect on the authorities. Our inability to comply with their wishes was taken as defiance on our parts . . . . Thereafter, an unending process of harassment and victimization was unleashed upon us.[14]

By early 2007, with the advent of a sustained campaign of vigilantism by his students, Abdur Rashid was picking new fights with the government. These, too, he justified in the name of an immutable shariah. He argued, in contradiction to established Sunni jurisprudence, that "land that does not belong to an individual must be treated as the property of the community" and when challenged, claimed that "this is not a matter of law. Shariah comes first, the law later."[15] Repeatedly, he drew distinctions between "law of the land" and the "law of Allah," and maintained that he was within his rights to carry out his own justice, since he had reported a complaint about the massage parlors to the government and they had ignored him.[16] Local officials, for their part, insisted that the charges were never reported to authorities.

Eventually, President Musharraf and his security agencies grew frustrated with the Ghazi brothers.[17] As negotiations dragged on through April and May, the Red Mosque appeared increasingly fortified, and its leaders increasingly resistant to compromise. On July 3, the conflict escalated when security forces engaged some of the militants, leaving ten dead and over a hundred

[12] Ahmed, *Religious Developments in Pakistan: 1999–2008*, 2: 316.

[13] Mariam Abou Zahab, *A Kaleidoscope of Islam* (New York: Oxford University Press, 2020), 136–37.

[14] Quoted in Noreen Haider, "Spreading the Writ of God," *The News*, July 1, 2007.

[15] Rubab Karrar and Umer Farooq, "'If the Government Does Not Heed Our Call, the People Will Rise': Interview with Maulana Abdul Rashid Ghazi," *Herald*, May 2007, 50.

[16] Quoted in Haider, "Spreading the Writ of God"; Rubab Karrar, "Inside the Mosque," *Herald*, May 2007.

[17] For a good history of the crisis and its implications, see Manjeet S. Pardesi, "The Battle for the Soul of Pakistan at Islamabad's Red Mosque," in *Treading on Hallowed Ground: Counterinsurgency Operations in Sacred Spaces*, ed. C. Christine Fair and Sumit Ganguly (Oxford University Press, 2008), 88–116, https://doi.org/10.1093/acprof:oso/9780195342048.003.0005.

wounded. The following day, about 1,200 students from Jamia Hafsa surrendered to authorities.[18] The casualty count increased over the subsequent days as the government moved more forces into place around the mosque, and continued to negotiate with the Ghazi brothers. Finally, on July 10, after a week of skirmishes and failed on-and-off negotiations, Musharraf ordered a full-scale operation against the forces holed up in the Red Mosque and the adjacent Jamia Hafsa. In the course of the operation, which was bloody but tactically effective, Abdul Rashid Ghazi and scores of students were killed.[19]

The reaction to the army's siege, which was dubbed "Operation Silence," was swift. A wave of political protests criticized Musharraf for his heavy-handed response to the students, sectarian killings against Shia in the tribal areas were carried out as reprisals for the operation, and self-styled "Taliban" groups—including Baitullah Mehsud in Waziristan and affiliated organizations in Swat—unleashed a spate of suicide bombings that continued throughout the summer and fall of 2007.[20] Musharraf's handling of the crisis turned out to be a major political liability for his government, and was viewed by many Pakistanis as yet another indication that he was beholden to American, rather than Pakistani national interests.

8.3 The Role of the Islamist Parties

8.3.1 The Brewing Crisis

Like most other political parties in Pakistan, the Islamist parties saw the Red Mosque crisis as an opportunity to criticize President Musharraf and paint his military rule as un-Islamic, or at the very least illegitimate. Even the PPP led by then-exiled Benazir Bhutto, which welcomed military action against the Red Mosque clerics, and which many expected would come to an agreement with Musharraf to form a government after the 2008 general elections, took pains to highlight its view that extremism was a direct consequence of military rule and the suppression of democracy.[21]

[18] Umer Farooq, "Red Seige in Capital," *Herald*, July 2007, 73.

[19] The best estimates put the number killed at about 200, though the Islamist parties have claimed that the true number was several times higher. Interior Minister Aftab Sherpao, speaking before parliament, claimed that there were only 103 casualties, including security personnel. "National Assembly of Pakistan Debates: Official Report," 2007, vol. 42, no. 2 (Islamabad, July 31, 2007).

[20] Zahab, *A Kaleidoscope of Islam*, 137.

[21] See, for example, Benazir Bhutto, "A Conversation with Benazir Bhutto" (Council on Foreign Relations, Washington, DC, August 15, 2007), https://web.archive.org/web/20240329225035/https://www.cfr.org/event/conversation-benazir-bhutto-0.

The involvement of the Islamist parties in the Red Mosque crisis remains opaque. In early 2007 as Jamia Hafsa students began their vigilante campaign in Islamabad, both the JI and the JUI-F responded to these provocations in more or less the same manner. Both parties affirmed the general goals of the students' Islamist agenda; counseled the state to negotiate with the activists; and blamed the government for targeting Islamic madaris and seeking their reform in order to curry favor with the West. At the same time, the JI and JUI-F leaders criticized the students for attacking local houses (such as massage parlors), noting that "such things [are] not allowed in civil society" and that only the state had the authority to determine which citizen to apprehend for which crime.[22] Both parties also initially shared a reluctance to becoming embroiled in the Red Mosque controversy; JI leader Liaquat Baloch insisted that "we have nothing to do with the issue" of the students' vigilantism, while Fazl ur-Rahman refused to answer questions on the matter. "If you want to talk on the madrassah Hafsa issue," Rahman's assistant told a journalist, "the Maulana will not talk to you."[23]

Soon thereafter, however, the JI's leadership began to qualify its criticism of the students. Recognizing that taking a harsh stand against burqah-clad, shariah-promoting female students would likely prove unpopular among its rank-and-file, one JI spokesman declared that his objection was not simply to the students' actions *as such*. His objection, instead, was to the fact that the vigilante campaign against such vulgarity was being led by *women*—which, he claimed, was clearly forbidden by Islam.[24]

It was not long before the official JI and JUI-F positions on the madrassah-based vigilantism began to diverge. By mid-April, the JI's amir, Qazi Hussain Ahmad, had begun to speak more forcefully in favor of the Jamia Hafsa.[25] Although he reiterated that "the MMA does not want to implement shariah by force," he described the Ghazi brothers' new qazi court a "positive" step and lent his support to the Red Mosque's administration.[26] After mid-April, the JI leadership was quite consistent in its support of the clerics; there was, noted the party's Deputy General Secretary Khalid Rehman in an interview

[22] JI leader Liaquat Baloch, quoted in "Jamia Hafsa and MMA's Reprimand," *Daily Times*, April 6, 2007. See also "Qazi Demands Withdrawal of Warning Notices," *Daily Times*, February 16, 2007; "Qazi Blames Govt for Jamia Hafsa Issue," *Nation*, April 8, 2007.

[23] Amir Wasim, "MMA in a Fix Over Lal Masjid Issue," *Dawn*, April 7, 2007.

[24] Nauman Tasleem, "MMA Raps Capital Clerics," *Daily Times*, April 5, 2007.

[25] Iqbal Khattak, "Durrani Denounces 'Islamisation' Drive Against His Government," *Friday Times*, April 20, 2007.

[26] This statement was provided by Qazi Hussain on behalf of the MMA, but does not appear to have been representative of opinion within the alliance as a whole. "JUI-F, JI Differ Over Jamia Hafsa Issue," *Daily Times*, April 12, 2007.

with the author, "no confusion" within the JI about whether to back the Ghazi brothers.[27]

The JI was also quick to downplay the notion that the Red Mosque clerics were challenging the state in any meaningful way. Even in interviews conducted after the events, JI leaders who were eyewitnesses to the crisis seemed almost bemused at the idea that the vigilantes were challenging the writ of the state. Dr. Farid Paracha, another of the JI's deputy general secretaries who was involved as a go-between throughout the crisis, argued that the Ghazi brothers did not challenge the state, but only "created some fear" in the community.[28] Syed Belal, a prominent leader of the JI Islamabad office only blocks from the Red Mosque, similarly expressed puzzlement: "What sort of challenge they were posing to the writ of the government, I don't know."[29] The consensus within the JI was that the students in Islamabad were at best fearless advocates of shariah, and at worst victims of a repressive military state.

The JUI-F, by contrast, looked at the same actions of the students and came to a different conclusion. When Maulana Muhammad Abu Bakar, deputy general secretary of the party in Punjab, asked with incredulity, "How is it possible that 400 girls wearing the veil and using the club can change the state?" he was not concerned with the resilience of the state, but with the futility of the students' protest.[30] Again and again in interviews and publications, the JUI-F expressed the view that the students' protests were fruitless and even dangerous. (According to one party insider, when Fazl ul-Rahman finally visited Abdul Aziz Ghazi in prison after the siege, he chided him for waging a failed effort at reform.[31]) While blaming the intelligence agencies for fomenting conspiracies to create "a pretext for taking . . . action against seminaries across the country," the JUI-F also urged the Red Mosque's administration to be wary of being manipulated by the state.[32]

In hindsight, it appears that this statement from JUI-F was meant to signal to the Red Mosque that the party did not approve of its actions and would not agree to agitate on its behalf. Internally, according to senior party leader Maulana Gul Nasib Khan, the party met early on at the markazi

[27] Khalid Rehman, interview by Joshua White, English and Urdu, trans. Shuja Malik, February 23, 2011.
[28] Farid Paracha, interview by Joshua White, English and Urdu, trans. Shuja Malik, March 8, 2011.
[29] Syed Belal, interview by Joshua White, English, February 18, 2011.
[30] Muhammad Abu Bakar, interview by Joshua White, Urdu, trans. Shuja Malik, May 16, 2011.
[31] Fatahullah Sajjad, interview by Joshua White, Urdu, trans. Shuja Malik, March 6, 2011.
[32] See Nisar Mehdi, "Jamia Hafsa Issue Called a Conspiracy," *Nation*, April 13, 2007; "Agencies Behind Hafsa Standoff: Fazl," *Dawn*, April 10, 2007; "Agencies Behind Lal Masjid Controversy: MMA Leader," *Dawn*, April 10, 2007.

majlis-e-shura and markazi majlis-e-amala levels and took that position that "we wanted to prevent fighting if we could, but didn't want to support either group."[33] As the crisis unfolded, this position of effective neutrality meant that the JUI-F's close associates within the Deobandi madrassah community began openly calling for greater restraint on the part of Jamia Hafsa in particular.

In April, many of the leaders of the Wafaq ul-Madaris al-Arabia, the leading Deobandi madrassah board in Pakistan, voiced concerns over the escalation of vigilante violence from the Jamia Hafsa. The Deobandi Wafaq then took the further—and highly unusual—step of revoking the madrassah's certification, and the board's secretary general Qari Hanif Jalandhri tried to insert himself as a mediator in the talks between Abdul Aziz Ghazi and the Pakistan government.[34] Jalandhri voiced the Deobandi leadership's delicately balanced position, arguing that, "We are against a policy of taking on the government in a head-on fight, as such a policy can only lead to damage," but noting in the next breath that he supported Abdul Aziz's demands "one-hundred-and-one percent."[35] Another leading Deobandi cleric, Mufti Rafi Usmani, tried a similar balancing act: "We should continue the struggle that they have started . . . [but their path] leads to violence and fighting, which we do not at all condone or permit."[36] By May, one journalist noted that no prominent Deobandi group or institution had come out in support of the Ghazi brothers.[37]

The JUI-F's ambivalence about the Jamia Hafsa took many observers by surprise. After all, as one up-and-coming JUI-F politician put it, "the madaris are our number one priority," and many expected that this meant that party would strive to defend the Red Mosque.[38] But as it turned out, the Deobandis were making a second, parallel political calculation: They were afraid that one high-profile case of violent vigilantism would tarnish the reputation of Deobandi madaris throughout the country. Much of this fear was articulated by the Wafaq ul-Madaris al-Arabia leadership and former politicians such as the influential Maulana Hassan Jan in Peshawar rather than by JUI-F officials as such.[39] Interviews in Islamabad and Peshawar with party leaders in the

[33] Gul Nasib Khan, interview by Joshua White and Niloufer Siddiqui, Urdu, May 26, 2011.

[34] "No Compromise on Sharia, Says Ghazi," *Daily Times*, April 12, 2007.

[35] "No Wafaqul Madaris Support for Jamia Hafsa," *Daily Times*, April 15, 2007.

[36] "No Wafaqul Madaris Support for Jamia Hafsa." See also Muhammad Qasim Zaman, "Pakistan: Shari'a and the State," in *Shari'a Politics*, ed. Robert W. Hefner (Bloomington: Indiana University Press, 2011), 227.

[37] Farooq, "Deceptively Smart," 48.

[38] Shuja ul-Mulk, interview by Joshua White, Urdu, trans. M. Asif Gul, July 26, 2007.

[39] Maulana Hassan Jan, a staunchly conservative Deobandi cleric who was perhaps the most respected religious leader in the NWFP, came out forcefully against Maulana Abdul Aziz. He was assassinated in September 2007 by unknown assailants believed to be associated with the Waziri Taliban. See Akhtar

summer of 2007 confirm that the position of Deobandi Wafaq leaders such as Jalandhri's were in fact broadly representative of the party's own thinking, especially as it concerned the risks associated with appearing to be too supportive of the Ghazi brothers. As if reading from talking-points (a practice at odds with the otherwise chaotic nature of Deobandi politics), one party leader after another declared, "Ghazi's objective is right, but his path is wrong."[40]

The preoccupation with protecting its madaris network was the dominant theme in the JUI-F's rhetoric, and that of its partners among the ulama. Clerics in Karachi encouraged their students to remain peaceful, and fretted that the "unwise activities" of the Jamia Hafsa students would tarnish madrassah students throughout Pakistan, as well as reduce donations by the public to the local madaris.[41] An influential cleric in KP laid out his fears more explicitly: "Through this act, all of the country's madrassas will be accused of training militants."[42] According to JUI-F insiders, this reputational risk weighed heavily on party leaders as they considered how to respond to the Red Mosque movement.[43]

The JUI-F also seems to have been spooked that the Red Mosque confrontation in Islamabad could create a pretext for terminating its tenure in NWFP—where it was still the leading and most visible party of the MMA government. The JUI-F could not openly oppose the Jamia Hafsa's establishment of qazi courts, since the MMA itself had proposed a similar arrangement in its ill-fated Hisbah bill. But the party was concerned that if it was seen as legitimizing vigilante Islamism against the central government, it would have no credible reason to oppose those same activities perpetrated against its *own* government in the Frontier. This was more than an academic concern. In the spring of 2007, the Islamist government in Peshawar was dealing with a vigilante Islamist of its own—Maulana Yousaf Qureshi of the Muttahida Shariat Mahaz. Qureshi was threatening to close music shops and launch a unilateral "jihad" against brothels in Peshawar. The JUI-F-affiliated chief minister of the NWFP pleaded, "Some people are violating the law in the name of 'religious sentiment' because they want to topple my government. I ask these clerics: what they want to do through force—can it not be done through democracy?"[44]

Amin, "Govt Engineering Jamia Hafsa Crisis," *Daily Times*, April 8, 2007; "Noted Religious Scholar Maulana Hassan Jan Gunned Down," *Associated Press of Pakistan*, September 15, 2007.

[40] For a longer exposition of this argument, see K͟hālid Mahmūd Somro, "kyā nifāz̠-e islām kā maṭālibah karnā jurm hai? [Is it a Crime to Demand the Enforcement of Islam?]," *al-Jam'iyat* 8, no. 11–12 (October 2007): 15.

[41] "Karachi-Based Madaris Distance Themselves from Lal Masjid Issue," *The News*, July 5, 2007.

[42] Amin, "Govt Engineering Jamia Hafsa Crisis."

[43] Mahbub ur-Rahman Qureshi, interview by Joshua White, Urdu, trans. Shuja Malik, May 24, 2011; Mufti Ibrar and Lutf ur-Rahman, interview by Joshua White, Urdu, trans. Shuja Malik, May 27, 2011.

[44] Khattak, "Durrani Denounces 'Islamisation' Drive Against His Government."

8.3.2 Operation Silence and Beyond

As the crisis peaked in early July, both parties began to recalibrate their language, emphasizing their support for the Red Mosque movement. After a scuffle between madrassah students and police on July 3, which left several students dead, JI amir Qazi Hussain Ahmad declared the state "wholly responsible," and Maulana Fazl ur-Rahman of the JUI-F thundered that the government was playing a "game of blood and fire."[45]

This rhetoric notwithstanding, the JUI-F was in practice quietly working to defuse the situation by assisting the central government as an intermediary, with Chief Minister Akram Khan Durrani meeting clerics from the Wafaq ul-Madaris al-Arabia as well as representatives of the Ghazi brothers at the government-run Frontier House in Islamabad.[46] The JI also inserted itself into the negotiations, with Islamabad leader Syed Belal taking a prominent role in reaching out to the Red Mosque clerics, who were holed up just blocks from the JI offices in Melody Market.[47] For a moment, it looked as though a compromise agreement might be reached: The Jamia Hafsa would be transferred to the control of the Deobandi Wafaq, thus satisfying both government concerns as well as the Deobandi ulama's concerns over state interference in the madrassah system.[48] But the agreement soon fell apart—apparently for reasons of mutual inflexibility, as Jalandrhi later implied—and the Pakistan Army proceeded with its siege.[49]

By the time the dust settled, political realities had clearly begun to change, and the JUI-F did not waste time further revising its earlier position. Although in theory it remained opposed to the vigilantism of the Jamia Hafsa students, it felt pressure to distance itself from the government and accede to the hagiographical narrative regarding the Red Mosque that was being promulgated by the JI and other Islamist groups. Abdul Rashid Ghazi, who was killed in the operation, was hailed as a martyr by the JI amir Qazi Hussain,

[45] Khattak, "Durrani Denounces 'Islamisation' Drive Against His Government"; "Rallies Against Lal Masjid Operation," *Dawn*, July 5, 2007.

[46] Ismail Khan, "A Marriage on the Rocks," *Dawn*, October 10, 2007. Other MMA leaders, from both JI and JUI-F, also met with the Lal Masjid clerics to seek a peaceful resolution of the standoff. Muhammad Anis, "MMA MPs, 18 Ulema Attempted to Broker Ceasefire," *The News*, July 4, 2007.

[47] Belal insisted that a deal in which Abdur Rashid Ghazi would give himself up was close to fruition when the army stepped in and carried out its operation. Syed Belal, interview.

[48] The Wafaq ul-Madaris al-Arabia gave Interior Minister Aftab Sherpao a statement, in writing, attesting that the Ghazi brothers were not implementing real shariah. Once it became clear, however, that they would not be given control of the sizeable Jamia Hafsa and Faridia madaris, they "lost interest" in the negotiations. Aftab Sherpao, interview by Joshua White, English, February 17, 2011.

[49] Naveed Butt, "Ulema Blame Govt for Sabotaging Talks," *Nation*, July 11, 2007. See also Rājah Bashīr 'Uṣmānī, "āpareshan sā'īlins: ḥaqā'iq kyā haiṅ? [Operation Silence: What are the Facts?]," *Haft Rozah Aishyā (Asia)* 56, no. 30 (July 19, 2007): 19–22.

and Fazl ur-Rahman praised the Red Mosque fighters as "mujahideens who fought for enforcing Islam in its true spirit."[50] Even acknowledging that the students fired first, JI leaders were adamant that they were not culpable for the violence.[51]

In a very real way, Operation Silence transformed the role of the Red Mosque in the debate over vigilante Islamism. Gone was the symbol of Ghazis-as-vigilantes that had proved so vexing for the JUI-F. In its place emerged a picture of the Ghazis-as-martyrs that was to prove a much more potent symbolic weapon for the Islamist parties to use against the government. On one level, Operation Silence came as a welcome relief for the JUI-F: The public's attention was diverted away from illicit activities of Deobandi madaris and toward the heavy-handed and widely condemned actions of the government. And if the Deobandis were relieved, the JI was ecstatic. Sensing a political opening against President Musharraf, the JI tacked heavily in support of the Red Mosque movement, stoking public anger against the government's handling of the crisis. Party amir Qazi Hussain Ahmad resigned his National Assembly seat in protest (his tenure was nearing its conclusion) and JI leaders unloaded an intense rhetorical barrage against Musharraf. Liaquat Baloch was particularly exercised: "The blood of martyrs will bear fruit. This struggle will reach its destination of an Islamic revolution. Musharraf is a killer of the constitution. He's a killer of male and female students. The entire world will see him hang."[52]

Unfortunately for the JI, the expressions of support for the students in Islamabad were not entirely mutual. This was not so much a case of a party engaging in "alliance formation with violence specialists" as it was an attempt to gain credibility from a loose and relatively low-risk association with a violent movement.[53] Prior to the army operations, the relationship between the Red Mosque leadership and the JI had been mutually advantageous; the Ghazi brothers used the JI to amplify their political voice, and the JI used the Red Mosque crisis to impugn President Musharraf. But after the military intervention and the dead from Red Mosque were hailed as martyrs, the JI found that it was no longer "needed" by the very movement that it was trying to defend and helped to lionize.

[50] Dilshad Azeem, "1000 Killed in Operation, Claims MMA," *Nation*, July 13, 2007; "Suicide Attacks, Lal Masjid Raid Mar NA Session," *Nation*, July 31, 2007.

[51] Yousaf Ali, "Political Parties Condemn Action," *The News*, July 4, 2007; Asif Luqman Qazi, interview by Joshua White, English, May 25, 2011.

[52] Muhammad Anis, "Qazi to Quit NA to Protest Lal Masjid Operation," *The News*, July 15, 2007; "Riots Mar Reopening of Lal Masjid," *The News*, July 28, 2007.

[53] Niloufer A. Siddiqui, *Under the Gun: Political Parties and Violence in Pakistan* (Cambridge: Cambridge University Press, 2023), 48, https://doi.org/10.1017/9781009242530.

Several weeks after Operation Silence, when the government attempted to re-open the Red Mosque for Friday prayers, it again was confronted by mobs of young madrassah students. As police (and this author) looked on, the students promptly re-took the mosque, hoisted the black flag of jihad, repainted the dome of the mosque a vibrant red, and yelled from the roof, "Ghazi, Ghazi, from your blood the revolution will come!"[54] Perhaps most tellingly, when two senior members of the JI attempted to enter the mosque and lead prayers in Ghazi's honor, they were forcefully rebuffed by angry students, and pressed to retreat to the courtyard, where they prayed and then hosted a news conference.

The Deobandi political leadership faced its own conundrum in the wake of Operation Silence. It was forced to confront deep internal rifts over its relationship to vigilante groups. These rifts erupted into view during the Wafaq ul-Madaris al-Arabia meetings in early August 2007.[55] The madaris board was split between those, like JUI-F leader Maulana Fazl ur-Rahman and Qari Hanif Jalandhri, who wanted to downplay the Red Mosque issue; and those like Maulana Sami ul-Haq of the JUI-S and JUI-F politician Hafiz Hussain Ahmad from Balochistan, who wanted to launch a mass protest against the Red Mosque operation and agitate in support of Maulana Abdul Aziz, who was by that time in government custody.[56] Although he played only a bit role in the crisis, Sami ul-Haq and his party—which historically had more overt ties to militant groups than the JUI-F—were particularly vocal in support of the Ghazi brothers, and blamed the Deobandi Wafaq for failing to mediate in time to avoid a tragedy.[57]

The Wafaq-ul Madaris al-Arabia itself had reason to be worried about defections from member institutions; more than a thousand madrassahs had reportedly filed for membership with an alternate, Red Mosque-supporting wafaq in the months leading up to Operation Silence.[58] After the operation, the board supported protests, and also moved to file a writ petition before the Supreme Court, charging the government with intentionally defiling the Quran in the course of its raids on the mosque.[59] The JUI-F was, in theory,

[54] Observations by the author, July 27, 2007, Islamabad.

[55] Nadeem Shah, "Wafaq-Ul-Madaris Faces Split," *The News*, August 8, 2007.

[56] Hafiz Hussain Ahmad was interested in leveraging Abdul Aziz's situation in order to shame President Musharraf and thwart what he believed to be malicious American designs on Pakistani sovereignty. Hafiz Hussain Ahmad, interview by Joshua White, English and Urdu, trans. M. Asif Gul, August 7, 2007. For his part, Fazl ur-Rahman argued unconvincingly that the divisions within the Wafaq were Musharraf's doing. Yousaf Ali, "Resignations to Be Decided by APDM," *The News*, August 26, 2007.

[57] See Rāshid al-Ḥaq Samīʾ Ḥaqqānī, "lahū rang lāl masjid kā alam nāk ḥādiṣah [The Alarming Tragedy of the Bloody Lal Masjid]," *al-Ḥaq* 42, no. 10 (July 2007): 1–4.

[58] Muhammad Amir Rana, "A Court of One's Own," *Herald*, May 2007.

[59] See Abdul Qudus Muhammadi, "vafāq ul-madāris kī sāniḥah lāl masjid par riṭ paṭīshan [Wafaq ul-Madaris' Writ Petition Over Red Mosque Tragedy]," *Islam*, April 29, 2012; "SC Moved Against Lal Masjid Operation," *Dawn*, August 5, 2007.

not opposed to these decisions of the Deobandi Wafaq—indeed, party leader Abdul Ghaffur Haidri led one of the Wafaq-inspired protests in Islamabad—but it remained opposed to the madaris board actively endorsing the Red Mosque clerics' actions.[60] Fazl ur-Rahman worried that the Deobandi Wafaq, whose functional mandate was in principle limited to officiating the national madrassah examinations, would begin driving the debate within the JUI-F about radical methods of shariah enforcement. The minority faction in the JUI-F, led by Hafiz Hussain Ahmad and Maulana Noor Muhammad from Balochistan, was known to be more fiercely anti-Shia, supportive of both the Afghan Taliban and the nascent Pakistani Taliban, and bent on disassociating the party from Musharraf's PML-Q.[61] Even more troubling to Rahman was that Qazi Hussain Ahmad, who led the "non-sectarian" Jamaat-e-Islami but whose father was a Deobandi cleric, appeared to be making moves to coordinate with the Deobandi Wafaq's hardline faction, going over the head of the JUI-F leadership.[62]

These moves within the Wafaq-ul Madaris al-Arabia only compounded the JUI-F's already delicate position in the weeks following Operation Silence. There were indications that the party was having trouble controlling its affiliated madrassah students who were upset with the party's tepid response to the operation.[63] And at the national level, the party was dealing with pressures to quit the government coalition in Balochistan, calls to adopt a harder line against Musharraf, and scattered resignations of local party officials.[64] Some of these political pressures became moot by 2008, as attention turned to the general elections. Others were mitigated over time by the JUI-F's shrewd use of symbolic endorsements of the memory of Red Mosque—seen, for example, in Fazl ur-Rahman's meeting with Abdul Aziz Ghazi; the party's call for the government to rebuild Jamia Hafsa and cease with the ongoing police presence at Jamia Faridia; and the party's embrace of the new Red Mosque prayer leaders (who happened to be sympathetic to the JUI-F).[65]

The JI continued its efforts to take advantage of the Red Mosque crisis well into 2008. Both major Islamist parties referenced Operation Silence as a rationale for the restoration of democracy, but whereas the JUI-F's focus

[60] Muhammad Anis, "Rallies Assail Raid on Lal Masjid," *The News*, July 14, 2007.

[61] "Rift in JUI-F Over Support to Taliban," *Dawn*, May 28, 2006; "Radicalisation of Wafaq Seminaries," *Daily Times*, August 11, 2007.

[62] Khaled Ahmed, "Making Chaos?," *Friday Times*, July 20, 2007.

[63] Umer Farooq, "Repainting It Red?," *Herald*, August 2007.

[64] Muhammad Ahmad Noorani, "Jamia Hafsa Students Urge Fazl to Quit Assemblies," *The News*, September 24, 2007; "Two Leaders of JUI-F Resign," *Dawn*, July 24, 2007.

[65] "Despite the 'Unilateral Ceasefire', Things Are Not Good," *Daily Times*, February 11, 2008; Delawar Jan, "Independence, Protection of Seminaries Demanded," *The News*, July 5, 2008; Asad Kharal, "Lal Masjid Deputy Cleric Likely to Face the Chop," *Express Tribune*, October 11, 2011; Saba Imtiaz, "People with Luxurious Lifestyles Cannot Bring Islamic Revolution," *Express Tribune*, January 27, 2012.

was on empowering the country's religious (read: clerical) leadership, the JI focused its attacks squarely on Musharraf.[66] This can be seen most clearly in the remarkable document produced by the MMA Fact-Finding Commission that investigated the events surrounding the Red Mosque.[67] The commission included thirteen parliamentarians, including members of both the JI and JUI-F, and ostensibly represented the views of the entire alliance. An interview with the report's author, Dr. Farid Paracha, made it clear that the commission's work and the resulting document were almost entirely the product of the JI's parliamentary staff office in Islamabad.[68] The report documents the JI's impressive organizational efforts surrounding the Red Mosque events: They set up two on-site coordination centers, managed by the JI's affiliate the Al-Khidmat Foundation; established a telephone help line; arranged for a psychologist to be on call for affected families; set up special centers for affected women; and offered prayers at the graves of the "martyrs" in Islamabad.[69]

Rhetorically, the report aptly captures the JI's propagandistic use of the Red Mosque as a symbol of Musharraf's perfidy. Containing nary a criticism of the mosque's clerics or the madrassah students, it presents a lyrical *memoriam* to their deaths:

> Our sisters, daughters, elders prayed with their broken hearts for the lives of those besieged innocent children, female students and other guiltless inmates of the masjid and madrassah. But at last, in the late night (or at dawn) of 10th July 2007, in the metropolis of [the] Islamic Republic of Pakistan; in the city developed in the name of Islam; [by the] Brigade 111 of [the] Pakistan army, bearing the motto of Faith, Jihad and Taqva [piety]: masjid and madrassah, stairs and camber, dome and minarets, male and female students, hafiz and hafizaat—all were sprayed with heavy gunfire and shelling.[70]

Abdur Rasheed Ghazi, the report, affirms, "has made unmatched and everlasting sacrifices."[71] The commission concluded, not surprisingly, that "all

[66] For a representative view of the JUI-F's perspective, see Abū al-Muṣadiq Ḥaddād, "ḥukūmatī roshnī k͟hayāl se lāl masjid kī lālī tak [From the Goverment's Enlightened Moderation to the Redness of the Red Mosque]," *al-Jam'iyat* 8, no. 10 (August 2007): 19, 44.

[67] Muttahida Majlis-e-Amal Fact-Finding Commission, *sāniḥah lāl masjid o jāmi'ah ḥafṣah qarṭās abyaẓ [White Paper on the Lal Masjid and Jamiah Hafash Tragedy]* (Lahore: Jamaat-e Islami Pakistan, 2007). Translations are taken from the English version, provided by the MMA: Muttahida Majlis-e-Amal Fact-Finding Commission, *The Mishap of Lal Masjid and Jamia Hafsa: A White Paper* (Lahore: Jamaat-e Islami Pakistan, 2007).

[68] Farid Paracha, interview.

[69] Muttahida Majlis-e-Amal Fact-Finding Commission, *The Mishap of Lal Masjid and Jamia Hafsa*, 7.

[70] Muttahida Majlis-e-Amal Fact-Finding Commission, *The Mishap of Lal Masjid and Jamia Hafsa*, 5.

[71] Muttahida Majlis-e-Amal Fact-Finding Commission, *The Mishap of Lal Masjid and Jamia Hafsa*, 16.

the male, female students, teachers and ulema-e-kiram [religious scholars], passer byes [sic] and journalists who embraced martyrdom during the mishap of Lal Masjid and Jamia Hafsa are absolutely innocent" and that Musharraf, his prime minister, and members of the military should be booked under the Pakistan Penal Code, the Anti-Terrorism Act—and the High Treason Act.[72] Where the JUI-F was primarily concerned with protecting its madaris from internal dissent and external pressures, the JI saw in the Red Mosque crisis something much grander—an opportunity to press for Musharraf's downfall, recapitulate the party's anti-American agenda, and advocate for the emergence of a new, more suitably Islamic, political order.

It is worth noting that this was far from the end of the story for the Red Mosque itself. The mosque continued under the leadership of Abdul Aziz Ghazi. In some respects, its radicalism muted after the crisis; its leaders were less openly provocative in behaving as a vigilante force in the capital, or in using the mosque and associated facilities as brazen militant redoubts. In other respects, however, the institution was largely unchastened and unchanged.[73] Under Abdul Aziz Ghazi's leadership, the Red Mosque, its seminaries, and its network of affiliated mosques continued to grow, and occasionally clashed with local officials over its suspect land acquisition practices.[74] Ghazi himself was charged multiple times with a variety of serious crimes, but was repeatedly acquitted for lack of evidence.[75] Ghazi and his acolytes also appeared to retain their ties to a range of sectarian organizations, such as the Sipah-e-Sahabah Pakistan, and to anti-state militants including the TTP, which threatened to the government not to interfere with the Red Mosque's leaders or activities.[76]

8.4 Conclusion: The Logics of Anti-State Violence

The JI and JUI-F diverged in their responses to the rise of the radical Red Mosque clerics. In supporting the Jamia Hafsa and embracing the Ghazi brothers, the JI leadership was testing the limits of Islamist party support for insurgent action against the state. The JUI-F, by contrast, seemed to be actively testing the limits of Islamist party rejection of vigilantism—whether

[72] Muttahida Majlis-e-Amal Fact-Finding Commission, *The Mishap of Lal Masjid and Jamia Hafsa*, 20.
[73] See *Among the Believers* (First Run Features, 2015).
[74] See, for example, Kalbe Ali, "Lal Masjid's Expansionism, Militant Links Alarms Agencies," *Dawn*, January 4, 2015.
[75] See, for example, Ziad Zafar, "The People Versus Abdul Aziz," *Dawn*, July 9, 2017.
[76] "TTP Issues Strong Warning Against Any Action On Maulana Aziz," *The Friday Times*, June 23, 2023.

Islamist parties could in fact disassociate themselves from madrassah students taking the law into their own hands.

What explains this divergence? Here again, purely ideological explanations are unsatisfying. If anything, the JUI-F ought to have been more sympathetic than the JI toward the Ghazi brothers, as the JUI parties shared with the Red Mosque clerics Deobandi interpretive traditions and networks. It is perhaps even harder to explain the rift between the JUI-F and JUI-S, or the emergence of two distinct factions within the JUI-F, as a product of ideological differences. These organizations and leaders espoused similarly vague aspirations for an Islamic state and drew on common Deobandi traditions, educational experiences, and interpretations about the state, shariah, and the legitimacy of violence.

The parties' structural vulnerabilities more coherently explain their behavior over the course of the Red Mosque crisis. Consistent with the first hypothesis from Chapter 1, the JUI-F felt more vulnerable to the state on account of its political investment in the ruling MMA government in NWFP, as well as the prospect that the state would use the crisis to regulate the Deobandi madaris.[77] The party also felt vulnerable to those who were undertaking violence against the state, as seen in the defections that began within the Wafaq-ul Madaris al-Arabia, which was a major affiliate, partner, and power center for the party.

By not aggressively throwing his support behind the actions of the Ghazi brothers, the JUI-F's Maulana Fazl ur-Rahman risked exposing himself and his party to attacks from other Islamist groups as well as to internal dissent.[78] Indeed, contemporaneous press reports suggest that the Deobandi Wafaq had received threats from a Pakistani Taliban leader in the South Waziristan tribal agency (most likely from the late insurgent leader Baitullah Mehsud) warning of severe punishments if the board continued to "compromise with the government."[79] The meeting of the Deobandi Wafaq in early August was itself so contentious on this point that when one JUI-F senator criticized the Red Mosque administration, reports say that he was "thrashed by enraged clerics amid calls for his death."[80] Although the JI believed that it had little to lose

[77] See Ḥafiẓ 'Azīzullah Paktvī, "dīnī siyāsī quvatoṅ kī jamhūrī jidd o jahd meṅ musalmānoṅ kī baqā' hai [The Prosperity of Muslims Lies in the Democratic Struggles of Religious Political Forces]," *al-Jam'iyat* 8, no. 10 (August 2007): 12–13; 'Abd al-Jalīl Jān, "madāris kā maqṣad: 'ilmī varṣe taḥaffuz [The Objective of the Madaris: Protection of Learning Heritage]," *al-Jam'iyat* 7, no. 8 (May 2007): 7–8; Ḥafiẓ 'Azīzullah Paktvī, "shara'ī 'adālatoṅ kā qayām aur pas pardah maḥarkāt [The Establishment of Shariah Courts and Behind-the-Curtain Actions]," *al-Jam'iyat* 7, no. 8 (May 2007): 17, 40; Mufti Ibrar and Lutf ur-Rahman, interview.

[78] Khaled Ahmed, interview by Joshua White, English, May 19, 2011.

[79] Shah, "Wafaq-Ul-Madaris Faces Split."

[80] Shah, "Wafaq-Ul-Madaris Faces Split."

by pushing the envelope in advocating for the Red Mosque clerics, the JUI-F senior leadership feared, in the words of one insider, that by testing the limits of their rejection of the vigilantes, they might "lose support in their own constituencies."[81] Comments like these suggest that the party was, consistent with the second hypothesis, acutely sensitive to the vulnerabilities that flowed from its loosely clientelist relationships with the Deobandi madaris.

Although I hypothesized (H2b) that weakly institutionalized parties such as the JUI-F would be more vulnerable both to the state and violent anti-state movements, this case admittedly provides some confounding evidence. Both the JI and JUI-F demonstrated relatively coherent decision-making during the crisis, even as both parties' leaders were in London at the All Parties Conference when the events of the Red Mosque reached their culmination. Both parties held multiple rounds of internal consultations about the problem, and deputed local party officials to make time-sensitive decisions. The former chairman of the Council of Islamic Ideology, who interacted extensively with the MMA parties, observed that local party members of the JI and JUI-F were generally quite eager to support the Red Mosque clerics—even compared with their senior leadership.[82] This presented a more pronounced principal–agent problem for the JUI-F, which was trying to maintain a nuanced policy, than for the JI, for whom the enthusiasm of local cadres played nicely into the party's broader attempts to leverage the crisis as a catalyst for removing Musharraf. But overall the JUI-F showed an unusual degree of party coherence in managing these internal contradictions.

The parties' messaging to their members about the Red Mosque did, however, reflect their vulnerabilities and their broader political objectives. The JI tended to write about the events in the context of national and global power struggles. The Red Mosque crisis was, in this view, merely one stage in a "massive war" against Pakistan, one that was prompted by Western discontent over Pakistan's nuclear arsenal and the world's embrace of India.[83] Musharraf, as a puppet of the West, was both illegitimate in his authority and un-Islamic in his actions.[84] To the extent that madrassahs were mentioned, it was usually as a secondary theme, if at all. The JI publications also more deeply romanticized

[81] Mufti Ibrar and Lutf ur-Rahman, interview.

[82] Khalid Masud, interview by Joshua White, English, February 22, 2011.

[83] 'Abd ur-Rashīd Turābī, "lāl masjid aur jāmi'ah ḥafṣah kā sāniḥah': pākistān ke khilāf baṛī jang kā ek marḥalah [The Tragedy of Jamia Hafsa and Lal Masjid: One Stage of a Massive War Against Pakistan]," *Haft Rozah Aishyā (Asia)* 56, no. 32 (August 2, 2007): 11–12.

[84] Rājah Bashīr 'Uṣmānī, "lāl masjid aur jāmi'ah ḥafṣah meṅ maujūd hazāroṅ qur'ān pāk aur kutub aḥādīṣ kahāṅ ga'īṅ: kyā yih qur'ān kī tauhīn aur be ḥurmatī nahīṅ hai? [Where are the Thousands of Holy Qurans and Books on Hadiths that were Present in the Lal Masjid and Jamiah Hafsa? Is This Not a Disgrace and Insult on the Quran?]," *Haft Rozah Aishyā (Asia)* 56, no. 32 (August 2, 2007): 13–14.

the crisis than those of the JUI-F.[85] Months after the crisis, the JI weekly ran a long, two-part article claiming that if the Ghazi brothers and their ilk came to power in Pakistan, there would be "the rule of truth, fairness and justice," and evoking the image of the female students' bloodied headscarves crying up from the ground in condemnation of the country's turn away from its Islamic faith ("People! Do the Sons of Qasim Yet Live in Pakistan?").[86]

The JUI-F messaging referenced global themes similar to those in JI articles, but focused more heavily—particularly in party publications directed at general members and youth—on the threat to the madaris.[87] The moves against the Jamia Hafsa were, in this narrative, part of a long history of state interference in the affairs of religious institutions in Pakistan, and one which opened the door for the madaris to be branded "sanctuaries of terrorism" by domestic and foreign observers alike.[88] Parties often engage in hyperbole, but as this messaging by the JI and JUI-F was directed specifically to party members in relatively obscure publications, its contents can be taken as representative of how the parties wished to frame the event for their own constituents.

In summary, the behaviors of the main Islamist parties during this crisis can largely be explained in light of their vulnerabilities to the state and to anti-state movements. Consistent with the first hypothesis from Chapter 1, the JI, which faced low vulnerability to the state and low vulnerability to the Red Mosque clerics, adopted a policy of praising and supporting the anti-state movement. It exhibited this behavior in public, and also to its own constituents through party-specific media outlets.

The JUI-F leadership found itself in a much different and more complex situation. It was vulnerable to both the state and the Red Mosque clerics, which, consistent with the hypothesis, led it to "prevaricate and undermine" the anti-state movement. According to interviews with party elites and analysis of party publications, JUI-F leader Maulana Fazl ur-Rahman mildly

[85] The party published a twenty-two-page pamphlet on the events written by Samihah Rahil Qazi, daughter of the former amir, which was printed with a back cover showing Abdul Rashid Ghazi's dead visage, and a graphic depicting blood dripping down the page. Samīḥah Rāḥīl Qāẓī, *lāl masjid sāniḥah: karb o balā [Tragedy of Lal Masjid: Anguish and Calamity]* (Lahore: Department of Broadcast and Communications, Jamaat-e Islami Pakistan, n.d.).

[86] Bilqīs Saif, "sāniḥah' jāmi'ah ḥafṣah o lāl masjid: sangīnauṅ meṅ uljhe khūn ālūd dūpaṭe kahte haiṅ, logo! pākistān meṅ kyā ibn-e qāsim rahte heṅ? [The Tragedy of Jamia Hafsa and Lal Masjid: Stuck Among Bayonettes, Bloodied Dupatte Say, 'People! Do the Sons of Qasim Yet Live in Pakistan?']," *Haft Rozah Aishyā (Asia)* 56, no. 39 (September 20, 2007): 7–13.

[87] "vāqi'ah lāl masjid aur pākistānī ḥukmrānoṅ kā sharamnāk kirdār [Lal Masjid Event and the Shameful Role of Pakistani Leadership]," *'Azm-e Nau* 21, no. 4 (August 2007): 5; Muḥammad Abū Bakr Sheikh, "sāniḥah' lāl masjid aur jāmi'ah ḥafṣah: madāris kā tārīkhī kirdār [Tragedy of Lal Masjid and Jamiah Hafsah: Historical Role of the Madaris]," *al-Jam'iyat* 8, no. 10 (August 2007): 9–10.

[88] Muftī Muḥammad Ḥanīf Ḥaẓarvī, "dīnī madāris ko lāḥaq khaṭrāt [The Dangers Being Faced By the Dini Madaris]," *al-Jam'iyat* 8, no. 11–12 (October 2007): 24–25.

criticized the Ghazi brothers in public; encouraged party workers not to join anti-government protests that were closely linked with the Red Mosque supporters; quietly pressed the Wafaq ul-Madaris al-Arabia to isolate the rogue clerics; advocated publicly for a peaceful solution; positioned his party leaders as natural intermediaries between the Ghazis and the state; and remained focused on his party's core objective: the "survival of the religious schools."[89] The party leadership's behavior during the crisis was clearly focused on trying to manage competition from within the Deobandi fold, and preventing the Ghazi brothers from precipitating wider state interference in the Deobandi madaris.

There are indications that Rahman went even further, taking steps to actively undermine the Red Mosque clerics. One former official, serving in President Musharraf's cabinet during the crisis, recalled a chance encounter with Fazl ur-Rahman on an airplane traveling to Lahore, just as the Red Mosque events were beginning to unfold. Rahman, he said, told him in no uncertain terms how he wanted the government to deal with the Ghazi brothers. His advice: "Get rid of them."[90] The JUI-F leadership was displeased with the outcome of Operation Silence, but it was also relieved that the state subverted a movement that threatened to displace its prominent position within the wider Deobandi community.[91]

This ambivalence was captured by Mufti Ghulam ur-Rahman, the head of the MMA's shariah council. Writing in a JUI-F party publication after the crisis, he admitted: "If we side with the Ghazi brothers, it will be used in the future as enough proof to declare us terrorists; while on the other hand, if we agree with the stance of government then we will be blamed for behaving without enthusiasm with respect to the Lal Masjid and Jamia Hafsa."[92] The party leaders clearly felt that they were damned if they supported the Red Mosque movement, and damned if they did not.

[89] Maulānā Faẓl ur-Raḥmān, "sāniḥah' lāl masjid: ham ne kyā kirdār adā kyā? [Tragedy of Lal Masjid: What Role Did We Play?]," *al-Jam'iyat* 8, no. 10 (August 2007): 14–16.

[90] Former cabinet official, interview by Joshua White, February 2011.

[91] Muḥammad Iqbāl A'vān, "sāniḥah' lāl masjid kā almīah aur ham . . . [The Conundrum of the Lal Masjid Tragedy, and Us . . .]," *al-Jam'iyat* 8, no. 10 (August 2007): 11, 25.

[92] Muftī G̱ẖulām ur-Raḥmān, "sāniḥah' lāl masjid: cand g̱ẖaurṭalab pahlū [Tragedy of Lal Masjid: A Few Aspects Worth Noting]," *al-Jam'iyat* 8, no. 11–12 (October 2007): 18–21.

9

Good Taliban, Bad Taliban

Negotiating the TTP's Rise

9.1 Introduction

One of the most important developments following the Red Mosque crisis in the summer of 2007 was the emergence of a more active and cohesive movement of Pashtun militants in the tribal areas opposed to the Pakistani state. Throughout the summer and fall of 2007, this network of antigovernment militants clashed with the Pakistan Army in Waziristan, attacking military and intelligence targets. In December 2007, the movement formally coalesced into the Tahrik-e-Taliban Pakistan (TTP) under the leadership of Baitullah Mehsud. The TTP, which became known informally as the Pakistani Taliban, was organizationally distinct from the Afghan Taliban, though the two movements—both Deobandi and largely Pashtun—retained significant ties.

By early 2008, it had become apparent that the TTP presented a potent challenge to the military and security services. It was largely responsible for a dramatic wave of violent attacks within Pakistan that crested in 2009, but continued through approximately 2015. The rise of the TTP prompted the military to launch a series of major operations in the tribal areas that continued for several years.

The TTP focused on confronting the state, but it also presented unique challenges to a number of the Islamist parties. It began as a Pashtun movement, which drew the attention of parties such as the JUI-F, JUI-S, and JI that had substantial Pashtun support. It emerged in the southern tribal areas, where the JUI-F in particular had a rich vote bank. It capitalized on very real grievances related to the army's operations in the tribal areas after 2001, many of which were shared by the Islamist parties. And it threatened to ideologically outflank the Islamist parties by arguing that *all* of Pakistan's political parties, together with the democratic system as a whole, were insufficiently Islamic.

This case study examines the ways in which the Islamist parties responded to the challenges posed by the rise of the Pakistani Taliban. It begins by providing background on the movement and its emergence circa 2005, and the

Vigilante Islamists. Joshua T. White, Oxford University Press. © Oxford University Press (2025).
DOI: 10.1093/9780197814178.003.0009

Islamist parties' early responses to the TTP. It then examines in detail the role of the Islamist parties during a critical period in which they were engaged as intermediaries between the government and the TTP—from February 2013, when the TTP publicly announced their conditions for peace talks, until June 2014, when the talks collapsed and the military began Operation Zarb-e-Azb against TTP strongholds in South Waziristan. The final section concludes with an analysis of the factors that shaped the parties' divergent responses to the anti-state Pakistani Taliban.

9.2 Background to the Case

Since the early nineteenth century, the Waziristan region has been a hotbed of resistance—first against the British, who clashed repeatedly with Wazir and Mehsud tribesmen, and later against the state of Pakistan and its security services.[1] To some extent, the emergence of the TTP can be seen as a continuation of this pattern of tribal resistance to what were perceived to be outside and illegitimate authorities.

But it was also more than that. After U.S. and NATO forces overthrew the Taliban government in Afghanistan following the attacks on September 11, 2001, much of the senior leadership of the Taliban fled into the Pakistani tribal areas, along with the al-Qaeda leadership and other Arab, Chechen, and Central Asian fighters. Many of these militants, foreign to the tribal areas, were given safe haven in Waziristan.[2] Those tribes that welcomed foreign militants were then subjected to Pakistan Army operations, which sometimes imposed collective punishment on families or tribes who refused to give up foreigners.[3] According to C. Christine Fair and Seth Jones, "[t]hroughout 2004 and 2005, the United States and Pakistan conducted a range of precision strikes against further targets, many of which were in North and South Waziristan."[4] Military operations in Waziristan were successful in degrading the capabilities of al-Qaeda, but had the perverse effect of radicalizing some Pashtun tribal elements against the Pakistani state and generating new incentives for anti-Pakistan militants throughout the border region to cooperate with each other.[5]

[1] B. D. Hopkins, "Jihad on the Frontier: A History of Religious Revolt on the North-West Frontier, 1800–1947," *History Compass* 7, no. 6 (2009): 1459–69, https://doi.org/10.1111/j.1478-0542.2009.00640.x.

[2] Shehzad H. Qazi, "Rebels of the Frontier: Origins, Organization, and Recruitment of the Pakistani Taliban," *Small Wars & Insurgencies* 22, no. 4 (2011): 578.

[3] Qazi, "Rebels of the Frontier: Origins, Organization, and Recruitment of the Pakistani Taliban," 579.

[4] C. Christine Fair and Seth G. Jones, "Pakistan's War Within," *Survival* 51, no. 6 (December 2009): 170, https://doi.org/10.1080/00396330903465204.

[5] Syed Manzar Abbas Zaidi, "The Taliban Organisation in Pakistan," *The RUSI Journal* 154, no. 5 (October 1, 2009): 40–43, https://doi.org/10.1080/03071840903411954.

Following military operations in South Waziristan in 2004, in which the Pakistan Army sustained heavy casualties, the government pursued a deal with one prominent Waziri militant leader, Nek Muhammad.[6] The Shakai agreement was brokered in part by the JUI-F, and the meeting was held at a Deobandi madrassah rather than a neutral site, which legitimized and emboldened the militants.[7] The deal quickly fell apart. This failure did not, however, dissuade the government from continuing to pursue in the tribal areas what Paul Staniland has called a "limited cooperation order," characterized by "formal ceasefires or informal live-and-let-live bargains between a state and armed group" that "limit[] mutual violence without formal demobilization, a peace settlement, or military victory."[8] Subsequent attempts by the government to establish limited agreements of this kind with anti-state militant groups also ended in failure.[9]

By 2005, violence in then-NWFP and the tribal areas was rising.[10] Until that time, the frontier province had had the lowest levels of violence per capita of any of Pakistan's provinces.[11] Pakistani Taliban militants began co-opting and displacing the state at the local level in the tribal areas and some adjacent regions of NWFP. Their expansion often followed a predictable pattern: Well-armed groups of young men entered an area with Kalashnikovs and white pickup trucks, calling themselves Taliban; they won the favor of the community by taking on local criminal elements and prohibiting certain un-Islamic behaviors; they established qazi courts for the quick adjudication of disputes; and, having garnered some measure of local support, they set about solidifying their control by marginalizing or killing notable tribal leaders or government officials, enacting even stricter Islamist measures, and establishing environments conducive to their own criminal networks.[12] By taking advantage of local discontent with the judicial system, policing, and

[6] Daud Khattak, "Reviewing Pakistan's Peace Deals with the Taliban," *CTC Sentinel* 5, no. 9 (September 2012): 11–13. For a subtle account of the Pakistani military's shifting postures toward Pakistani Taliban groups, see Paul Staniland, *Ordering Violence: Explaining Armed Group-State Relations from Conflict to Cooperation* (Ithaca, NY: Cornell University Press, 2021), 190–97.

[7] Fair and Jones, "Pakistan's War Within," 170–71.

[8] Paul Staniland, "Armed Politics and the Study of Intrastate Conflict," *Journal of Peace Research* 54, no. 4 (July 1, 2017): 461, https://doi.org/10.1177/0022343317698848.

[9] Thomas H. Johnson and M. Chris Mason, "No Sign until the Burst of Fire: Understanding the Pakistan-Afghanistan Frontier," *International Security* 32, no. 4 (Spring 2008): 56; Khattak, "Reviewing Pakistan's Peace Deals with the Taliban."

[10] Saira Yamin and Salma Malik, "Mapping Conflict Trends in Pakistan," Peaceworks (Washington, DC: United States Institute of Peace, 2014), 11.

[11] Jacob N. Shapiro, C. Christine Fair, and Rasul Bakhsh Rais, "Political Violence in Pakistan 1988-2010: Patterns and Trends," IGC Working Paper (London: International Growth Centre, February 2012).

[12] Author interviews, Peshawar, August 2008. See also Johnson and Mason, "No Sign until the Burst of Fire: Understanding the Pakistan-Afghanistan Frontier," 57; Adnan Naseemullah, "Shades of Sovereignty: Explaining Political Order and Disorder in Pakistan's Northwest," *Studies in Comparative International Development* 49, no. 4 (December 1, 2014): 518, https://doi.org/10.1007/s12116-014-9157-z.

other state services, the insurgents were often able to gain a foothold that they then used to reinforce their local positions.

The new Pakistani Taliban groups were coalescing in the tribal areas at about the same time that Afghan Taliban leaders, most of whom had fled to Pakistan for safe haven, were working to infiltrate fighters back into Afghanistan to fight as insurgents against the U.S.-backed government of Hamid Karzai. By 2005, with support from the Pakistani security services, the Afghan Taliban had gained significant footholds in rural eastern and southern Afghanistan, and in 2006, there was a three-fold increase in suicide attacks over the previous year.[13] Even as the Pakistani military supported the Afghan Taliban insurgency that sought to topple the Islamic Republic of Afghanistan, it was increasingly struggling to manage the Pakistani Taliban insurgency within its own borders that was challenging the Islamic Republic of Pakistan.

The TTP was formally established in December 2007 under the leadership of Baitullah Mehsud. Although Mehsud had a local following in South Waziristan, he "broke out of the normal boundaries of tribal leadership" by forming the TTP as a collection of militants disaffected with the Pakistani state and the army's role in the tribal areas.[14] Unlike most other Deobandi groups operating in Pakistan, the TTP was politically rejectionist; its leaders dismissed the legitimacy of the Pakistani state, either for ideological reasons or on account of the state's ostensible failure to live up to its Islamic political commitments. It justified its attacks on the Pakistan Army on the basis of prosecuting a defensive jihad.[15] It did not, however, limit itself to military targets; it attacked civilian and political elites. Most prominently, Baitullah Mehsud was widely blamed for the assassination of former Prime Minister Benazir Bhutto in December 2007.[16]

Throughout 2008, 2009, and 2010, the Pakistan Army conducted a number of major operations in the tribal areas, some of which were punctuated by abortive or failed peace agreements with TTP and other anti-state militants.[17]

[13] Seth G. Jones, "The Rise of Afghanistan's Insurgency: State Failure and Jihad," *International Security* 32, no. 4 (April 1, 2008): 7–40, https://doi.org/10.1162/isec.2008.32.4.7; Johnson and Mason, "No Sign until the Burst of Fire: Understanding the Pakistan-Afghanistan Frontier," 66.

[14] Shuja Nawaz, "FATA—A Most Dangerous Place" (Washington, DC: Center for Strategic and International Studies, January 2009), 18.

[15] Qandeel Siddique, "Tehrik-e-Taliban Pakistan: An Attempt to Deconstruct the Umbrella Organization and the Reasons for Its Growth in Pakistan's North-West," DIIS Report (Copenhagen: Danish Institue for International Studies, 2010); Mariam Abou Zahab, *A Kaleidoscope of Islam* (New York: Oxford University Press, 2020), 126. For more on the TTP's views on defensive jihad, see Mona Kanwal Sheikh, *Guardians of God: Inside the Religious Mind of the Pakistani Taliban* (New Delhi: Oxford University Press, 2016), 66ff, https://doi.org/10.1093/acprof:oso/9780199468249.001.0001.

[16] "We Killed Benazir Bhutto, TTP Claims in Its Book," *Express Tribune*, January 16, 2018.

[17] See Zahid Ali Khan, "Military Operations in FATA and PATA: Implications for Pakistan," *Strategic Studies* 31, no. 4 (Winter 2011): 129–46.

With the death of Baitullah Mehsud by a missile strike in 2009 and the ascension of Hakimullah Mehsud to the leadership of the TTP, the organization entered an even more brutal phase. Hakimullah deepened cooperation with al-Qaeda and sectarian organizations and extensively targeted civilians.[18]

The wave of violence brought on by the TTP made the organization profoundly unpopular in Pakistan. In a 2009 survey, a majority of respondents in all four provinces of Pakistan considered the "activities of the Taliban and Religious militants in FATA and settled areas of Pakistan" to pose a "critical threat."[19] Surveys conducted by the Pew Research Center between 2010 and 2015 show that the percentage of respondents who had a "very favorable" or "somewhat favorable" view of the TTP specifically peaked at 19 percent in late spring of 2011, and by 2015 had declined to a mere nine percent.[20]

In early 2013, after five years of conflict, the government and TTP again entered into negotiations, this time with the Islamist parties playing an important role. This period from early 2013 until the summer of 2014, when talks broke down and the military launched another major named operation, is the central focus of this case study and is explored in detail in the section that follows. The 2014 operation, Zarb-e-Azb, was widely considered a success. It significantly degraded the group's operational capabilities, and drove many TTP members to take safe haven across the border in the mountains of eastern Afghanistan.[21] The group, further weakened by the killing of Hakimullah Mehsud in 2013 (discussed in greater detail later) also suffered from internal fractures and leadership disputes. Its subsequent leader, Maulana Fazlullah, was from Swat rather than Waziristan, and could not command the same breadth of allegiance as his precedessors.[22] (He may have been chosen as a consensus candidate to avoid conflict between rival Mehsud factions.[23])

Diminished by the sustained military campaign against it that continued until early 2017, and enervated by its leadership woes and the allure of the Islamic State, which began to take root in eastern Afghanistan in 2014 and

[18] Amira Jadoon, "The Evolution and Potential Resurgence of the Tehrik-i-Taliban Pakistan" (Washington, DC: United States Institute of Peace, May 2021), 6–9.

[19] C. Christine Fair, "Pakistan's Own War on Terror: What the Pakistani Public Thinks," *Journal of International Affairs* 63, no. 1 (Fall/Winter 2009): 45.

[20] "Pew Global Attitudes & Trends, Question 842" (Pew Research Center, 2015), https://web.archive.org/web/20220323171945/https://www.pewresearch.org/global/question-search/?qid=842.

[21] Abdul Sayed and Tore Hamming, "The Revival of the Pakistani Taliban," *CTC Sentinel* 14, no. 4 (2021): 29.

[22] Abdul Basit, "Mullah Fazlullah: A Journey from 'FM Mullah' to Head of the Pakistan Taliban," *Counter Terrorist Trends and Analyses* 6, no. 10 (November 2014): 16; Arif Rafiq, "The Pakistani Taliban's Radical Rebranding: Is There More Than Meets the Eye?" (Washington, DC: Middle East Institute, February 24, 2022).

[23] Declan Walsh, "Pakistani Taliban Pick Hard-Liner as Leader, Imperiling Proposed Peace Talks," *The New York Times*, November 7, 2013.

drew recruits from disaffected Pakistani Taliban, the TTP lay relatively fallow during Fazlullah's tenure. After he was killed by a U.S. strike in Kunar, Afghanistan in June 2018, the TTP chose Mufti Noor Wali Mehsud as the new leader of the group.[24] Under Noor Wali's leadership, the TTP began to experience a revival of influence. It pivoted away from attacks on civilian targets, bolstered its ties with the Afghan Taliban after the latter's takeover of Afghanistan in the summer of 2021, and expanded its presence in Pakistan beyond the border areas and its safe havens in Afghanistan.[25]

9.3 The Role of the Islamist Parties

9.3.1 The TTP's Political Disruptions

The formation of the TTP in late 2007 was, for most of the Pakistani political establishment, a clarifying moment. The anti-state militants who had been clashing with the Pakistan Army could no longer be dismissed as a disorganized collection of disaffected tribal leaders; the inchoate group now had a name, a leader, and a set of specific criticisms of the state and of Pakistan's political parties.

No political party was as conflicted by the TTP's rise as the JUI-F. The party had longstanding links with Afghan Taliban groups dating back to the mid-1990s, particularly in the southern part of NWFP.[26] And although (until 2013) elections for National Assembly seats from FATA were conducted on a non-party basis, independent candidates affiliated with the JUI-F were often successful; in 2002, the Islamist parties' high water mark, eight of the twelve FATA MNAs had MMA links, most with JUI-F.[27] The party was also closely tied with some militant factions in the FATA that were at the time more amenable to the military, such as the group led by Wali ur-Rahman, and elements of the Hafiz Gul Bahadur faction.[28]

[24] DoD Inspector General, DoS Inspector General, and USAID Inspector General, "Operation Freedom's Sentinel: Lead Inspector General Report to the United States Congress, April 1, 2018, to June 30, 2018," Quarterly Report, Quarterly Report to Congress (Washington, DC: U.S. Department of Defense, 2018), 25; "Pakistani Terrorist Leader Who Ordered Malala Shooting Killed in Drone Strike: Afghan Officials," ABC News, June 16, 2018, https://abcnews.go.com/International/pakistani-terrorist-ordered-malala-shooting-killed-drone-strike/story?id=55939214.

[25] Abdul Sayed, "The Evolution and Future of Tehrik-e-Taliban Pakistan" (Washington, DC: Carnegie Endowment for International Peace, December 21, 2021) .

[26] See, for example, Imtiaz Gul, "The Fog of War in Waziristan," *Friday Times*, March 17, 2006.

[27] "Eight Fata Seats Go to MMA Supporters," *Dawn*, October 12, 2002; "Major Changes Made in FCR: Fata People Get Political Rights," *Dawn*, August 12, 2011.

[28] Mansur Khan Mahsud, "The Battle for Pakistan: Militancy and Conflict in South Waziristan" (Washington, DC: New America Foundation, April 2010); Zia Ur Rehman, "Militants Turn Against Pakistan's JUI-F Islamist Party," *CTC Sentinel* 5, no. 4 (April 2012): 15–17.

As the TTP spread throughout the FATA, its targeted killing of tribal leaders threatened the JUI-F's political base. This came at a time when the party was already facing internal pressures to more vocally endorse the Afghan Taliban and support al-Qaeda and other transnational militant groups. As evidence of these internal tensions, a group of party leaders in Balochistan had broken away and formed a rival party, the JUI-Nazryati (JUI-N), in 2007.[29]

Eventually, the TTP began to threaten and target the JUI-F itself. This became apparent during the general elections in February 2008, held in district Bannu—a traditional JUI-F stronghold bordering North Waziristan, in which Maulana Fazl ur-Rahman was contesting the National Assembly seat. The election provided a window into the party's internal turmoil.[30] On the one hand, Fazl ur-Rahman was concerned about his party's declining influence in the southern settled districts and adjacent tribal agencies, including North and South Waziristan. The Pakistani Taliban had established a strong presence in the area, and on more than one occasion had instructed people not to vote, based upon the premise that "democracy is un-Islamic."[31]

Fazl ur-Rahman sought to counter this politically rejectionist message by dismissing TTP concerns in public, while lobbying in private for them to remain neutral. He reportedly requested a "no-objection certificate" from Pakistani Taliban commanders in the Bannu area, as a result of which he was able to minimize militant opposition to the election process.[32] Although Fazl ur-Rahman clearly required at least tacit support from certain Pakistani Taliban groups, he was also wary of siding too closely with the militants; since the relatively liberal PPP seemed poised to do well in the upcoming election, he could not afford to alienate a potential coalition partner.

Prior to the polls, the JUI-F had fragmented into at least two factions over what to do about the Pakistani Taliban, and, in a sense, the Pakistani Taliban had fragmented into at least two factions over what to do about the JUI-F. Fazl ur-Rahman avoided campaigning in Bannu out of concerns for his own safety, but eventually won the seat due to the support of certain militant factions from the nearby Frontier Region Bannu, who reportedly commandeered polling stations with rocket launchers and dismissed election observers.[33]

[29] Zia Ur Rehman, "The F and N of JUI," *The News*, February 28, 2016.

[30] At the time of the elections, the party was still facing internal dissension. See "Postponement of Polls Won't Be Accepted, Says Fazl," *Dawn*, January 17, 2008.

[31] Iqbal Khattak, "Taliban Leader Warns Against Using Religion for Electoral Gains," *Daily Times*, December 28, 2007.

[32] "JUI (F) Seeks Taliban NOC for Elections," *Frontier Post*, December 1, 2007.

[33] Author interview with an election observer based in Bannu, February 2008, Islamabad.

9.3.2 The 2013 Negotiations

The events of 2013 and 2014 revealed the complex decisions that all of Pakistan's major Islamist parties faced in responding to the TTP's extraordinary campaign of violence. In the lead-up to the spring 2013 general elections, the JUI-F continued to be the most wary of—and frequently targeted by—the Pakistani Taliban. By that time, dozens of party leaders and parliamentarians had been killed through targeted assassinations, attacks on madrassahs, and other violence.[34] Mainstream political parties had been resoundingly opposed to the TTP, and Islamist party leaders had often remained silent, or offered at most tepid support for negotiations.

With a general election on the horizon in the spring of 2013, public concern over TTP attacks and the prospect of peace talks quickly became a campaign issue. In early February, the TTP spokesman announced that the movement would be willing to engage in talks, but demanded that "if the government wants the peace talks to make headway, it has to give us three guarantors."[35] It listed the leaders of three parties: the PML-N, the JI, and the JUI-F. If any of Pakistan's parties had hoped to avoid the topic of peace negotiations in the course of campaigning, they now had no choice but to stake out their respective positions.

All of the major Islamist parties agreed that peace talks with the TTP were necessary, but they disagreed about the timing and structure of the negotiations. The Jamaat-e-Islami, which under its amir Munawar Hasan had been fiercely critical of the PPP-led government in Islamabad, took the position that undertaking a negotiation with a weak central government at the end of its term would be pointless. Better, noted a senior JI leader in early February, to wait for a "strong a sovereign government" that could bargain credibly with the Pakistani Taliban.[36] The JUI-S, which frequently sought to align itself with the Taliban movement writ large—but not necessarily the anti-state TTP—also expressed skepticism about the utility of talks at a time when both the parties lacked seriousness.[37] (This may have been because Sami ul-Haq felt snubbed that he had not been proposed as a "guarantor" by the TTP.)

[34] See, for example, Joshua T. White, "Pakistan's Islamist Tightrope," *Foreign Policy Af-Pak Channel*, April 19, 2011, https://web.archive.org/web/20110625100043/https://afpak.foreignpolicy.com/posts/2011/04/19/pakistans_islamist_tightrope; Rehman, "Militants Turn Against Pakistan's JUI-F Islamist Party"; Saleem Shahid, "16 Killed in Blast at Quetta Seminary," *Dawn*, June 8, 2012.

[35] Zahir Shah Sherazi, "TTP Willing to Talk Under Guarantee from Nawaz, Fazal and Munawar Hasan," *Dawn*, February 3, 2013.

[36] Peer Muhammad, "Talks with Taliban: JI Will Only Be Guarantor for a 'Strong' Govt," *Express Tribune*, February 6, 2013.

[37] "Taliban, Govt Not Serious in Peace Talks: Samiul Haq," Khyber News TV, February 14, 2013, http://khybernews.tv/newsDetails.php?cat=3&key=MjkxMjk.

The JUI-F, battered by the TTP's campaign of violence against its workers and leaders, took a more enthusiastic line regarding talks between the government and the militants. It welcomed the "positive" demands by the TTP, and—seeking to leverage its own influence among the Pashtun population—encouraged the PPP leadership to convene a grand jirga for negotiations.[38] This idea gained traction in the months before the election. The JUI-F took a leadership role in convening an All-Parties Conference in late February that affirmed the need for peace talks and validated the grand jirga concept.[39] Of all of Pakistan's major parties, the JUI-F was clearly the most publicly invested in the talks at a time when they were a campaign issue, even though the party leadership had the luxury of knowing that the discussions were unlikely to materialize immediately before an election.

Even after Nawaz Sharif won the May 2013 election and called for peace talks with the TTP, it took nearly eight months for the negotiations to materialize. Whatever momentum there might have been following the election was abruptly halted in late May after the TTP deputy amir Wali ur-Rahman was killed in a strike that media reports attributed to the United States.[40] The next day the TTP withdrew its offer for peace talks. The death of Wali ur-Rahman put an end to the nascent discussions about negotiations, but also represented a blow to the JUI-F's position as a potential mediator between the state and the militants. Wali ur-Rahman had formerly been a member of the JUI-F, and was seen as something of a "moderate" in TTP circles.[41] His death meant that the JUI-F lost an inside track to the Pakistani Taliban leadership, and thus diminished their confidence that they could play a substantive mediating role without being dominated or alienated by the hardliners within the TTP movement.

Throughout the summer and autumn of 2013, the Islamist parties continued to posture in support of talks with the TTP. But as their domestic political fates diverged, their views on peace talks began to do so as well. The JUI-F joined the new PML-N government and reaffirmed its offer to convene a jirga and be a guarantor of peace talks.[42] At about the same time, the party leadership began to shy away from a mediating role with the TTP, instead

[38] "Fazl Welcomes Pakistani Taliban's Conditions for Peace Talks," *Dawn*, February 4, 2013.

[39] "APC Calls for Immediate Peace Talks with Pakistani Taliban," *Dawn*, February 28, 2013.

[40] Mark Mazzetti and Declan Walsh, "Drone Strike Is Said to Kill a Pakistani Taliban Leader," *New York Times*, May 29, 2013.

[41] Daud Khattak, "A Profile of Khan Said: Waliur Rahman's Successor in the Pakistani Taliban," *CTC Sentinel* 6, no. 6 (June 2013): 16–18.

[42] Javaid-ur-Rahman, "JUI-F, JI 'Willing' to Act as Guarantors," *The Nation*, August 18, 2013; Syed Irfan Raza, "JUI-F Joins Govt, Backs Taliban Talks," *Dawn*, August 30, 2013.

proposing that they create the jirga forum and sit on the government bench during negotiations.[43]

The Jamaat-e-Islami, by contrast, was in a tenuous political position after the May elections. The party received four National Assembly seats in total from Khyber Paktunkhwa and was shut out from the other provinces and from the FATA.[44] Compared with the JUI-F's thirteen seats, the JI's take was embarrassingly meager.[45] The amir, Munawar Hasan, offered to step down, but his resignation was not accepted by the rest of the leadership. He continued on as the party's leader, and throughout 2013 became increasingly strident in support of negotiations with the TTP, and in opposition to the new PML-N government.

9.3.3 Responding to Hakimullah Mehsud's Death

Sometime on the evening of November 1, 2013, in the tribal agency of North Waziristan, TTP leader Hakimullah Mehsud was killed in a strike that Pakistani and Western press reports widely attributed to a U.S. drone.[46] Many Pakistani commentators cheered the passing of a menace who had targeted civilians—even the visiting Sri Lankan cricket team—and sown fear throughout the country's urban heartland. The government in Islamabad reacted cautiously, gratified to see Mehsud dead but wary of inviting backlash from his compatriots in Waziristan, or having to answer questions about the nature of its counterterrorism cooperation with the United States. Right-of-center commentators were more critical, acknowledging Mehsud's role in sponsoring violence against Pakistani civilians but condemning the strike for short-circuiting promising peace talks with the Pakistani Taliban.

[43] "Preparing an Olive Branch: Panel of Prominent Figures to Hold Taliban Talks, Fazl," *Express Tribune*, August 31, 2013; Umer Farooq, "Talks with Taliban: Empty Claims by Sami and Fazl," *Dawn*, September 7, 2013; Ikram Junaidi, "JUI-F Reiterates Need for Jirga," *Dawn*, September 28, 2013; Jan Achakzai (@Jan_Achakzai), "OFFICIAL: Neither Interior Minister Asked Maulana Fazalur Rahman 2 Lead Taliban Talks, nor Maulana Sb's Job Is to Lead. A Jirga Best Forum.," Twitter, November 1, 2013, https://web.archive.org/web/20240925184858/https://joshuatwhite.net/wp-content/uploads/2024/09/archive-20131101-twitter.pdf.

[44] "Party Position (National Assembly)" (Election Commission of Pakistan, 2013), https://web.archive.org/web/20140222025005/http://ecp.gov.pk/overallpartyposition.pdf. Note that these figures include both general and reserved seats.

[45] "Party Position (National Assembly)." The difference in Provincial Assembly seats was 24 for the JUI-F, and 9 for the JI..

[46] Zahir Shah Sherazi, "Pakistani Taliban Chief Hakimullah Mehsud Killed in Drone Attack," *Dawn*, November 1, 2013, http://www.dawn.com/news/1053410; Declan Walsh, Ihsanullah Tipu Mehsud, and Ismail Khan, "Drone Strikes Are Said to Kill Taliban Chief," *The New York Times*, November 1, 2013, sec. World, https://web.archive.org/web/20140405020938/https://www.nytimes.com/2013/11/02/world/asia/drone-strike-hits-compound-used-by-pakistani-taliban-leader.html.

In the days following Mehsud's death, the leaders of the JI and JUI-F faced a particularly fraught public relations challenge. Mehsud had been a fierce critic of the United States, a strident if vague champion of Islamic law, and a self-appointed successor to the spirit of the "reformist" Afghan Taliban of the 1990s. These traits made him an appealing symbol to the Islamist parties. And yet they could not afford to openly endorse a man who had violently and decisively rejected democratic politics, targeted the army—the country's most respected institution—and killed untold numbers of women and children. There had to be a middle way.

For the Jamaat-e-Islami, the middle way skirted dangerously close to endorsing the state's most-despised militant organization. Party leader Syed Munawar Hasan, in an appearance on the popular Urdu talk show *Jirga*, introduced the JI's position by staking out the easy high ground: The United States was at fault for violating Pakistan's sovereignty and foiling efforts at peace talks.[47] He then waded into controversial territory, suggesting that Mehsud should be considered a martyr, and asking why it was that if American soldiers who die on the battlefield are not martyrs, their backers in the Pakistan Army could nonetheless be granted that honor? His comments provoked a sharp and unprecedented public rebuke from the military's Inter Services Public Relations, which demanded an apology for Hassan's "irresponsible and misleading remarks . . . declaring the dead terrorists as *shaheeds* [martyrs] while insulting the *shahadat* [martyrdom] of thousands of innocent Pakistanis and soldiers of Pakistan's armed forces."[48] Hassan stubbornly stood by his comments, putting on record his party's own "middle way" that stopped just shy of aligning itself with the military's most prominent domestic security threat.

The JUI-F, by contrast, charted a more subtle course. When asked about Hakimullah Mehsud's death in an interview outside the parliament in Islamabad, Maulana Fazl ur-Rahman affirmed the view that Mehsud was a martyr but later added coyly that "anyone killed by the U.S. is a martyr, even if it is a dog."[49] The cleric's statement was just ambiguous enough to cover all the party's bases: support the Pakistani military, give underhanded approval to Mehsud's martyrdom without endorsing the TTP, and refocus attention on the supposed perfidies of the United States. Whereas the JI doubled down on its criticism of the government, the JUI-F solidified its establishment

[47] "Jirga with Saleem Safi" (Geo News, November 9, 2013) .

[48] Inter Services Public Relations, "Press Release No. PR182/2013-ISPR," November 10, 2013, https://web.archive.org/web/20240925185815/https://joshuatwhite.net/wp-content/uploads/2024/09/archive-20131110-ispr.pdf.

[49] "Anyone Killed by US Is a 'Martyr': Fazlur Rehman," *Express Tribune*, November 5, 2013.

credentials, joining the governing coalition in Islamabad just two months after the controversial Mehsud strike.[50]

9.3.4 The Islamist Parties as Mediators

From late 2013 into early 2014, Islamist parties continued to jockey for influence as to who would reach out to the new TTP leadership to broker peace talks with the government. Unlike the JUI-F, the JI was not a member of the new PML-N government, and neither was the JUI-S, which had won no seats in the general election. Both of the JUI parties at various times claimed to have been deputized by the prime minister to broker talks, and both parties sniped that the other was not up to the task.[51]

In the end, and to the surprise of many, it was not the government that chose the Islamist parties as mediators, but the TTP that did so. In early February 2014, the Pakistani Taliban nominated its own negotiating committee, which included JUI-S chief Sami ul-Haq, JI leader Muhammad Ibrahim Khan, and JUI-F party member Mufti Kifayatullah.[52] In doing so, the TTP was effectively corralling Islamist parties to represent its interests to the government. The Jamaat-e-Islami embraced Muhammad Ibrahim's role as "mediator" and "messenger," as did Sami ul-Haq and the JUI-S.[53] But the JUI-F was not so enthusiastic. The Pakistani Taliban proposition put the party in an awkward position. It was a member of the governing coalition, so it could not represent the TTP across the table. At the same time, it may have been wary of ceding credibility as a mediator to the JUI-S or even the JI. It knew, moreover, that it could not afford to disassociate itself entirely from the Taliban's agenda, given its own constituent base and rhetoric of Islamization.

Following a hastily convened leadership meeting, the JUI-F decided that Mufti Kifayatullah would not be permitted to sit on the Pakistani Taliban's negotiating committee. Fazl ur-Rahman gave a narrow procedural justification for the decision—citing the party's longstanding position that talks should happen by way of a jirga—but it was widely believed that the party

[50] "Much Awaited Decision: JUI-F Agrees to Join Federal Govt," *Express Tribune*, January 16, 2014.

[51] See, for example, Mian Abrar, "Fazl to Break the Ice in Talks with Taliban," *Pakistan Today*, November 13, 2013; Jan Achakzai, "Proper Mechanism, Not Individuals Can Render Successful Taliban Talks: Jan Achakzai," Facebook, January 1, 2014, https://web.archive.org/web/20240925192150/https://joshuatwhite.net/wp-content/uploads/2024/09/archive-20140101-fb.pdf; Javaid-ur-Rahman, "JUI-S Sets Peace Talks Process into Motion," *The Nation*, January 4, 2014; "Feeling Sidelined? JUI-F Chief Downplays Sami's Role in Proposed Peace Process," *Express Tribune*, January 5, 2014.

[52] "Govt, TTP Negotiators Chart Roadmap for Peace Talks," *Dawn*, February 6, 2014.

[53] Zulfiqar Ali, "Peace Talks: TTP Lists Imran Khan, Samiul Haq in 5-Member Committee," *Express Tribune*, February 2, 2014.

did not want to jeopardize its position in the governing coalition.[54] When Mufti Kifayatullah publicly complained about the party's decision and said that he had wanted to join the TTP team, a JUI-F spokesman distanced himself from the party member and posted a public reminder that workers "are subservient to party's collective decision and wisdom."[55] Kifayatullah later fell in line, but made a point of thanking the Pakistani Taliban for inviting him to represent their interests.[56]

Talks between the TTP and the government continued episodically throughout the spring of 2014. Progress was halting. On one occasion in February, talks were suspended after a TTP faction kidnapped and executed Frontier Corps soldiers.[57] In March, both sides agreed to a ceasefire but could not translate the opportunity into direct talks. Dissension within TTP ranks began to break into the open in April, as factions turned against each other in local power disputes.[58] The government negotiators were also facing competing pressures, as Pakistani military planners began to speak more openly about the prospect of an army operation to dislodge anti-state militants from Waziristan.

Eventually, the splits within the Pakistani Taliban and the pressures from the military to commence operations drove the peace talks into irrelevance. In late May, the Pakistan Army began isolated ground operations in North Waziristan.[59] This was followed by a retaliatory attack by the TTP against civilians at the Karachi airport in early June, killing three dozen people.[60] On June 15, the military announced Operation Zarb-e-Azb, focused on clearing North Waziristan.[61] The operation, one of the largest that the military would

[54] "Fazl Dissociates JUI-F from 'Ineffective' TTP Talks," *Dawn*, February 3, 2014; Tahir Khan and Qamar Zaman, "Negotiating Committee: JUI-F, Imran Say 'Goodbye' and 'Good Luck,'" *Express Tribune*, February 4, 2014.

[55] Jan Achakzai, "JUI-F Has Nothing to Do With Mufti Kafautullah Affairs," Facebook, February 4, 2014, https://web.archive.org/web/20240925192355/https://joshuatwhite.net/wp-content/uploads/2024/09/archive-20140204-fb.pdf; Khawar Ghumman, "Peace Talks Hampered by Exchange of Accusations," *Dawn*, February 5, 2014.

[56] "Mufti Kifayatullah Backs JUI-F's Stance on Talks," *The News*, February 6, 2014.

[57] Haq Nawaz Khan and Tim Craig, "Pakistani Taliban Says It Executed 23 Captured Pakistani Soldiers," *Washington Post*, February 16, 2014.

[58] Saeed Shah and Safdar Dawar, "Pakistani Taliban Infighting Stalls Peace Talks," *Wall Street Journal*, April 11, 2014; Tim Craig and Haq Nawaz Khan, "Pakistani Taliban Splits into Two Major Groups Amid Infighting," *Washington Post*, May 28, 2014.

[59] Jon Boone, "Pakistani Ground Troops Escalate Hostilities in North Waziristan," *Guardian*, May 22, 2014.

[60] Raza Rumi, "What the Karachi Airport Attack Says About the Pakistani Taliban," CNN, June 10, 2014, https://web.archive.org/web/20170730032000/http://www.cnn.com/2014/06/10/opinion/karachi-airport-attack-analysis/index.html.

[61] Inter Services Public Relations, "Press Release No. PR124/2014-ISPR," June 15, 2014, https://web.archive.org/web/20240925192613/https://joshuatwhite.net/wp-content/uploads/2024/09/archive-20140615-ispr.pdf.

undertake in the tribal areas, and squarely focused on the TTP, was seen by the Islamist parties as marking the end of any efforts to bring the TTP into constructive dialogue with the government.

9.4 Conclusion: The Logics of Anti-State Violence

The Islamist parties did not, in the end, play a decisive role in bringing the TTP to the negotiating table, or ensuring the success of the subsequent talks between the group and the state. Nonetheless, their participation as mediators and public commentators during the 2013–2014 discussions can shed light on the ways in which they approached their decision-making with respect to anti-state movements. What explains the observed variation in their behaviors—the willingness of the JI and JUI-S to go so far as to sit on the TTP's negotiating committee, and the unwillingness of the JUI-F to do so?

9.4.1 Ideological Factors?

One possible explanation would look to ideological factors. But here the evidence is thin. The JUI-S and JUI-F emerged from essentially the same Deobandi tradition, and there is no obvious ideological difference that would drive the JI to take a different position from the JUI parties. Indeed, ideological or theological questions were almost completely absent from the public commentary of the Islamist parties during the course of the state's outreach to the TTP. The parties rarely suggested that there was an ideological gap between the state's position and that of the TTP. In fact, Sami ul-Haq, arguably one of the most proudly ideological of Pakistan's Islamist party leaders, went so far as to say that there is "no ideological, religious or constitutional conflict between the Taliban and the government," suggesting that ideological questions were not driving his party's posture.[62]

An analysis of the TTP's negotiating demands, and the Islamist parties' long-standing positions on those demands, also suggests that ideological differences between the parties were not major factors in shaping their respective behaviors. Figure 9.1 lists the TTP's negotiating demands to the government. These were reported by news sources on February 10, 2014, approximately

[62] Qamar Zaman, Jehanzeb Khattak, and Kamran Khan, "Stalled Peace Talks: Govt Is Apparently Going for Operation, Says Prof Ibrahim," *Express Tribune*, February 23, 2014.

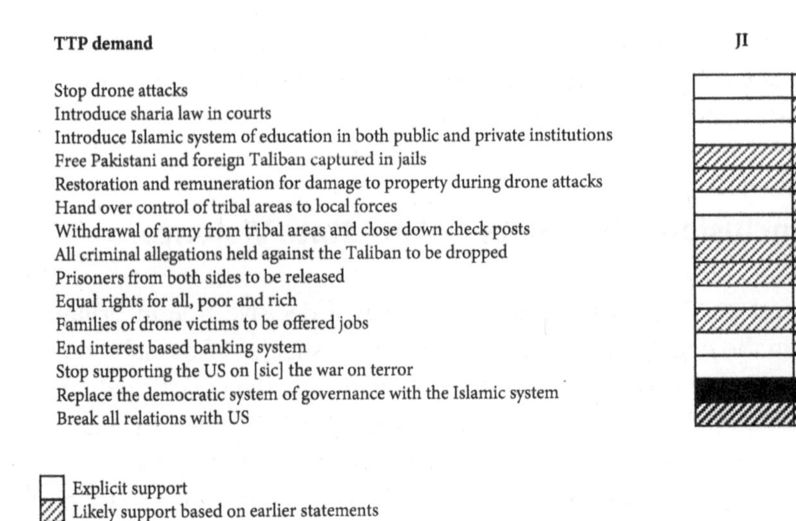

Figure 9.1 Islamist Party Support for 2014 TTP Demands.

Note: Support as reflected in the parties' respective 2013 manifestos, or the All Parties Conference statements in 2013. TTP demands drawn from Zahir Shah Sherazi, "TTP Finalises 15 Point Draft for Talks: Sources," Dawn, February 10, 2014

one week after the Islamist parties decided on their participation in the Pakistani Taliban's peace committee. The list, however, merely collates public demands that the TTP had been making for months.

When these demands are compared against the established policy positions of the JI and JUI-F, two patterns emerge. (The JUI-S is not considered here, as it did not release its own 2013 party manifesto.) First, the vast majority of the TTP's demands were, on their face, either part of both major Islamist parties' 2013 manifestos and joint statements from recent All Parties Conferences, or were likely to have garnered support from the JI and JUI-F based on past party statements. At the very least, the religious parties had not in prominent policy documents foreclosed their possible support of any of the first thirteen of fifteen Pakistani Taliban demands. There were two areas in which they differed with the TTP. One was the demand to "break all relations" with the United States, a position somewhat more definitive than either party had—notwithstanding their anti-American rhetoric—consistently advocated. The other, and perhaps most significant, difference with the TTP was the latter's demand to replace "the democratic system" with "the Islamic system" of governance.

This demand stood in direct opposition to the manifestos of the JI and JUI-F. Both parties were clear that they would not accept a shariah agenda that was in contravention to the democratic process. Writing in the March

2014 issues of its flagship journal, the Jamaat-e-Islami amir Munawar Hasan reminded his members that the party "has always been a staunch supporter of government transitions in a constitutional, traditional, and democratic manner." Perhaps chastened from the blowback he received after his comments regarding Hakimullah Mehsud in November 2013, he went on to affirm that the JI is opposed to factionalization in the country "and the use of violence to achieve goals."[63]

The second pattern that emerges from this analysis is that there was no significant difference between the positions of the JI and the JUI-F on the issues germane to the TTP negotiations with the government. Both parties naturally rejected the Pakistani Taliban's demand to replace the democratic electoral system. Both parties also appeared to be open to most of the remaining demands, many of which reflected long-standing Islamist party positions (e.g., more shariah in courts) or effective campaign issues (e.g., a cessation of drone attacks).

We do not have any authoritative statements by the Islamist parties regarding their views on the TTP, and even if we did, some of those views may well have evolved over time. It is worth recalling from Chapter 3, however, that only a few years after this series of negotiations in 2013–2014, the Government of Pakistan sponsored a major (if belated) effort to gather support from clerics and influential Islamic leaders to denounce the ideology of the TTP and its theological justifications for vigilantism and anti-state violence. This project, *Paigham-e-Pakistan*, began in 2017. The document was drafted with the support of all five major Wafaq-ul-Madaris boards, including one associated with the Deobandi sect and one associated with Jamaat-e-Islami madaris. A number of leading JUI-F-affiliated clerics and scholars were involved in the drafting process, as was Sami ul-Haq's son.[64] Although this deliberation was not contemporary with the negotiations in 2013–2014, it suggests that the Islamist parties likely held similar views about the TTP's justifications of violence against civilians and state institutions.

9.4.2 Structural Pressures

It therefore seems unlikely that the JI and JUI-F decided on their respective roles in the negotiations on the basis of ideological or religious issues. Rather, the parties' decisions during this tumultuous period appear to have been

[63] Munawar Hasan, "muẕākarāt, faujī āpareshun aur ḥukūmat [Negotiations, Military Operation and the Government]," *Tarjumān al-Qur'ān*, March 2014.

[64] Islamic Research Institute, *Paigham-e-Pakistan*, trans. Muhammad Ahmad Munir (Islamabad: Islamic Research Institute, International Islamic University, 2018).

subject to other considerations. The first of these was patronage. Throughout the spring of 2014, the JUI-F was involved in negotiations with the government of Nawaz Sharif to increase its profile as a coalition partner. The party had been given two cabinet positions, but these were as ministers without portfolio, an arrangement that limited the political visibility and patronage opportunities available to the party leadership.[65] Reports suggested that the JUI-F had been offered the Ministry of Religious Affairs, but sought a more important ministry.[66] The negotiations dragged on for months, and on several occasions the party threatened to resign the coalition, but was persuaded not to.[67] Finally, after five months, the JUI-F received two portfolios of its choice: state minister for postal services, and federal minister for housing and works. Both provided, incidentally, notable patronage opportunities to the party. It is reasonable to assume that the party's interest in securing these senior patronage opportunities inclined them to side with the government in the negotiations with the Pakistani Taliban, and made the party leadership wary of having one of their members participate as part of the TTP's negotiating committee.[68]

Indeed, the March cover story in the JUI-F's flagship magazine, *al-Jam'iyat*, explained that the party "retracted the name of its nominee not on religious grounds, or because of any feelings of inferiority, but because of the government's lack of principles *and because of being sidelined by them.*"[69] It went on to lament that the "the government should have taken its ally party into confidence and taken steps collectively based on JUI's previous efforts" but that instead the government took a path that "flies in the face of all JUI recommendations"—particularly, its recommendation for a jirga-based process.[70]

A plaintive editorial in the same issue suggested that the party distanced itself from the negotiations because of these process issues, and because of government incompetence:

> In the beginning it seemed like the government was earnest and serious about negotiations, recognized the urgency of the situation, and was progressing with

[65] A FATA senator informally affiliated with the JUI-F, Abbas Afridi, was given the textile portfolio in March 2014. "Abbas Afridi Gets Textile Portfolio," *The News*, March 19, 2014.

[66] Amir Wasim, "PML-N, JUI-F Differ on Portfolios," *Dawn*, January 27, 2014.

[67] Irfan Haider, "JUI-F Announces Withdrawal from Government," *Dawn*, April 11, 2014; Iftikhar Firdous, "Growing Rift: JUI-F Set to Join Opposition Benches," *Express Tribune*, June 9, 2014.

[68] For more on the JUI-F's efforts to position itself as a mediator with Taliban groups, see International Crisis Group, "Pakistan's Tribal Areas: Appeasing the Militants," Asia Report 125 (Islamabad: International Crisis Group, December 11, 2006), 15–20.

[69] Muḥammad Fārūq Qureshī, "muẕākarāt, ā'īn o sharī'at [Negotiations, Constitution and Shariah]," *al-Jam'iyat* 14, no. 6 (March 2014): 4–5. Emphasis added.

[70] Qureshī, "muẕākarāt, ā'īn o sharī'at [Negotiations, Constitution and Shariah].

> the matter carefully. But now it appears that the government has become helpless, or that its previous actions were a mere show.[71]

This may be true, but notably fails to mention the political context, in which the party leadership was angling for more significant representation within the coalition, and may have believed that siding with TTP elements explicitly opposed to the Constitution would have alienated the party from the government in Islamabad.

In fact, part of the JUI-F's value proposition to the new PML-N government and the military and security services was that its inclusion in the government would position it to rein in anti-state militant influence.[72] As Fazl ur-Rahman argued in an interview with the author in 2007, the "JUI is like a wall. If that wall falls, the extremists will come."[73] The theme of JUI-as-bulwark against a rising tide of radicalism may have been self-serving, but reflected the party leadership's interest in sustaining support from political and military elites and positioning itself as a broker between the state and the TTP.

The second dynamic that appears to have shaped party responses was their internal vulnerabilities to competition. This was most evident between the JUI-F and JUI-S, both of which sparred frequently during this period over which party was better qualified to serve as an interlocutor to the Pakistani Taliban. On the face of it, competition between the two JUI parties made little sense. In the 2013 general election the JUI-S had been completely shut out of National or Provincial Assembly seats. With no parliamentary footprint, the JUI-S could not have presented meaningful electoral competition to the JUI-F, particularly in the near term. And yet, there is considerable evidence that the JUI-F took Sami ul-Haq and his party as a threat, both in late 2013 as both parties were offering their good offices for outreach to the TTP, and again in the spring of 2014. There was reason to worry; as a member of the Pakistani Taliban's negotiating committee, Sami ul-Haq went on the record more than once to criticize the JUI-F's ostensibly pro-government position.[74]

Since there was no meaningful electoral competition between the two parties, any jockeying between them can be taken as evidence of ongoing non-electoral forms of competition. For example, concerned about party

[71] Abūbakar Shaikh, "qaumī salāmatī pālīsī aur jīopoliṭikal manẕar nāmah [National Security Policy and the Geopolitical Landscape]," *al-Jam'iyat* 14, no. 6 (March 2014): 2–3.

[72] Nazar Ul Islam, "The Beauty of Democracy: An Interview with Maulana Fazlur Rehman," *Newsweek Pakistan*, June 24, 2011.

[73] Fazl ur-Rahman, interview by Joshua White, English and Urdu, trans. M. Asif Gul, July 23, 2007.

[74] "Sami Warns of Fallout in Case Peace Talks Fail," *Pakistan Today*, May 15, 2014; "Include Army in Taliban Talks, Demands JI Negotiator," *Pakistan Today*, May 16, 2014.

discipline or recruitment, the JUI-F might have worried that Sami ul-Haq and his madrassah network were capitalizing on their reputation for being pro-Taliban, and would cut into the JUI-F's recruits. A source within the JUI-F claimed in March that Sami ul-Haq's prominence in the peace talks "has sent ripples through the party's ranks" and suggested that the JUI-F was being undermined as the party that traditionally represented the tribal areas.[75] This would be consistent with evidence earlier in this book that the JUI-F felt particularly vulnerable to defection by its cadres to other Deobandi parties, or to fringe Pakistani Taliban groups such as the TTP.

Although JUI-F leaders argued that links between its party workers and Pakistani Taliban groups did not necessarily constitute official endorsement by the party, it was widely believed that low-level party workers were the segment most inclined to join militant groups.[76] In numerous interviews by the author, JUI-F leaders expressed concern about their ability to hold the loyalty of the party's constituents—especially madrassah students—in the face of emerging Pakistani Taliban groups. Ulama affiliated with the party similarly complained that madrassah students failed to heed their fatawa denouncing suicide attacks.[77] "As a party, we don't support the [Pakistani] Taliban," explained a JUI-F leader in Punjab. "But some individuals do . . . on the basis of [their] *ẓulam* [oppression], they support them."[78]

The third notable dynamic that emerges from this period of negotiation is the ways in which the Islamist parties perceived differing levels of vulnerability to the TTP. The Jamaat-e-Islami appeared to feel significant freedom to calibrate its positions with respect to the Pakistani Taliban without incurring costs to party cohesion or retribution from the security establishment or the TTP. As noted earlier in this chapter, the JI's amir Munawar Hasan earned a rare rebuke from the military after referring to the brutal TTP leader Hakimullah Mehsud as a martyr in November 2013. Rather than issue an apology, the JI senior leadership defended Hasan's remarks and dismissed the military's criticism as interference in political affairs.

Munawar Hasan softened his tone somewhat in early 2014, emerging as a proponent of direct peace talks and encouraging military stakeholders to participate directly in the Taliban negotiations.[79] The party's tone moderated even further with the election in late March of Siraj ul-Haq as the new party

[75] Omer Farooq Khan, "Fazl Conveys Concern on Peace Talks to Govt," *Daily Times*, March 19, 2014.
[76] M. A. Niazi, interview by Joshua White, English, May 16, 2011; Muhammad Amir Rana, interview by Joshua White, English, February 14, 2011.
[77] Zakir Hassnain, "Clerics Worried by Lack of Respect for Fatwas on Suicide," *Daily Times*, May 7, 2007.
[78] Muhammad Abu Bakar, interview by Joshua White, Urdu, trans. Shuja Malik, May 16, 2011.
[79] "Munawar Hasan Welcomes Govt's Direct Talks with Taliban," *Dawn*, March 7, 2014.

amir. His election was something of a surprise. It was the first time in the party's history that a sitting amir who was standing for election had not been re-elected.[80] In contrast to his predecessor, Siraj ul-Haq took a more conciliatory and constructive line. Interviewed in April about his perspective on peace talks, he pitched the Jamaat-e-Islami as an enthusiastic and willing supporter of the government on this issue: "We are ready to do anything for the talks if the federal government asks us. I am earnestly praying for the government to succeed. Fortunately, in my opinion, the Army and civilians are on the same page."[81]

The shift in tone between Munawar Hasan and Siraj ul-Haq may have been one of temperament alone. Or perhaps the heated rhetoric in late 2013 reflected internal competitive struggles within the party, and Hasan's attempt to reassert authority after an embarrassing showing in the general election. Regardless, it appears that, for several reasons, the Jamaat-e-Islami was able to adjust its policy toward the TTP over time without having to worry much about the implications for the party. For one, its electoral prospects were not tied to the southern areas of Khyber Pakhtunkhwa and FATA where the TTP presence was strongest. Additionally, having taken the decision not to join the federal coalition government—and choosing instead to join as a minority partner with the Pakistan Tahrik-e-Insaf in Khyber Pakhtunkhwa—the party was relatively insulated from pressures from the military or intelligence services. It also had little to fear in the way of attrition of its party workers, because, as described earlier in this volume, for reasons of geography and demographics its cadres would be unlikely to defect to anti-state shariah movements en masse.

The JUI-F felt considerably more pressure from the TTP. Its leadership worried that the criticism from Sami ul-Haq, together with the JUI-F's unwillingness or inability to participate on the Pakistani Taliban benches during the negotiations, would put the party at risk from the new anti-state Taliban groups. By the spring of 2014, this was not an idle worry. The JUI-F leadership was under increasing pressure from the hardline factions of the TTP. An unconfirmed report on March 19, 2014 suggested that Maulana Fazl ur-Rahman had complained to "key federal ministers" that the government's negotiation process should also include the Taliban leaders such as Hafiz Gul Bahadur, who had deep ties to the party.[82] He also reportedly fretted that

[80] Noman Ahmed, "Changing Traditions: Sirajul Haq Picked to Head JI," *Express Tribune*, March 31, 2014.

[81] Benazir Shah, "'True Mujahid,'" *Newsweek Pakistan*, April 9, 2014.

[82] Shah, "'True Mujahid'"; "Prime Minister to Take Nation into Confidence Today," *Business Recorder*, June 16, 2014.

the government's direct negotiations had "unduly elevated the stature" of the TTP, "and brought them at par with the state."[83]

Just days later, Fazl ur-Rahman survived two consecutive attacks in Khyber Pakhtunkhwa, both of which were believed to have been undertaken by Pakistani Taliban groups. Before the year was out, he would survive another major attack, this time in Balochistan.[84] The JUI-F's strategy for dealing with this growing threat appears to have been multifaceted. As it had done since at least 2006, the party tried to position itself as the most prominent supporter of the broader "Taliban" project (that is, implementing shariah) and to minimize the role of the JUI-S. The party highlighted its historical electoral and jirga convening roles in the FATA, even though a number of its affiliated MNAs and tribal leaders had been targeted by the anti-state Pakistani Taliban, and it tried to side rhetorically with the TTP by, for example, praising its desire for shariah and criticizing the government's use of the term "militant" to describe the group.[85]

In the months following the failed attacks against him, however, Fazl ur-Rahman began to draw a clearer line between the party and the anti-state factions of the Pakistani Taliban:

> We cannot call the people who killed religious scholars including Maulana Hassan Jan [a prominent cleric in Peshawar affiliated with the JUI-F] and carried out attacks against me and other learned clerics as mujahideen . . . . We are not supportive of armed struggle in the country and the religious circles have no link with the elements involved in militant activities.[86]

The targeting of senior JUI-F leaders made it inevitable that the party would switch from lauding the TTP—likely a means of protecting the party's reputation among the Deobandi elite, and stemming defections of low-level cadres—to selectively criticizing them. Still, the party's critique of the Pakistani Taliban was limited. When asked in early 2011 why the party did not speak out more clearly against militancy, one leader in Fazl ur-Rahman's inner circle laughed and drew his finger across his throat: "Do you want to get me killed? . . . [if] I am sitting at a madrassah, they're going to chop my head off!"[87] He went on to describe that party leaders felt directly threatened

[83] Khan, "Fazl Conveys Concern on Peace Talks to Govt."
[84] Zia Ur Rehman, "Fallout," *The Friday Times*, October 31, 2014.
[85] Rehman, "Fallout"; Owais Jafri, "Peace Talks: Negotiations with the Taliban Without Army's Representation to Fail, Says Fazl," *Express Tribune*, March 22, 2014.
[86] Yousaf Ali, "Killers of Scholars Not Mujahideen: JUI-F Chief," *The News*, October 24, 2011.
[87] Interview by the author with a senior JUI-F politician, May 27, 2011.

by the TTP and other anti-state Taliban groups, and had to be discreet and indirect in their public statements.

In summary, the behavior of the Islamist parties during the course of the 2013–2014 negotiations with the TTP were generally consistent with Hypothesis 1 from the first chapter. The JI had relatively low vulnerabilities to the state and to the TTP, and proved most willing to praise the Pakistani Taliban. The JUI-S also had relatively low vulnerability to the state, and modest concern about the ability of the TTP to draw away its party workers and madrassah students; it praised the TTP, but it is difficult to assess whether it took any actions to limit the influence of the TTP over its institutions and students.

The JUI-F faced considerable vulnerabilities, both to the state and the TTP. Hemmed in by its interests in sustaining patronage networks, and in needing to recruit a new generation of young madrassah graduates, the party appears to have tried to thread the needle by sustaining rhetorical support for a wide range of self-described "Taliban" organizations in order to protect itself from retaliation and bolster its credibility. Consistent with the "praise for protection" behavior described in Chapter 1, the party continued this approach until, following TTP attacks on its leadership, it could no longer pretend to share a mutual understanding with the anti-state movement and pivoted to a more openly critical posture.

10
Barelvi Street Power
The TLP

10.1 Introduction

This final case study traces the rise of Barelvi political activism and vigilantism following the 2011 assassination of Punjab Governor Salman Taseer by his Barelvi bodyguard, Mumtaz Qadri, who opposed the governor's support for a Christian woman accused of blasphemy.[1] Barelvism, as noted throughout this book, has a large following in Pakistan, but Barelvi parties such as the various JUP parties and the Sunni Ittihad Council have historically performed very poorly at the polls, winning few seats. The Barelvi parties have also been highly fractious.

The trial and eventual hanging of Mumtaz Qadri in 2016 provided a catalyst for a new generation of activists to create a broad-based and energetic Barelvi movement.[2] This movement was formed with a clear ideological premise, oriented around the protection of the prophet Muhammad's honor and the rejection of "blasphemy," broadly construed. It had a sectarian objective as well, seeking to mobilize Barelvi leaders, institutions, and devotees in their competition with Deobandis for resources, students, and followers. And third, the movement staked out political objectives, coalescing into a political party, the Tahrik-e-Labbaik Pakistan (TLP), which contested seats in vote-rich Punjab and Sindh provinces.[3]

In a few short years, the TLP emerged as a potent pressure group, organizing huge rallies that shut down the capital Islamabad. The party won only two provincial seats in the general 2018 election but secured more than two

[1] For a rich narration of Governor Taseer's actions in the lead-up to his killing, see Adeel Hussain, *Revenge, Politics and Blasphemy in Pakistan* (London: C. Hurst & Co., 2022), 144ff, https://doi.org/10.1093/oso/9780197659687.001.0001.

[2] I will generally refer to this new movement by the name of its prominent political party, the Tahrik-e-Labbaik Pakistan (TLP), rather than the movement from which it emerged, the Tahrik-e-Labbaik Ya Rasool Allah (TLYRA).

[3] See Joshua T. White, "Beyond Moderation: Dynamics of Political Islam in Pakistan," *Contemporary South Asia* 20, no. 2 (June 2012): 179–94.

Vigilante Islamists. Joshua T. White, Oxford University Press. © Oxford University Press (2025).
DOI: 10.1093/9780197814178.003.0010

million votes overall, demonstrating its potential as a new political contender that could sap votes from both mainstream and Islamist parties. The TLP also developed a contentious relationship with the Pakistani security services, as might have been expected from a group whose original rallying cry was in support of a vigilante assassination of a sitting governor. Between 2017 and 2021, party activists attacked and killed police and injured hundreds of civilians; received funds and accolades from serving military officers; were banned under the Anti-Terrorism Act; and were subsequently un-banned.

This chapter begins by briefly tracing the rise of the TLP, from Governor Taseer's assassination in 2011 through the lifting of the ban on the party in 2021. It then examines two key episodes in this story: first, the responses of established Islamist parties such as the JI and JUI-F to the 2011 assassination and the emergence of a new kind of Barelvi activism that might challenge those parties' influence; and second, the ways in which the TLP itself, as a new Islamist party, made decisions regarding its protests, vigilantism, use of violence, and challenges to state authority during the contentious 2017–2018 period.

10.2 Background to the Case

Following the assassination of Governor Salman Taseer in January 2011, his bodyguard Mumtaz Qadri was placed in custody and, in October of that year, sentenced to death for murder.[4] Qadri garnered support from a number of prominent Barelvi figures, including religious leaders and lawyers who showered him with flowers as he appeared before a court in Islamabad. Many of the early demonstrations in support of him and his vigilantism were organized by the Sunni Tahrik party, which had a small following but took advantage of Qadri's popularity among Barelvis to build support.[5]

Soon, however, another political party emerged that more successfully capitalized on pro-Qadri sentiment among Barelvi voters.[6] The TLP was established in 2015 by Maulana Khadim Hussain Rizvi as the political wing of the Tahrik-e-Labbaik Ya Rasool Allah (TLYRA), a movement he founded in 2013 to defend prophet Muhammad's honor, oppose changes to the blasphemy

[4] Nasir Jamal, "The Wages of Capitulation," *Dawn*, November 14, 2021.

[5] Alix Philippon, "Sunnis Against Sunnis: The Politicization of Doctrinal Fractures in Pakistan," *Muslim World* 101, no. 2 (April 2011): 359ff, https://doi.org/10.1111/j.1478-1913.2011.01360.x; Fahad Nabeel, Muhammad Omar Afzaal, and Sidra Waseem, "Profile of Sunni Tehreek," Briefing Report (Islamabad: Center for Strategic and Contemporary Research, 2016), 8.

[6] See Farhat Haq, *Sharia and the State in Pakistan: Blasphemy Politics* (Milton: Taylor & Francis Group, 2019), 94–96.

laws, and secure Qadri's release.[7] Rizvi had served as a minor official in the Punjab Auqaf Department, which oversaw religious endowments, but after Taseer's assassination he was fired for his outspoken views and began traveling and preaching.[8]

Rizvi organized his first major public rally in January 2016 in Lahore, in which his followers clashed with police and were forcibly dispersed. The tempo of protest rallies increased following Qadri's execution in March. Rizvi, in cooperation with other Barelvi groups, led a days-long sit-in in Islamabad that precipitated further confrontations with police.

It was not, however, until November 2017 that the TLP rose to prominence as a disruptive political force.[9] The party organized a march near Islamabad and encamped at the Faizabad Interchange on the perimeter of the city, creating gridlock along a major route between the capital and nearby Rawalpindi. As protests spread to other cities across the country, Rizvi continued his sit-in for nearly three weeks. His supporters dispersed only after the federal law minister resigned and the government capitulated to Rizvi's demands and withdrew proposed changes to the Election Bill 2017 that, he claimed, weakened the government's commitment to the finality of the prophethood and represented a concession to the Ahmadi sect.[10] As described later in this chapter, the TLP garnered attention during this episode not only for its ability to organize mass protests, but also for its apparent ties to—and support from—the security services that were seeking to use the TLP to advance the standing of the political opposition in the lead-up to the July 2018 general elections.

The TLP launched another major round of protests in the spring of 2018. This time Rizvi mobilized Barelvi activists around reports that Asia Bibi, the Christian woman accused of blasphemy who had received support from Governor Taseer, was going to be released and allowed to leave the country. The TLP organized a set of road-blocking protests in Punjab province, and relented only when it secured amnesty for those who protested and received guarantees from the government that Ms. Bibi would be banned from leaving the country.[11]

Encouraged by its strong showing in the general elections in July, the party continued to exert its political leverage, this time with the newly installed

[7] Jamal Malik, "The Prophet, Law, and Constitution in Pakistani Society," in *The Presence of the Prophet in Early Modern and Contemporary Islam*, ed. Rachida Chih, David Jordan, and Stefan Reichmuth, vol. 2, Handbook of Oriental Studies (Leiden: Brill, 2021), 311.

[8] Ali Kalbe, "Who Is Khadim Hussain Rizvi?," *Dawn*, December 3, 2017.

[9] Jamal, "The Wages of Capitulation."

[10] Malik, "The Prophet, Law, and Constitution in Pakistani Society," 311.

[11] Deutsche Welle, "Pakistan Blasphemy Protests to End After Deal Struck," dw.com, March 11, 2018, https://web.archive.org/web/20230405151022/https://www.dw.com/en/pakistan-blasphemy-protests-to-end-after-deal-struck/a-46141302.

PTI government led by Imran Khan. In August, Khadim Rizvi threatened to organize country-wide protests if the government did not rescind the appointment of Princeton University's Atif Mian, an Ahmadi, to serve on the prime minister's economic advisory council. The prime minister relented.[12] Then, in October, the TLP returned to the streets, taking advantage of the Supreme Court's acquittal of Asia Bibi to organize huge protests that were again marked by violence. The party disbanded its sit-ins only after securing an agreement from the religious affairs minister that the government would challenge the court decision and put Bibi's name on the no-fly list.[13]

The party's victory was, however, short-lived. Following inflammatory and accusatory remarks against the Supreme Court judges, Chief of Army Staff Javed Bajwa, and Prime Minister Khan by senior TLP leader Afzal Qadri, and promises to renew their protest meetings, both Rizvi and Qadri were taken into "protective custody" by police.[14] After several months in jail, Qadri announced his retirement from politics and released a video apologizing for "hurting the sentiments of the government, the judiciary and the chief of army staff."[15] Both leaders were eventually released on bail in May 2019.[16]

The TLP leadership kept a relatively low profile for about a year and a half before again diving into the fray. In September 2020, it took to the streets to protest the decision of a French magazine to republish cartoons of the prophet Muhammad.[17] The party organized rallies in major cities across the country, and marched on Islamabad demanding that the French ambassador be expelled. In November, the group again encamped at the Faizabad Interchange, and this time the sitting government decided to quickly negotiate. The resulting agreement represented a striking concession by the government, which capitulated to all of the TLP's major demands. It agreed to seek a decision from the parliament regarding expulsion of the French ambassador within three months, to decline to appoint its ambassador to France, to release arrested TLP protesters and to refrain from filing any cases against protesters.[18]

[12] Ahmad Sabat, Muhammad Shoaib, and Abdul Qadar, "Religious Populism in Pakistani Punjab: How Khadim Rizvi's Tehreek-e-Labbaik Pakistan Emerged," *International Area Studies Review* 23, no. 4 (December 1, 2020): 369, https://doi.org/10.1177/2233865920968657.

[13] Jamal, "The Wages of Capitulation."

[14] Arif Malik et al., "TLP Head Khadim Rizvi Taken into 'Protective Custody', Scores of Workers Arrested in Crackdown," *Dawn*, November 23, 2018.

[15] Javed Hussain, "TLP Patron-in-Chief Pir Afzal Qadri Quits Party Citing Health Issues," *Dawn*, May 1, 2019.

[16] Sushant Sareen, "Tehrik-E-Labbaik Pakistan: The New Face of Barelvi Activism," Occasional Paper (New Delhi: Observer Research Foundation, September 2021), 20.

[17] Sareen, "Tehrik-E-Labbaik Pakistan," 20.

[18] Mohammad Asghar and Munawer Azeem, "TLP Claims Govt Accepted All Its Demands," *Dawn*, November 17, 2020.

When Khadim Rizvi died unexpectedly shortly after the agreement was signed, many observers anticipated that the party's influence would wane. It did not. Rizvi's son, Saad Rizvi, assumed leadership of the TLP and continued pressing the government to fulfill the extraordinary commitments it had made in the November agreement. When, in January 2021, it appeared as though the government might not follow through on these commitments, the TLP again threatened to launch protests and again signed an agreement with the government—this time extending until April the deadline for the parliament to consider expulsion of the ambassador.[19]

April 2021 marked a turning point in the relationship between the TLP and the state. Anticipating the return of disruptive protests by the party, the government preemptively arrested Saad Rizvi in Lahore on April 12 and charged him under the Anti-Terrorism Act (ATA), 1997.[20] TLP organizers responded by organizing violent protests and blocking key transportation routes across the country. Multiple police officers were killed and scores of protesters were injured.[21]

On April 15, the government banned the TLP, adding the party to the list of proscribed organizations under the ATA.[22] The National Assembly did subsequently take up the question of expelling the French ambassador, but after a contentious debate could not reach consensus and the session was adjourned.[23] The government's decision to ban the TLP was met with a mixed reaction by Pakistani political elites, but was notably criticized by the anti-state Deobandi TTP, which said it would avenge the death of TLP workers killed by police and urged armed struggle against the state.[24]

For an organization that had been formally banned, and had been embraced by the most prominent militant group targeting the Pakistani state, the TLP remarkably continued to function as a political party. More than 200 TLP candidates contested local government elections for cantonment boards, and the party also fielded candidates for elections in Pakistani Kashmir and in

[19] Mian Abrar, "Govt, TLP Reach Agreement, Demands Will Be Put Forward in Parliament," *Pakistan Today*, February 11, 2021.

[20] Imran Gabol, "TLP Chief Saad Hussain Rizvi Released from Jail," *Dawn*, November 18, 2021.

[21] Jamal, "The Wages of Capitulation."

[22] "Government Bans TLP Under Anti-Terrorism Law," *Dawn*, April 15, 2021. Organizations are listed in the First Schedule, and individuals in the Fourth. See Government of Pakistan, "The Anti-Terrorism Act, 1997," 1997, https://web.archive.org/web/20240119232720/https://nacta.gov.pk/wp-content/uploads/2017/08/Anti-Terrorism-Act-1997.pdf.

[23] Mujib Mashal and Zia ur-Rehman, "Caving to Islamists, Pakistan's Parliament Debates Expelling French Ambassador," *The New York Times*, April 20, 2021.

[24] Ihsan Tipu Mehsud (@IhsanTipu), "TTP Expressed Solidarity with TLP and Its Leader Saad Rizvi. In the Statement, TTP Vowed to Avenge the Death of TLP Workers, Killed in Clashes with Police. 'Don't Trust Pak State Institutions and Their Promises. Armed Struggle against Them Is the Only Solution,' Statement Says.," Twitter, April 14, 2021, https://web.archive.org/web/20240925195752/https://joshuatwhite.net/wp-content/uploads/2024/09/archive-20210414-twitter.pdf.

by-elections.[25] The Imran Khan government could have permanently banned the party and halted its election activities, but it declined to send the requisite reference to the Supreme Court, perhaps because the TLP had been a thorn in the side of its political rival the PML-N.

Emboldened by the government's half-hearted attempt to restrict its activities, the TLP once again took to the streets in October 2021, pressing for the release of Saad Rizvi, the expulsion of the French ambassador, and the end of the ban on the party. Following yet another round of violent clashes that left six police dead and over 500 injured, the TLP and the government announced in early November that they had reached a "secret agreement."[26] Under the terms of the agreement, the TLP would be removed from the list of proscribed organizations under the ATA; the TLP would withdraw its demand for the expulsion of the French envoy; and the party agreed not to resort to violence or challenge the state. Shortly after the agreement was signed, TLP protestors were released without charge, and Saad Rizvi was removed from the ATA's list of proscribed individuals and was released.

10.3 The Role of the Islamist Parties

This section examines two key episodes related to the TLP's rise: first, the responses of established Islamist parties to the 2011 assassination of Salman Taseer, and the emergence of a new kind of Barelvi activism that might challenge their influence; and second, the TLP's choices regarding its protests, vigilantism, use of violence, and challenges to state authority during the contentious 2017–2018 period.

Both of these episodes involve Islamist party responses to, or instrumentalizations of, accusations of blasphemy or disrespect of the prophet Muhammad. As discussed in Chapter 3, Deobandi and Barelvi clerics and political leaders draw on the same Hanafi fiqh but have at times had somewhat different understandings of the applicable punishments for those accused of blasphemy or apostasy. Moreover, the development of Pakistan's own penal code on these matters has reflected a step-wise expansion of the law to encompass a wider and wider range of potentially criminal actions.

The Pakistan Penal Code (PPC) sections 295 and 298 deal with offenses related to religion and were derived from the same sections of the Indian Penal Code (IPC) of 1860, which, as an instrument of colonial management,

[25] Shehryar Warraich, "Banned, but Not Quite," *The News*, September 26, 2021.
[26] Jamal, "The Wages of Capitulation."

was used by British colonial officers to deter and suppress inter- and intra-sectarian disharmony that could destabilize the colonial regime. In 1980, President Zia ul-Haq modified the PPC to add section 298-A, which criminalized derogatory remarks regarding the prophet Muhammad, his family, "the righteous Caliphs," and the prophet's companions.[27] Importantly, and unlike earlier language in sections 295 and 298, this new addition did not require "deliberate" or "malicious" action, but sanctioned "whoever by words, either spoken or written, or by visible representation, or by any imputation, innuendo or insinuation, directly or indirectly" defiled one of the protected figures. As Farhat Haq has chronicled, these changes, taken together, empowered Sunni clerics at the expense of their Shia rivals (who held a different view about the prophet's succession) and made it easier to weaponize accusations of disparaging Muhammad.[28]

In 1982, Zia ul-Haq further modified the PPC to add 295-B, which criminalized defiling the Quran, and proscribed a mandatory life sentence as punishment.[29] Perhaps most important was the addition in 1986 of section 295-C, which criminalized, without any qualification of intent, the defilement of "the sacred name" of the prophet Muhammad, and proscribed that the offense was punishable by death.[30]

This expansion of the PPC in the 1980s provided Islamist activists and parties with a newly potent tool for political agitation—one that the Barelvis were best positioned to benefit from, given their longstanding focus on the honor of the prophet. Even though it has been widely documented that, in the words of the International Commission of Jurists, "[m]any blasphemy-related allegations are motivated by personal vendettas and political interests," it is equally clear that no one in Pakistani public life has wanted to be seen countenancing inaction in the face of (supposed) disparagement of Muhammad.[31] Thus, as Gabriela Knaul, UN Special Rapporteur on the Independence of Judges and Lawyers argued in her 2013 report, the blasphemy laws "serve the vested interests of extremist religious groups and are not only contrary to the Constitution of Pakistan, but also to international human rights norms, in particular

[27] Ministry of Law and Justice, Government of Pakistan, "Pakistan Penal Code, 1860 (As Amended)" (n.d.), secs. 298-A, https://web.archive.org/web/20240925200019/https://pakistancode.gov.pk/pdffiles/administratord5622ea3f15bfa00b17d2cf7770a8434.pdf.

[28] Haq, *Sharia and the State in Pakistan*, 142ff.

[29] Ministry of Law and Justice, Government of Pakistan, Pakistan Penal Code, 1860 (As Amended), secs. 295-B.

[30] Ministry of Law and Justice, Government of Pakistan, Pakistan Penal Code, 1860 (As Amended), secs. 295–C.

[31] International Commission of Jurists, "On Trial: The Implementation of Pakistan's Blasphemy Laws" (Geneva, November 2015), 6.

those relating to nondiscrimination and freedom of expression and opinion."[32] It is in this legal context that the Islamist parties made their calculations about the benefits of political agitation and violence pertaining to the issue of blasphemy.

10.3.1 Islamist Party Responses to the Taseer Assassination

Although Barelvi activists have often taken the lead in protesting proposed changes to Pakistan's blasphemy laws, they were not the only ones to have used the blasphemy issue to mobilize support and criticize sitting governments. In December 2010, the JUI-F, which had been a minority member of the governing coalition led by PPP Prime Minister Yousuf Raza Gilani, left the government over a dispute that centered principally around patronage positions.[33] This freed the party to protest even more loudly the government's consideration of a bill introduced earlier that year by PPP Senator Sherry Rehman that would have enacted modest amendments to the blasphemy laws.[34] The JI, JUP, and other Islamist parties had been vocal in their criticism of the bill and in late December, just days prior to Governor Taseer's assassination, the secretary-general of the JUI-F warned the government from even considering the legislation and ominously told a gathering in Karachi that he regretted that action had not already been taken against Taseer and Rehman.[35]

In the wake of Taseer's assassination, the Islamist parties doubled down on their criticism of the government, their opposition to changes to the blasphemy laws, and their narrative that the preponderance of the blame for Taseer's death rested with him rather than with his assassin. All of the Islamist party representatives refused, for example, to attend Taseer's burial or to recite traditional Fatiha prayers for him during a late January Senate session.[36]

The various JUP parties were, unsurprisingly, among the most strident in their defense of Mumtaz Qadri. Senior JUP(N) leader Abul Khair Mohammad Zubair reportedly told a rally that Pakistani leaders had ignored public sentiment on blasphemy and should now "learn a lesson" from

[32] United Nations Human Rights Council, "Report of the Special Rapporteur on the Independence of Judges and Lawyers, Gabriela Knaul (A/HRC/23/43/Add.2)" (New York: United Nations General Assembly, April 4, 2013), 13.

[33] "JUI-F Chief Slams Govt's Aim to Amend Blasphemy Law," *Express Tribune*, December 26, 2010.

[34] "Sherry Submits Bill for Amending Blasphemy Laws," *Dawn*, November 30, 2010.

[35] Imtiaz Gul, "Pakistan's Dangerous Blasphemy Laws Claim the Governor of Punjab," *Foreign Policy*, January 4, 2011, https://web.archive.org/web/20240620220236/https://foreignpolicy.com/2011/01/04/pakistans-dangerous-blasphemy-laws-claim-the-governor-of-punjab/.

[36] "Taseer Laid to Rest with Full State Honours," *Dawn*, January 6, 2011.

Taseer's assassination, and admitted that he could not "express grief or offer condolence" for the death of someone who criticized the blasphemy laws.[37] One senior figure in the JUP went so far as to declare that Taseer had become *wājib ul-qatl* (someone that must be killed) on account of his supposed disobedience to divine law.[38]

The Jamaat-e-Islami, too, took a strident line. "If the government had removed [Taseer] from the governorship," the party asserted in a statement shortly after the assassination, "there wouldn't have been the need for someone to shoot him."[39] The party's amir, Syed Munawar Hasan, told a rally that "all the inhabitants of Pakistan back Qadri" and blamed Taseer for his own death.[40] Other party officials were even more enthusiastic; the party's provincial amir in Sindh exulted that Taseer's assassin would go directly to the "seventh heaven."[41]

One modest note of caution from the JI's senior ranks came from Farid Paracha, the party's respected deputy secretary general. Speaking on a popular TV news show, Paracha argued that officials should not make public statements on sensitive issues that might hurt the sentiments of Muslims, but also asserted that Taseer's murder "cannot be justified."[42] He similarly told a newspaper reporter that "I don't condone such a blatant killing in the name of religion."[43] Dr. Paracha's comments may have reflected a concern that an embrace of vigilantism could endanger the Islamist parties themselves by emboldening anti-state militants such as the TTP.[44]

Perhaps reflecting this concern, the party later sought to underscore the unique nature of the Taseer case. After the anti-terrorism court sentenced Mumtaz Qadri to death in October 2011, the JI shura issued a resolution calling on President Asif Ali Zardari to use his constitutional powers to grant Qadri an amnesty.[45] In explaining the resolution, Senator Khurshid Ahmad reasoned that while in principle the party believed "the law of the land was supreme and all citizens must be treated equally," Qadri deserved amnesty

[37] "Rally Demands Abolition of Committee Formed to Amend Blasphemy Law," *Pakistan Press International*, January 9, 2011; "Murder Elicits Only Vague, Equivocal Condemnation," *Dawn*, January 4, 2011.

[38] Salman Siddiqui, "Hardline Stance: Religious Bloc Condones Murder," *Express Tribune*, January 5, 2011.

[39] Rob Crilly, "Clerics Applaud Murder of Punjab Governor," *Daily Telegraph*, January 5, 2011.

[40] Quoted in Mosharraf Zaidi, "Having the Wrong Debate," *The News*, January 11, 2011. See also "Rally Demands Abolition of Committee Formed to Amend Blasphemy Law"; Saeed Shah, "Mainstream Pakistan Religious Organisations Applaud Killing of Salmaan Taseer," *The Guardian*, January 5, 2011.

[41] Shamim Bano, "JI Sees Taseer's Assassin in 'Seventh Heaven,'" *The News*, January 5, 2011.

[42] "Lekin" (Karachi: Geo TV, January 4, 2011).

[43] "Murder Elicits Only Vague, Equivocal Condemnation."

[44] Muhammad Khalid Masud, interview by Joshua White, English, August 15, 2012.

[45] Zahid Gishkori, "JI Seeks Presidential Pardon for Mumtaz Qadri," *Express Tribune*, October 21, 2011.

because Taseer had been seeking amnesty for Asia Bibi, the woman accused of blasphemy. Qadri's case, he conveniently concluded, was "special and represents [the] nation's feelings."[46]

In the years that followed, the party continued to use Qadri's case as a tool for political mobilization. Senior JI leaders joined rallies in support of Qadri both before and after his sentencing. In November 2015, a few months prior to his hanging, a local JI candidate in Karachi added Qadri's picture to an election poster, prompting a party spokesman to explain with disarming candor that there is "nothing wrong with these pictures and they have only been printed to motivate our voters."[47] Nearly a year and a half after Qadri was hanged, the JI amir announced at a conference that "to pay tribute to Qadri's sacrifices," the party would cover all of the educational expenses of his young son.[48]

Many prominent Deobandi leaders echoed similar criticisms of Taseer as their Barelvi and Jamaat-e-Islami colleagues, and many joined antiblasphemy rallies with other parties, particularly after Qadri's sentencing.[49] But on the whole, Deobandi clerics were more likely to qualify their support for Qadri and his vigilante assassination. JUI-F amir Maulana Fazl ur-Rahman blamed Taseer for his own death, but more obliquely than other leading Islamist political leaders had done. He attributed Taseer's killing to a failure by the government to implement Islamic laws in Pakistan.[50] Just hours after the assassination, Rahman called into Hamid Mir's popular TV program *Capital Talk*. Asked whether the shooting was justified, Rahman at first equivocated, but when pressed by Mir eventually condemned Qadri's action.[51] At subsequent rallies and press conferences, the JUI-F amir continued to criticize both Taseer and Qadri, and express his reservations about the legitimacy of violence against accused blasphemers.[52] He was also one of the few prominent Islamist party figures who, following the assassination by the TTP of Federal Minister for Minorities Affairs Shahbaz Bhatti in March 2011, expressed a willingness to discuss blasphemy "if a law is being misused against minorities."[53]

[46] Irfan Haider, "JI Urges Govt to Spare Salmaan Taseer's Killer," *Islamabad Dateline*, October 23, 2011.

[47] "JI Candidates Using Convict Mumtaz Qadri to Garner Votes," *Express Tribune*, November 26, 2015.

[48] Izhar Ullah, "JI to Bear All Educational Expenses of Mumtaz Qadri's Son: Siraj," *Express Tribune*, October 19, 2017.

[49] See, for example, Javaid-ur-Rahman, "Religious Parties Enhance Contacts to Evolve Strategy," *The Nation*, October 3, 2011.

[50] "Murder Elicits Only Vague, Equivocal Condemnation."

[51] "Capital Talk" (Karachi: Geo, January 7, 2011); Hamid Mir, "We Need a 'Made-in-Pakistan' Solution for Fighting Terrorism," *The News*, January 11, 2011.

[52] See, for example, "Pakistan: Religious Issues: Fazl Warns Against Crossing Limits," *Right Vision News*, January 15, 2011.

[53] "Fazl Says Misuse of Blasphemy Law Can Be Discussed," *Dawn*, March 5, 2011.

The JUI-F appeared to tolerate a wider range of views about Qadri than the Barelvi parties or even the JI. Speaking on TV the evening of the assassination, JUI-F Senator Muhammad Ismail Buledi of Sindh noted that while Taseer spoke irresponsibly, his words did not justify the violence against him, and that he considered Qadri a criminal.[54] Senator Buledi reiterated similar comments in the days that followed, noting that it was not good when individuals took the law into their own hands.[55]

Some of the most critical comments about Qadri, both in the early days after the assassination and later after his hanging, emerged from prominent Deobandi clerics who had links to the JUI parties. Mufti Muhammad Naeem, co-founder of the prominent Jamia Binoria madrassah in Karachi, and a member of the executive committee of the Wafaq ul-Madaris al-Arabia, condemned Taseer for inviting trouble on himself, but rejected Taseer's actions: "The blasphemy law was made exactly to prevent such incidents. Else there will be chaos in the country and everyone would kill everyone."[56] Tahir Ashrafi, a Deobandi, former member of the militant Sipah-e-Sahabah Pakistan, and leader of the Pakistan Ulama Council that had ingratiated itself with successive governments, condemned Taseer's killing, but also rejected any changes to the blasphemy laws.[57] Perhaps most notably, Maulana Muhammad Sherani, a conservative JUI-F MNA from Balochistan who served as chair of the Council of Islamic Ideology from November 2010 through November 2016, spoke out about Qadri shortly after he was hanged in late February 2016. "No one is above the law," he noted. "I respect Qadri's religious sentiments but I respect Pakistan's Constitution more."[58]

10.3.2 The TLP and the State: Collusion to Confrontation?

The most interesting and puzzling chapter of the TLP's rise to prominence was the one-year period from November 2017 through November 2018. During this short span, the party established itself as a disruptive force with its Faizabad sit-in; brought down a sitting federal law minister; demonstrated

[54] *NEWSNIGHT: Salman Taseer's Assassination: Part 1*, 2011, https://www.youtube.com/watch?v=Bn0UzRh2-4A.
[55] Javaid-ur-Rahman, "JUI-F Asks Sherry to Withdraw Bill," *Nation*, January 6, 2011.
[56] Siddiqui, "Hardline Stance."
[57] Michael Georgy, "Pakistan Governor Buried as Clerics Warn Against Grief," *Reuters*, January 5, 2011; Mehreen Zahra-Malik, "Pakistani Senate Group to Debate How to Prevent Misuse of Blasphemy Laws," *Reuters*, January 12, 2017.
[58] Sarfaraz Memon, "I Respect Pakistan's Constitution More Than Qadri's Religious Sentiments: CII Chairman," *Express Tribune*, March 1, 2016.

its rising electoral potential by receiving the fifth-largest number of votes nationwide; and saw its most prominent leaders arrested and jailed.

It has been widely asserted that the TLP's rapid ascent was due to its collusion with Pakistan's security services, or at the very least its unwitting use by the services. Two arguments support this assertion. First, there is substantial documentation of efforts, dating back decades, by the security services to instrumentalize Islamist parties for the purpose of disrupting sitting civilian governments and perpetuating military dominance. Some of these are documented in Chapters 2 and 5. Chapter 7 also describes the ways in which the MMA alliance benefited from the support of the Pakistani military. More recently, critics pointed to the curious case of Dr. Tahir ul-Qadri, a Pakistani-Canadian Barelvi scholar who returned to Pakistan in 2012 to organize a series of "Long Marches" that weakened the sitting PML-N civilian government.[59] Tahir ul-Qadri appeared to be on good terms with both the opposition PTI and the security services, prompting speculation that his activities were designed to increase the military's leverage over the civilian government.[60] In light of the Tahir ul-Qadri case, it is no surprise that many Pakistanis saw the TLP as yet another instrument of the state. That the TLP's electoral strength appeared to draw from some of the same areas in urban Punjab in which the PML-N had traditionally dominated merely reinforced this view.[61]

The second argument supporting collusion was more straightforward: There was evidence that the military aided the TLP during this contentious 2017–2018 period.[62] In November 2017, a reporter filmed Major General Azhar Navid Hayat, Director-General of the Punjab Rangers, handing out envelopes of cash to protestors at a TLP rally in Islamabad, along with words of encouragement: "This is a gift from us to you."[63] This was, Hassan Javid has noted, "seen as evidence for the idea that the military had a working relationship with the TLP" who otherwise would not have been able to sustain such a disruptive sit-in in the capital.[64] TLP leaders also admitted that they

[59] See Alix Philippon, *Soufisme et Politique au Pakistan: Le Mouvement Barelwi à L'heure de "La Guerre Contre Le Terrorisme"* (Paris: Éditions Karthala and Sciences Po Aix, 2011), 80–83.

[60] S. Akbar Zaidi, "Resilience in Pakistan's Democracy? The Tahir-Ul Qadri Episode," *Economic and Political Weekly* 48, no. 5 (February 2, 2013): 12; Huma Yusuf, "Tahirul Qadri's Rise and Its Potential Impact on Pakistan's Stability" (Oslo: Norwegian Peacebuilding Resource Centre, February 2013).

[61] Ejaz Haider, "PTI's TLP Problem: Irony Smiles," *The Friday Times*, October 29, 2021.

[62] Kalbe, "Who Is Khadim Hussain Rizvi?"

[63] "Why Was Pakistan General Giving Money to Protesters?," *BBC News*, November 29, 2017, https://web.archive.org/web/20240910033457/https://www.bbc.com/news/world-asia-42149535.

[64] Hassan Javid, "The Limits of Possibilities of Religious Politics: The Case of the Tehreek-i-Labbaik in Pakistani Punjab," *Sociological Bulletin* 70, no. 4 (October 1, 2021): 502–21, https://doi.org/10.1177/00380229211051041.

were negotiating their demands directly with army and ISI officials, not with central or provincial civilian leaders.[65]

In a *suo moto* report on the violent TLP protests issued by Justice Qazi Faez Isa of the Supreme Court in November 2018, he observed that "ISI's report [to the court] identified 'Channel 92' as a television channel supporting TLP and stated that its owners had supplied food to the protestors occupying the Faizabad Interchange."[66] Later, it emerged that the then-head of the media regulatory authority PEMRA had received a call from a senior ISI official telling him to reinstate Channel 92's live coverage of the TLP protests.[67] The Justice Isa report called out the intelligence agencies, asserting that "they should not ignore those who promote violence and hate" and that such groups "should never be pampered" by the state.[68] And, reviewing the role of the intelligence agencies in the TLP protests, Justice Isa wryly concluded that "[t]he perception that ISI may be involved in or interferes with matters with which an intelligence agency should not be concerned with, including politics, therefore was not put to rest."

Whatever implicit or explicit understandings the TLP may have formed with the Pakistani security services broke down in November 2018. Following Asia Bibi's acquittal, the TLP began publicly criticizing not only the civilian government, but the military. Whether this pivot was the result of a deeply held ideological position or merely a misreading of the party's political leverage vis-à-vis the security services is unclear.

What is clear is that TLP leaders targeted the military in ways that directly challenged its religious and political legitimacy. Senior TLP leader Afzal Qadri told his followers that "Muslim generals" should rebel against Chief of Army Staff Bajwa, falsely labeling him a Qadiani—a pejorative for a member of the ostracized Ahmadi sect.[69] He also asserted that the judges who acquitted Asia Bibi deserved to be killed.[70] This crossed a line for the security services, which moved swiftly to detain TLP leaders and rein in the party's activities.[71]

[65] Ali Arqam, "Rise of the TLP," *Newsline*, October 2018.

[66] Mushir Alam and Qazi Faez Isa Isa, Suo Moto Case No. 7/2017 (Supreme Court of Pakistan November 22, 2018).

[67] Absar Alam [@AbsarAlamHaider], "novambar 2018 meṅ...," Tweet, *Twitter* (blog), April 18, 2021, https://web.archive.org/web/20240925201049/https://joshuatwhite.net/wp-content/uploads/2024/09/archive-20210418-twitter.pdf.

[68] Alam and Isa, Suo Moto Case No. 7/2017.

[69] *Pir Afzal Qadri Speaking Against Army Chief of Pakistan*, 2018, https://www.dailymotion.com/video/x6wgtsa.

[70] Arslan Ahmed and Bilal Zafar Ranjha, "Salafising Barelwiyat: Salafi Doctrine of Al Wala' Wal Bara and TLP Politics in Pakistan," *Journal of Research in Humanities* 56, no. 2 (2020): 139–64.

[71] Umair Jamal, "How the Pakistani State Cracked Down on Tehreek-e-Labbaik," *The Diplomat*, December 7, 2018. https://web.archive.org/web/20240826162152/https://thediplomat.com/2018/12/how-the-pakistani-state-cracked-down-on-tehreek-e-labbaik/.

10.4 Conclusion: The Logics of Anti-State Violence

10.4.1 The Established Islamist Parties

What lessons can we draw from the emergence of the TLP about the ways in which Islamist parties enable religiously justified anti-state violence? We will begin with observations about the reactions of the more established Islamist parties, and then we will grapple with the complexities of the TLP itself and its contentious interactions with the state.

The responses of the established Islamist parties to the rise of the TLP were similar but not uniform. The JUP parties were the most outspoken in their support, followed by the JI, and finally the JUI-F—which offered only qualified support to the new party. The Deobandi clerical establishment was even more critical of the TLP than the JUI-F.

This pattern of reactions can be explained in part by ideological factors. As Barelvi institutions, the JUP parties had a sectarian affinity with the TLP, and shared with its leaders devotional practices regarding the prophet Muhammad and theological views about the centrality of protecting the prophet's honor. These affinities help to explain the JUP parties' support for Tahir ul-Qadri and, later, the TLP. The JUI-F and leading Deobandi clerics, by contrast, were more qualified in their praise of the TLP, possibly reflecting the discomfort among some Deobandis of giving too prominent a place to the prophet Muhammad in devotional practices.

In other respects, however, theological differences seem inadequate to explain this pattern of party reactions. Consider ideological views regarding anti-state violence, as examined earlier in Chapter 3. Although there is some precedent in the early Barelvi tradition for apostatizing those who hold competing interpretations of shariah, the Barelvis in Pakistan were, until 2011, widely considered to be more pacific than their Deobandi counterparts, and considerably more reluctant to take up arms against the state. It was the Barelvis who had been improperly elevated, in SherAli Tareen's sharp critique, with a kind of "international and national valorization . . . as the true banner-bearer of 'moderate Islam' in Pakistan."[72] And it had been Deobandi movements, after all—including the Red Mosque clerics and the TTP chronicled in earlier chapters—that had confronted the Pakistani state with violence.

Although ideological factors may indeed help to explain JUP support for TLP, and the reticence of Deobandi leaders to embrace the new Barelvi party,

[72] SherAli Tareen, "Commentary on Part III: The Problems and Perils of Translating Sufism as 'Moderate Islam,'" in *Modern Sufis and the State: The Politics of Islam in South Asia and Beyond*, ed. Katherine Pratt Ewing and Rosemary R. Corbett (New York: Columbia University Press, 2020), 179.

structural and institutional factors more coherently explain the established Islamist parties' reactions to the rise of the TLP. Many aspects of these parties' behaviors toward the TLP, including their nonpublic activities to support or undermine the new party, remain opaque. But their patterns of public behavior and comments generally comport with the first hypothesis from Chapter 1—that an Islamist party's willingness to enable anti-state violence in the name of advancing Islamic law is principally a function of its structural vulnerabilities to the state and to anti-state movements, rather than a function of its ideological commitments—and with the typology presented in Figure 1.1 that associates these vulnerabilities with particular party strategies and discourses.

The JUP parties praised the TLP. At least publicly, they supported the rise of a vigorous new Barelvi party and movement. How should we assess these parties' vulnerabilities? While in principle the JUP parties might have had high vulnerability to the state on account of their small size, they had such a meager track record of electoral success that they effectively had nothing to lose by embracing a new movement that could reenergize the Barelvi community both socially and politically. Their vulnerabilities to the TLP itself are harder to discern. The JUP parties, particularly JUP-N, might rightly have worried about defections of their cadres, particularly in pockets of Karachi that had long been contested among the MQM, the JI, and JUP parties, but were now part of the prime TLP electoral "hunting ground."[73] On the other hand, the rise of a new TLP movement and its anti-blasphemy platform on balance could, over time, create enormous opportunities for all of the Barelvi parties to raise their political profiles in the vote-rich provinces of Punjab and Sindh. Consistent with Hypothesis 1 but reflecting this ambiguity, it appears as though the JUP parties praised the TLP in public, but may not have developed clear policies of supporting or opposing the TLP with respect to on-the-ground activities.

The JI praised the TLP, but did so less fulsomely than the JUP parties. As has been well documented throughout this book, the JI's vulnerability to state pressure is relatively low—in part due to intentional efforts by the party to retain its freedom of action. The JI's vulnerability to the TLP was arguably low to moderate. The JI likely did not worry much about its cadres

[73] Talat Aslam (@titojourno), "Looks like the TLP's Strong Showing in Karachi in 2018 Was Not a Flash in the Pan. Its Performance in the Malir by-Election Suggests the Death of Its Leader Hasn't Made a Big Difference to Its Appeal in Sindh's Urban Areas. Also Shows the Party Enjoys Cross-Ethnic Appeal. Ominous," Twitter, February 16, 2021, https://web.archive.org/web/20240925204817/https://joshuatwhite.net/wp-content/uploads/2024/09/archive-20210216-twitter.pdf.

defecting to the TLP, given its ideological differences with the Barelvi party, and its rigid and disciplined institutional structure. In certain Karachi constituencies in 2018, the JI did contest against TLP politicians, and may for that reason have worried about the risks of too directly embracing the TLP and its platform.

More cautious still than the JI, the JUI-F offered only qualified praise of the TLP. The party's vulnerability to the state was, for the reasons noted throughout this volume, moderate to high, given its weakly institutionalized party structure and its longstanding concerns about state control of the Deobandi madaris. Its vulnerability to the TLP was moderate. At the time of the Taseer assassination, the JUI-F had recently left the coalition government, and thus felt at relatively greater liberty to support opposition elements such as the TLP. Moreover, there were few if any constituencies in which the JUI-F had historic strength and in which the TLP could be considered a credible threat. On the other hand, the JUI-F leadership would have been concerned about the rise of the TLP's national profile, which might sideline the JUI-F as a leading Islamist party and sought-after coalition partner for the larger mainstream parties. There is no direct evidence to this effect, but the equivocation of the JUI-F leadership in the wake of Taseer's killing suggests that they might also have worried that an endorsement of the TLP could validate the kind of religious logic of violence that the TTP had employed in their attacks against the Deobandi Islamist parties.

It is, finally, worth noting the responses of mainstream Deobandi clerics, who exhibited a complex mix of praise and prevarication regarding the assassination of Salman Taseer and the rise of the TLP.[74] These clerics are not a central subject of this study, but their responses provide a useful point of comparison to their close sectarian allies within the JUI-F. Leading Deobandi clerics arguably had even higher vulnerabilities to state pressure than the JUI-F, given that they were directly affiliated with a madrassah, or responsible for the regulation of broader Deobandi madaris networks. Some also had stakes in government institutions, such as the CII, or government-recognized bodies such as the Pakistan Ulama Council. And their exposure to violence from anti-state groups such as the TTP had been quite high. Their complex response to the TLP is thus consistent with the theory put forward in Chapter 1, reflecting their considerable vulnerability to both the state and an anti-state movement.

[74] For a review of these responses, see Mashal Saif, *The 'Ulama in Contemporary Pakistan: Contesting and Cultivating an Islamic Republic* (Cambridge, UK: Cambridge University Press, 2020), 122–29.

10.4.2 The TLP's Decision-Making

We now turn to assessing the TLP itself. How to explain the party's decisions to confront the state? And what does this case tell us about how Islamist parties reckon with the use of violence or endorsement of violence against the state? This element of the TLP case study is most analogous to the MMA case in Chapter 7, in which we explored the MMA's logic of confrontation with the state. Here also it is important to note that much of the TLP's decision-making remains opaque.

There appear to have been both ideological and organizational drivers that might explain the party's decision to confront the state. From the party's earliest days, the TLP leadership cultivated a theology of violence that set it apart from most other organizations and leaders in the modern Barelvi tradition. As noted in Chapter 3, Barelvi parties have, following Hanafi fiqh, typically been cautious about endorsing violence against the state. Even parties such as Sunni Tahrik, which had a long tradition of sponsoring violence, distanced themselves from the TLP and its radical positions in the years following 2011.[75] Other leading Barelvi figures, such as the cleric Dr. Tahir ul-Qadri, disagreed with the TLP's hardline rejection of any attempts to reform the blasphemy laws.[76]

The TLP took a distinctive element of its sectarian tradition—a high theology of the prophet Muhammad—and fused it with a takfiri theology of violence that until that time had taken root more in Salafi circles than in Barelvism. As Mashal Saif has noted, there was a particularly robust debate among Barelvi scholars and activists regarding this theology of violence between Taseer's assassination in 2011, and the emergence of the TLP as a social and political force in 2016.[77] Khadim Hussain Rizvi extended his critique of Deobandi leaders for not sufficiently protecting the honor of the prophet Muhammad, and it was the TLP that most successfully amplified the view that individuals and nongovernment actors could legitimately punish so-called perpetrators of blasphemy apart from the state.[78]

It would be indefensibly reductionist to conclude that the TLP's theological position regarding the honor of the prophet Muhammad was merely

[75] For a review of Sunni Tahrik's violent history, see Mujeeb Ahmad, "The Rise of Militancy Among Pakistani Barelvis: The Case of the Sunni Tehrik," in *State and Nation-Building in Pakistan: Beyond Islam and Security*, ed. Roger D. Long et al. (Routledge, 2016); Philippon, *Soufisme et Politique au Pakistan*, 86ff.

[76] Abdul Basit, "Barelvi Political Activism and Religious Mobilization in Pakistan: The Case of Tehreek-e-Labaik Pakistan (TLP)," *Politics, Religion & Ideology* 21 (August 20, 2020): 378.

[77] Saif, *The 'Ulama in Contemporary Pakistan*, 116–22.

[78] See Jazib Rehman Khan, "Spread of Religious Hatred through Digital Media in Pakistan: The Case of Tehreek-E-Labbaik Pakistan," *Journal of Media and Communication Studies* 1, no. 1 (January 2021): 51.

derivative of its material or electoral interests. The blasphemy issue was clearly at the center of the party's agenda and indispensable to its public appeal. The TLP also had the benefit, as it were, of the legal infrastructure of sections 295 and 298 of the PPC. These provisions, as written and interpreted, dramatically advantaged those who made accusations about blasphemy or dishonoring the prophet Muhammad, and provided few legal avenues of recourse to the accused. As the International Commission on Jurists noted in 2015, "All institutions of the Pakistani State . . . have effectively abdicated their responsibilities under human rights law when people are accused of committing blasphemy, knowingly leaving them either at the mercy of mobs and organized extremist religious groups or facing trials that are fundamentally unfair."[79] The TLP thus had at its disposal a potent if politically volatile set of legal tools to advance its ideological agenda.

As with all parties, the TLP's organizational structure determined in part its ability to capitalize on these legal and political tools. Throughout this period, the party appeared weakly institutionalized. It exhibited characteristics of both programmatic and charismatic linkage patterns—the former can be seen in its use of a single policy issue to drive political mobilization, and the latter in its reliance on a key leader (and later, his son).[80] The party suffered from internal divisions and factionalization, and did not appear to have developed robust internal norms and procedures.[81]

What the TLP lacked in structure it partially compensated for with energy and innovation. Leveraging Barelvi mosque networks, the party aggressively built out a presence in urban and peri-urban Punjab, areas where Islamist parties had, with the occasional exception of the JI, performed poorly.[82] It sought—with decidedly mixed results—to reorient the locus of authority among the Barelvis away from the class of wealthy pirs, shrine caretakers, and madaris leaders toward a new and largely younger generation of social and political activists.[83] Although it was not electorally successful in 2018, this network allowed the TLP to demonstrate its broad appeal in Punjab and Sindh and its ability to generate a significant quantity of votes.

Ultimately, while the behavior of the established Islamist parties toward the TLP is generally consistent with the hypotheses presented in Chapter 1, the

[79] International Commission of Jurists, "On Trial," 6.

[80] See Sabat, Shoaib, and Qadar, "Religious Populism in Pakistani Punjab."

[81] Basit, "Barelvi Political Activism and Religious Mobilization in Pakistan: The Case of Tehreek-e-Labaik Pakistan (TLP)."

[82] Umair Javed, "Checkmate," *Dawn*, November 1, 2021.

[83] See Javid, "The Limits of Possibilities of Religious Politics," 508ff; Ayesha Siddiqa, "Imran Khan's Secret Agreement with TLP Has Brought the Barelvi Jinni Out of the Bottle," *The Print*, November 3, 2021, https://web.archive.org/web/20230812035356/https://theprint.in/opinion/imran-khans-secret-agreement-with-tlp-has-brought-the-barelvi-jinni-out-of-the-bottle/760968/.

behavior of the TLP itself is harder to fully square with those hypotheses. The party had ample reason to fear financial or legal retaliation by the state, and yet its leaders endorsed and participated in violence against state institutions. It appears, with the benefit of hindsight, that party leaders were simply more vulnerable to the state than they had originally believed, and that at key moments they misjudged their leverage vis-à-vis the security services.[84]

There is, on the other side, ample evidence that the party was unusually resilient. It continued to contest elections after being banned, used its public influence and religious discourse to successfully pressure the government to reverse its ban, and got the better of the government in a series of negotiations over the course of several years.

Given these contradictions, it is not surprising that the TLP does not neatly fit the typology proposed in the second set of hypotheses in Chapter 1. As a party with programmatic and charismatic linkage patterns, it should have been relatively less vulnerable to state influence, compared with those that relied on clientelistic patterns (Hypothesis 2a). But as a weakly institutionalized party, it should have been relatively more vulnerable to state influence than its more institutionalized peers (Hypothesis 2b).

The TLP thus defies easy categorization. Because it is still a relatively new entrant to the Pakistani political scene, it is too early to judge with confidence its underlying calculations about religiously justified anti-state violence. Even so, we can make four observations about its behavior and possible future trajectories.

First, the TLP's activism appears to be more deeply ideologically anchored than that of the JUI parties, and more narrowly focused than that of the JI. The party's leaders pursued an ideological agenda, and at times chose to confront the security services in ways that would not have served their interests had they been principally interested in electoral gain. Their ideological agenda was also considerably more bounded than that of the JI, which historically directed its efforts into a broader systemic project of state Islamization.

Second, the party championed an ideological issue, that is, the protection of the honor of the prophet Muhammad, that had competitive utility in advancing the profile of Barelvis against rival maslaks such as the Deobandis. Blasphemy can be instrumentalized as a highly emotive issue, and it is one that appeared to engage the interests and feelings not only of Barelvis, but of those who identified more generically as Sunni. Whether or not the TLP leadership intentionally designed its campaigns during this period from

[84] A key example is the decision by Pir Afzal Qadri to engage in inflammatory rhetoric against the Chief of Army Staff. See Khan, "Spread of Religious Hatred through Digital Media in Pakistan: The Case of Tehreek-E-Labbaik Pakistan," 51.

2011 through 2018 to maximize its standing vis-à-vis its Deobandi rivals is unknown and perhaps unknowable. But the party's actions do appear to have raised the national profile of Barelvi leaders, possibly advancing their efforts to gain adherents, donations, and state patronage.

Third, as noted above, the TLP was plainly susceptible to state intervention given its weak organizational and structural vulnerabilities, but these frailties did not seem to constrain the party's leadership as much as might have been expected. This may have been due in part to the party's inexperience. Unlike the mainstream Islamist parties, it had little track record of confronting the state. Its often-shifting public postures toward state institutions—at times militant, at times accommodating—could have been products of this inexperience, or of a poorly organized decision-making structure.

Fourth, the party's decision to focus on blasphemy gave it an unusually strong hand to play in its negotiations with both the state, and with its ideological rivals. As explained earlier in this chapter, Pakistani state institutions have gradually acceded, both in law and in practice, to the notion that there is limited room for regular judicial process to be carried out on matters of blasphemy. Judges, lawyers, police officers, and administrative officials often rightly fear vigilante violence if they try blasphemy cases with the same due process and evidentiary standards as other criminal matters.[85] This has the effect of insulating activist groups such as the TLP from the ordinary consequences of political violence. It has made mainstream Islamist parties wary of challenging the TLP's ideological premise regarding blasphemy, and may have made the security services wary of cracking down too quickly—or too severely—on the party when it engaged in violence.

Of the preceding four observations about the TLP, only one of them—the third, pertaining to its organizational coherence and experience negotiating with the state—seems as though it could plausibly change in the short- or medium-term. This does not suggest that the party will suddenly (or indeed, ever) become more successful at converting its agitation into electoral victories. This will likely remain difficult, particularly given that the TLP's rivals in Punjab and Sindh are principally mainstream parties rather than other Islamist parties. But it does suggest that the TLP and other Barelvi activist groups have good reason to believe that they can, for their own ideological and competitive reasons, continue to normalize the use of violence—including anti-state violence—in ways that were once largely outside the Barelvi mainstream.

[85] This is extensively documented in International Commission of Jurists, "On Trial."

11
Conclusion
The Conflicted Islamists

11.1 Ideological and Structural Logics of Islamist Violence

This book describes and demonstrates the centrality of organizational rather than ideological explanations for Islamist party decision-making in Pakistan. While not discounting these parties' ideological agendas, or their reliance on Islamic discourse, I have argued in the preceding chapters that the ways in which they decide to enable religiously justified anti-state violence has more to do with their structural constraints than with their ideological or theological positions. Fundamentally, this book posits a vulnerability-oriented model of Islamist behavior: Parties respond to their political environments and opportunity structures, and are shaped by their weaknesses relative to the state and to other Islamic movements. These structural incentives are often at least as important as a party's ideological predispositions.

In the opening chapter I introduced two overarching questions. The first was *why* Islamist parties enable anti-state violence, particularly when doing so could undermine their standing as legitimate political actors and the benefits that they derive from political participation. I posited several reasons, each of which also pertain to mainstream parties, but which are often more acute for Islamist parties. The first was that they do so because they have ideological sympathies for the stated objectives—if not the means—of groups that promote anti-state violence. Each of the five case studies in this volume includes examples of Islamist parties supporting or endorsing anti-state groups because they advocated, usually in vague terms, for a greater role for shariah in the Pakistani legal or political systems. This much is clear: Islamist parties often make the calculation that they will benefit indirectly when an outside movement focuses public debate on issues of Islam and shariah, even when it does so through provocation or violence.

The second reason that Islamist parties sometimes enable anti-state violence is because they find it valuable in targeting their political opposition.

Vigilante Islamists. Joshua T. White, Oxford University Press. © Oxford University Press (2025).
DOI: 10.1093/9780197814178.003.0011

Chapter 5 provides many examples of Islamist parties' relationships with militant groups—such as those operating in Afghanistan and Kashmir, and violent sectarian movements—but most of these militant partners did not direct their energies against the state; rather, they acted in ways that supported the objectives of the security services. There were, however, some exceptions, particularly in the behavior of the Jamaat-e-Islami. The party took advantage of violence by its own youth cadres during its tenure in then-NWFP, and violence by the Red Mosque clerics, to exert pressure on the Musharraf government. The JI's later praise of Hakimullah Mehsud, chronicled in Chapter 9, may have been an attempt to gain popular support and leverage over the Pakistani military.

Perhaps the most complex and compelling reason that Islamist parties sometimes support anti-state violence is that they are seeking to manage competition. Fearing defection of their own cadres to more radical anti-state organizations, the parties sometimes decide to publicly support those organizations rather than risk challenging them. This behavior was on display frequently throughout this volume's case studies. For example, worried about the TNSM's potential to cut into its electoral stronghold, the JI praised the new movement while actively working to undermine it. The JUI-F, anxious about the TTP gaining influence among the Deobandi madaris and eventually targeting the party leadership, sought to manage this competition as long as possible through "praise for protection" behavior. And the Deobandi parties all, to varying degrees, publicly acclaimed the TLP, worried that outright criticism of the new Barelvi movement might subject them—and the wider Deobandi movement—to accusations that they were not sufficiently devoted to defending the honor of the prophet Muhammad.

The second and more significant major question introduced in this volume is *under what conditions and in what ways* do Islamist parties enable religiously justified anti-state violence? In other words, how can we explain puzzling observed variations in Islamist party behavior? Hypothesis 1 posited that an Islamist party's willingness to enable anti-state violence in the name of advancing Islamic law is principally a function of its structural vulnerabilities to the state and to anti-state movements, rather than a function of its ideological commitments. Corollaries 1a and 1b further described the relationship between parties' structural vulnerabilities and their public and private postures toward anti-state movements. These corollaries predicted a pattern of four distinct Islamist party strategies, as shown in Figure 1.1. And Hypotheses 2a and 2b provided supporting arguments about the ways in which specific structural factors—party linkage patterns and institutionalization—generate party vulnerabilities.

Much of the analytical work of this book has focused on testing these hypotheses and the predicted pattern of Islamist strategies. I will not recapitulate the case studies, each of which examines evidence for these hypotheses in its concluding section. But taken together, the case studies present a sustained argument that, in most cases, structural factors provide the best explanation for the variations in Islamist party strategies. There are, to be sure, some puzzling party behaviors within the case studies that do not seem to support the hypotheses. For example, the JUI-F mustered a much more coherent response to the Red Mosque crisis than would be expected of a weakly institutionalized clientelist party. And the TLP's repeatedly aggressive posture toward the state is simply hard to square with its pronounced structural vulnerabilities. Overall, however, the case studies largely support the structuralist arguments that are at the heart of this work.

There are several broad lessons to be drawn from this volume's analysis of Islamist party behavior. The first is that Islamist parties have established a unique and resilient place in the Pakistani political system, and that the nature of Islamist discourse allows these parties to exert influence well beyond their size. Islamist parties are not major electoral entities in Pakistan; their share of votes has been consistently small, and with few exceptions they have not governed as majority parties even at the provincial level. Some, like the JUI-F, have been large and active enough to extract concessions at the federal level in exchange for their participation in coalitions. But none seem likely to govern outright. Nonetheless, the way in which these parties leverage the language of shariah gives them meaningful advantages in the Pakistani system.

To adopt the language of political party theory, shariah is a good subject to extreme valence competition; that is, it is considered a universal good, and one for which—in the vaguest terms—more is always better than less.[1] ("The demand that Pakistan should be an Islamic state," observed Wilfred Cantwell Smith presciently in 1957, "has been a Muslim way of saying that Pakistan should build for itself a good society."[2]) In such an environment, Islamist parties are able to muster disproportionate influence. So long as they can position themselves in the public square as the legitimate and rightful champions of shariah, they can pressure all other parties to adopt their religio-political program, or at the very least can insulate themselves to some extent from state pressure. Even when they function in highly constrained political

[1] A 2009 survey conducted in Pakistan revealed that nearly 80 percent of respondents believed that a greater role for shariah in Pakistani law would result in "a lot more" or "a little more" fairness in the administration of justice. Graeme Blair et al., "Poverty and Support for Militant Politics: Evidence from Pakistan," *American Journal of Political Science* 57, no. 1 (2012): 30–48. See Q170.

[2] Wilfred Cantwell Smith, *Islam in Modern History* (Princeton, NJ: Princeton University Press, 1957), 239.

and electoral environments, Islamist parties around the world can use this shariah "ratchet effect" to amplify their influence in political debates.

The most salient question, then, is usually not whether these parties will lead an "Islamist takeover" of the political process in Pakistan or elsewhere, but whether and how they might incrementally promote the Islamization of political discourse and institutions, or provide legitimacy to anti-state groups that seek to do so with violent means. Pakistan's Islamist parties are well positioned to continue to play this role, provided that they remain reasonably competitive and organizationally coherent. The JI's electoral fortunes have declined notably since its electoral high-water mark in 2002, and it has struggled to identify policy issues that motivate its core lower-middle-class constituency. The principal risk to the JUI parties is that they are famously fractious, and they may lose their ability to influence national policy-making if they do not form a minimally cohesive political bloc. The TLP, for its part, could eventually face competition from other Barelvi movements or parties that are able to effectively tap into the blasphemy issue to exert pressure on the government.

The second lesson is that while the commonalities among Islamist parties' rhetoric and support for shariah makes it tempting to see them as relatively homogenous, they often face distinctive incentive structures, have distinctive capabilities, and perceive distinctive vulnerabilities. Their relationships with both the state and with violent anti-state groups are patterned by these particular distinctions. The JI, for example, as an ideological, modernist, largely urban party, is policy-oriented and willing to sacrifice electoral participation in the short term in order to advance a systemic Islamist agenda in the long term. With its high levels of ideological commitment by members and robust institutionalization, it believes that it has little to fear from other Islamist organizations or from the state; such confidence gives it the freedom to embrace anti-state Islamists when it can do so for political benefit. And while public support for some radical organizations such as al-Qaeda would violate the party's ideological principles and invite unwanted interference by the state, the party seems to be in no rush to abandon its strategy of occasionally offering quiet, qualified, or indirect support for a host of other Islamist groups that embrace violence against the Pakistani state.

The JUI-F, as a clientelist party, has rather different incentives: it values political participation and patronage, focuses on short-term gains, and works principally to protect the madaris. It is highly susceptible to inducements and pressures by the government, and is willing to embrace ambiguous policy positions when necessary. In keeping with a long tradition of the ulama in South Asia, the JUI-F leaders have learned to cultivate a "studied ambiguity" that gives them maximum room to maneuver.[3] What the party gains in flexibility from this decentralization, however, it loses in resilience to external challengers. A poorly organized, weakly institutionalized party is uniquely vulnerable to outside groups that might gain a constituency within the party apparatus itself. In this way, the JUI-F has struggled to develop a coherent policy toward anti-state groups that does not alienate key internal leadership blocs. Given that this challenge is structural rather than ideological, it is not likely to change in the near future.

The TLP is unlike the Islamist parties that came before it. It rose to influence on an antiblasphemy platform that mobilized Barelvi activists outside the traditional channels of the madaris, shrines, and JUP political parties. Building charismatic and programmatic linkages with its constituents, it was able to garner significant votes before it had established a robust party structure. Its innovative forms of outreach and lack of institutionalization helped to drive its early success and made it an attractive instrumental partner for the Pakistani security services to undermine the civilian government. These same qualities, however, made it unusually vulnerable, and it was unable to sustain its campaigns of political violence once the state had decided to rein them in. It also found that there was an upper bound to its support from the ulama, who were often wary of precedential implications of the party's support for the assassination of a sitting politician.

The third lesson is that Islamist parties and the Pakistani security services have consistently worked to co-opt each other, and that these relationships, too, are shaped by the structural vulnerabilities of the parties. The analytical narratives in Part I and the case studies in Part II both repeatedly showed that Islamist parties seek from the state access to patronage, protection, and validation as authoritative voices on shariah. The state, too, has a set of longstanding strategies for co-opting the Islamist parties. As Vali Nasr has observed,

> The state has followed two general approaches to regulating Islamic activism. The first was directed at incorporating Islam into the state's discourse on sociopolitical change while simultaneously limiting the role of Islamic parties—the self-styled advocates of Islamization—in the political process . . . . The second incorporated Islamic politics into the state's discourse by including Islamic parties in the political process and even in the running of the state, all with the aim of establishing control over them.[4]

[3] Muhammad Qasim Zaman, "Pluralism, Democracy, and the 'Ulama," in *Remaking Muslim Politics: Pluralism, Contestation, Democratization*, ed. Robert W. Hefner, Princeton Studies in Muslim Politics (Princeton, NJ: Princeton University Press, 2005), 70.

[4] Seyyed Vali Reza Nasr, "Islamic Opposition to the Islamic State: The Jamaat-i Islami, 1977–88," *International Journal of Middle East Studies* 25, no. 2 (May 1993): 142.

Put another way, the state can incorporate the parties' discourse while marginalizing their political participation, or can encourage their political participation while finding ways to temper their influence. At least since the 1990s, the military has generally adopted the former approach with the JI, which it has generally sought to keep outside the halls of power, and the latter approach with the JUI-F, which it has generally welcomed as a coalition partner to its favored political blocs while working to limit the party's influence on the political system as a whole.

But to these two strategies we can add another: The state has consistently co-opted Islamist parties to endorse, validate, and recruit for militant groups that use violence against Pakistan's adversaries in Afghanistan and India. This has required that the Islamist parties cultivate and promote theologies of violence that allow them to selectively endorse militant actions in Pakistan's neighborhood, but reject violence against the Pakistani state itself. As the case studies amply demonstrate, the Islamist parties and their members do not always make clear distinctions between the two types of violence, and the ways in which they choose to enable vigilantism do not always sit well with the security officials who are seeking to co-opt them.

The fourth lesson is that when Islamist parties perceive that they are in competition with anti-state groups that are willing to employ violence, it can prompt them to adopt counterintuitive rhetorical strategies. This book documented several "praise for protection" efforts, in which an Islamist party's often lavish commendation of an anti-state movement belied its quiet attempts to undermine the very same group. Parties with high vulnerability to ideologically similar anti-state challengers are most likely to undertake these efforts as a way to hedge against diminished legitimacy, and to protect themselves against political or even physical attack by the challenger movement. This pattern was evident with the JI in the TNSM case from the 1990s, with both the JI and JUI-F during the Red Mosque crisis, and with the JUI-F in its interactions with the Pakistani Taliban after 2008. In each instance, there came a point at which the behavior of the anti-state group became so egregious, or so clearly directed at the Islamist party, that the party could no longer credibly associate itself with the challenger, and it pivoted to criticism instead.

This pattern of "praise for protection" behavior suggests that Islamist party rhetoric is not always a reliable indicator of that party's actual position regarding a violent anti-state challenger movement. Consequently, observers should be somewhat more cautious about taking Islamist party rhetoric about shariah, or their endorsements of new and more radical movements, at face value. In an environment of armed competition, affirmation of an anti-state shariah narrative might be nothing more than a desperate act of self-preservation.

11.2 Islamist Political Futures

These four lessons are drawn from, and apply to, Pakistan's unique political environment, but may with some caveats be relevant to other contexts as well. The shariah "ratchet effect" is most likely to be found in relatively open political milieus that are free from heavy-handed state censorship or repression of Islamist parties. Arab states have frequently exerted a strong hand in effecting precisely this sort of suppression. In Muslim-majority states in Southeast Asia and the Indian Ocean, however, there is considerably more room for this dynamic to take root. Islamist parties such as the Malaysian Islamic Party (PAS) and the Prosperous Justice Party (PKS) in Indonesia have occasionally been successful enough to negotiate with larger parties for coalition formation at the national level, and they operate in Muslim-majority political environments in which their discourse about Islamization or shariah has the potential to shape government policymaking even if these parties remain outside of direct decision-making roles. In the Maldives, the small Islamist-oriented Adhaalath Party has helped to form and sustain coalition governments, has at times dominated the Ministry of Islamic Affairs and the government's Fiqh Academy, has lobbied the government to adopt anti-Israel policies, and has used its public profile to pressure larger parties by accusing them of being irreligious.[5] Even in Türkiye, where the right-of-center Justice and Development Party (AKP) has dominated politics since 2002, smaller Islamist parties such as the New Welfare Party (YRP) have shown that they can generate some political leverage that could be deployed to shape policy-making on a narrow set of issues.[6]

The lessons from this book about the distinctive incentive structures and vulnerabilities faced by Islamist parties may also have wider applicability. Some of these vulnerabilities are constraints imposed by federalist systems.

[5] Boris Wille, "Defending Islam in an Islamic State: Islamic Nationalist Discourse, Democratic Reform, and the Religious Commitment of the State in the Maldives," *Asian Ethnology* 80, no. 1 (2021): 199–226; Aditya Gowdara Shivamurthy, "Trouble in Paradise: Endorsed Extremism and Sustained Extremist Ecosystems in the Maldives," *ORF Online* (blog), July 1, 2022, https://web.archive.org/web/20240417125820/https://www.orfonline.org/expert-speak/sustained-extremist-ecosystems-in-the-maldives. For a deeper view of the debates on Islam and politics in the Maldives, see Azim Zahir, *Islam and Democracy in the Maldives: Interrogating Reformist Islam's Role in Politics* (Oxford: Taylor & Francis Group, 2021).

[6] M. Hakan Yavuz and Rasim Koç, "Do Turkey's 2024 Local Elections Signal the End of Erdoğan's Reign?," *Middle East Policy* 31, no. 2 (2024): 95–107, https://doi.org/10.1111/mepo.12747.

The MMA's complex decision-making about its Islamist agenda, its associations with vigilantism and violence, and its rhetoric about the Islamic legitimacy of the state, echo the decisions that Malaysia's PAS has faced during its various tenures in subnational governance in Kelantan and Terengganu states.[7] Other Islamist vulnerabilities outlined in this book are the product of dominant central authorities, such as militaries or monarchies, that constrain Islamist parties and exploit their institutional weaknesses. In Egypt, the Muslim Brotherhood-linked Freedom and Justice Party won the 2011–2012 parliamentary election and briefly held the presidency before the military took advantage of its numerous vulnerabilities, deposed the president, and subsequently banned the party. Somewhat less dramatically, the Ennahda party in Tunisia and the Justice and Development Party (PJD) in Morocco—both linked informally to the Muslim Brotherhood—felt pressures to moderate and demonstrate responsible rhetoric toward more radical groups when they had governance roles, but each faced significant vulnerabilities from the ruling elite and the monarchy, respectively.[8]

The "praise for protection" behavior described in this volume is a particularly overt outcome of the internal unease that many Islamist parties have confronted when they face the rise of new, more radical Islamic groups that justify the use of violence on the basis of Islamic law. Praising such groups often invites reputational damage to parties that wish to remain in the mainstream, while criticizing them risks losing dedicated cadres, or inviting direct violence from the more radical organization. It is here that most parties face strong incentives to prevaricate but quietly undermine these radical rivals. The Ennahda party, for example, grappled in this way after 2011 with the rise of an array of Salafi jihadi groups, before belatedly breaking decisively with them.[9] And in Yemen, as another example, both before and after the 2011 uprising the Muslim Brotherhood-linked Yemeni Congregation for Reform (Islah) struggled—and eventually failed—to navigate its governance

[7] See Ahmad Fauzi Abdul Hamid, "Islam and Violence in Malaysia," Working Paper No. 123 (Singapore: S. Rajaratnam School of International Studies, March 9, 2007); Mohd Faizal Musa, "Post-Islamism Battles Political Islam in Malaysia," Trends in Southeast Asia No. 2023/17 (Singapore: ISEAS-Yusof Ishak Institute, 2023); Azmil Tayeb, "Delivering Development, Enforcing Shariah: PAS's Dilemma in Terengganu," Trends in Southeast Asia No. 2024/14 (Singapore: ISEAS-Yusof Ishak Institute, 2024).

[8] See, for example, Monica Marks and Sayida Ounissi, "Ennahda from Within: Islamists or 'Muslim Democrats'? A Conversation" (Washington, DC: Brookings Institution, March 23, 2016); Avi Spiegel, "Succeeding by Surviving: Examining the Durability of Political Islam in Morocco," Working Paper, Rethinking Political Islam (Washington, DC: Brookings Institution, August 2015); Shadi Hamid, "The End of the Moroccan 'Model': How Islamists Lost Despite Winning," Brookings Institution, January 31, 2023, https://web.archive.org/web/20240921013423/https://www.brookings.edu/articles/the-end-of-the-moroccan-model-how-islamists-lost-despite-winning/.

[9] Monica Marks, "Tunisia's Ennahda: Rethinking Islamism in the Context of ISIS and the Egyptian Coup," Working Paper, Rethinking Political Islam (Washington, DC: Brookings Institution, August 2015).

ambitions with the rising power of both Houthi militants and radical Salafis linked to al-Qaeda in the Arabian Peninsula, both of which eventually turned on the party.[10]

There are of course limits to how far these analytical observations from the Pakistani context can reasonably travel. As a state that has from the outset defined itself in relation to Islam, and has from its earliest days instrumentalized Islamic militancy for foreign policy ends, Pakistan has cultivated an unusually permissive environment for the use of religiously justified violence, even when that violence is at times directed toward the state itself. The often lethargic or even deferential behavior of the Pakistani government toward groups that engage in anti-state violence is on display in nearly every case study in this volume. In such a context, Islamist parties naturally have more political space to engage with anti-state militants than they would in many of the other countries referenced above, in which it is simply too dangerous for relatively small and vulnerable political parties to be seen as endorsing violence against the state.

In Pakistan, at least, there is ample reason to believe that violent anti-state Islamist movements will unfortunately continue to thrive—at least episodically. If anything, the takfiri justifications for violence against the state have become more widespread with the rise of the Islamic State Khorasan Province in 2015, and the subsequent cross-pollination of Islamic State fighters with the TTP and sectarian organizations in both Afghanistan and Pakistan after the fall of Kabul in 2021.

As these anti-state movements evolve, so will the complex political and organizational challenges that they pose to Pakistan's Islamist parties, which represent perhaps the most important potential political competitors to, and enablers of, anti-state violence. The political science literature suggests that political parties often struggle most in responding to external groups that share similar ideologies or policy goals, as it is these groups that present competition for members, funds, or public status. Comparative examples of such competitive relationships have included the Green parties and the radical environmentalists in Europe; socialist parties and labor unions in Sweden

[10] Laurent Bonnefoy, "Sunni Islamist Dynamics in Context of War: What Happened to Al-Islah and the Salafis?," in *Politics, Governance, and Reconstruction in Yemen*, vol. 29, POMEPS Studies (Washington, DC: George Washington University, 2018), 23–26; Farea Al-Muslimi, "In Exile in Turkey, Yemen's Muslim Brothers Cling to Caliphate Dreams," *New Lines Magazine*, May 23, 2024.

and Britain; the Republican party and the Tea Party movement in the United States; and rightist parties and anti-immigrant lobbies in Europe.[11]

In similar ways, if and when future Islamist movements declare the Pakistani state un-Islamic and mobilize violence against it, Pakistan's Islamist parties will likely be forced to grapple with an unattractive set of options that result from their own vulnerabilities and their stark dependency on a simplistic political narrative that more shariah is always better. They can embrace anti-state violence, risk the ire of the security services, and put their patronage and political access at risk. Or they can speak out against these anti-state movements, who will in turn target them for being insufficiently religious—intimidating them into silence, or weakening their credibility as representatives of a "true" Islamic political agenda.

If the case studies from this book provide any guide, the Islamist parties will often respond with ambivalence. Thrust into the heart of the debate as de facto public arbiters of shariah, pressured to side with the newest champions of Islamic practice, and aware of their institutional vulnerabilities, they will be forced to weigh the risks and opportunities that come with embracing a vision of Islamic law that elides the authority of the state.

[11] See, for example, Clive S. Thomas, "Studying the Political Party–Interest Group Relationship," in *Political Parties and Interest Groups: Shaping Democratic Governance*, ed. Clive S. Thomas (Boulder, CO: Lynne Rienner, 2001), 20ff; Herbert Kitschelt, *The Logics of Party Formation: Ecological Politics in Belgium and West Germany* (Ithaca, NY: Cornell University Press, 1989); Ruud Koopmans, "Explaining the Rise of Racist and Extreme Right Violence in Western Europe: Grievances or Opportunities?," *European Journal of Political Research* 30, no. 2 (September 1996): 185–216.

Index

For the benefit of digital users, indexed terms that span two pages (e.g., 52–53) may, on occasion, appear on only one of those pages.

W

Z